Chiang Kai-shek

ASIA'S MAN OF DESTIN[Y]

BY H. H. CHANG

DOUBLEDAY, DORAN AND COMPANY, INC.

Garden City   1944   New York

COPYRIGHT, 1944
BY DOUBLEDAY, DORAN & COMPANY, INC.
ALL RIGHTS RESERVED

PRINTED IN THE UNITED STATES
AT
THE COUNTRY LIFE PRESS, GARDEN CITY, N. Y.

FIRST EDITION

*To the unknown, unsung soldiers
and people of my country who die
that the nation may live and
the world be free.*

Acknowledgments

THANKS are due to the following authors, publishers, publications, and agents for permission to use the material indicated:

Constable and Company, Ltd.—for selections from *The Chinese Revolution, 1926–1927*, by Herbert Owen Chapman.

The Cresset Press Limited—for selections from *China: A Short Cultural History*, by C. P. Fitzgerald.

Current History and Forum—for an extract from *Forum* magazine.

Doubleday, Doran & Company, Inc.—for selections from *General Chiang Kai-shek*, by General and Madame Chiang Kai-shek; published in England by Faber & Faber, Ltd.

Lewis Gannett—for extracts from his articles in the New York *Times*.

Harper & Brothers—for an extract from *The Far Eastern Crisis*, by Henry L. Stimson; and for quotations from *Resistance and Reconstruction*, by Chiang Kai-shek; published by Hutchinson & Co., Ltd., in England.

Carol Hill, agent—for two quotations from *Personal History*, by Vincent Sheean, published by Doubleday, Doran & Company, Inc.

Luzac & Company, London—for extracts from *The Art of War*, by Sun Tse, translated by Lionel Giles.

The New York *Times*—for selections from several issues.

Charles Scribner's Sons—for an extract from *My Life*, by Leon Trotsky; published in England by Eyre & Spottiswoode, Ltd.

Simon & Schuster, Inc.—for quotations from *One World*, by Wendell L. Willkie.

Richard Steel, agent—for extracts from *The War of Civilization*, by George Lynch; published in England by Longmans, Green & Company.

H. G. W. Woodhead—for selections from various issues of the *China Yearbook*.

The Genesis of the Book

When I came with my family to this country some three months before Pearl Harbor was attacked, the war in China was already fifty months old. We disembarked at San Pedro. Before we landed a reporter asked some pertinent questions about the war with Japan. He wanted to know if the Burma Road was in danger. He also wanted to know how it was that a peace-loving country like China could fight alone against a strong military power like Japan for so long without adequate modern equipment. Above all, he wanted to know all that I could tell him about the remarkable man who had become the acknowledged leader of his people. That was my first contact with American public opinion.

I intended to make a short stay in Los Angeles and complete my arrangements for the family before proceeding to my own duties. The openness and climatic wonders of southern California were indeed marvelous. Though we knew no one there, it was not long before we had a circle of friends who were all kind and anxious to be of help. They were especially anxious, however, to know about conditions in my country. Theirs was a lively and healthy intellectual curiosity. But I soon realized that in spite of the many channels of information which were open to the American public, the understanding of China and things Chinese was both limited and quite often inaccurate. It was not America's fault. It had been brought up on information that somehow did not seem to offer a satisfactory explanation for the phenomenon of a brave and sustained war of resistance.

Interest in the Chinese personalities behind the war was naturally keen. What kind of man is your Chiang Kai-shek? What was his training? What is the background of his thoughts and beliefs? How does he rule his country? These and many others continued to be baffling questions. "We don't know him at all," many of them would tell me. Others would say, "He is so far away from us. He is so very Chinese, and frankly there is no common medium through which we can understand or appreciate him."

Requests soon came in from many quarters for both my wife and myself to speak, with which we gladly complied. I accepted the invitation of the Institute of World Affairs at Riverside. We appeared before clubs, churches, and public forums; and in a few months we were happy in feeling that we were supplying a need which the American public was anxious that we fill. Finally we were invited to speak on the radio, where our voices could reach not only a few thousand, but hundreds of thousands or perhaps even millions of listeners. And with the hearty response that we received through the mail from people of all walks of life we felt increasingly convinced that here was a piece of work that we must perform as a matter of duty.

But the immediate stimulus for the present volume came at an informal gathering of writers and men of letters who had come to California from all parts of the world. It was natural that the conversation should drift to political matters. The crisis in India was then on everybody's lips, and Mr. Louis Bromfield, the author of *The Rains Came*, had much to say on the subject. From India we turned our attention to China. "How do you account for the magnificent stand that you are making in China?" "What are the factors behind this success?" were among the many questions that were asked. As one member of the gathering remarked, "Surely a China that is showing such heroism, on such an epic scale, completely upsets all the traditional notions that we have been brought up to believe about that country. We must have been quite mistaken, but then how can we understand the real situation?"

I made the observation that China in fact remains the same China she has always been. There have been no basic changes in her culture or in the quality of her people. But I added that there was a new feeling in that country today. The war in the East, I said, was being fought between a highly organized and powerful country with no leadership and a weak and comparatively disorganized country that happened to have a strong personality and a great leader. It was, moreover, a war between militarism and aggression on the one hand and justice and a righteous cause on the other: there should be no doubt as to the eventual outcome of that gigantic struggle. The presence of Chiang Kaishek had made all the difference in the world.

"Then, why don't you, for heaven's sake," said one of them, "write a biography of that man? Surely it should be your duty to bring us and the Western world nearer to him and him to us." But I said I did not enjoy the reputation as a writer that most of those present did. I was willing, however, I explained, to help gather the material and perhaps to collaborate with one of them in particular who was considered one of the greatest living biographers in the world. The little group remained adamant; it insisted that only one of Chiang Kai-shek's own countrymen, who was at the same time familiar with the West and its literature and history, should undertake the task.

The idea was a challenge to me. But I hesitated. For I had doubts that a book written by me would do justice to so great and difficult a subject. If I were back in China it would probably be a different thing. But here in America I would have difficulty in collecting Chinese material, which was the only source that an adequate biography could draw upon. However, I proceeded with the plan, and before I knew it I had assembled a large amount of relevant documentation in the Chinese language upon which I thought I could base my endeavors. I also talked with people who had known the Generalissimo intimately. I talked with those of my countrymen who had just come from Chungking, and gradually I felt that the plan was taking shape in my mind. I could, moreover, draw from my own experience, gained from many years of active service in the government. As a counselor in the Chinese Foreign Office and as director of one of its important departments, I was obviously placed in an advantageous position from which to observe the leader of the government at close range. I had also attended meetings where he spoke and had met him at banquets and many other functions.

In 1933 I was appointed to head a diplomatic mission in Europe and proceeded to Nanchang to bid farewell to the Generalissimo, who was then engaged in the bitter war against the Communists in Kiangsi Province. When I arrived he was at the front. I suggested that I see him there. But he returned to his headquarters before I was ready to leave. He invited me to have lunch with him, and I will never forget the utter simplicity of the man on that occasion. His quarters knew no luxury whatever and were no more comfortable than those of an ordinary civil servant. All the ranking generals were present. They had been trained under strict military discipline. The lunch was eaten with almost military precision, and it was to be expected that there was no free and lively conversation at the table. I was especially honored, however, with a half-hour interview when the lunch was over and the party dispersed. The Generalissimo made me feel at home and asked me many questions on the international situation, regarding which I found he was unusually well informed. When the interview was over, he escorted me to the door and gave instructions to his chauffeur that I be sent back to my hostel. That deep sincerity, that ease of manners, that courtesy and graciousness that we usually associate with the Chinese scholar were all there, and he was the first soldier in China! I at once recalled a famous saying by Confucius, which no doubt the Generalissimo knew. "Let the prince," said Confucius, "treat his public servant with honor and consideration. The public servant must then serve the prince with loyalty." Before I went back to Nanking the Generalissimo presented me with an autographed photo of himself.

Surely a man with so many interesting facets in his remarkable personality should be the subject of a full and adequate biography. But more than that, he is the epitome of his race. The Chinese war of resistance, which incidentally has now become the longest war in the history of the modern world and which seems to have baffled almost everybody outside of China, cannot be properly appraised without an understanding of its leader.

It may seem unusual to bring the name of Lytton Strachey into this foreword, but he it was who started to write biography in the manner of fiction. For better or for worse the method has come to stay, and its influence has been extensive. I wish, however, that it were possible for me to say, as he said of his eminent Victorians, *"Je n'impose rien; je ne propose rien; j'expose."*

It will be difficult to enumerate the many people who have helped me in the preparation of this book. To all of them I owe a debt of gratitude. I have also made copious use of material from various sources for which I am thankful. A portion of the book was prepared while I was on official duties in Washington, where I had the good fortune to pass the hottest summer on record. But then the Library of Congress came to the rescue and defied the weather by maintaining a consistent 78 degrees in its annex, where I spent many pleasant weeks. The staff was unfailingly helpful, and I am grateful especially to those in the Jefferson Reading Room who in one way or another placed their services at my disposal.

The greatest of all debts is one which I can only mention; to do more than that would be an impertinence. For how can I describe in words the quiet but sustained courage, the patience, the fortitude,

THE GENESIS OF THE BOOK

and the constant encouragement of a loving and devoted wife who is, incidentally, my best and severest critic?

And now a last word. Although during the preparation of the book I had access to a variety of source material and discussions with many people, it is free from any official inspiration or authorization. The opinions are entirely my own, and I alone am responsible for them.

Riverside Drive
New York City
October 1943

Contents

	PAGE
The Genesis of the Book	vii

DEVOTION

1. Parting of the Ways	3
2. Farmers and Traders	10
3. "Greater Than She There Is None"	14
4. School of the Keeper of the Phoenix	23
5. The Dragon's Anger	29
6. The Interval	33
7. And So It Happened	41
8. The Career Begins	45
9. A Military Classic	51

LOYALTY

10. Across the Sea	61
11. Revolutionary Contacts	65
12. A Leader Inspires Him	68
13. The Flowering of a Faith	74
14. A Tragic Overture	86
15. Going into Action	91
16. Shifting Fortunes	98
17. The Revolution Continues	106

CONTENTS

		PAGE
18.	Abiding Loyalty	114
19.	Genius for Military Organization	123
20.	The Russian Interlude—I	132
21.	The Russian Interlude—II	139

Fulfillment

22.	The Legacy of Inequality	151
23.	The Northern Expedition	158
24.	The Split	168
25.	Marriage	185
26.	The Peking Drive and After	193
27.	The Road to Manchuria	203
28.	The Communists Again	214
29.	The Sustaining Power of the Past	220
30.	They Start a Movement	225
31.	He Starts Another Movement	230
32.	Half a Century	234
33.	Sian Incident	241
34.	Denouement	253
35.	The General Surveys the Field	263
36.	The Sword Is Unsheathed	272
37.	Planning a Strategy	277
38.	Stiffening Resistance	287
39.	Constructing from Within	298
40.	And in Other Ways?	307
41.	A Policy of Conciliation	320
42.	China Looks Ahead	331
	An Appendix on the Cairo Conference	345
	Index	349

Illustrations

	FACING PAGE
Dr. Sun Yat-sen	64
Generalissimo Chiang Kai-shek Reviewing His Troops	120
Generalissimo and Mme. Chiang Kai-shek Emerging from Their Dugout in Chungking	192
Generalissimo Chiang Kai-shek Taking a Walk with the Venerable President Lin Sen	224
Generalissimo Chiang Kai-shek Being Decorated with the Legion of Merit Order	256
The Visit of Mr. Wendell Willkie with Generalissimo and Mme. Chiang Kai-shek	296
Generalissimo and Mme. Chiang Kai-shek Visiting India	328
General Sir Archibald Wavell, Now Viceroy of India, and General George Brett, of the U.S. Air Corps, with Generalissimo and Mme. Chiang Kai-shek	336

Devotion

I

Parting of the Ways

ON AUGUST 29, 1842, at about eleven o'clock in the morning, when the day's heat was already becoming oppressive, three representatives of the Imperial Chinese Government went on board H.M.S. *Cornwallis,* which was anchored near the bank of China's mightiest river, the Yangtze, and soon after the Treaty of Nanking was signed with the British representatives.

That was the end of the Opium War and the beginning of China's international woes.

One hundred years afterward, on October 10, 1942, the thirty-first anniversary of what has now become one of the youngest republics, the Government of the United States, in association with the British Government, announced that it was "prepared promptly to negotiate a treaty providing for the immediate relinquishment of extraterritorial rights" in China.

That marked the end of one century of impairment of Chinese sovereignty and independence and the beginning of a new era in which China will regain her equal status among the free peoples of the world.

When the United States made this move with Britain, she was aware of its deep significance, and the Liberty Bell in Independence Hall, symbolic of America's own love of freedom and liberty, rang thirty-one times as a fitting commemoration of an important event taking place on the thirty-first anniversary of the Chinese Republic. It was an unprecedented act in America's international relationship. Three days afterward the leader of the Chinese people responded to this gracious expression when he said:

"I, personally, am so deeply moved by this beautiful and touching gesture that I cannot find words adequate to express my feeling.

"As a boy the very words 'Liberty Bell' and 'Independence Hall' fired my imagination and made a profound and lasting impression on my mind.

"Throughout my struggle to secure national freedom for China I have continuously dreamed of the day when she would assume the full stature of an independent, democratic nation.

"Today this ideal has been realized."

The man who said this was Generalissimo Chiang Kai-shek. To the statesmanship, vigor, and personality of this one man more than to any other single factor must be given the credit for having realized this ideal. Dr. Sun Yat-sen preceded him, through forty years of unremitting toil, in keeping this ideal of a free and democratic China alive in the minds of his countrymen. But he died before his country became politically united. When he closed his eyes on March 12, 1925, at Peking, he was surrounded by those same war lords whose chronic civil wars it was his ambition to terminate as a first step in the unification of the country. Although to all appearances China remained as much confused as when he started out on his revolutionary career, the seeds had been sown; and in seventeen short years, through the devotion and energy of his young follower, those seeds have grown and flowered, until today, not only is China's position as a great power assured, but the history of the Asiatic continent and of the world will be different because of this altered position of China. Generalissimo Chiang Kai-shek is in the prime of life, having celebrated the fifty-sixth anniversary of his birth on October 31, 1943. It is safe to say that what he will still be able to accomplish in the years to follow may yet exceed all expectations. Certainly the life of China and eventually of Asia would not be what it promises to be if Chiang Kai-shek had not appeared on the scene.

One hundred years, from 1842–1942, is indeed a short period in the life of a nation having an unbroken history of from four to five thousand years. But no nation has known, within the same number of years, an equal intensity in the change of national moods. To feel, as China felt, the immense pride in being the most cultivated and civilized people in the world, and then, in a few short years, to see all pride, whether justified or not, completely suppressed and trampled into the dust, is to pass from one extreme of national feeling to another. And this transformation took place within the brief span of two generations!

When King George III, that amazing monarch who lost a whole continent in the New World and acquired another in India, sent his first embassy to the court of the Chinese Emperor in 1793, this was how Emperor Chien Lung addressed him through Lord Macartney:

"You, O King, lie beyond the confines of many seas, nevertheless, impelled by your humble desire to partake of the benefits of our civilization, you have despatched a mission respectfully bearing your memorial. . . . To show your devotion, you have also sent offerings of your country's produce. I have perused your memorial: the earnest terms in which it is couched reveal a respectful humility on your part which is highly praiseworthy. . . .

"Swaying the wide world, I have but one aim in view, namely, to maintain a perfect governance and to fulfill the duties of the state: strange and costly objects do not interest me. . . . Our dynasty's majestic value has penetrated unto every country under Heaven, and kings of all nations have offered their costly tribute by land and sea. As your ambassador can see for himself, we possess all things. I have expounded my wishes in detail and have commanded your tribute Envoys to leave in peace on their homeward journey. It behooves you, O King, to respect my sentiments and to display even greater devotion and loyalty in future, so that, by perpetual submission to our Throne, you may secure peace and prosperity for your country hereafter. . . ."

George III must have received the shock of his life on reading such a message. But for Chien Lung the attitude was a most natural one. It was not a case of false pride. For was he not the lord of a domain that stretched all the way from the Amur River to Burma and from the China Sea to the heart of Central Asia? Within the circumscribed knowledge of the world that the Chinese then possessed, and with their vast cultural background extending to the early days of recorded history, it would be surprising if a Chinese Emperor did not feel that he alone was entitled to an exalted position over the rest of mankind.

The tragedy was that this exalted position should have been humbled within so short a period of time. The Treaty of Nanking of 1842 was the first official announcement of a changed order when the Chinese, whether they liked it or not, were asked to accept an inferior status in the family of nations. But in spite of this diplomatic instrument whose significance they did not fully realize at that time, the Chinese continued to believe that they were immeasurably superior. Even though they were defeated in the Opium War, they considered it no more than "a rebellious irruption of a tribe of barbarians." Some of the ideas about Europe and America among the best-educated Chinese were so farfetched that they were quite pathetic. The prevailing notion was that, China being such a large and fertile country abounding in all good things, and all other places being so small and barren, the most important possessions of Europe and America must therefore all come from within the confines of China. Their belief was that the merchants who came to China constituted the sum total of all the important people or chiefs of the foreign countries. This belief existed to the last days of the nineteenth century.

A carpenter who worked for many years in the building of the British Consulate at Shanghai, soon after the Opium War, took for granted that "with the exception of the Queen of England all Englishmen of any consequence personally knew me." So also thought even the educated Chinese. He would regard everything foreign as being the reverse of what it should be. When a book was shown to him he could not see how these "barbarians ever managed to read." "Ah, it's all confused, I see," he would say. "You put the words anywhere, just as it suits your fancy." Or he would think to himself, "These are funny people. They write their language backwards. Instead of beginning from the right, they began from the left or the tail end. Instead of running perpendicularly down the page, they read sideways, and the words are written like the crawling of a crab." In order to realize that these remarks are not so fantastic, all we need to do is to listen to what the average European or American has to say about China today. For the tables have been turned and, in spite of the enormous advance the world has made in the knowledge of foreign peoples, exactly the same remarks which the Chinese used about the perversity of the foreigners are now being used by the foreigners to describe the Chinese.

The amazing phenomenon was that the educated Chinese could not see, in spite of the Treaty of Nanking, that the countries which could produce, for instance, so large and so beautiful a thing as a ship involving, obviously, in the course of its construction, a high degree of technical skill, must be inhabited by people who had attained a high degree of civilization. He refused to be impressed by these sights. T. T. Meadows, who arrived in Canton in 1843 as interpreter to the British Consulate, was much exasperated by the stubborn and unreasonable attitude of the typical mandarin. "We have, it is true," he said, in interpreting that attitude, "the power to do some great and extraordinary things, but so have the elephants and other wild animals he occasionally sees or hears of; in his eyes, therefore, we are all barbarians, possessing perhaps some good qualities, congregated perhaps together in some sort of societies, but without regular government, untutored, coarse and wild."[1]

A state of mind so incapable of understanding realities and of knowing the actual conditions in those far-off countries that had the strength and power to defeat the Chinese in their own territory, both on land and on sea, must inevitably lead to further disasters and unhappy consequences. And so it did. The Opium War was soon followed by what is known as the Arrow War, again fought with the British and won by them in 1856-58. That was terminated by the Treaty of Tientsin, which imposed further limitations on China. From that time on the decline of Chinese prestige was precipitate. The Taiping Rebellion, which ravaged the country for at least fourteen years ending in 1864, further reduced the energy of a country whose vitality was already at a low ebb. Until then Britain and, to a lesser extent, France were the only countries that delivered blow after blow against a big and helpless China. But from then on other countries followed and demanded their share of the privileges. Russia, who always loomed ominously in the north, became active, but the worst was yet to follow. In 1894 the impossible happened. Japan, little Japan, which could not even be classed among the "barbarian" nations, but was merely a country of "dwarf slaves," regarded by the Chinese as being on the same level as Siam, Burma, Indo-China, and other tribute-bearing tribes on the border, now also heaped indignities on China by roundly defeating her in a war over the question of Korea. That was indeed the last straw. The "paper tiger" had until then at least the semblance of a tiger. The fate of China was now almost sealed. The processes of disintegration worked relentlessly and mercilessly on a country that, by all standards, was highly civilized and refined, possessing a rich treasury of the arts of peace, but lacking the energy and the means to withstand the forces of spoliation that were invading her from all directions.

Such was the condition of China when Chiang Kai-shek was born on the thirty-first of October 1887.

It was the year in which Sun Yat-sen, then a young man of twenty-one, entered the Medical College at Hong Kong after having spent a number of years of his boyhood in Hawaii. When China was humbled by the Japanese in the war of 1894-95, Chiang Kai-shek, then known

[1] *Desultory Notes on the Government and People of China*, Thomas Taylor Meadows.

to his parents as Chou-tai, was only seven years of age. He was playing on the cobblestone streets of Chikow or catching fish from the surrounding streams, a delight which to this day he has not forgotten. Nor was it likely that either his family or his immediate environment was at all affected by the great disaster that had befallen the country. Wars in China in those days were curiously localized though their consequences were national.

In the war with France in 1884, for instance, the Chinese soldiers actually routed the invading forces at Langson, while the government at Peking was signing the terms of capitulation. The war with Japan was fought along the coast of Shantung and to the north. News spread slowly to other parts of China. In time it reached the ears of the Chikow villagers, but life flowed on placidly as if nothing had happened.

No one had any premonition that Japan was to become such an enormous factor in Chiang Kai-shek's life or that he would be called upon, less than half a century later, to solve the same Japanese problem once and for all in the interest of world peace, and to lead in the progressive development of his own country.

In accomplishing these ends Chiang Kai-shek was fortunate in having a mother who had unusual vision for a woman of her training and environment, and a great leader in Dr. Sun Yat-sen, who was singularly pure in his ideals and whose charm and character left a deep and lasting impression upon all who came into close contact with him. Above all, Chiang was fortunate in having behind him a rich and abundant cultural heritage. For in both the case of Sun Yat-sen and Chiang Kai-shek it has not been simply a matter of taking over foreign ideas and institutions as a means of developing their country. Rather has it been necessary for them to urge their countrymen to rediscover the essential virtues and qualities that have been the mainstay of their history. It cannot be a mere accident that China has had such a long and unbroken history. To acquire genuine strength is to find out what these qualities are, to have abiding faith in their efficacy even under the conditions of modern society, and to give them every opportunity for further development.

It has been said of the Renaissance in Europe that it was the discovery of man and the discovery of the world. The same remark can be applied to what has happened in China since Sun Yat-sen conceived the idea of overthrowing the Manchu Dynasty. Both Sun and Chiang desired that China should know a larger world, but above all they desired that China should know herself. Their work has been, in the first instance, political and military; but their ultimate objectives are moral and spiritual. It is impossible to understand the accomplishments and the influence of Chiang Kai-shek without knowing that he has been continuing the work where Sun Yat-sen left off. And the highest thought of Sun Yat-sen was the creation of a great commonwealth which in essence was a conception of Confucius. "When the great way prevails," says that sage, "the world becomes a common state." Everything in China ultimately goes back to the pattern of thinking that Confucius and his followers wove. It was the conviction of Sun Yat-sen and now of Chiang Kai-shek that the old concepts and virtues not only retain their fullest value but must also serve as a foundation for the progressive social and political evolution of China as a modern nation. It is Chiang Kai-shek's task thus to create a new and better China and, through China, a new and better world.

To the student of sociology and history, the interesting question is whether it is possible to create a new and progressive society that can withstand the strain of modern conditions on the basis of values that are an inalienable part of a society that was so radically different in structure. Many are inclined to believe that the two are incompatible and that one must give way to the other. It is Chiang Kai-shek's belief that they are compatible. And I think that he has thus, either consciously or unconsciously, grasped the secret of China's long and vigorous history. The secret is in China's ability to absorb the new into the matrix of the old. The principle of continuity has ever been the most vital principle in the history of China. Archaeologists have recently discovered in their excavations stone sickles, in use during the Stone Age in China four thousand years ago, that are almost identical with the iron sickles now in use in different parts of northern China. When metal was first introduced and proved to be more efficient, the peasants did not discard the old instruments but adapted the new to the old requirements. This is even truer of moral values which, if they contain any truth, must possess an element of permanency about them. Chiang Kai-shek considers it essential that the new society should be constructed on the basis of these values. It is a great and interesting experiment that deserves close observation, sympathy, and understanding.

2

Farmers and Traders

THE NAME of the little village of Chikow where Chiang Kai-shek was born means the Mouth of the Brook, and today has a population of less than four thousand. It is tucked away among the hills and is surrounded by lovely natural scenery. The village is part of a larger community called Chinchi, or the Embroidered Brook, under the jurisdiction of Fenghua. It is now on a highway some twenty miles to the south of Ningpo, the city of vigorous men and of still more vigorous language.

The big, sprawling country of China, for all its size, is unusually unified in its social organization and mental outlook, though naturally there are striking local differences. The people of Ningpo and of the surrounding villages, of which Chikow has now become the most significant, very definitely constitute a unit all by themselves. Over on the other side of the Chientang River from Ningpo to the north, there is the delicate and sophisticated beauty of China at its best. Nature is graceful, the climate mild, and both the men and women enjoy the easy comforts of life. The city of Soochow has attained the highest development in this kind of life. It also produces the largest number of singsong girls whose soft, languorous graces and gentle, modulated accents are known throughout the land.

Once you cross south of the river and come to the city of Ningpo, you have come into a totally different environment. Nature becomes more rugged as you penetrate more deeply into the south. The rivers are just as picturesque as the mighty Yangtze above Ichang. They are on a smaller scale, but the grandeur is all there. The coast also is deeply indented, and when you walk through the congested streets of the cities and villages surrounding Ningpo you find men and women of astounding vitality doing their daily work with all the noise and bustle of the bazaar. There is no trace of the delicacy and effeminacy of Soochow. They talk in loud, firm, vigorous tones. They indulge in broad humor and laugh in the Rabelaisian manner. There is a proverb in Shanghai that it is more pleasant to quarrel with the man from

Soochow than to talk with the man from Ningpo. But what of it? The man from Ningpo does not mind being known for his brusque manners. He overflows with energy, and that energy carries him to the big centers of trade all over the country. The Ningpo guild is the most powerful in Shanghai, and there is not one branch of trade in that metropolis in which the people from Ningpo do not have a predominating interest.

Nowhere are such sharp contrasts in temperament seen within so short a distance. The man from Ningpo and the surrounding neighborhood is always downright, straightforward, and definite. He is assertive. His very food is strong and pungent. His mind is not accustomed to the oversubtle and tortuous reasoning which makes the men in the triangle formed by Hangchow, Soochow, and Shanghai as slippery as the eel. Whether the sea has anything to do with this temperament it is hard to say, but it is true that a large percentage of the population of the Ningpo area is devoted to sailing and owns practically all the picturesque fleets of large wooden boats in China. These are the colorful junks that painters from foreign lands have often reproduced on canvas and which, from the early days of the Tang Dynasty, sailed through the China Seas, across the Indian Ocean, and over to Arabia, where brisk trade was maintained for some seven hundred years until the early period of the Ming Dynasty. That is why a large portion of Chinese crews in ships that travel all over the world today consists of daring and adventurous people from Chiang Kai-shek's district.

But if there are merchants and seafaring people from that district, at least one third of the population remain as farmers, always a most highly respected class of people in China, surpassed in respect only by the scholars. Even they—and, indeed, all self-respecting men when their career is run—long to go back to the farm. Chiang Kai-shek himself, as late as 1935, when he was making one of his periodic visits to his native village, said in the course of an address to the village school, of which he is the principal, that political life was merely superficial. "Agriculture is the primary consideration. You must learn to work on the farms. It is only when you love the land and the soil that you begin to love your country."

The Chiang family had been farmers for generations. It was in Chiang Kai-shek's grandfather's time that it shifted to trade. The grandfather became a salt and tea merchant, and through application and industry acquired moderate affluence. He had the reputation of being a fine and honest country gentleman, much respected by his fellow villagers. He was devoted to social welfare and gave funds generously for the building of roads and the construction of dikes and bridges over the many waterways in the surrounding area. To all these public works he gave freely not only his money, but also his time, for he personally supervised their building. Friends and relatives could also count upon his support and assistance whenever they needed him.

One of his good acts is remembered to this day. Chinchi, to which the village of Chikow belongs, is situated on the border of the three big cities of Ningpo, Shaoshing, and Taichow, where there is a range of mountains in the neighborhood called Wuling, or the "Military Range." It is a lonely spot, but the inhabitants of these three cities must pass through it in going from one city to another. Nowhere could these people get a drink or buy food while they were on their way. Chiang's grandfather arranged with a Buddhist temple on the range to supply tea and other necessities to travelers for many long years; and to this day the people speak of this act with affection and gratitude.

It frequently falls on the shoulders of good village gentry to perform such deeds for the welfare of the community, because until recently public utilities in China were not encouraged by the government, and the practice of individual interest and private donations is being maintained to the present day by good, honest people in the villages that are removed from the centers of life. My own father, for instance, also considers it almost a religious duty to go to the country two or three times a year to see that the roads and stone bridges are kept in good repair. The feeling of belonging to the village where one is born, and where one's ancestors are buried, is strong in China, and acts of goodness performed in the village, aside from being contributions to public welfare, are also considered as seeds sown for the future prosperity of the family. "To do good for one's children and for posterity" is a part of the Buddhist belief that good begets good as evil begets evil.

Chiang's grandfather was a devout Buddhist and took greater delight in helping those around him than did the ordinary run of the gentry. He also had knowledge of medicine, not the modern scientific medicine which has now come into China to stay, but the traditional type of Chinese medicine that involved a deep knowledge of the healing qualities of herbs. Yu-piao, for such was the name of the grandfather, was always prepared to place this knowledge at the disposal of the villagers, to whom he was kind and devoted, though toward the members of his own family he was inclined to be a strict disciplinarian. That again is a trait of the typical Chinese paterfamilias. The relationship between father and son or between elders and the younger members of the family is not placed on the basis of easy fellowship, though with the coming of the new knowledge from the West it is now rapidly developing in that direction.

When a grandfather is still alive, his influence in the family is twice as important as the father's, for isn't he the father's father? The impression this stern and yet kindly Yu-piao made on the young Chou-tai must have been deep, for there is much in the leader of contemporary China which recalls the sterling qualities of his grandfather.

But what was Chou-tai's father, Su-an, like? He would often gather his children around him and say to them: "When I was young I had to struggle and continue the work of my father. I was not in a position to do much for the good of the country. But I did manage to do some good for the villagers. I promoted education and did all I could for the public welfare. What I want from you is that you pursue your studies diligently so that when you grow up you may do what I couldn't do and thus make good my deficiencies." He was a stern person. A man of great firmness and determination, he started to rebuild the fortunes of his father, which all but vanished as a result of the ravages of the Taiping Rebellion. He was then in his early teens, and the province of Chekiang, as I heard from my own grandmother, was more seriously affected than many other parts of China. The rebels pillaged and slaughtered until some twenty million people had perished during the uprising. No wonder the fortunes of the Chiang family were depleted. The devastation was so thoroughgoing that it was quite some time before Su-an got on his feet again. But through perseverance and determination, which his son has inherited in good measure, he recovered all that the family had lost by continuing to trade in salt, and in time he managed to carry on his father's social activities also.

Su-an died in 1896, soon after China's first humiliating defeat at the hands of Japan. He was then fifty-three, leaving a comparatively large family to be brought up by his widow. Chou-tai was only nine years of age. There were four other children, two sisters and two brothers, the younger of whom died during childhood, while the older brother lived till 1938. One of the sisters passed away in 1939 at the age of seventy, and the other sister, who married into the family of a well-to-do landlord, lived only a few miles away from the village of Chikow until the Japanese invaded the southern part of the Chientang River in 1941. With her three sons, she alone of the immediate Chiang family has lived to see the phenomenal transformation of a small and unknown village into what has today become a national shrine.

3

"Greater Than She There Is None"

THERE IS indeed no more charming spot than Chikow to become the mecca for a nation which does not generally take to hero-worshiping. The Chinese are strong individualists and like to believe that one man is just as good as another. Even though an extraordinary person does appear and prove his mettle, they are not apt to be in a hurry to idolize him. It is safer to leave that to posterity. Then legends begin to be woven around him. He may even become a saint and be worshiped in temples erected to honor his memory. Such a hero was Kwan Yu of the Three Kingdoms. Such also was Yo Fei of the Sung Dynasty. But it was centuries before these heroes captured the popular imagination. No one in Chinese history while still alive has received so much respect and admiration as Chiang Kai-shek. His name became really well known abroad after the Sian episode of December 1936 and as the leader of China's heroic resistance against Japanese aggression after July 1937, but in his own country his position was established long before those dates, and the little village which gave him birth was a popular spot for visitors even before the present war.

From Shanghai it used to be a pleasant four-hour drive to Hangchow, an ancient city with a lovely lake, long and richly associated with the art and poetry of the romantic history of China during the best days of the Sung Dynasty. From there one crossed the Chientang River, and, passing through beautiful landscape, entered the bustling city of Ningpo. From there, for another twenty miles, the highway ran straight into Fenghua and the village of Chikow. The highway, however, is now torn up as a military measure against the Japanese invaders.

The village of Chikow is situated on an elevation, and all around there are mountains that are ageless and serene. The rocks are of all shapes, as if they were the figures of buddhas and bodhisattvas carved by the hands of nature. Among the hills to the west there are waterfalls and cascades, and down in the valleys are wild flowers and groves of bamboos. The bamboos, which grow with especial luxuriance in that section of China, are so clean, so straight, and so gaunt that they are loved by painters and poets alike for being symbolic of great moral virtues, of character and personal integrity.

These were the favorite haunts of Chou-tai until he grew into early manhood, and they were a deep influence on him during the formative years of his life. Mountains and water are, in fact, considered in China as dominant factors in the molding of character, for didn't Confucius say that the wise derive joy from water and the virtuous gain joy from the mountains?

Close by, however, there is also the sea, and the villagers traffic their wares and produce to other parts of the coast in those gorgeously colored junks. After the evening sun has set these plain boatmen are happy and content to rest with their pot of tea in the teashops, puffing their long bamboo pipes filled with a local tobacco. Many of them bring in a few fish they have caught from the sea, and it was these people who delighted Chou-tai most of all. He mingled with them, overheard their talk, understood their joys and sorrows and, in this way, acquired a knowledge of the problems of the common man of China. It is fortunate that China has had no aristocracy, except that of the truly noble in character. All her great historic leaders have grown from the ranks of plain, ordinary people. They knew the problems of the masses, for whom they were willing to work, and Chiang Kai-shek has been no exception. He spent his entire boyhood in this little village, and there he saw in miniature the many social problems that he was later to be called upon to solve.

"When I saw these social inequalities," he once said, referring to his experiences as a boy in the village, "I kept asking myself the questions, 'Why must a poor man go through such hardships and difficulties and live a life of bitterness? Why should the children of the rich, doing no productive work, enjoy such plenty and luxury?' I have always wondered, and I have been persistently haunted by the thought that, if the poor must have such bitterness and the rich enjoy such plenty, this is certainly not the right way of life, and measures of improvement must one day be found and introduced."[1]

Looking around the village of Chikow today, one realizes that it is no longer the same village that Chou-tai knew. It is no longer a typical traditional Chinese village. It has acquired a modern appearance. The streets are well paved and clean. On their way to the modern schools or to their places of work, the boys and girls are all properly and tidily dressed. There is electricity in the village, although that is no longer a novelty to most villages in that section of China. But the shops are also modern, and motor vehicles, before the troubles started in 1937, were common sights.

One of the most modern achievements of Chikow is the school of which Chiang Kai-shek is the principal. In spite of his heavy duties with affairs of state, he very carefully supervises every part of its curriculum. The actual work is done by a trusted dean. Between this school and the typical village school where Chiang Kai-shek himself spent some eight years of his life there is a wide difference. In the first place it has an enrollment of some six hundred and fifty students, coming from all parts of the province of Chekiang. Classroom work is done in the morning, and the afternoons are devoted to practical experimentation. The school is meant to be the center from which modern influences may radiate to all the surrounding country, and agriculture and forestation are its principal concerns. The problems of soil improvement, of irrigation, of the care and nurture of plants are all studied to make farming a more scientific undertaking. Those things were, of course, unheard of in the village school.

The school also maintains a hospital where girls receive training in nursing and the domestic sciences. It also dispenses daily medical care to large numbers of villagers. All this work of modernization receives the personal attention of Chiang Kai-shek and is a continuation of the philanthropic efforts of his grandfather and father. He does in a modern way what they did in their traditional way. Nor is it surprising that he should be interested in his native village, even though his constructive labors are today primarily on a national scale. The sense of continuity is strong among all self-respecting Chinese. "Never forget the roots from which you spring." Or: "While you drink the water, think of the source." The odium and moral disap-

[1] Weekly Memorial Address before the Central Military Academy, July 8, 1929.

probation attached to any person turning his back on his benefactor after he has achieved success is stronger in China than in any other country I have known.

Even though a Chinese may be confined to his duties far away, his ties with the village from which he and his ancestors sprung are never cut from him. It makes little difference if he was himself not even born there: the fact that his immediate ancestors were from that village and are buried in the family graveyard is sufficient to make him a product of that village. That might seem to the average European or American a part of ancestor worship, which they think of as a kind of religion. But there is nothing mysterious or esoteric about it. It is rational and has nothing to do with religion as religion is usually understood. It grows out of a feeling that social order would be precarious without it.

All moral virtues, so the Chinese believe, spring from love and devotion to one's parents. It is through their care and self-denial that the next generation is able not only to survive but also to grow and prosper. The least, therefore, that the young can do is to show their gratitude and reciprocate the love and affection of their parents by honoring and remembering them and making them feel proud even though they may have passed into another world. It is a part of the Chinese belief that the dead continue to exist among the living whom they have created, and to exercise an influence over their fortunes. The living, on their part, also believe that their ancestors maintain an eternal vigil over their welfare, and at least once a year, during the Chin-ming festival, when the warm breezes of spring begin to blow, it is usual for a family to gather and "sweep the tombs" of the ancestors and to pass a few days in the company of the departed spirits. It is in this way that a kind of continuity is firmly established with what has gone before. The past, present, and future are merged into one time-pulse and exist as one unit in the consciousness of the living. A society with such beliefs tends to be conservative but also stable, and stability is not the least of conservatism's virtues.

Chiang Kai-shek is an orthodox Chinese in what he has done for his native village of Chikow. It was there that he acquired the roots of his life, and the fact that he is a national leader makes it still more important that he maintain a proportionately large interest in the villagers among whom his family spent their days.

The most impressive structures in Chikow are those which constitute part of the temple or shrine of the Chiang family. The central edifice is the ceremonial hall, where the living members, at certain festivals of the year, pay respects to the departed. It is constructed in the manner of the old architecture, away from which it is impossible to conceive these old rituals for the dead. It is a hall into which all people, paying a short visit to Chikow, desire to enter and roam about, for it is the visible symbol of the national leader's devotion and filial love for his ancestors. As one approaches the entrance to the hall one is impressed by its quiet grandeur and simple dignity. The roofs are made of glazed tiles of different colors, and some of the woodwork is delicately and elaborately carved. Immediately above the entrance is a large wooden scroll dedicated to the mother who gave so illustrious a son to the nation. On it are written four bold Chinese words, meaning "You have labored hard for your country." And as one enters the spacious hall one sees that all the arrangements are rigidly symmetrical. Set up in rows are the tablets or the "seats of the spirits," on each of which is a description of the relationship of the man or woman, while alive, to the rest of the family. It is interesting to observe how Chinese society, even for those who are departed, exists in such stern orderliness. Each person has his allotted position which follows him even to his grave. This conception, like many others, grew from the fertile mind of Confucius, who insisted upon proper definition as the beginning of all moral and social development. In order to realize what a strong hold this belief has on the Chinese consciousness one has only to visit these ceremonial halls in one village after another. Some are sumptuous, as in the case of the Chiangs', and some much more modest, but all Chinese who are financially able build their halls as a mark of devotion to their parents and their families.

In the neighborhood of this hall for family worship is the grave of Chiang Kai-shek's mother. To her more than to anyone else Chiang Kai-shek owes what he is. Today, in the maturity of his life, he is often heard to say, "Greater than my mother there is none." The grave commands a beautiful position with vistas all around to the surrounding mountains in the distance. There are always verdure and wild flowers on the mound, violets that are as big as daisies, and it is even said by some villagers that when it rains, though the surrounding area is wet, the grave remains dry.

No subject in China has been so long and profoundly studied as that of *feng shui*, meaning, literally, the study of wind and water. It is believed that, if the ancestors are buried well and their remains lie at the proper angle, position, and elevation, then they are in complete harmony with the natural elements, and such harmony brings lasting blessing upon the living members of the family wherever they may be and whatever they may be doing. This may sound mystical and irrational, but when there are great personal calamities and misfortunes for which he can find no adequate reason the orthodox Chinese, no matter how thoroughly he may be baptized with the water of modern education, instinctively thinks of *feng shui* of his departed ancestors. At any rate, thousands of Chinese have remarked about the unique position of the grave of Chiang Kai-shek's mother. A whole nation has indeed reason to be thankful for the beneficent influence that continues to flow over the soul of its leader.

When the Sian incident occurred in December of 1936 it was undoubtedly the greatest crisis, the greatest personal calamity in the life of Chiang Kai-shek. It was also a national calamity of the first magnitude. When the crisis was over the Generalissimo and Mme. Chiang immediately repaired to Chikow as the only place in the world where they could be spiritually and mentally rested. Chiang Kai-shek came back to his mother's grave and was comforted.

Chiang's mother was an unusual woman. She was the daughter of the modest Wang family of Fenghua. When she was married and came over to the Chiang family, it was probably not as the "original spouse," for Su-an had already lost two wives. Su-an was happy in finding in this new wife a woman who had as determined a will as his own. She was able, energetic, had no taste for luxury, and soon became a model mother. She was accomplished in embroidery, and as education went in those days for girls of modest families, she was well versed in the classics. It was a happy marriage. Though Su-an was not a man of great wealth, he had sufficient means to maintain the family in a reasonably comfortable way and enough left over to satisfy the zeal for philanthropic work that he had inherited from his father.

When he died at the comparatively early age of fifty-three it was a severe blow to the family. There was little in the way of inheritance and days were hard. It fell entirely upon the shoulders of the widow to maintain a family of five children, some of whom were left behind by the previous wife. There were moments, which was understandable, when life became so unbearable that she thought it best to follow her husband into the other world, as women were taught to do by social custom. But even in those moments of darkness and utter dejection her sense of responsibility and moral courage never deserted her. An ancient proverb in China says, "It is easier to die than to maintain the life of a widow." But she chose the harder way. Once she made up her mind to carry it through, she found herself in possession of abundant energy. She made a living through her ability as an embroiderer and managed not only to keep the family alive but also to promote, so far as possible, the work of her husband as a public benefactor.

She demanded a stern discipline from her children and made them account for every one of their activities. Their help with the household chores was the least that she asked of them. When these were over their attention must be directed to books and to serious study. Young Chou-tai went to school at a somewhat later age than other children who were more fortunately situated, because his mother had to accumulate sufficient means to enable her to send him to school. The school was some distance away from home, and Chou-tai went to live with one of the relatives. When holidays came he would return home. Except for about one month at New Year's, there were few other holidays to break the monotony of the school routine. On Saturdays and Sundays there was work as usual, for there were no such days on the Chinese calendar. As soon as the holidays were over Chou-tai went straight back to school. On the eve of one of these departures from home his mother gave him some valedictory instructions with tears in her eyes. "Since your father's death," she said, "I have worked hard so that you may go to school. But remember it is not my aim that you become a great official or a wealthy person. My only hope is that you always retain your self-respect and do something for the country so that you do not go against the words of your parents."

He was then thirteen years of age and his heart must have been heavy, for those were weighty words for a child to carry back with him to school. But that has been the ideal of the orthodox good mother in China. Between mother and son there was, of course, the usual fun and a great amount of love. Young Chou-tai enjoyed life as much as any child, especially as the rivers and brooks were full of fish and the bamboo groves yielded delicious shoots. Fishermen coming home in the evening in their colorful junks, with big eyes painted on them to frighten away the evil spirits of the sea, would have their usual quota of fish stories, and young Chou-tai, along with other children, would sit with open mouth and listen entranced to the yarns.

But beneath this fun and play there was a note of sternness that the mother would never allow Chou-tai to forget. The duties of the day must be performed, and after that he had to learn Chinese words and practice writing them even before he was formally sent to school. Those tasks were arduous and difficult. It was during those moments that the mother's face would sometimes become long and taut, but she would not give in until the words had made some impression on the youngster's mind. Like all good mothers in China, she knew the story of Mencius. For it was said of that sage, the great and illustrious follower and expounder of Confucian thought, that even he was apt to find fun and amusement more appealing than serious application to studies. And when one day he found it more agreeable to stay at home than join the other children in learning the classics, his mother, while working at the loom, took up a pair of scissors and cut straight across it, to the horror of the young scholar. "To stay away from your studies is like my cutting this loom," she explained. "All the previous labor which you have put into your studies has been wasted." Young Mencius evidently took the episode to heart, for from that day on he never missed his studies.

This little incident is a favorite story with mothers in China, and Chou-tai's mother must have had it in mind as she trained the future leader of his people. It is for this reason that, as early as 1916, Sun Yat-sen, with whom Chiang Kai-shek was then beginning their close association, presented the old lady with a scroll on which he wrote four words, *"chiao-tse yu-fang,"* meaning: "You have educated your children on sound principles."

Chou-tai's mother was also a devout Buddhist. That did not involve any regular attendance at Buddhist temples in the same way that Christians attend church, although occasionally during the spring she might go to a famous temple to "burn incense." But as she had increasingly more time to herself toward the latter part of her life, she grew fond of reciting to herself the great sutras of the Buddhist religion. On certain days of the year she would become a strict vegetarian out of compassion for the animals that were slaughtered for meat. Those days were usually the first and the fifteenth of the lunar month. Her heart was full of kindness and mercy, and praying and worshiping became an indispensable part of her life. She would also visit some of the neighboring temples. These have now been repaired by Chiang Kai-shek as another expression of his devotion to his mother.

On the anniversary of his birthday in 1936[2] Chiang issued a message to the nation called "Reflections on my Fiftieth Birthday," otherwise known as "Performing Duties for My Country and Thinking about My Parents," in which he spoke at length on the virtues of his mother. He recounted the days when, as a fatherless child, he and his mother struggled hard so that he would not suffer from cold and hunger. There was no one upon whom they could depend for support. The mandarins and officials of the tottering Manchu Dynasty were cruel and corrupt, and what his father had left in the way of land and property was lost through blackmail and usurious taxes. "It came even to pass that we were brought before the courts of justice and publicly humiliated," Chiang recalled. Friends and relatives alike would merely look on and even throw ridicule and slander instead of demanding justice and fair play. "Those were indeed difficult times, but it was the loving-kindness of my mother, her firmness and determination and, above all, her great moral courage that saved the day. At any cost she must have the family maintained and the children properly nurtured and brought up."

She loved him, put him through school, and later, in spite of opposition from many quarters, even sent him abroad to Japan to learn military science. "If I finally succeeded in pursuing my course of study, it was because of my mother's efforts." When he grew older and decided to dedicate his life to revolutionary activities, again he had to encounter many obstacles. "If I managed to continue these activities and to become more determined in my resolves, it was because of my mother's efforts." When, still older, his work as a revolutionary repeatedly failed and bore no fruit, "it was again my mother who counseled me not to lose heart and to fight to the very end."

For the first twenty-five years of Chiang's life his mother was his unfailing guide and counselor. She was the determining factor of his life. She laid the foundation for his moral development and the growth of his personality. We can understand now why his mother, though departed from this earth, remains the center of the life of Chikow. The new edifices, the temples, the household hall of worship, all that is likely to attract public attention, are the symbols of a devoted son to a great and loving mother.

As for Chiang himself, he is satisfied with a simple and unpreten-

[2] It should be 1937, but the Chinese count one year more than is done in the West.

tious little house perched three thousand feet high on a mountain some distance from the village itself. There, if he could afford now and then to put aside the cares and worries of state, he would rest with Mme. Chiang. Even this simple enjoyment has been denied to him since 1937. But before that year they would often walk up the mountain, passing by lovely waterfalls and through row upon row of young pines, whose numbers have been increasing every year. There, through the foliage, one can see the small unpretentious structure built on a rock that juts out like the prow of a ship. Above, all around the upper part of the structure, is a spacious walk. Here Chiang was in the habit of meditating as he looked out into the distance through the tranquil surroundings. What a modest architect! For him there is no need for any elaborate and fortified Berchtesgaden, no eagle's nest in which to escape from the rest of humanity. A clean and honest soul is its own fortification. And China's leader is happiest when, with his wife, he finds himself in the midst of his unostentatious mountain resort looking over the distant horizon, just as statesmen of his country have done from time immemorial.

4

School of the Keeper of the Phoenix

WHEN CHOU-TAI'S MOTHER decided that he must be sent away to school to receive proper training, she was making a great resolve. For Chou-tai it was also the first important move in his life. The school to which he was to be sent was some miles away from home. It was out of the question for Chou-tai to be a day student, and yet the school, as was usual in those days, took no boarders. Fortunately there was a relative of the family in the neighborhood of the school with whom arrangements were made for the young scholar to stay. He could naturally come back to his mother whenever there were special occasions at home or when there were festivals and holidays.

Chou-tai started for school shortly after the death of his father, and leaving home meant for him the beginning of a life of independence. Upon arrival at school, however, he found that most of the boys were older than he. Some were even in early adolescence, and life for a new student who was younger than his schoolmates was no easy matter. It involved tact and diplomacy to make up his deficiency in physical strength, and young Chou-tai proved that he was equal to the task.

The school had the colorful name of School of the Keeper of the Phoenix. The founder evidently thought that the scholars who were placed under his charge would become select and rare specimens of the feathery world. It is not known whether he is still alive. But if he is, he can now be justly proud that he has been true to the name of the school in having brought into the world at least one unusual graduate. The institution was actually no more than an average village school, having an enrollment of perhaps seventy or eighty pupils. The teachers, of course, knew nothing of modern education, and boys of any age, mostly the sons of farmers and traders, were admitted at any time that they applied for admission.

When modern trends set in, these village schools disappeared in China, just as the old mandarins cast off their colorful robes to put on simpler and perhaps more efficient garb. This particular school where Chou-tai spent some eight years of his early life has now yielded place to a middle school named after the larger community of Chinchi, the village of the Embroidered Brook. It was among the first of the modern schools in the province of Chekiang, and official reports also consider it the best organized and equipped school of its kind. It now has an enrollment of over a thousand students, considerably more than ten times what it was over forty years ago, and counts among its graduates some of the leading men of the province.

But when Chou-tai was a student there it had a life of its own. It belonged to another world and had very little in common, either physically or spiritually, with its prosperous successor of today. The students were then of all ages and were probably lumped in the same classes. The curriculum was the same one that had been in existence for perhaps two thousand years. It consisted of the equivalent of the trivium and quadrivium or the seven liberal arts of medieval Europe. It included, in other words, practice in handwriting, composition, and the committing of the classics to memory. But the classics vary in their degree of difficulty, and there was a prescribed course that all the students were required to go through.

The first book was the *Three-Word Classic,* in which each sentence is arranged in three words. In the first few sentences the child receiving his preliminary formal education, after having acquired a knowledge of a few hundred words, was taught the astoundingly true philosophy that all men are good. It says literally: "At man's beginning his nature is basically good. Through their nature men are drawn together. It is practice that leads them apart." These few sentences embody a philosophy and an attitude toward human society that only the most advanced and mature minds can comprehend, and yet the minds of the Chinese children have been impressed with these ideas for two thousand years. No one ever thought of protesting against this type of education. Judged by all the standards of modern pedagogy, it was altogether a waste of time. And yet after making due allowance for all its faults and defects, which were many, I am not so sure that this system of teaching did not have something solid and substantial to contribute. The old pedagogues had enough sense to realize that the words were far above the heads of the youngsters, but they were convinced of the intrinsic value of the message and its wholesome view of life. They were therefore anxious that the pupils commit the words to memory so that they might be stored for later years when they would be understood and comprehended.

Next to the *Three-Word Classic* on the curriculum of those days was the *Classic on Filial Love,* which is a small book of some twenty pages. On the very first page young Chou-tai was taught the following sentence: "Love and devotion to one's parents, or filial piety, is the foundation of all virtues. All education and moral training is based on it." This was supposed to have been said by Confucius to his great disciple Tseng-tse. When the disciple, who was then also young and impatient, was getting up to go away, Confucius made him sit down again and said: "Wait, let me tell you. You should cause no damage to be done to your body, which you have inherited from your parents—this is the beginning of filial devotion. When you accomplish great deeds and develop into a noble character so that your name will be handed down to posterity as a tribute to your father and mother—this is the highest you can reach in the devotion to your parents. Remember that the end of this devotion is the complete fulfillment of your moral being."

And this little classic goes on in a similar vein. It now sounds old-fashioned and antiquated and difficult to understand. The children in Chou-tai's village school could have not paid more than lip service to these fine and noble sentiments. But the fact remains that these old-fashioned teachings, so long as they contain vital truths, continue to exercise a great and important influence on large sections of Chinese society today.

To give one example. A friend of mine who enjoys considerable wealth and is a self-made man is always proud to let his friends know that he owes nothing at all to his parents. He treats his father and mother well enough, providing them with the best food and giving them a beautiful suite in his palatial residence; and yet just because he says that he has nothing to be grateful to his parents for, even his business associates consider him to be morally dwarfed and shun him, with the result that his business has been seriously affected.

It is thus impossible to understand the mind of Chiang Kai-shek, the habits of his thought, and his accomplishments without knowing that he went through a course of training based upon ideas found in such books as the *Three-Word Classic* and the *Classic on Filial Love* which have nourished Chinese culture through the ages. Chiang Kai-shek's roots are deep in the past and he knows that they are strong. What he is now doing for the nation can be explained on the strength of this early training. To think of Chiang Kai-shek as attempting to break from the past or as having started China entirely on the lines of mechanical progress and modernization is to misunderstand him completely. The essence of the orderly progress of China is China's rediscovery of her historic personality and her infinite faith in her own power. Thus the supreme task for Chiang Kai-shek, as for Sun Yat-sen before him, is to make his countrymen realize the full value of China's classic lore. Having made it an integral part of their lives, he thinks and believes that the people of China can proceed with their work of modernization without danger to China as a nation.

When Chou-tai was being taught Chinese literature, ranging from the simplest subjects to the Four Books and the Five Classics, we need not feel that he worked and acted like a young sage. Boys are boys even when their minds are being drilled in the abstruse thoughts of moral philosophy. Chou-tai and his companions carried their fun and amusements even into their classrooms. These village schools conformed pretty well to a set pattern. Every new student who came in offered some diversion. His first duty was to pay his respects to the teacher, which was usually quite a little ceremony. The teacher ranked in importance next to the parents in helping to form the character of the boy placed under his charge. Their relationship was based upon the assumption of the vital importance of personal influence, a point of view which is now practically non-existent since modern education has become increasingly a matter of conveying instruction. In those days, when the student was brought into the presence of the master, his first act was to give deep and respectful bows and even to kowtow on the red felt spread over a cushion specially prepared for the occasion. He would partake of a pot of sugared tea with the other students to symbolize that the relationship between them would be sweet and one of harmony. But no sooner had the new student taken his seat than the older ones would perform their first prank on him. In order to see whether he could take it, they would tie his pigtail, which everybody then wore, to his chair, or, if it was long enough, to the leg of the table or bench. The fun was sure to begin even before the class was dismissed.

Committing the classics to memory meant reading the passages over and over again as loudly as possible. When half of the school was reading the same passages a leader, acting as a moderator or conductor, would use his hand to indicate whether the voices should be raised or lowered. The noise at times was deafening. But it was fun for the children.

The teacher, seeing that his students were applying themselves to the task of serious study, would also sometimes risk taking a nap. When he began to nod it was a signal for one of the braver boys to fill his teacup with water to the brim, cover it with a piece of paper, and then overturn it on the table so that the water would remain inside. While this difficult and audacious task was being performed, the class would read out in unison more loudly than ever in order to produce the impression of being well behaved. When it was done the teacher would at last wake up and push the inverted cup, whereupon the water would flood the table. The angry teacher would then go on the warpath. The culprit would be found, and the punishment would sometimes consist of having him lie face downward on the bench with his pants lowered sufficiently for the teacher to exercise the rod.

These were some of the variations that relieved the monotony of the classics within the classrooms; and as soon as the boys were out in the open they had, of course, tops to spin, shuttlecocks to play, and kites to fly. No Chinese boy who is worth his salt can pass his childhood without being proficient in some one of these extracurricular games or even in a combination of all of them. For they are the channels through which his native intelligence and ability can find full and spontaneous expression, while aptitude for the classics, without his having at the moment any understanding of their meaning, is after all merely the training of his memory. Chou-tai, like the rest of the children, was passionately devoted to these games.

He was one day confronted with a group of older boys while he was playing seesaw with another boy of his age. These demanded immediate possession of the wooden structure. The younger boys accepted the inevitable and gracefully retreated, only to prove later, however, that the retreat was a strategic move. They simulated defeat so well that no one paid them any attention. Chou-tai, however, whispered a few words into the ear of his companion, and the two of them disappeared into the house. When they came out again they each concealed a basin of water. It was already dusk; and as the seesaw came down to the ground the basin was gently placed at one end, so that when it went up again the water went into the air and drenched the rider. In the meantime the other end had come down, allowing the second basin of water to be placed in a similar way, to be followed by the same result.

Chou-tai had an enjoyable time as a child, but only when the cares and worries of his mother were not brought to his attention. The death of his father not so long before had created important changes in the life of the family, and the mother naturally had great difficulty in adapting herself to a situation in which she had to depend entirely upon her own resources. She was poor, and friends and relatives were not inclined to offer much help to a widow who showed little prospect of ever being completely on her feet again. The children were young and still unknown quantities.

Those were indeed hard times for Chou-tai's mother. To struggle against such trying circumstances was difficult enough. But that was not all. There were people, even some relatives and friends, who took advantage of her lack of protection and tried to take away what little she had in the way of worldly possessions. It was then that young Chou-tai saw the sadness on his mother's face and learned the cruelties and afflictions of human life.

Chou-tai's love and deep devotion to his mother were, however, a source of unfailing comfort to her, but he was young, and what could he do to help out? He would be lucky if other children who were more fortunately situated did not attempt to cause him misery, of which his mother had already had her share.

One such day came. Chou-tai's mother as usual went out to call on the relatives, leaving him and his younger sister in their modest home. The day was growing dark, and still the mother had not returned.

That came to the knowledge of the neighboring children, who would not allow the opportunity to go by without doing something to frighten the anxious brother and sister. Soon a strange sound was heard on the other side of the wall. It was meant to be the sound of a ghost from the tomb. But Chou-tai's intelligence was keen. He was not fooled. He knew at once who the children were who wanted to frighten them. He held his little sister close to him, explained to her who they were and what the noise was, but she burst out crying all the same, much to the delight of the mischief-makers. Their object having been accomplished, they left the frightened little sister and went their way. But Chou-tai's mind worked quickly; he was just one step ahead of them. In a moment he was ready for reprisals. He seized a near-by bamboo basket, which he overturned and fitted over his head. Covering it with a piece of white cloth, he quickly left by the back door and ran for the nearest big tree which he knew his enemies would pass on their way home. Soon they came, happy over the results of their adventure. The moment for revenge had arrived. Chou-tai moved forward, and yelled at the top of his lungs. The erstwhile heroes collapsed to the ground, thought they had really met a ghost, and cried out for help. The villagers came with their lanterns and discovered the boys still struggling to stand on their shivering legs, but Chou-tai was already home relating the story to his frightened sister.

When the mother returned after another day with friends and relatives, with perhaps nothing accomplished to win them over, she found her children sound asleep.

5

The Dragon's Anger

WHEN, in Chou-tai's thirteenth year, on his return to the village school, his mother reminded him that he must apply himself to serious study so that he might eventually do something for the good of his people, she had a great deal on her mind. Vast changes were going on in the country. She probably felt the devastating effects of the war with Japan five years before more than she had those of previous wars. The country was in a feverish state of excitement. The treaty ports where the foreigners were residing in increasing numbers had become busy not only as centers of trade but also as clearinghouses for plans and schemes affecting the future of China.

The people from Ningpo and the surrounding areas, including Fenghua and Chikow, were carrying on most of the bigger business transactions in those ports and especially in near-by Shanghai. When they made their periodic visits back to their villages, they would tell their families of the sights they had seen, of the strange warships, more powerful by far than their own bulky junks, that were plying the Whangpoo River. They would not know exactly what was taking place, but they heard rumors and gossip, and the districts all along the coast to the south of Shanghai felt more keenly than any part of China the impending changes in the life of the nation.

Chou-tai's mother, intelligent as she was, knew that her children, when they grew up, were not going to have an easy time. Yet there was nothing they could do. They were still young, and the only course that was open to them was to study hard and fortify themselves with knowledge and virtue. There is no record that she had definite plans for their future: her financial condition would not allow them to be made. But the decisions she had in mind for shaping the course of Chou-tai's scholastic career showed that she had vision and foresight.

Three years after China's defeat by Japan the controversy between the leaders of the tottering dynasty came to a head, while the foreign powers looked on and proceeded with their plans for the impending breakup of the country. The year 1898 was a memorable one. It was the year of the battle for concessions. It was a year of feverish changes, of defeated hopes, and the return of reactionary forces.

The foreign powers rivaled each other in the outright seizure of Chinese territory and the establishment of spheres of influence. The whole of the coast line from Manchuria in the north to Kwangtung in the south was full of scars through which spearheads of penetration had been thrust into the body of China.

The name of the great Li Hung-chang was on the lips of everyone. He had been in Russia, had traveled in Europe and America, and had gone through the intricacies of foreign diplomacy. He was the logical person to save the situation. But the foreign powers in their mad scramble for concessions made a great display of force. The only formula that Li Hung-chang could devise to protect the interests of his country was to play on the desires of the powers and dissipate their force by causing them to fight among themselves. The plan worked to a certain extent, but it was plain that something much more fundamental was needed.

It was then that cries for reforms were raised everywhere. Even mandarins like Chang Chih-tung whose knowledge of the world never extended beyond the limits of the Chinese classics began to clamor for radical changes. "The study of the old is not urgent; the call for men of attainments in useful knowledge is pressing." That was the gist of an essay entitled "Persuasion to Learn" which was a great literary piece of the period.

From June 11, 1898, for a hundred days, the Emperor Kuang Hsu, young, progressive, though somewhat lacking in force of personality, issued decree after decree calling for radical reforms in every branch of the national life. But it was not long before the reactionary elements, under the protection of the Empress Dowager, assumed complete control of the situation and broke up the reform movement before it really got started. She was a woman of strong resolves, a powerful character, but willful and ignorant. Cruel and possessed of execrable taste, vulgar and vain, she was pampered by a group of mean eunuchs and sycophants who knew how to strengthen their own positions but cared nothing about the real interests of the country. The reactionary forces grew and spread. Their country continued to be mercilessly devastated by the foreign powers, and their hatred for the foreigners and for everything foreign became a mania. The uprising of the I-ho Tuan or the Group of Righteous Harmony, popularly known as the Boxers, was the logical result of this policy of unending insult and continual impairment of Chinese sovereignty.

The rebellion, as Sir Robert Hart said, "was patriotic in its origin, and that it was justifiable in much that it aimed at cannot be questioned and cannot be too much insisted upon." But it was a movement based upon ignorance all the same, and the consequences were painful. Chou-tai's mother knew what a shameful episode it was and wondered to herself what career her son could follow after the nation had been so deeply humiliated. There was the father's profession and that of his grandfather which he could step into. Yet the atmosphere even in the quiet village of Chikow was too tense for that. There were rumors that among the villagers were actually young men and even young women who were joining the ranks of the secret societies, who, by means of mysterious incantations, believed that they had the power to drive away the foreigners. But the numbers of such people in the south were small compared with those in the northern provinces. Chou-tai's mother, however, did not believe in this supernatural power. She knew that strength could come only through serious application. She also knew that when her boy grew into manhood he was not going to receive any official emoluments from so rotten and decadent a regime as that of the Empress Dowager.

The ancestors of the Chiang family had settled in Chikow near the end of the Ming Dynasty, which was a Chinese dynasty, when the Manchus were beginning to entrench themselves in Peking. As descendants of the Ming people it was understood that, like many others who were loyal to that dynasty, they would remain clear of any official connections with the new alien house. Chou-tai's forebears therefore took to farming as the only commendable form of activity, and remained farmers until his grandfather became a merchant.

The time had come, so Chou-tai's mother thought, when the life of this alien dynasty was rapidly nearing its end. Chou-tai must be trained for the great opportunities that would come in the wake of its downfall. But before she knew it Chou-tai had become a lad of seventeen, just when Japan and Russia began their struggle for supremacy on the Manchurian plains.

For the first time the word "Manchuria" acquired a deep significance in Chou-tai's mind. It was no longer a child's mind. The land was an integral part of China, so he had learned, both from the elementary village school from which he was soon to graduate and from the scholars of the village who talked about the war between Japan and the Russian colossus. Yet Manchuria had become a battleground for two foreign powers. Chou-tai sought illumination on the subject from the old and the wise among the villagers, but received no satisfaction. Some had heard that Russia was a big and strong country that had only recently grown in territory at the expense of China. Large slices of China's northern territory beyond Manchuria had been cut away and annexed to Russia without China's full realization that they were being taken. And as regards Japan, the village scholars had heard nothing about her beyond the fact that she possessed a potent army and navy.

When the news finally came that Japan had actually defeated the great and powerful country of Russia, the effect on China generally and on Chou-tai in particular was great. Occasionally there were villagers who, on their return to Chikow from Shanghai, would tell of the sights they had seen in the growing metropolis. For the Russo-Japanese War, though it was fought in northern China, was felt even in Shanghai. The foreign settlements there had converted the city into a neutral area, and wounded Russian soldiers were pouring in by the thousands. Many of them were taken care of in factories and warehouses; and as they began to convalesce, they were happy that the war was over and appeared in the streets in full view of the pedestrians. They sometimes amused themselves, while moving about with amputated arms and legs and bandaged heads, by throwing chunks of bread and cubes of sugar onto the streets, and children would crowd around to see what they were. For in those days even objects so common as bread and sugar cubes, because they were foreign, were a source of curiosity.

Chou-tai wondered as he listened to the accounts of this strange war.

6

The Interval

CHOU-TAI WAS now entering the eighteenth year of his life. He had just completed a course of instruction extending over seven years such as every Chinese boy had received for hundreds of years, with perhaps a smattering of modern knowledge added. He had a good foundation in the classics, but that did not enable him to come confidently into contact with a larger world. The country at last was beginning to show an interest in foreign learning, for there was a decided change of attitude after the Boxer troubles and the Russo-Japanese War, but Chou-tai had had no training in any foreign language. In the treaty ports, and more particularly in Shanghai, Chinese children were being brought up under new influences, but life in the little village of Chikow went on much as it had always done. It knew little of the world outside, and Chou-tai's soul yearned for experiences that could be gained only by leaving this quiet life. His mother was also aware of the fact that her son required fresh mental food on entering early manhood.

However, it was time that her boy, who had now come of age to face a larger world, should no longer be known by the "little name" of Chou-tai. In the China of the past, the changing of a boy's name when he entered adolescence was celebrated by an elaborate ceremony. It involved changes in the manner of dressing his hair, which before had hung loose around the head and was neatly trimmed, but which from now on was to grow long and be tied in a knot perched on the crown. It involved also changes in the style of dress much in the same way that boys in England discard knickerbockers and don the full-length trousers of a man. The ceremony was elaborate, and like many other ancient practices it is no longer followed, the change of the name being about all that remains of the custom today.

To begin with, there is the "milk name," which is used exclusively by the parents. That is followed by the "little name," which is used by members of the family and is therefore a very intimate name. It is sometimes carried into the school, though a child is usually given an additional name, the "school name." When a boy comes of age, however, he assumes the name with which he faces the world and which remains with him for the rest of his life.

Chiang's mother decided to change the name of Chou-tai to Chung-cheng, *chung* meaning middle and *cheng* meaning just or right. Chinese names consist of three words, the first of which is the name of the family and the next two the personal name. There are slight variations. In rare cases a man has four words, in which the first two are the family name, as for instance, Ou-yang. There is not much to choose from for a family name, for theoretically there were only one hundred families in China, of which all the millions of families today are branches, and so there are only one hundred or so family names for the total of four hundred and fifty million people. There are therefore millions of Changs, Wangs, and Lees, which are among the commonest of family names. The family name of Chiang is not so popular, though it is found throughout the country. In order to distinguish one person from another with the same family name, there are different personal names consisting either of one word or, which is far more common, of two words. For these personal names there is a great variety of choice. The name usually describes some virtue or is the name of some illustrious person whom the boy aspires to emulate in later life.

Chou-tai's mother chose the name Chung-cheng to mean center and justice. But in addition to this name it is customary to have a courtesy name that is used by friends out of personal respect. Chung-cheng thus acquired the additional name of Kai-shek. The proper pronunciation of these words is really Chieh-shih, *chieh* meaning ambition and loyalty to ideals that marks a person from other people, or just great and luminous; and *shih* means a stone that is hard and durable. Kai-shek was the Cantonese pronunciation of these two words which became popular in those days when he spent so much of his time with Dr. Sun Yat-sen and the Kuomintang party in southern China. The name Kai-shek thus became known to the foreign world and has remained so to this day.

Chiang Kai-shek thus stayed at home with his mother, thinking and planning what to do next. The most serious obstacles were, of course, financial. A less determined mother would probably have acted differently under the weight of those financial difficulties. But Chiang's mother was not to be beaten. In her quiet way she was making contacts and finding the means to send the boy to a larger educational institution.

While she was thus planning, Chiang Kai-shek was himself passing through a period of mental agitation. He looked placid and complacent, continuing the pursuit of his studies through self-application. Methodically he practiced his Chinese handwriting, a form of exercise that scholars indulge in as much for the spiritual and moral qualities which it develops as for the mastery of the brush. For it is a widely prevailing belief that, until the opportune moment arrives, a person's energy and vitality should not be dissipated and squandered but should be properly harnessed, controlled, and harmonized as a part of his moral force. Constant practice at handwriting, like painting, evokes an aesthetic sense and develops at the same time a moral personality.

For fully half a year Chiang Kai-shek led the life of a young recluse, thinking and planning ahead for the years that were to follow. He was laying the broad foundations of his character. He read and studied once more the classics which for a period of seven or eight years he had only learned like a parrot, singing and shouting with the rest of the class more as a matter of fun and routine than of serious study. He was then too young to have an understanding of the abstruse truths of the ancient moral philosophy. But now it gradually became clearer. His mind was going through a period of illumination. The words conveyed a significance that was not present before. That brief span of a few months was for Chiang Kai-shek a real turning point in his life. The period of fun and amusement was over; from now on he was determined to be earnest and serious-minded.

Many other manifestations of the important changes which were going on within were now apparent. He became quiet in his manners and was not given to flippancy. He was not inclined to talk much. His whole moral inspiration was derived from the classics that were unburdening their treasures to him. To his mother he was always the devoted and loving son, for now he understood why it was said in the little *Classic on Filial Love* that devotion to one's parents was the foundation of all moral virtues.

Above all, poor as he was, he hoped that he would soon have an opportunity to enter a more advanced school where modern training would be offered so that he could discover what was going on in the outside world. He had to be patient, however, and to wait for the good news that some satisfactory financial arrangement was forthcoming.

Finally the news arrived. The mother was able at last to say to her son: "Here, child, take this money and go find for yourself a modern school of learning." She produced forthwith a small bundle wrapped up in a handkerchief in which, when she untied the knots, there lay before the thankful eyes of the son a hundred and more silver coins. "These," she continued, "are all that I have saved after years of toil with my needle and as a result of prolonged negotiation with friends and relatives."

With this money young Chiang Kai-shek took leave of his mother and went north to Ningpo, crossed the Chientang River and found himself in the large and populous city of Hangchow. It would have been better, he thought to himself, if he could proceed to Shanghai, where people from foreign lands congregated and where boys from inside the country went if they had the money. However, that was still beyond his means. Hangchow was the capital of the province and could already boast that it was the seat of many new schools of learning, among which was the recently established School of Law and Politics. There were then few such schools anywhere in China. They were being slowly and grudgingly established by the government only as a concession to the invasion of foreign ideas. The day had at last arrived when it became clear even to the reactionaries that to maintain the status quo was to court disaster.

The School for Law and Politics in Hangchow was therefore a new institution worthy of some consideration. Chiang Kai-shek went there as a lonely boy with big resolves in mind. At first he was overwhelmed by the beauty of the city, about which he had heard so much. There was the enchanting lake, long associated with the muses, and all along its shores were monuments and tombs of great historic figures and personalities. There were two beautiful pagodas on either side of the lake, redolent with romance and legends that stretched back into the medieval days of the Tang Dynasty. There were picturesque villas of the rich with lovely gardens that seemed to float with fairylike lightness on the water of the lake. It was altogether fascinating, this city which became the capital of China in the twelfth century, when the nomadic hordes sweeping down from the cold, bleak lands of the north threatened the serenity of the imperial house of the Sung Dynasty.

There was one monument in particular that attracted the attention of young Chiang Kai-shek. It was hidden behind a temple on the shore of the lake. It was a tomb lying peacefully under a canopy of old pine trees. In it was buried a hero, Yo Fei by name, who gave his life at the age of thirty-nine in defense of his country against the invasion of the Kin barbarians from the north. He died as a victim of betrayal and treachery at the hands of an important minister of state.

Chiang Kai-shek loved to walk over the spacious grounds surrounding this tomb and think about those difficult days of the Sung Dynasty. He could not help comparing the condition of the country during those days with that of his own time, when it was again in danger of being invaded by foreign foes. What similarities there were between then and now, he thought, and yet there was a difference. The reigning house then was a Chinese house, but the reigning house now belonged to the Manchus, a nomadic tribe that was once scattered along the borders of Manchuria. The task of saving the country was now twofold. It was necessary first to abolish the Manchu rule, and then on the destruction of the old to build a new edifice powerful enough to resist the forces of foreign invasion. It was a long and arduous task, but someone must rise to accomplish it. And as he sat thinking beside the tomb he looked across the lake at the new buildings of the School of Law and Politics. If he finished his course of study at this institution, he had been told, he could become a lawyer. But what point was there in being a lawyer or a mandarin of a decaying alien dynasty? Were not all his people direct descendants of those who swore loyalty to the Chinese house of the Mings? The more he thought about the prospect of a legal career, the less attractive it seemed.

So for many days he wavered between carrying out his original plan and making a new resolve. All the arguments seemed to be in favor of his giving up the contemplated career of a lawyer and an official. More especially, his daily visits to the tomb of the hero who brought so much honor and glory to his race left no room in Chiang's bosom for anything but the strong desire to emulate him. How he admired this great soldier who for ten long years had fought not only a foreign foe on the battlefield but also strong enemies within the court itself. Chiang sat on one of those stone benches near the tomb surrounded by the lovely old trees, and there he gazed at the image of the hero and at the two kneeling figures in front of it, Chin Kuei and his wife, by whom Yo Fei had been betrayed and killed.

The Kin barbarians, or the Golden Hordes as they are more popularly known in history, began devastating the northern borders of the Chinese Empire when Yo Fei was a lad of twenty. That was only slightly older than himself, Chiang Kai-shek thought, and curiously enough, there were a number of similarities in their personal fortunes and environment. Yo Fei also belonged to a family of farmers and was so poor that he had no money even to buy the candles he needed for the studies that he pursued deep into the night. He studied almost the same books that Chiang had become familiar with during those years at the village school. But there was one book that especially intrigued Chiang, one about which he had heard but had not yet read or studied. He found that Yo Fei was a passionate student of the *Art of War*, written by one Sun Tse in the fifth century B.C. It was that work which had contributed so much to Yo Fei's success as a soldier.

Also, Chiang thought as he sat musing among the old ruins, Yo Fei's father reminded him of his own father and grandfather, except that Yo Fei's father had been even poorer. Often as Yo Fei's father cooked his evening meal he would keep only one half of it for himself and his family, leaving the other half to be distributed among those who were without food. It was the same kind of generosity and the same kind of desire to work for the common good that, Chiang knew, his own immediate ancestors had shown.

Most of all Chiang admired Yo Fei's military ability and his deep loyalty to his country. By the time Yo Fei was twenty-five, in 1127, the Sung emperors were actually kidnaped by the foreign invaders. It was a deeply humiliating chapter in Chinese history. And as the invaders pushed steadily southward, the reigning house was compelled to establish its temporary wartime capital in Hangchow, the very city where Chiang was passing his days. All the Chinese territory to the north, including Honan and Shantung, became occupied territory and was placed under those whom the invaders chose to set up as the rulers.

It was then that Yo Fei took up the sword in defense of his country and his race. He was then a young military officer, and in a series of brilliant victories he managed to push the invaders far back into the north. He had his own strategy and tactics, based on the element of surprise and quickness of action. Although he was in command of only a few thousand soldiers, he managed to defeat an enemy of vastly superior numbers. These historical facts made a profound impression upon Chiang Kai-shek. How did he manage to do all that? What superior power did he possess? These and other questions assumed paramount importance to Chiang. Then he recalled that, even as this leader struck terror into the heart of the invading foe, there were people within the Chinese court itself who grew jealous of his power. The invaders were driven to a point where they actually sued for peace, but the great minister Chin Kuei still allowed large portions of Chinese territory to be occupied by them. Yo Fei protested and swore that he would have only complete victory. He would continue to fight until he reached the last base of the enemy. The invaders accepted the challenge and called out their ablest general with a force of fifteen thousand cavalry. Yo Fei met the attack by ordering his soldiers to lie flat on the ground and to hold their big knives ready for the charge. The horses, each with a rider on it, came tied to one another in groups of three. Yo Fei saw at once that as long as his enemy could advance they were unbeatable, but that there was no way for them to retreat. As the enemy advanced toward the defenders, they found Yo Fei's soldiers spread on the ground, which was covered by carefully scattered hemp. The horses' feet became entangled, and when one horse fell with a stroke of the knives the other two had to fall also. The riders fell with them, and the invading force was all but wiped out.

Yo Fei's armies advanced so far north as to recover all of Honan, where the Sung emperors lay buried. He was in a position to say to his commanding officers: "Let us go straight to the city of the Yellow Dragon[1] and there we shall drink to our hearts' content." It was then that Chin Kuei called for a truce. He recalled all the commanders from the various warring sectors. Yo Fei's army alone remained in the field. But orders inscribed on slabs of gold, supposed to have been

[1] In Manchuria, the seat of the government of the invading hordes.

issued by the Emperor himself, came thick and fast. In one day Yo Fei received twelve of them asking him to come back. There was no way out of the difficulty. He was alone and ran the risk of disobeying the imperial commands. Treachery had won the day. And so it is said: "From time immemorial it has been true that if there is a powerful enemy within no general, however able he may be, can ever hope to accomplish anything on the field of battle." This is indeed true not only of military leadership but also of Chinese political life generally, even down to the present day.

Upon Yo Fei's return he asked that he be relieved of his military duties so that he could go back to his farm, but the request was not granted. His political enemy, Chin Kuei, could not allow him to disappear from the scene so peacefully and accused him of harboring rebellious desires against the reigning house. As a Chinese proverb says, "If one decides to create trouble for a person, there is no difficulty in finding some cause to condemn him." In the courtroom when the trial was on, Yo Fei stripped himself to the waist, and there revealed on his back four words inscribed deep in his flesh: *"tsin-chung pao-kuo,"* meaning: "Exert the utmost of your loyalty for the welfare of your country." Nonetheless, it was Chin Kuei's desire that Yo Fei must die. He was thrown into prison and in two months the hero was dead.

Chiang Kai-shek thought long about the extraordinary career of this patriot whose great deeds had never been forgotten by his countrymen. As Chiang looked at the tomb he felt close to this young soldier. But he saw also those two small kneeling figures of a man and his wife who, through jealousy and treachery, murdered the savior of their country. For the first time in Chiang's life it dawned upon him that human life was a dual battle—a struggle to assert the very best which one was capable of for constructive enterprise, and a struggle against the dark and sinister forces which continued to seek one's ruination because of that capability. Of the two, the second battle was even more difficult.

7

And So It Happened

AND SO IT HAPPENED that as he left the tomb Chiang Kai-shek was deeply engrossed in thought. It was time for his noonday meal, and he walked slowly toward the shore of the lake and turned in at a near-by restaurant.

He sat there alone at a table that gave him a full view of the lake. In the distance was a range of mountains within whose valleys were the ancient Buddhist temples. He heard a few notes from the distant bells. The lake itself was also a delightful sight. On one side was the inner lake, which was separated from the outer lake by a dike of earth that was completely covered with weeping willows. And there were those fairylike boats which plied from one villa to another. Purity, quietness, and peace!

The waiter came, and Chiang ordered his food. It was a simple repast that he wanted, and the fish and shrimps were so fresh and tastily cooked that they became a regular part of everybody's menu. The cook went straight to the shore of the lake, and there took out of a bamboo basket fish and shrimps that had just been caught.

Chiang's thoughts continued to eddy around the personality of the hero. Aside from being purely a military hero, he must have been a great moral force as well. For though he was a great general, he lived a most frugal and abstemious life. When friends wanted to present him with servants Yo Fei replied, "How can I think of personal comfort when the country is having such difficulties?" When he scored victories over the enemy and the imperial court wanted to build a house for him Yo Fei said, "If the Kin barbarians are not destroyed, I have no need for any house." Yo Fei was once asked when there would be peace in the country, and his reply was, "When civilian officials do not covet money and when military officers are not afraid of death, that will be the day when there will be peace in the country." It was Yo Fei's policy to treat his soldiers with kindness and consideration, but he enforced the strictest discipline. If they went to the extent of taking anything from the people without paying for it, the penalty was death. But if the soldiers were wounded he would personally see that they were attended to. He would send his own wife to the families of the commanders in the field when they received orders to take up service far away. And even if it was necessary to store up food for the soldiers he would constantly remind his officers that the people's ability to contribute had been taxed to the utmost. His favorite remark which he rigidly applied to himself was, "If a man really wants to perform immortal deeds he must consider all other desires as obstacles." This great military leader was also a scholar who could write a beautiful hand. Greatness in any field in China must be built on moral strength. A soldier is not really great simply because of his military ability; he must be reinforced by character and a strong moral personality before he is recognized as being truly great.

Young Chiang Kai-shek was so deeply impressed by these qualities and so absorbed in them that he did not realize that other guests had come into the restaurant. The waiter came up and whispered a few words into Chiang's ear. "I beg your pardon, but those two guests over there . . ." And he made a gesture in the direction of a middle-aged man and a boy younger than Chiang himself. "Won't you please give up your table to them?"

"But why?" Chiang wanted to know.

"Well, excuse me for saying so," replied the waiter, "but those two people are so powerful that I run some risk if I do not satisfy their desires. The younger of the two is the son of the mayor of this city and is related to the imperial house. The older one is an official in the mayor's office. How can I say no to anything they want?"

The request came just at the moment when young Chiang's mind was overwhelmed by thoughts of the deep patriotism of Yo Fei.

"I drink my wine and they drink theirs," Chiang replied. "I have my table and they have theirs. Why should I give up what I have in order to please them? Haven't they occupied the beautiful mountains and rivers of this fair land long enough? Can't they allow me to occupy so small a thing as a table? What right have they to demand that I give it up to them?"

The waiter was in a most embarrassing situation and immediately went over to the couple and apologized. "I'll give you a good table tomorrow. That youngster happens to have had more wine than is good for his health. Well, yes, so please you, what would you have for your lunch?" But the older one would not be so insulted and insisted upon having the table because it commanded the best view of the lake.

He must do something to please his young master. The younger one, however, was more sensible.

"Why spoil an enjoyable afternoon by working up your passion like this?" And so the incident came to an end.

Chiang drank a few more cups of rice wine and recalled, during this moment of emotional stress, the great poem that Yo Fei had written, at the age of thirty, when he was engaged in the military campaign against the foreign foe. Chiang repeated aloud the closing lines of the poem.

> *The national shame has not been wiped off,*
> *When will my sorrows be appeased?*
> *Let us ride in the long war chariots,*
> *And cross the northern range.*
> *Let the soldiers, when they are hungry,*
> *Feed on the flesh of the barbarian hordes!*
> *Let them laugh and drink*
> *The very blood of these Huns!*
> *These ancient hills and valleys—*
> *Let them be taken over and reconquered.*
> *For then and only then can we face*
> *The imperial court.*

Young Chiang had learned to read poetry in the village school, and he recited it well. It made an immediate impression on the guests who were present. But those were the days of the Manchu monarchy, and no one dared recite patriotic songs and poems without suspicion falling upon him. The guests, perhaps, liked it but they were visibly afraid. There was one among them, however, who did not seem to be overly concerned. He smiled and glanced approvingly in the direction of Chiang.

"Your bill, sir, has been paid," said the waiter, coming back to the young visitor from Chikow.

Chiang did not wish to allow such a thing, but the stranger insisted that he should at least show some respect to the young man who had won his admiration. They went through the formalities of introducing themselves and continued their lunch together. They discussed the problems of the day and agreed that the only salvation for the country was the overthrow of the existing incompetent government in order to make room for a new regime. Before they realized it they were expressing the sentiments of revolutionaries, and in doing so they were exposing themselves to personal danger. For the official in the mayor's office to whom young Chiang would not give up his table had determined that it was his duty to notify the authorities of the existence of such revolutionaries and have them properly taken care of.

When Chiang and his older friend, who had introduced himself as a Mr. Tao, finally left the restaurant for their hotels, they were followed. Tao was more experienced in these things, because he actually was a revolutionary, and he suggested that they move to new quarters. Whereupon young Chiang left Hangchow and went back to his native Chikow across the Chientang River. His mind was now made up, for the influence of Yo Fei had been decisive. He wanted to follow a military career.

The sojourn in Hangchow had been a short one, but for Chiang it had been a visit packed with fresh impressions and significant experiences. It was the first time that he had left his native village for a big city, and he came back a changed person. He became stronger, spiritually more fortified, and his outlook upon life became more definite and purposeful. For the city of Hangchow, with all its seductive charms, taught him that it was, after all, a city full of inadequacies. Delicacy, poetry, romance, gracefulness—it had all of these qualities, which indeed touched a very genuine part of human life, but still it remained a symbol of softness and frustration. It lacked the vigor and the vitality to stand as a citadel of strength against the evil forces that kept battering it both from within and without. It had become the capital of China when the life of the nation was at a low ebb; and if Yo Fei, whose like appeared only once in many centuries in any country, had failed to rally the manhood of the nation and succumbed to meanness and treachery, it meant to Chiang that the city and the people living in it were lacking in those virile qualities that alone could command the respect of so purposeful a young man. He had talked with the people of Hangchow and from them had gained the same impression. Their language, their manners, their pettiness, their ways of doing things, all seemed soft and effeminate to Chiang.

8

The Career Begins

Upon his return to Chikow after his short stay at Hangchow, Chiang Kai-shek did everything he could to further his dream of a military career. It was an unorthodox career, and there was naturally a good deal of opposition. There was first of all a social stigma attached to anyone who wanted to be a soldier. No boy who had any self-respect or was from an honorable family would ever think of descending to such a level. For there is a widely known saying in China, "No good iron is cast into nails as no good man ever becomes a soldier." How far back this sentiment goes it is difficult to say. But it is interesting to bear in mind that, though the Chinese as a race are a peace-loving people, they have experienced war in its many phases as often as any modern state. But it remains true that the Chinese believe military measures to be only a means to an orderly and peaceful government and that military careers must be rounded off by more than purely military accomplishments. They show no respect to the military man as such and erect no monument to perpetuate his memory.

The relatives of the Chiang family also objected, not perhaps because they had any special love for the family, but because they did not particularly desire to be known as relatives of a boy who was not doing them honor.

Chiang's decision was obviously a grave matter. But the fact that the young man ultimately succeeded in following his own desires shows that even in those early days he had a will of his own. Once he had made up his mind, he would not change it even in the face of the bitterest opposition. He was known in those days of early manhood to have a peculiar habit. He rose early, and after completing his daily morning tasks he would stand with his eyes closed and his mouth tightly shut for a quarter of an hour or more as if he were going through some exercise to strengthen his will power. Perhaps all young men of ambition, during this formative period, undergo some form of test to prove to themselves the existence of an inner power. If so, Chiang Kai-shek was no exception.

In addition to making important resolutions for his future, Chiang was systematically persistent. He would not wax enthusiastic one day and then allow his fervor to cool the next. His habits were orderly and, once formed, they were apt to take root. After careful consideration he had made up his mind to follow a military career. He was not going to give it up simply because he could not please other people. Chiang's mother, as always, was a great help at this critical period of his life. She stood solidly on the side of her son. She understood him as she understood conditions in the country. She knew what it meant to be defeated by Japan when, in addition to territorial concessions, including Formosa and the Pescadores, China had to pay an indemnity of $200,000,000. So, when her son decided that he wanted to follow the life of a soldier as the only effective means of making the country strong and powerful, she gave him every encouragement and support. It was a rare thing for a woman in her position to do.

In 1906 Chiang departed for Japan to begin his military studies, but on his arrival he made the painful discovery that all Chinese students entering a Japanese military academy had to be sponsored by the Chinese Government. No Japanese military academy could take a private student from China. Chinese students must first go through a preparatory course of training at home. So after a few months Chiang returned to sit for the examination of the Military Academy at Paoting in North China.

The few months in Japan, however, did Chiang a world of good. In the first place, passing from Shanghai to Japan, he saw an enormous difference between the conditions in the two countries. Shanghai was growing into a great metropolis, but its growth was largely due to the initiative and effort of the foreign community there. The special privileges which the foreigners enjoyed in the settlements and concessions were all symbols, to a young man like Chiang, of the weakness and incompetence of the government. The foreigners were clearly pursuing a policy of exploitation which the government had no power to resist. In Japan, however, he found a new and energetic nation whose government was strong enough to take care of the interests of its own people. It was making rapid progress in every line of work, and Chiang could now see for himself why China continued to be defeated in all her wars and why Japan could even win a victory over so powerful a nation as Russia.

Shanghai and Nagasaki, the Japanese port where he landed, were both rapidly growing cities; but one symbolized the inefficiency and corruption of the Chinese Government, because it was the foreigners who were behind its growth, while the other symbolized progressiveness and enterprise.

Chiang's belief in the necessity of overthrowing the existing government, therefore, grew deeper, and his first contacts were naturally with members of the Chinese revolutionary party, of whom there were large numbers in Japan. One man in particular, who later was destined to have an important influence on Chiang both as friend and superior, now came into his life. This was Chen Chi-mei, eleven years his senior, who next to Sun Yat-sen did more for the revolutionary cause in China than any other single person. Chen was already active as a leading member of the Tungmenghui, the revolutionary party of which Sun Yat-sen was the founder. The Kuomintang party which today guides the destiny of China is its lineal descendant. Chen's two nephews, Chen Ko-fu and Chen Li-fu,[1] remain important members of the party and government to this day.

The academy to which Chiang had to return to sit for the examination was the only military academy from which students were sent to Japan at government expense. The academy was a new institution, having been established only recently by Yuan Shih-kai, who was a potent force close to the imperial throne. A very able man, Yuan had confined his activities exclusively to the court and showed no sympathy with the revolutionary movement that had grown up in the south under the leadership of Sun Yat-sen, who was constantly having to find refuge with his associates in Japan.

Chiang passed the examination with distinction. He was one of a group of sixty students who were chosen from the province of Chekiang. The Paoting Military Academy, as the only institution of its kind, wanted all of the provinces of the country to be represented. The quota for Chekiang, Chiang's native province, was, however, unusually large. Most of the successful candidates were well advanced in years and, although the examination was conducted entirely on the basis of merit, political influence had much to do with the choice of candidates. There was no one to give Chiang a helping hand. It was only through his own ability that he succeeded in passing the examination.

One of the examiners did complain, however, that a boy of nineteen was too young to enter the academy.

[1] Chen Li-fu, a mining engineer from the University of Pennsylvania, is now China's Minister of Education.

"I beg your pardon, sir," the young man exclaimed with all due respect, "but as you can see, I am in the best of physical condition. I am anxious to serve my country, and it has been my ambition for many years to be a student of this academy. Please allow me this opportunity, and you need not be concerned with my age."

His earnestness took effect. Chiang at once made preparations to go north. The journey in those days from Chikow to Paoting was a long one. The first stop was Shanghai, through which he had previously passed. But, as usual, he had to wait for many days before he could get a steamer to Tientsin, where he would have to disembark for the academy at Paoting. It was tiresome having to wait, but fortunately it was not time wasted. He again saw the degradation into which his countrymen had fallen in this big and growing city. Laborers were working like beasts of burden for a mere pittance. Their life was pitifully poor. All their energy was being expended so that a few foreign capitalists might carry on their trade and grow rich. And although the territory was Chinese, frightful treatment was meted out to the population, who were treated worse than dogs. For as Chiang walked along the Bund, along the river where so many foreign steamers were anchored waiting to carry rich merchandise into the far corners of the world, he saw that he and his countrymen were not even allowed to step into the park enclosures, which were reserved exclusively for the small foreign community. And his thoughts went back to the few months that he had spent in Japan, where an energetic nation was master of its own household.

The day arrived when he was to take the steamer that was to carry him north. There again foreign passengers traveled in what was known as the saloon passage, clean, comfortable, and airy, all on the upper deck. The decks down below, dirty, squalid, and smelly with overcrowded humanity, were for the Chinese passengers, who were placed in two classes, the first Chinese class being euphemistically called "the mandarin's cabin."

For one week the young candidate for the Military Academy at Paoting was on board this ship. The experience was frightful; it was not only uncomfortable, it was degrading. Chiang passed that week of torture in deep meditation and thought. "Yes, the foreigners are cruel and hateful," he must have thought to himself, "but after all, we have our own shortcomings. If only we become strong ourselves, if only we become strong ourselves . . ." He probably recalled the four words of antiquity, *tse-chiang pu-shi*—to increase and work unceasingly for one's own strength. That became the motto of his life. It remains his motto to this day.

Upon his arrival at the academy he found that it was a fine institution with good equipment and a faculty of well-trained instructors from many lands. There were Japanese and German as well as British and French instructors. For although the school was newly established, it was part of an ambitious scheme of Yuan Shih-kai's to assume military control of China. Yuan was the recognized leader of the Pei-yang military party, and since the country's defeat by Japan in 1894-95, he had become the creator of China's "modern" army. He inherited all the power of Li Hung-chang, and although for a time he had a number of rivals, he virtually became a military dictator immediately after the Boxer troubles in 1900. He began with the creation of two modern military divisions, which grew to six divisions by 1906, the year in which young Chiang Kai-shek enrolled as a student in the academy. When, in that year, Yuan was appointed a minister of state in control of the military power, he helped create a Central Military Board of which he became the director. Although the soldiers were officially under the supervision of that board, they were actually Yuan's own soldiers, who were primarily loyal to himself. At any rate, all the officers in command of those troops were appointed by Yuan. The Military Academy at Paoting was organized to supply those officers. In the normal course of affairs, therefore, Chiang Kai-shek would become an officer under the command of Yuan Shih-kai.

It did not take Chiang long to see that Yuan was feathering his own nest, but the young student had to be patient: any carelessness on his part would spell disaster. He had to be especially circumspect about his revolutionary sympathies, which had by that time already become quite pronounced. As it was, he came into the academy without a queue, a fact that did not fail to excite a good deal of interest and curiosity, both among his fellow students and among the faculty. For to go about without that ornament was equivalent to a declaration of his disbelief in the existing monarchy. There was only one course open to Chiang, and that was to be as observant as possible and to apply himself vigorously to his studies so that he might be sent to Japan for further study with the least possible delay.

His observation of conditions in the Chinese Army in those days led him to one conclusion that was later to be exceedingly important. He realized that, incompetent as the Chinese Army as a whole might be, the individual soldier was fine military raw material. He was hardy, brave, intelligent, and obedient. He was capable of extraordinary endurance and could go through the bitterest fighting with a minimum amount of subsistence. Given the right type of training and leadership, he could be transformed into an excellent soldier.

But the Chinese soldier in those days was led by incompetent officials whose physical and moral energy had been sapped through contact with an effete and degenerate officialdom. As regards equipment, the Chinese soldier had to depend upon a variety of weapons ranging from those of feudal times to the most modern. But the important factor, as Chiang observed, was the quality of the soldier himself, and that was indeed very good. All he needed was training and leadership, which Chiang made up his mind he would one day supply.

These observations seem to have been borne out by disinterested observers of that period. An Irishman by the name of George Lynch, who fought against the Boxers in 1900, had the following to say about the Chinese soldier:

> I got some interesting glimpses of the Imperial troops and of their quaint armament which is composed of a mixture of the most modern rifles and field-guns with the bows and arrows of centuries ago. I saw them practicing with the latter at targets when riding on horseback at full gallop, and taking apparently as much interest in this practice of archery as they did in rifle practice. This is not so much to be wondered at when we consider that the Chinese officers are men who have been successful at examinations in which they have shown their proficiency in the use of the bow and arrow as well as in the knowledge of the tactics of the time of Confucius. From what I saw of the Chinese soldiers here as well as Chinamen in general all over the country, I came to the conclusion that a Chinaman is capable of being manufactured into a really good soldier. He is very quick to learn anything taught him, he is obedient, hardy, capable of enduring great fatigue, and either extremity of heat and cold, and is extremely simple in his mode of living. With great individual strength, he combines a fineness of hand and touch which would enable him to manipulate with facility the most delicate machinery of our modern killing machines.
>
> But none of these qualities can be used or brought into play until he has officers capable of teaching and leading. The present men are incapable both from temperament and qualifications. Their qualifications are antiquated and on obsolete subjects, their temperament is that of scholars, not of fighting men, still less of leaders of fighting men. The Chinaman would make a very different soldier if properly drilled, taught and led.[2]

[2] George Lynch, *The War of Civilizations*, 1901, p. 281.

It is the truth of this observation and the resulting confidence in the quality and capabilities of the individual Chinese soldier that has sustained Chiang Kai-shek's abiding faith in the prospects of a first-class Chinese Army. But he had to wait eighteen years before he was placed in a position to provide the leadership and the equipment necessary for such an army.

9

A Military Classic

CHIANG KAI-SHEK had no time to lose at the Military Academy. He had made some careful observations, but he wanted above all to apply himself vigorously to his studies.

The instructors in the academy were of various nationalities, but Chiang had been to Japan, and his immediate purpose in attending the institution was to pass the final examination so that he could enter an advanced Japanese military college and rejoin his revolutionary comrades, with many of whom he had only a fleeting acquaintance. He therefore confined himself largely to the Chinese and Japanese instructors. From the Chinese instructors he gained a historical view of the art of war as practiced in China through the different dynasties. From the Japanese instructors, even though some of them were unbearably haughty and repugnant, being intoxicated by their recent successes against the Russians, Chiang learned their language, which was important if he planned to return to their country for further study.

The reasons why Japan had been giving asylum for many years to young revolutionaries from China were interesting. The Japanese themselves have to this day never tolerated any anti-monarchical movement, and yet they openly encouraged the activities of a group of young Chinese whose one ambition was to overthrow the existing Manchu monarchy and establish a republican form of government. The Japanese gave this support not because they hoped that the young men would really succeed in making China a modern and progressive country. That was the last thing they wanted, for it has been Japan's consistent policy to keep a weak and divided China across the sea, and the young revolutionaries would supply just the right amount of chaos and confusion which the Japanese desired to introduce into China.

There were occasions when a few Japanese really became friendly and sympathetic to Sun Yat-sen and his followers, but the Japanese Government maintained a strict viligance so that the revolutionary ideas were confined mainly to the Chinese. The Chinese, on the other hand, welcomed this arrangement as a splendid opportunity. They knew they were undertaking a task which would mean the supreme punishment if they were apprehended by the Manchu authorities, and Japan, being so near China, was the only base from which they could operate. All they wanted was the freedom and sense of security which the Japanese willingly provided. The young followers of Sun Yat-sen could thus openly plan their revolutionary activities right under the nose of the official representatives of the Manchu court in Japan without fear of any harm being done them.

There was one book in particular that Chiang studied during this period. It was the book which was constantly referred to by Yo Fei and which became Chiang's main preoccupation when, during his short sojourn in Hangchow, he considered the extraordinary career of the patriot. The *Art of War* of Sun Tse was written in the Age of the Contending States (480-221 B.C.), during which period a group of seven states struggled and fought for supremacy in China. Throughout his military career Chiang has made constant reference to this military classic, written nearly twenty-five hundred years ago. One of the most familiar quotations is this: "He is not the best soldier who fights a hundred battles and wins a hundred victories. The best soldier is one who, without being engaged in any battle, wins over the enemy and makes him willingly submit."

It sounds strange, this idea of defeating your enemy without having recourse to actual combat, nor is it an ideal that is frequently realized, but it is interesting that such an ideal exists in China. To the Chinese, genuine conquest must be of the heart, and as long as the heart is not conquered victory achieved through superior military ability, which in essence is physical, is only a temporary victory. The aim of all military conquest is that the enemy completely submit to the conqueror's will for as long a time as possible. That clearly involves not only his defeat in actual combat but also a genuine willingness for co-operation afterward. Military victory is therefore the beginning, not the end, of real conquest. The Chinese ideal, as expressed by Sun Tse, maintains that, if it is possible to conquer the heart of your enemy without having recourse to arms, it is a more real and permanent conquest. We shall see later how Chiang Kai-shek made full use of this idea some thirty years later in the liquidation of China's modern feudalism and thus united the country under his control.

The many kinds of propaganda which nations at war commonly resort to are, in a sense, one expression of this idea. The famous Fourteen Points of President Wilson are in this category. There is no denying that they brought the first World War to an end earlier than it would have otherwise ended; and if those points had been more scrupulously carried out, it is possible that the present war could have at least been delayed. It was a case of the heart of the enemy being conquered, and that precipitated his downfall and collapse; but victory remained temporary because the Versailles Conference brought forth a new crop of hatred and bitterness: the heart did not remain conquered.

However that may be, the *Art of War* by Sun Tse, which Chiang Kai-shek so closely studied during this early period of his life, laid the foundations of his career both as a soldier and as a statesman. Sun Tse lived at a time when China was divided into seven powerful states. It was an interesting period and offers many striking resemblances to what is taking place in the world today. In the west of China was Tsin, the biggest and most powerful state of them all. In the south, in what is now central China, was the state of Chu. There was Chi in the east (present-day Shantung), and then there were the Yen, Han, Chao, and Wei states. They had some difficulty in maintaining a balance of power, and the result was the development of a number of alliances and counter-alliances. Military measures became an essential adjunct to diplomatic negotiations. It was in that atmosphere that Sun Tse wrote his remarkable treatise on war, which is perhaps the earliest document to be written on that subject in any language, and remains to this day a classic. It discusses the principles of military science and military strategy, which are permanently true, even though there had been a complete revolution in the weapons of warfare.[1]

[1] In an article, "Armies That Win," which was published in *Life* magazine, October 5, 1942, the author, David Cort, said: "The first organized warfare began on the other side of the world, in China, where by 500 B.C. Sun Tse had written down the rules by which the Chinese conquered. His lessons on discipline, deception, maneuver, terrain are good today."

We shall have occasion later to see how Chiang Kai-shek applied the principles of Sun Tse to the training of his army and to his conduct of war. For the present, we find Chiang an ardent student of this military classic. What then were some of the ideas he learned from this book that was written at least a generation before Aristotle had Alexander the Great as his private pupil?

This is what Sun Tse had to say about discipline. "If soldiers are punished before they have grown attached to you, they will not prove submissive, and unless submissive they are practically useless. If, when the soldiers have become attached to you, punishments are not enforced, they will still be useless. Therefore soldiers must be treated, in the first instance, with humanity, but kept under control by means of iron discipline. Regard your soldiers as your children and they will follow you into the deepest valleys; look on them as your beloved sons and they will stand by you even unto death."

About leadership, Sun Tse says: "The general who advances without coveting fame and retreats without fearing disgrace, whose only thought is to protect his country and do good service for his sovereign, is the jewel of the kingdom." And this: "At a critical moment, the leader of an army acts like one who has climbed up a height and then kicks away the ladder behind him."

On deception: "All warfare is based on deception. Hence when able to attack, we must seem unable; when using our forces, we must seem inactive; when we are near, we must make the enemy believe we are far away; when far away, we must make him believe we are near.... Therefore attack the enemy when he is not prepared, catch him when he is napping."

Another principle of successful warfare is that, though the soldiers must obey orders, they should not commit themselves to any hard and fast rule. It is important that they should be intelligent enough to know how to be elastic. "While reaping the profit of my counsel, avail yourself also of any helpful circumstances over and beyond the ordinary rules. According as circumstances are favorable, one should modify one's plans." The lack of elasticity has repeatedly been the cause of many cases of Japanese failure in the war with China. When Lord Uxbridge, commanding the cavalry units on the eve of the Battle of Waterloo, went to the Duke of Wellington for final instruction, it was reported that the Duke grew impatient and asked who was going to attack. "Bonaparte," replied Lord Uxbridge.

"Well," continued Wellington, "Bonaparte has not given me any ideas of his projects, and as my plans will depend upon his, how can you expect me to tell you what mine are?"

Here are some ideas on offensive and defensive warfare which seem to be relevant to the present war: "You are on the defensive when you are not sure of victory. You are on the offensive when you are sure of victory. To be on the defensive shows that you feel your inadequacy. To be on the offensive means that you have an overflowing amount of energy. He who knows how to be on the defensive conceals his strength under the nine layers of earth. He who knows how to be on the offensive moves from among the nine layers of heaven. This is the secret of self-protection and leads one to victory. . . .

"Security against defeat implies defensive tactic: ability to defeat the enemy means taking the offensive. . . .

"Rapidity is the very essence of war. Let your rapidity be that of the wind, your compactness that of the forest." Or: "Let your plans be dark and impenetrable as night, and when you fall, fall like a thunderbolt. Therefore the good fighter will be terrible in his onset and prompt in his decision." These ideas seem to indicate that blitzkrieg tactics were not unknown in one of the most peace-loving countries more than two thousand years ago.

The most interesting chapter is, I think, the last one, which is Chapter 13, on spying and espionage.

Sun Tse says: "The enlightened sovereign or able general who, whenever he moves, brings victory, must depend for his success upon previous knowledge of conditions with enemy ranks. This knowledge cannot be elicited from spirits, it cannot be obtained inductively from experience nor by any deductive calculation. Knowledge of enemy dispositions can only be obtained from other men. Hence the use of spies of which there are five kinds: local spies, internal spies, converted spies, doomed spies and surviving spies. If all five kinds of spies are at work, none can discover the secret of the system. This is called 'divine manipulation of the threads.' It is the sovereign's most precious faculty.

"Having local spies means employing the services of the inhabitants of districts within enemy territory. Having internal spies means making use of the officials of the enemy. Having converted spies means getting hold of the enemy's spies and using them for our own purposes. Having doomed spies means doing certain things only for purposes of deception and allowing our own spies to know of this and report them to the enemy. Surviving spies finally are those who bring back news from the enemy's camp."

The scheme is, in fact, so all-embracing that it covers all we know today about espionage. Fifth-column activities are not new. Sun Tse's conclusion is: "The success of military activities depends so much upon the right use of spies. Spies should be treated royally. The secrecy of everything depends upon how well the spies can keep their secrets. It is only the saintly wise who can use spies. It is only the really virtuous and the morally upright who can control spies. It is only when one is meticulously careful that the real value of spies can be extracted. Everything depends upon the successful use of spies."[2] Though an immensely practical measure, the success of the system must depend upon the virtues and moral probity of the man who uses it. That is the ultimate criterion of everything in China.

Those ideas were to be applied to practical advantage later in Chiang Kai-shek's life, when he extended his military control to include all of China, and in the present war against the Japanese. But the principle which remains uppermost in his mind is that, while not forgetting military tactics, one must also not forget that over and above military success there is something even more important. It is not enough to defeat your enemy through military ability; you must conquer the enemy's heart, and that is not done by skillful use of your weapons, but by real moral superiority and the integrity of your being.

For did not Mencius say, "When a person subdues other men by force, they do not submit to him in heart. They submit because their strength is not adequate to resist. When he subdues them by virtue, in their heart of hearts they are pleased and sincerely submit."

That may sound metaphysical, but it is nonetheless the active principle in the lives of all Chinese heroes who started out as soldiers. It has been also the active principle in Chinese history in the gradual extension of its cultural influences to areas which came into contact with them.[3] As early as the period of the Three Kingdoms, during the

---

[2] There is a good translation of Sun Tse's *Art of War* by Lionel Giles, Luzac & Co., London, 1910. He calls it "the oldest military treatise in the world." The quotations, with slight modifications, are from that translation.

[3] This phenomenon has led one modern and competent historian of China to make the following significant statement: "No territory once fully subjected to this civilization has ever been wholly lost, and no territory permanently incorporated in the Chinese area has withstood the penetration of Chinese culture. The process of absorption has sometimes been slow, but always complete and final. . . . The history of China is the record of an expanding culture, not that of a conquering empire." C. P. Fitzgerald, *China: A Short Cultural History* (The Cresset Press, London), p. 1.

second century, the story was told of Chu-ko Liang, who, in his military conquest of present-day Szechuan Province in southwestern China, caught and set free seven consecutive times the tribal chief of the aborigines, Meng Ho. When the chief was captured alive in his own territory and brought before Chu-ko Liang, the Chinese statesman asked him, "You said originally that if I caught you in your own home, then you would submit to me. Now that I have done so, what have you to say?"

Meng Ho replied: "We have really delivered ourselves into your hands through carelessness. It was not your ability. My heart is not subdued."

Chu-ko Liang then said: "I have caught you six times and still you don't submit. When shall I wait for you to submit then?"

Whereupon Meng Ho said: "If I am captured for the seventh time, then I shall really submit."

So Chu-ko Liang let him go again, treating, in the meantime, the people of the conquered territory with the utmost consideration as if it were his own country. The rebel chief, however, made elaborate preparations for the reconquest of the land. But unfortunately he was captured for the seventh time and brought before Chu-ko Liang. He knelt before the Chinese statesman, who ordered that the manacles be taken away and that there should be a banquet prepared for the chieftain.

Thus Meng Ho enjoyed the feast with his wife, who was also captured. Presently a messenger from Chu-ko Liang came to visit him and said, "My lord feels ashamed and has no desire to have any interview with you. He has ordered me to come and set you free so that you are at liberty to go back and, if you so desire, to fight back."

Upon hearing this, Meng Ho wept profusely and said: "Captured seven times, and seven times I am set free. Why, such a thing has never occurred in all history. Although I am outside of the pale of Chinese culture, I know what personal honor and integrity are. I too have a sense of shame." Thereupon Meng Ho brought his wife, his brothers, and all the members of his clan to the tent and knelt before the Chinese general, imploring mercy and expressing the deepest gratitude. "Your lordship," he said, "has such magnanimity and such great moral influence over me that I shall never think of turning on you again."

Chu-ko Liang then invited the chieftain and his retinue to be seated at the same table with him and to continue the feast. He congratulated them upon their new resolve and ordered that all the territory which was taken from them should be returned. Meng Ho was completely overwhelmed and willingly allowed his territory to become an integral part of China.

This was how the Chinese nation grew from the valley of the Huang Ho into an extensive empire. This was how Chinese culture spread to the farthest reaches of southeastern Asia. It expresses a principle upon which the historical evolution of China has been based, and no true Chinese leader has ignored it. Chiang Kai-shek learned it in those early formative years at the Paoting Military Academy.

Loyalty

10

Across the Sea

IN 1907, after having been a student of the Military Academy at Paoting, where he passed the final examination with honors, Chiang Kai-shek was sent to Japan for further studies. That year was an important landmark in his life. From that time to the death of Sun Yat-sen in 1925 and the Northern Expedition in the following year, when he assumed command to unite the whole country under his military control, we have the second long period of his career, in which the predominating influence was that of Sun Yat-sen, as that of the first period was unquestionably his mother.

Chiang's mother lived until 1921, covering almost fifteen years of this second period, and all through those years no son could have been more devoted and loving. But from the day he landed in Japan for the second time his mind was absorbed by the larger world of revolutionary activities. He remained in that country for four and a half years, and during that period his major interest was the continuation of his military studies and the making of friends and contacts for the important work that was to follow. When the Chinese Revolution broke out in 1911 to overthrow the Manchu Dynasty and establish a republic, Chiang left Japan to take part in it. From that year to 1926 was a long period of disappointment, disillusionment, blasted hopes, and unrealized ideals. But whether as a student in Japan or as an active schemer and participant in the revolution, Chiang had only one aim from which he never swerved. It was the constant beacon in the midst of all the vicissitudes of his life: a deep and passionate loyalty to the ideals of Sun Yat-sen. Sun was the symbol of China's salvation. To him and to his ideals Chiang remained faithful, even though at times the hours were dark and gloomy.

There were four students from the Paoting Military Academy who traveled on the boat from Shanghai to Japan. Chiang was the only one who passed the examination through merit, the other three being appointees of Yuan Shih-kai, whose one aim in maintaining the academy and sending its graduates to Japan was to train a group of young officers who later would be in command of his own soldiers and thus help him to establish his power over the whole country.

When he arrived in Japan Chiang found that the number of Chinese students there was large. He was at once assigned to a preparatory military academy in Tokyo, known as Shinbo Gokyo, where he remained for the next two years, until 1909. There were altogether some fifty Chinese students specializing in military science in Japan, but there was slight relationship between them and Chiang, for though their main interests were identical, they had nothing else in common. Most of the students belonged to well-to-do families who had political influence in the court at Peking. They knew that when they completed their training they would be appointed to important posts upon their return to China. They were not chosen by merit in the first place; and the Japanese military academies, while they enforced the strictest discipline upon their own boys, purposely followed a policy of extreme leniency toward these Chinese students. It was clearly not to Japan's advantage to train them into really efficient and competent officers.

Chiang was reserved and kept to himself most of the time. He was studying seriously and making friends with those who in their quiet way were furthering revolutionary aims and ideals. The Manchu court, however, kept some check on these radical elements. But if the court was already showing signs of decay in its very center, those who were employed by the court to do its bidding and carry out its will could not be expected to perform their functions well. Chiang and his friends thus felt reasonably safe. As for the other students, since their scholarships and stipends had been granted to them through political connections, it really made no difference to them whether they worked hard or chose a life of ease. So they followed the line of least resistance and spent most of their time in the geisha houses rather than in the classrooms. A somewhat similar situation developed later on among Chinese students pursuing their studies in the United States. Twenty-five years ago the students who won scholarships were mostly earnest scholars who did credit to their country, but later on, when the sons of rich government officials began flooding the American colleges, they became more interested in having a good time than in serious studies. It is said that the son of one rich official hired a secretary to do all his studying for him!

Chiang Kai-shek realized how much the quality of the students depended upon the manner in which they won their scholarships. With these sons of rich officials, to get drunk was common enough; and during these moments of disturbed mental equilibrium these youngsters would indulge in loose and unbridled talk. One would say that his father was the most powerful official in the court, and that even the Emperor was afraid of him. Another would say that he used to have his living quarters right within the precincts of the Forbidden City itself, and that all the court ladies vied with each other for his love. And as Chiang looked on with amused interest, he thought to himself: "These are our students upon whom the future of the country is to depend." The more he watched, the more he realized how much there remained to be done. If the young had already become degenerate, what hope was there for the future? The building of character, if it was ever to have any effect, he thought, must begin in early youth. That was what he had done for himself. And seeing his fellow students frittering away their time with wine, women, and song, it is little wonder that he has ever since taken a profound interest in the youth of the country. However busy he may be, he is always prepared to meet and say a few words to boy scouts, to students of the high schools and sometimes even of the elementary schools.

Having finished his two-year course at the Shinbo Gokyo in 1909, Chiang Kai-shek was transferred to the 13th Field Artillery Regiment of the Japanese Army for actual experience as a cadet before joining the more advanced of the Japanese military colleges. He continued to show devotion to his studies and duties. It was said that his deep and accurate knowledge of the construction of guns often placed his instructors in embarrassing situations. One instructor had to burn his midnight oil and bring three hundred and seventy different types of accessories to the classroom the next morning before he had the courage to face the young, inquiring student from China.

It was the performance of the regimental duties that was the most exacting part of his life as a cadet. The winters in Japan can be vigorously cold, and Chiang was frequently assigned, as a part of his regular work, to scrub the horses, polish the guns, and shine the boots of the officers. He accepted all this discipline as being essential to the life of a soldier, went through it cheerfully and with alacrity, and impressed his instructors as being quite different from the other Chinese students. To this day Chiang Kai-shek remains a mystery to the Japanese. It is part of the Chinese cult of self-development that one's qualities should be as little obvious as possible. Even in those early days Chiang knew how to conceal his strength.

One Japanese officer, General Nagaoka, who had commanded a division in one of whose regiments Chiang was a cadet, gave an interview to a Japanese newspaper in 1928 which is interesting. He said:

In those early days there were some fifteen or sixteen Chinese students of the Military College who were assigned to the Takada Artillery Regiment. The present chairman of the Chinese Government was one of them. When the soldiers of Li Yuan-hung raised the banner of revolution at Wuchang in 1911, Mr. Chiang was anxious to return to his native country, and I remember some of his friends held a feast in his honor to bid him farewell.

One of the friends said: "Military people do not drink saké. Please drink pure water instead. For according to the *bushido* spirit of Japan, drinking water means that the soldier will not return alive."[1]

Upon saying this, a cup of water was passed around. When it came to Mr. Chiang he drank to the last drop and replied: "Gentlemen, thank you for the honor you have done me."

And as he drank his face was red with emotion. Who ever dreamt that the student of those days would become the chairman of the Chinese National Government? None of us thought that Mr. Chiang was going to be an historic personality. He must have had the great merit of being able to conceal his strength and of not allowing other people to appreciate his rare qualities. How did he become such a great man? This is the most interesting of questions. It was only last year, in 1927, that I was able to answer that question. For in that year Mr. Chiang resigned from all his positions and was planning to take an extended trip abroad. He first came to Japan. When he arrived at Tokyo on October 23 he rang up from the Imperial Hotel where he was staying and paid me his respects.

"I should have come to pay my respects to you earlier, my former com-

---

[1] This is one of the many feudal practices which flourish in modern Japan. The farewell cup of water known as *mizu-sakazuko* or water-wine cup is given by the nearest relative to the dying man to drink as an act of purification for the next life. The use of water in one way or another as a symbol of purification is common in Japan. In the tea ceremony, when the guests enter the front gate leading into the garden of the host, the first act they perform is to dip their hands into a basin of running water coming through a bamboo tube. That means they leave behind the life of sordidness and enter into a new world of purity. It originated perhaps from Zen Buddhism. Somewhat in the same sense, a person leaving his family for a task for which he is expected to sacrifice his life, as for instance a soldier leaving for the front, does not drink the Japanese rice wine or saké, which is a symbol of cheer and good-fellowship, but a cup of water, which means that he purifies his life so as to be prepared to enter the next one.

Chinese News Service

DR. SUN YAT-SEN

mander," he said, "but I am indisposed and must hurry to the hot springs. When I am better, I shall at once come in person. All respects also to my regimental commander."

When, a few days later, I invited Mr. Chiang and the regimental commander to have tea with me, I realized that he has become a completely different man. There was such nobility in his expressions. He had altogether the attitude of a great statesman and a great soldier. He had also the attitude of a young diplomat. And as we talked of former days he continued to address me as his divisional commander. So also he addressed his regimental commander, although he knew that I am no longer a commander. And before he returned home to his own country he wrote four words as a gift to me: "Show no ingratitude to the teaching of your instructor." I have had so much contact with young men from China, but not one like Mr. Chiang, who is so loyal to those from whom he has derived benefit. Now I understand why he is head and shoulders above others, although he did not appear remarkable during his student days. It is this deep sense of loyalty and gratitude for which I must show him my unbounded respect.

II

Revolutionary Contacts

WHILE A GOOD NUMBER of the Chinese students, children of the rich and privileged official classes, were wasting their time in Japan, there were others who were busy with patriotic activities. These activities all centered around Sun Yat-sen who, since the time of his graduation from the Medical College at Hong Kong, where he enrolled as a student in the same year that Chiang Kai-shek was born, had been dominated by one passion—the desire to overthrow the Manchu regime. Sun had traveled widely, stimulating interest in his revolutionary work wherever he could find his countrymen. He was now back in Japan, having arrived a few years before Chiang came to join the Shinbo Gokyo. The number of his followers was then already quite large, but there were varying degrees of devotion to him and to his ideals. There was, however, a small nucleus of passionate adherents. Not many of this original group are alive today. Among the most eminent was Hu Han-min, who played a consistently important part in Chinese politics until he died in 1936. A man of purpose, he unfortunately had an inflexible mind which sometimes prevented him from having a sympathetic understanding of the men and events of the constantly changing environment. Another man was Wang Ching-wei, who is still alive today. Wang is volatility itself, but has no center, no permanent principle which can guide him through a world of flux. For he has chosen to live the life of a quisling and is content to be a marionette at the hands of the Japanese.

In 1905, when Sun Yat-sen was gathering around him a group of young patriots, he felt that he was in a position to launch an official party, which he called the Tungmenghui, or the League of Common Alliance. It dedicated itself to the task of overthrowing the existing government in China and of establishing a republican government in its place. In those days Sun had not yet evolved the well-articulated principles that have since come to be known as the Three Principles of the People, based upon nationalism, democracy, and the economic welfare of the people. Even a simple formula based on the slogan of the overthrow of the Manchus was enough to fire the imagination of the small group of patriots.

The Tungmenghui, however, had to be careful about its activities. There were indeed a few Japanese sympathizers, but the Japanese Government sometimes felt compelled to give up its neutral attitude. While members of the Tungmenghui could be reasonably free in their movements, their activities would now and then be reported to the agents of the court at Peking, and returning to their own country to spread the revolutionary ideas was not an easy thing.

It was some time after Chiang Kai-shek's arrival in Japan that he officially became a member of the Tungmenghui. But before that time he was already in constant touch with the members of that group. The Tungmenghui was not in itself the beginning of the revolutionary movement. It was the successor to the Society for the Regeneration of China (1894-1905) and also brought to a focus separate revolutionary organizations, both in and out of China, which had been working as secret groups. When it came to the knowledge of the Manchu government that revolutionary forces were gathering strength on Japanese territory, Japan was regarded as performing an unfriendly act, and the government accordingly protested. For a time thereafter Chinese students were admitted into Japan only under strict regulation. But Chiang Kai-shek, fortunately, had come in under a different category. He was sponsored by the government itself, being one of the successful candidates sent by one of the most renowned of its own military academies, though his sympathies were definitely with those young men who were being spied upon and stigmatized by the government as undesirables.

One person in particular Chiang wished greatly to see again in Japan. He was the same Tao Huan-ching whom he had met in the restaurant when he first went to Hangchow. Tao was now in Japan as one of the most active exponents of the revolutionary cause and had become vice-president of the revolutionary Kwangfu Society. Chiang was also introduced to one Hsu Hsi-ling, many years Chiang's senior, for whom he had a warm admiration. The acquaintance was a short one, for not long after Chiang's arrival in Japan in 1907 Hsu went home to China, was captured by the authorities, and executed. He died as a martyr at the age of thirty-four. The Hsu Hsi-ling episode was typical of the uprisings that occurred during the fifteen years preceding the 1911 revolution.

Among those who died in this uprising was Chiu Chin, a woman whose memory lives on today, one of the greatest heroines in modern Chinese history. Miss Chiu Chin was in Japan and worked closely with Sun Yat-sen. She returned to China just before Chiang's arrival in Japan, so the two never met. But when the Nationalist Army under Chiang Kai-shek reached the Yangtze Valley in 1927, twenty years after her death, he gave instructions that a permanent memorial be erected in her honor. There is now a pavilion in Hangchow built on the spot where she was executed, bearing the inscription, "Autumn wind, autumn rain." These words are taken from a verse that Miss Chiu composed during her trial. When she was asked to make a full confession of her activities, all she wrote was seven words: "Autumn wind, autumn rain, how killingly sorrowful." She would write no further, and this line has now become immortal, being placed in the same category with the poem by Yo Fei which Chiang Kai-shek chanted so lustily during his first visit to Hangchow.

The person who exercised the most profound influence on Chiang Kai-shek during his student days in Japan, perhaps next only to that of Sun Yat-sen, was Chen Chi-mei. Chiang met him during his first short visit to Japan in 1906 and their friendship grew. Chen had to leave for China to direct revolutionary activities in 1908, but when the revolution broke out in 1911 the young man whom he befriended in Japan became one of his ablest and most trusted lieutenants. It was Chen who introduced Chiang to Sun Yat-sen. Sun was reported to be deeply impressed by the earnestness and deep sincerity of the young man in his first conversation with him, and is said to have remarked, "That man will be the hero of our revolution: we need just such a man in our movement."[1] It was Chen also who proposed Chiang's name and became his sponsor when Chiang decided to become a member of the Tungmenghui, over which the genius of Sun Yat-sen naturally prevailed, but where Chen also exercised great influence by reason of his organizing ability and practical sense.

Sun Yat-sen remained in the background as an inspiring figure. He was a colossus who created the firm spiritual bond among the group of young and ardent patriots. He encouraged them, enlarged their views, and provided them with a well-planned and consistent program upon which they based their activities. But Chen Chi-mei, a native of Wuchow, the city of rich silk merchants, not far from Chiang's own home village of Chikow, was the practical tactician. He was the man who galvanized his associates into action and carried out the schemes. A delicate and scholarly-looking man, in age midway between Sun Yat-sen, who was then in his early forties, and Chiang Kai-shek, who had just reached his twenty-first year, Chen had great physical courage. The revolution of 1911 was only the last of a series of outbreaks and insurrections which he engineered to bring about the downfall of the Manchu regime.

Sun Yat-sen and Chen Chi-mei were entirely different in temperament, but they had the same intense devotion to the cause of the revolution. Chiang Kai-shek drew strength and sustenance from them both. For over four years he listened, watched, and observed these two men. When the day arrived in 1911 on which he was called upon to put his strength to the test, he was ready to play his full part.

12

A Leader Inspires Him

DURING THE VISIT to Chungking of the British Parliamentary Mission in November 1942, one of its members, Lord Teviot of the Liberal party, was asked to respond to the speech of welcome by Generalissimo Chiang Kai-shek, who was presiding over the Tenth Plenary

[1] Hollington K. Tong, *Chiang Kai-shek, Soldier and Statesman*, p. 16.

Session of the Central Executive Committee. This was what Lord Teviot said:

"Dr. Sun Yat-sen has demonstrated to the world how a great man inspired by no other thought than the determination to bring reforms and benefits to his country and its people can succeed in laying, in a few years, the foundation of a new era. By creating the principles on which your party (the Kuomintang party) was founded China was quick to respond. The Japanese who meant war anyhow chose this moment to attack, as they realized that China would eventually become the dominant power in the East not through war, but by conferring on her people a new life of progressive development which would not only raise her to the highest importance in the East but in the world.

"Japan has been frustrated by your magnificent resistance. The work of your great founder has been and is being carried on by your Generalissimo. How remarkable it is China has produced two such men to follow each other."

Two great men following each other. This, I think, is one of the most remarkable phenomena in modern China. The succession was even chronologically perfect. The period of maturity and wide experience of the one synchronized with the period of active preparation and training of the other; and when Sun died in 1925 Chiang Kai-shek was in a position to begin his Northern Expedition and the unification of the country the following year. The one possessed a large and luminous mind, leaving a legacy of ideals and resolution that the firm and practical instincts of the other immediately executed on a national scale. What Chiang then started has been continued and amplified to the present day, with almost no intermission. The record has been a most impressive one, and it has been so because there has been such close continuity between the labors of the two men. Sun Yat-sen first tried to put his revolutionary ideas into practice soon after the collapse of the Boxer Rebellion, so that between then and now there is a consistent period of over forty years during which Sun's ideas, even though at times they may have been eclipsed, burned with a steady flame in the hearts of millions of his countrymen.

It was in September of 1900, at Canton, that Sun Yat-sen actually made the first serious attempt to overthrow the existing regime. The time was well chosen, coming as it did immediately after the court was humiliated by the total defeat of the Boxers. But the revolution proved to be short-lived, and Sun had to flee to Japan. His spirits were by no means dampened: the failure made him search for its causes. He realized that he had started the revolution before he was properly prepared for it, but he gained valuable experience. He started out with only three hundred poorly armed revolutionaries, and yet they had managed to capture large amounts of ammunition from the troops of the Manchu government. In less than three weeks they had won six battles and had taken possession of five cities. In time his army grew to the number of twenty thousand, but then they found that the ammunition that had been bought from a Japanese firm never arrived. With no cartridges on hand, the men had to be disbanded and were requested to go home, resume their work as farmers and trades-people, and await a better opportunity in the future.

Sun knew from this experience that the people could be relied upon. They had proved receptive to his ideas, and that was the principal factor to consider. As a matter of fact, the people had always been more ready than the mandarins and scholars to overthrow the alien rule. For generations they had been familiar with revolutionary ideas through the effective operations of secret societies and they were ready for action, while the scholars were more reconciled to the existing regime if only because their official careers or their hopes of obtaining official emolument required its maintenance. The most the scholars asked was a gradual and evolutionary process that would sometime in the future bring about reforms. Sun Yat-sen had no patience with this point of view and was all for revolution. A conversation which the Irishman, George Lynch, had with Sun shortly after his arrival in Japan, following the failure of the Canton uprising, gives, I think, a good picture of Sun's attitude at that time. The description is so colorful that it is well worth quoting at some length.

I did not meet Sun Yat-sen in Canton [said Lynch], but came upon him unexpectedly in Japan, where he had taken refuge, and was living under a Japanese name. Finding out his address, I wrote to him, asking for an interview, and received a courteous reply written in perfect English.

I went that evening at the time appointed. He was living in the Chinese quarter of the town of Yokohama. With some difficulty I found my way through the labyrinth of streets to the house where he was living. The street was a dark one, and there were no lights in the front of the house he was occupying. In answer to my knock a tall young Chinaman admitted me, and led the way along a dark passage, and opened the door of a brilliantly lighted room beyond.

A smart, dapper young man in European clothes stepped briskly forward with outstretched hand to greet me. At first there was little of the Chinaman about him, his brisk manner, the nervous firm grasp of his hand, with just a faint Oriental lingering of a caress about it. He spoke English almost perfectly, with the slightest possible American accent, which was accounted for by his having spent many years in America and only one in England.

The table in the middle of the room was strewn with books and papers, and the walls lined with books and maps. The books were chiefly English, with a few French among them, and were all dealing with war and the subjects connected therewith.

Carey on Minor Tactics, the last edition of Block's book, somebody on explosives, a history of the Franco-Prussian War, and a whole lot of later books which had just appeared on the South African campaign were there. It was a perfect arsenal of warlike literature. . . .

His ambition is to revolutionize China. . . . He is convinced that there is no chance of doing this otherwise than by doing away with the present dynasty; he said that what they would prefer would be a republic. As he pointed out, there is already in existence all the machinery for a great democracy in China. For practical purposes, it is already democratic; the governors of the great provinces, under them the governors of the districts, until we reach the Chinese villages with their headmen. And what more democratic institution is there in the world than that system of competitive examination which puts it within the power of the poorest villager in the Empire to attain by his own intellectual efforts to the highest positions in the state?

And then Lynch talked with the doctor on the prospects of the future.

So far from Sun Yat-sen being discouraged by the results of the insurrection, he said that he and his friends were quite pleased and full of confidence from the discovery that his followers could so easily defeat the Imperial troops and capture arms and ammunition from them. During the twenty days' war the fighting was carried on entirely with the captured arms and ammunition. He made no secret of the fact that when the time was ripe he was going to have another try, and the only fear he had about the result was that some of the European powers might interfere on the side of the Empire.

That was the mental state of Sun Yat-sen just when the twentieth century was dawning upon a decadent China; but even so, for him and his followers the prospects for their country were bright and hopeful. This conversation presents the broad outlines of Sun's revolutionary work and shows that he was aware of the international difficulties that would obstruct his way.

Between this time and the appearance of the Tungmenghui there was a period of some five years. It was an important period in the development of the revolutionary ideology. Sun Yat-sen was then the leader of the Hsingchunghui, or the Society for the Regeneration of China, which came into existence in 1894 after the defeat by the Japanese, but the society was really a congeries of secret groups not differing essentially from the secret societies that had been in existence for generations. From this time on there were forces working to make the society a more conscious and articulate political organization, with Sun Yat-sen as its central representative. One was the succession of major catastrophes to the Manchu dynasty which convinced the Chinese people generally that the whole system of government under that rule had become little more than an ornament. It had become so weak, effete, and disorganized that the only way to deal with it was to wipe it out completely. Another tendency was the accession in increasing numbers of overseas Chinese who had been brought up for years under the progressive governments of the West and who had practically nothing in common with the traditional elite of the country. Their dominating passion was the introduction of those modern scientific devices with which they had become familiar during their residence abroad.

When the Tungmenghui was organized in 1905, it was therefore not merely a change of name. It gathered in all the patriotic fervor of the secret societies and became something more: it acquired a more definite personality, became more aggressive and more militant. It showed the people that it was now in a position to sponsor movements and uprisings that could stir the mind of the Chinese public. The Hsu Hsi-ling episode of 1907 was an example of such movements. But in thus working for the total collapse of an outworn regime, the society needed a broad basis of positive values for constructive work. It needed a program. From a general feeling of patriotism, the time had come to evolve a planned nationalism and a consistent scheme of political and economic reconstruction.

Chiang Kai-shek had the advantage of being associated with Sun Yat-sen at this stage of critical formulation of policies which eventually gave birth to what is known as the *San-min chu-i,* or the Three Principles of the People. Chiang was impressed not only by the fervor and sincerity of Sun Yat-sen, but also by his intellectual powers and the scope of his knowledge of international affairs. Chiang's own education had been limited, but now he was constantly in the presence of a person who was mature in his experiences and who understood the conditions in the modern world as well as the historical values of ancient China. Chiang's head and heart were completely conquered: he adored Sun as his hero and leader. To this day any reference to Sun Yat-sen in Chiang's presence can be made only with the deepest reverence, even though Chiang's own work is now much wider in scope and answers more immediately the practical needs of the nation. However, Chiang Kai-shek does not consider his work as anything more than the practical application of the ideas and policies that he saw gradually taking shape in their final form during those early days of association with Sun Yat-sen.

Chiang had now come to a period in his life when it was necessary for him to possess an intellectual justification for his actions. He did not question his own patriotism, but a life of feeling for a young man was not enough; it had to be accounted for and sustained by mental content. That was why Sun's ideas gave such a tremendous fillip to his development. They provided a framework for his emotional energies. From that moment on Chiang's activities acquired meaning and significance. They became canalized and had direction where before they were apt to be somewhat vague and shapeless. It was all very well to overthrow the existing Manchu regime, for it was an alien rule that had reached the nadir of incompetence and corruption. The feeling for that need was shared by many others. But it had also become necessary for Chiang to ask himself many questions. When the existing government collapsed, what kind of a government was to take its place? What would be the responsibilities of the new regime to the people? What would be the position of China in the family of nations? What, in a word, was that new China going to be?

These and other related questions were pressing on Chiang Kai-shek's mind for full and adequate answers. In the meantime Chiang was submitting himself to rigid military discipline. But whether he was grooming the horses of the cavalry of the Takada Regiment or polishing the shoes of the officers, which had become his daily morning task, his mind was searching for a larger and firmer grasp of the intellectual issues involved than could be acquired by the fact that he had been sent to Japan to study by Yuan Shih-kai's Military Academy.

Yuan Shih-kai's power in China in those days was an obvious fact, but it was merely power to satisfy a personal ambition. It was at best a military feudalism in which loyalty was demanded as a quid pro quo for personal favors. It had no program, no platform, and therefore no intellectual justification. Even if Yuan was the most powerful man in China, as he became not many years later, he would merely substitute without effecting any real change. It was necessary for Chiang Kai-shek to have this understanding because he was, after all, receiving his military education on the strength of a scholarship provided by the Paoting Military Academy. The funds, however, were not personal funds; they came from the government treasury and therefore belonged to the country. Besides, he had won the scholarship not through influence but by personal merit. Chiang was loyal to his country but was certainly under no obligation to promote Yuan's ambition for personal aggrandizement.

Not that Chiang Kai-shek had any great doubt as to the objectives toward which he was going to direct his energy. He was loyal to Sun Yat-sen and to his ideals from the very beginning. But at this period, when Chiang was making an appraisal of the various forces, it was essential that he should clear the ideological deck, so to speak, and sweep aside all the intellectual debris. Having done this, he entered mentally and spiritually into the Sun Yat-sen ideology with the singleness of purpose that has made China what she is today—a united nation that is conscious of its strength and confident of its future.

13

The Flowering of a Faith

IT WAS during the Tungmenghui period that Sun Yat-sen felt the need of a political platform that would buttress his revolutionary activities. He had been toying with a number of ideas that he considered essential for a well-defined program. They were now slowly taking shape, and in the fullness of time came the flowering of an articulate and consistent ideology, a new social and political faith, that has since become the *raison d'être* of the party now called the Kuomintang party. It is fortunate for China that young Chiang Kai-shek was so closely associated with Sun at that time and was therefore in a position to observe every phase of the party's development.

One important element of Sun Yat-sen's doctrinal trilogy was nationalism. Sun considered the growth of a national spirit among the Chinese people a primary requisite without which it would be impossible to realize the other two social and political aims. The country was then falling to pieces under the impact of aggressive forces which not only brought China to the verge of ruin and dismemberment, but were also devastatingly successful in making the people lose faith in themselves. In order to survive as a nation it was clearly necessary to rally to the support and strengthening of a nationalistic faith. Territory that had been taken away could be regained; indemnities might be heavy and onerous, but they could be redeemed; but if a nation should lose faith in itself, it would indeed cease to exist. The times were critical. Sun Yat-sen decided that the process of demoralization and disintegration must stop immediately, and that the cult of nationalism was the only weapon that could save the situation.

Sun Yat-sen knew, however, that the type of national feeling he wanted for his countrymen would be in a sense similar to the nationalism that he had found in the Western nations. That would not be an entirely unqualified blessing. Nationalism in Europe had only a short history, having grown as an aftermath of the Napoleonic Era. It had brought wars and conflicts. National entities arose like powerful individuals, each of which struggled and clamored for its rights. They asserted their egos and a clashing of wills became inevitable. For Sun had discovered that underlying that nationalism was not the principle of harmony but the principle of secession. Harmony could not be built on a philosophy that recognized the ego as the supreme reality. The ego has its legitimate place in the scheme of things; but one must realize that it has its limitations, that it must allow for the existence of higher values without which orderly human society would be impossible. If that had been true of individuals who thus managed to live together because they were willing to submit themselves to a law over and above themselves, it must, so Sun thought, be true of nations also. The basic idea of nationalism as known in Europe Sun Yat-sen could not, therefore, accept. It was alien to his thinking, and, more particularly, it was at variance with the entire spirit of Chinese cultural development. But he was prepared to admit that there was one asset in the Western cult of nationalism: it made for compactness and solidity within the national group, and that was what he wanted for the moment. Compared with these European nations, his own people, as he described them, were but a "tray of loose sand particles." The problem which confronted Sun was thus an interesting one: how to develop that same compactness and solidity among his people without at the same time sacrificing the inherent virtues that had made Chinese culture and civilization so impressive a monument in human history.

Out of the desire to preserve and reconcile the two grew the first of Sun Yat-sen's social and political doctrines, and in studying them we must constantly bear in mind that at no time did Sun ever become anything else but what he actually was—a true-born Chinese. That fact made a deep and lasting impression on the young associate who was destined to carry on Sun's mission. Sun was then already a widely traveled man, speaking at least one foreign language with a fluency that must have astonished Chiang Kai-shek. His education too was foreign, and for long periods he had to make an enforced residence away from his country, so that a large number of his contacts were made either with foreigners or at any rate outside of China. In spite of all this, Sun not only remained true to his Chinese instincts but was to the end of his days a warm and ardent defender of the virtues of his race. That, in Chiang Kai-shek's estimation, was an extraordinary feat.

Sun Yat-sen made a careful study of Chinese history and found, to his immense satisfaction, that in its impressive record of nearly five thousand years of development there was an unmistakable racial consciousness which was itself a form of nationalism, and in its gradual expansion in southeastern Asia the motivating principle was always one of assimilation rather than the imposition of military force, of absorption through cultural harmony rather than conquest through the use of arms. As in the case of other races, the early beginnings of the Chinese race must have been modest, and yet today it has grown to enormous proportions with a deep underlying unity in social habits, in mental outlook, in its general attitude toward life, and even in physical appearance. That would not have been possible if, in its contact with alien races in the course of its development, it did not allow its cultural attributes to perform the miracle of transformation. It was always prepared to absorb and harmonize. The result was a complete elimination of all racial and other accidental differences so that they stood equal under the aegis of a common culture. There was no question of one race dominating another: it was a constant fusion of differences until a homogeneous civilization was evolved. This fact seemed to have existed from very early times, for it was said in the *Book of Poetry,* "The offsprings of Wen Wang [the first Chou emperor] branch to a hundred generations"; and also, "These people of a different race are all brothers, nephews and uncles."[1] So that when Confucius later developed his political philosophy from the assumption that "within the four seas all men are brothers" he was merely giving articulate expression to a state of things that had long been an established fact. From that position, however, Confucius went one step further. He showed that all men were brothers because they must all submit to the rule of the moral law that was the supreme reality. The distinction between races and nations was in Confucius' mind an artificial distinction; the real difference between them was the extent to which they succeeded in making the moral law prevail. It should, therefore, be the common effort of mankind to establish this moral order and thereby usher in the period of the great commonwealth.

When the Great Doctrine prevails, all under Heaven will work for the common good. They will choose men of virtue and ability. They will maintain sincerity and cultivate harmony. Thus they will not confine their love to their own parents, nor will they confine their affection to their own children. Sufficient provision will be secured for the aged till their death, there will be employment for the able-bodied, and the means of growing up for the young. Widowers, widows, orphans and childless men as well as persons disabled by disease will be adequately supported. All men will have their proper work and all women will be married. Although the people do not like to see wealth abandoned, yet they will not necessarily keep it for their own advantage. Disliking not to exert their own strength, it does not follow that they will exert it merely for their own benefit. In this way, selfish desires will be repressed; robbery, larceny, rebellion and treachery will not rise; and the outer doors will then remain open. This will be what we call the Great Commonwealth.[2]

[1] Mr. C. P. Fitzgerald, in his *China: A Short Cultural History,* which, in my estimation, is a very able and illuminating book, made the following observation: "From the earliest times it was acceptance of Chinese culture rather than racial ties which determined whether a people were to be regarded as Chinese or barbarian. Although such analogies must not be pushed too far, the relationship between the true Chinese states and the half-barbarous fringe was not unlike that which in classical times subsisted between the republics of the southern parts of Greece and the half-Greek northern lands of Epirus and Macedonia." P. 54.
[2] *Li Chi,* one of the richest repositories of Confucian wisdom.

In order to attain that universal peace, it is essential that a race should first preserve its entity. When China was the object of rival cupidities and the battleground for ruthless aggrandizement, it was clear to Sun Yat-sen that it was otiose to speak about this exalted view of human relationship, as it would be impossible of realization. His first task was, therefore, to call upon his countrymen to develop an awareness of their historic personality and the record of infinite good which it had established. Only in this way could they know a sense of pride and an unbounding faith in themselves as well as in the nation that nurtured them. Sun Yat-sen's principle of nationalism was therefore not expansion at any cost or even, as has happened with many European countries, at the expense of one's neighbors; it was not merely an assertion of right, but an understanding of one's own potentialities and capabilities to perform the highest good so that all might live in perfect accord and neighborly peace. It involved, in other words, a sense of responsibility to oneself as well as to others.

There is no doubt that this view of Sun Yat-sen's was thoroughly understood by Chiang Kai-shek even in those early days of their association, and that it remains today the informing principle of Chiang's statesmanship. As late as October 31, 1942, when Chiang was speaking before the People's Political Council, that representative body of Chinese who deliberate over national issues and present their recommendations to the government for action, he made the statement that "it is not for us boastfully to talk of China's right to a position of 'leadership' among those (Asiatic) countries. In the spirit of the saying that all men are brothers, we shall rather regard it as our responsibility to treat the peoples of Asia and elsewhere as equals whom we must help and support. Toward Asia as toward the whole world we wish only to do our duty to the exclusion of any lust for power. Our aim is a gradual advance of all nations from the stage of equality to that of ideal unity."

Sun Yat-sen discovered, furthermore, that it was because of this unfailing emphasis on responsibility so that all might share in the benefits of a unique culture that China has attained to its present territorial limits. There were periods when this steady development met immense difficulties and obstacles from without. When such contingencies arose, however, the Chinese were always prepared to rally their energy and offer stern resistance. As early as the Tsin and Han dynasties there were nomadic tribes that threatened to break in from the north. The Chinese Government accepted the challenge, though it was not interested in punitive measures as a form of retaliation. As a matter of protection, it began to build the colossal Great Wall which was meant to serve as a dike, as it were, to keep the mighty flood from inundating the Middle Kingdom, so that the constructive energy of the race might still be devoted to the peaceful exploitation of the areas both to the south and the west. During the period of the Three Kingdoms invasions from the north by foreign tribes became more frequent; but even when they succeeded in penetrating to the south it was only a question of time before they glorified in being transformed into an integral part of Chinese culture itself. The same process of fusion took place during the Sung, Yuan, and Ching dynasties when the Kitans, Nuchens, Mongols, and Manchus successively entered into the spirit of Chinese culture and willingly lost their identity. The same thing occurred in the intellectual and spiritual sphere where the question of degree in the stage of culture did not enter. For during the Tang Dynasty, when Buddhism was rapidly spreading over every part of the country, the Chinese intelligentsia felt the danger of the invasion and rose against it. The writings of Han Yu remain to this day a beautiful and vigorous defense of orthodox Chinese thinking.

From these historical facts we can draw, as Chiang Kai-shek recently observed, some definite conclusions. "The Chinese nation," he said, "in its historical evolution has developed so strong a purpose and has been so conscious of its strength that it will not allow itself for long to be the object of aggression. Nor, however, will it pursue a policy of aggression itself against other peoples. It is because it will not allow itself to be an object of aggression that, when alien forces begin to invade its territory, the race will rise and expel them from its confines so that what has been lost will be eventually recovered. It is because it will not pursue a policy of aggression itself that it is able to present its cultural accomplishments to those who are torn by conflict and rivalry and make them a part of itself. The Chinese race has always put up resistance against the military force of alien invaders, though it will not impose the same force on them. It has always been prepared to absorb what good there is in these invaders and pay them with its own cultural accomplishments."

Without any exceptions these cultural accomplishments have been freely and willingly accepted. This has been so not because the Chinese, through superior physical force, have been able to impose their will upon others, but because they invite them to understand that moral values are at the basis of all human relationship. It is on this foundation that Sun Yat-sen constructed his principle of nationalism. In the final analysis, therefore, it turns out to be something totally different from nationalism as generally understood in the West. It was essential, at a time when the Chinese people were beginning to lose confidence in themselves, that they rediscover China's historic personality. Only in this way could they acquire inner strength and union among themselves; and it is with these qualities that the battle for freedom and independence is won.

In an early speech before the members of the Kuomintang party on the general ideas underlying Sun Yat-sen's Three Principles, this was what Chiang Kai-shek had to say on the subject of nationalism:

"It is important to bear in mind that the Chinese race is not just one race of people. It embraces all the racial elements covering the territorial limits of China (proper), Manchuria, Mongolia (both Inner and Outer), Sinkiang and Tibet. From all historical, geographical and cultural considerations, these races have always held together to form a unity and cannot under any circumstances live separately from one another. In pursuing the principle of nationalism, we shall preserve the integrity and complete independence of these races which together form the Chinese race and shall not suffer any part to be invaded. We shall within ourselves seek complete equality and freedom so that there will be no oppression of one part over any of the rest. More than that, it is our purpose not only to seek the independence and equality of ourselves, but also to render all the assistance to those who are weak so that they in turn may ultimately rise to fight for their liberation and enjoy together freedom and independence as the fruits of their struggle. While we cannot suffer for a moment any oppressive measures from foreign sources, we shall likewise, under no circumstances, when our own strength has grown and developed, enforce any oppressive measures against other races. It is our mission, on the basis of the Three Principles, to lend succor to all the small and weak races and assist them to win genuine equality with the rest so that the world may really enter the age of the Great Commonwealth.

"I do not believe that there is much reason to quarrel over this point of view. Certainly to insist upon equality, freedom and independence for all should neither be new nor revolutionary; but there are nations, as there are men, who are disconcerted when they hear the still, small voice of conscience; and these will undermine what is obviously a perfectly sane and rational view by describing it as being too idealistic or utopian."

A word of explanation is also necessary for the territorial limits within which, according to Chiang Kai-shek, Chinese nationalism should be free to express itself. Those limits are the extent of Chinese cultural influences which have been at work during long historic periods. There are many differences in local customs and ways of living within these limits, but the fact remains that together these parts constitute a complete unity. Considered from a purely geographical point of view, these territorial limits likewise constitute a unity. The mountain ranges, branching out from the Central Asian plateau, stretch to the Tienshan and Altai mountains in the north and embrace the plains of Manchuria. The Kwenlun Mountains extend to the plains to the south and east while the Himalayas form a natural protection to all the land stretching from Tibet to the southwestern provinces and the Malay Peninsula. Intersecting these mountain ranges are mighty rivers that flow from the west in an easterly direction. The Amur in the north, the Yellow River, the Huai River, the Yangtze River, and the Pearl River in the south are all integral parts of a vast riparian system that is intimately related to the general configuration of the land. Furthermore there is no part of this geographical or natural entity that can be detached without bringing danger to all the rest, and it is because they constitute a unit that Chinese cultural influences, in varying degrees of intensity and effectiveness, have been at work throughout the centuries. The fact that Chinese population has been migrating into Manchuria within comparatively recent times, so that over ninety-five per cent of the total population there is now purely Chinese, is not the reason why Manchuria is an integral part of China: Manchuria became unmistakably Chinese from the time of the Chou Dynasty (1122–255 B.C.). So also the different tribes of Mongolia, going back to as early a period, became absorbed into the Chinese matrix. Sinkiang, otherwise known as Eastern Turkestan, has been Chinese territory for over two thousand years. The first contacts were made in the Chun Chiu Period (722–481 B.C.), and when the explorers Chang Chien and Pan Ku opened up the routes of commerce through this "new territory" to the heart of Asia, it became as much a part of China as any of the eastern provinces. In the case of Tibet, it has perhaps the shortest history of cultural contact. It began in the Sui (A.D. 589–618) and Tang (A.D. 618–

906) dynasties some thirteen hundred years ago, or some two centuries before the Danes invaded the British Isles.

In all these instances there were three stages of transformation. The first period was when the territories recognized the strength and agreeableness of the Chinese way of life, usually expressing this recognition in a periodic presentation of tributes to the court of the Chinese Emperor. The next period saw the territories become dependencies of the empire, and in the final stage they were accepted as integral parts of the empire, entirely on a par with the rest and enjoying perfect freedom and self-rule. Throughout these periods of contact military force, if it was present at all, merely lingered in the background, for the power of persuasion was not a physical but a moral one. In all the world's history there have been only two examples of a successful melting pot, each achieving unity in its own way: one is the United States, where the fusion of races and cultures has been going on for over a century; and the other is China, where the transformation began some forty centuries ago. Who can mistake the stamp of Americanism as who can mistake the characteristics of Chinese culture and civilization, whether they are found along the banks of the Amur River or in the mountain fastnesses of Tibet?

The first principle of the Sun Yat-sen trilogy is that of equality among nations. The second and third principles are political equality and the economic and social welfare of the people.

It is clear that political equality can be realized only under a democratic system of government. Here again Sun Yat-sen found it advisable to examine the political institutions of the West, though he never lost sight of the deep democratic spirit that has prevailed in China. As he said in his interview with George Lynch, the system of governors in the provinces and districts and of the village headmen was essentially a democratic system. So, also, the system of competitive examination in which, literally speaking, prince and pauper alike could sit and compete for the highest honors of the state, was one of the surest expressions of the democratic spirit.

Although there was no lack of the democratic spirit, there was, nevertheless, no permanently effective machinery by which its exercise and free expression could be maintained and guaranteed. This part of the argument made an especially strong appeal to Chiang Kai-shek at this period. In one of his early speeches, shortly after the Northern Expedition, Chiang recalled those days. "When I was sixteen or seventeen, I learned at school that the people who rule over us are a handful of Manchus and not the Han people. The four hundred millions of my countrymen have no share in the government under this autocracy. A few officials, out of their ignorance and corruption, can even go to the extent of damaging national prestige so seriously as to involve the loss of territory and the payment of enormous indemnities. National existence thus became impaired. I thought to myself then that we should not allow this Manchu house to rule over us, but that everybody should have the right and the initiative to be directly concerned with all the national affairs. It was then that thoughts stimulated me to become a member of the Tungmenghui and determined my life as a revolutionary."[3]

When Sun Yat-sen, therefore, began the construction of a democratic machinery in which the people would have the full share of responsible self-government, he provided the intellectual satisfaction that Chiang desired. It became clear to Chiang that such a government would be directly opposed to a rule by war-lordism or by a local bureaucracy that would in essence be personal and therefore feudalistic. Such a government would also provide an opportunity for political training on a large scale, and in consequence the people would be in a position to exercise the political powers that are inherently theirs.

The third doctrine of Sun Yat-sen, that of social and economic welfare, also became real to Chiang Kai-shek because he was overwhelmed, as a boy, by the wide differences between the rich and the poor. He lived under a system where the rich could grow richer and the poor poorer, so he vowed, as a result of his own sufferings, that he would do everything to fight for economic equality among the people. This last principle is, in fact, the basis of the whole ideological structure. It is the final objective, for without being able to improve the economic lot of the people the whole structure of government has no meaning and must collapse.

On this subject Sun Yat-sen was on surer ground than on any other subject, because he was supported by the whole trend of Chinese historical thought. Whichever page of the classics we turn, we find that from the very earliest day of recorded history the promotion of the welfare of the people was the principal concern of all good Chinese rulers. The only criterion of successful government was whether or not the people were happy, whether or not they were adequately provided for. The Chinese Government might be a

[3] Address before the Central Military Academy, July 8, 1929.

monarchy, but the Emperor was always the servant of the people. The people had the right to depose him and to call in another one to rule over them if they felt that he was incompetent in this regard.

Thus a political philosophy was conceived in which the central consideration was the happiness of the people. Confucius was a consistent exponent of this view, and the eloquence of his great disciple, Mencius, on the subject was one of the principal sources of his perennial charm. His books are full of references to the welfare of the people.

The great King Wen depended on the strength of the people to build a tower and a pleasure lake, and the people rejoiced to do the work. They called the tower the "spirit tower" and the lake the "spirit lake." They were happy that the king had deer, fish, and turtles. The rulers of ancient times shared their joy with the people, and that is why the people were happy.

Or again, Mencius said:

Let mulberry trees be planted about the homesteads with their five *mow*, and people of fifty years of age may be clothed in silks. In keeping fowls and pigs, do not let their time for breeding be neglected, and people of seventy years may enjoy eating meat. Let there be proper and timely cultivation of the farm with a hundred *mow* of land, and families with eight mouths to feed will know no hunger. Let careful attention be paid to education so that the children will know what it is to be devoted and loving to their parents and brotherly to other people. Persons covered with gray hair will then no longer be seen in the streets, carrying loads on their backs. The old will be clothed in silks and fed with meat, the people generally will know no hunger or cold. When your people attain such conditions, then truly you are a ruler.

This was almost a description of Chikow itself, and Chiang Kai-shek knew, remembering all that his mother had suffered and the wide discrepancies between the rich and the poor, that conditions were far from being what they should be. He agreed with Sun Yat-sen that the improvement of economic welfare for the people was the most important part of their revolutionary platform. That was where he differed from the other members of the Tungmenghui, who used to say to Sun Yat-sen that if the first two doctrines were realized he could leave the third behind and still attain the objectives of the revolution. Sun was vigorously opposed to this view and insisted that, if the revolution did not help to solve the economic problems of the

THE FLOWERING OF A FAITH

people and raise their economic level, then it had nothing to do with the people and was therefore not a revolution at all. A genuine revolution must be a people's revolution. If they accepted him as their leader they must help him to carry out this most essential part of the program.

Chiang Kai-shek agreed entirely with this view and has since taken upon himself the responsibility of carrying out this last principle as the most important of Sun Yat-sen's Three Principles. There are two measures which are indispensable to the realization of this principle—the equalization of land ownership and the limitation of private capital. No one, in other words, should be allowed to own large tracts of land or consider unearned increment as private profit. Likewise personal wealth should be placed under a limitation. There should be a ceiling on private income, and public utilities and big industries should be government-owned and -operated. The war has delayed the enforcement of these measures, but they will undoubtedly become an important part of the reconstruction program when the war is over. They are at the core of Sun Yat-sen's political and social faith; and if the standard of living of the Chinese people is not generally improved, the government will carry the onus of having failed to put into practice the ideals for which Sun Yat-sen worked during the forty years of his revolutionary career. The common people of China now, more than ever, after the enormous sacrifices they have endured and the epic heroism they have unfailingly shown in more than six years of bitter war, certainly deserve prior consideration. In the meantime we must admit that the discrepancies between their economic condition and that of the privileged classes remains as wide as ever.

Having made himself clear about the principal ideas of Sun Yat-sen's revolutionary program, Chiang Kai-shek, now a young man in the twenties, was prepared to plunge into the maelstrom of revolutionary activities. He has been consistently loyal to these ideas through all the vicissitudes of his life. To this day his work has been confined within the framework of these ideas. It is in this sense that he is the successor of Sun Yat-sen.

14

A Tragic Overture

BY 1910 OR 1911 the country was prepared for another revolutionary attempt. Sun Yat-sen had gathered around him a group of young men who were unquestionably patriots, mostly Chinese students in Japan. He had also completed the main outlines of a political platform, which was an essential part of the revolutionary scheme. While the emotional fervor of the students was deep and intense, they still required an intellectual appeal. That was provided by the Three Principles.

Outside of Japan there were other centers, such as the Malay States, Siam, Indo-China, and the Dutch East Indies, where the revolutionary agents of Sun Yat-sen had worked for years, and so the Chinese communities there had also long been agitating for a final showdown. By 1910, after having been on the Pacific coast of the United States, Sun Yat-sen was back in Penang, establishing contact with his followers, who in the meantime had grown in numbers in spite of the repressive measures against revolutionary tendencies which all countries surrounding China enforced in varying degrees of severity.

Ever since the defeat of China by France, shortly before the birth of Chiang Kai-shek, Sun had maintained that only a revolution could save the country. After the Chinese defeat in the Sino-Japanese War of 1894 his views developed even more rapidly, and between then and 1911 he undertook no less than nine revolutionary attempts, all ending in disaster; but he was not dismayed. Every defeat meant another period of gestation, during which he would travel and seek financial support from his compatriots abroad. Sun was a man of deep persistence and never lost faith in his cause. There was, in fact, no reason for him to lose courage, when, in spite of repeated failures, the response to his call was growing larger every day; Chinese laborers, farmers, workers, and, more especially, students, in all the countries where he traveled, flocked to him and received him as their unquestioned leader.

It is interesting to observe how widely the Chinese Revolution differed from revolutions in other countries. In the first place it received much of its strength from students. It reinforced the traditional belief that those who were devoted to books were somewhat better equipped mentally to initiate a large-scale social or political undertaking. Nor did the other classes question that leadership and privilege. The students, therefore, came to assume an importance that would be regarded elsewhere as out of all proportion. Since then they have continued to exercise an influence on Chinese politics which in the main has been wholesome. Their passion for reform has been prompted by genuine patriotism. They have a purity of motive which puts the officials as a class to shame. They have, generally, no ulterior motives to serve, and that is why they can be relied upon. They have not only a mental but also a moral integrity that raises them as a class to a position of respect. That respect was, to a certain extent, lost in 1919 when, during the so-called May 30 movement, some of the leaders were bribed into becoming officials themselves, and turned out to be as worthless as those whom they superseded; but in spite of occasional weaknesses, the student movement in Chinese politics has been a healthy influence. That was especially true of the students led by Sun Yat-sen. Failure then clearly meant the sacrifice of their lives, yet the students fearlessly went on with their work.

Another way in which the Chinese Revolution differed from revolutions in other countries was that it did not involve any mass struggle between the classes within the country. It differed, for instance, from the Russian Revolution, which involved a conflict between capital and labor. That was an uprising which tore society up by its roots, because one class of people rose to eliminate the other and all that it stood for. It differed also from the French Revolution, which was, in essence, likewise a struggle between the privileged class and the underprivileged class. In both cases the conflict rose out of some malady within the social structure that was attributed to a particular class, and in the effort to wipe out that class the conflict became perforce a bloody affair, accompanied by reigns of terror.

Not so the Chinese Revolution, in which there was merely a strong discontent on the part of a small enlightened group because of the government's inability to win for China the prestige to which she was entitled in the family of nations. Its origins, in other words, were to be found in the international background, in which the existing government failed to live up to the expectations of the Chinese people. There was obviously much bitterness of feeling against the Manchus as an alien race, but there was not so much animosity against them on this account as there was because they were incompetent, corrupt, and decadent. Unlike the French and Russian revolutions, the Chinese Revolution did not have convulsive qualities. It appeared to be more localized, less compelling, and more leisurely. It was satisfied so long as the reigning house was willing to renounce its claims to rule the country and give way to the demands of the revolutionary elements. When the republican regime finally came into existence the Emperor still enjoyed privileges within the precincts of the Forbidden City, and an annual stipend was even provided for him by the republican treasury. Surely this was a strange kind of revolution, when revolutions in popular imagination are not complete without the murder of some member of a royal household or the decapitation of a king.

While the Chinese Revolution was not a deeply stirring event, it was, within its sphere, interesting as a revelation of the quality of the men who took part in it. The incidents themselves might be circumscribed in their scope, but that did not prevent the individuals from showing patriotism, bravery, and a willingness to sacrifice their lives on the altar of a noble cause worthy of genuinely great heroes.

March 29, 1911, was such an incident and again an abortive attempt. It had to be followed by another uprising six months later, on October 10, which was finally successful in overthrowing the monarchy and establishing the new Chinese Republic. Chiang Kai-shek took no part in the March 29 episode, for he had remained in Japan, but actually he learned more from it than from all other previous revolutionary activities. It fully prepared him for his own work in October. It showed him why it had failed, and he learned to avoid the mistakes which his predecessors had committed. Those who participated in that incident were practically all young men in their twenties, some few even less than twenty, and some slightly over thirty. They were, in other words, of Chiang's own age, which was then twenty-four. They were mostly from the provinces of Kwangtung and Fukien, with a few from Anhwei and Szechuan. But there were more from Chiang Kai-shek's own province of Chekiang among the list of those who perished as a result of that revolt. That episode is known as that of the Seventy-two Heroes, whose brave deeds are still commemorated every year as one of the most glorious episodes in the history of the Chinese Revolution.

The uprising was planned by Sun Yat-sen during a meeting of the Tungmenghui among the local members at Penang. That was probably the reason why Chiang was not in it, for those who were in Japan kept to their own work. During that meeting in Penang, which took place on October 12, 1910, it was decided that on March 29 the revolution was to break out at Canton, when four separate groups were to storm the centers of Manchu authority in the city, the most important being the residence and yamen of the provincial governor.

Between the day of the meeting and the actual outbreak there was an interval of nearly six months, a much longer period than had been allowed on previous occasions. The students were determined that this time some tangible results must be accomplished. They made the fullest preparations. Among the first items attended to was ammunition, which was necessarily purchased abroad and then transferred to Canton and assembled there. They had recourse to ingenious devices for escaping the attention of the police. Some arranged to have elaborate wedding ceremonies or funeral services. In the wedding of a rich Chinese family, in those days, the bride was supposed to convey to her new home a large number of boxes, containing a complete wardrobe to be used during the entire period of her married life, sixteen to twenty-four soft, padded bedcovers, and a full set of wooden basins and tubs for laundry and miscellaneous kinds of washing. The conveyance of these articles formed a procession, attracting people from all parts of the city. The young revolutionaries took advantage of such arrangements and managed through a number of fake weddings to smuggle a portion of the ammunition they needed. In faked funerals, all they did was to put their guns and bullets in the spacious wooden coffin that was usually carried by eight to sixteen bearers. But too frequent weddings and funerals would arouse suspicion, so other devices had to be resorted to. Anything in the way of boxes or cases or even flowerpots was recruited into the service.

Most of this ammunition came from Japan, Indo-China, or Siam, and the first place of assemblage was Hong Kong, which was ideal because it was so near Canton and because it was also a seaport. Not all consignments, however, arrived safely. One student, while accompanying one of these major consignments, suddenly received a wire as he was embarking on a steamer from Japan, heading for Hong Kong, that customs officials had somehow begun to examine incoming steamers from Shanghai and that he had better be careful. The youngster grew so excited that he secretly threw all the ammunition overboard. It turned out that when he arrived in Hong Kong nothing at all happened.

The weapons which the revolutionaries needed most of all were bombs which could be thrown at some of the key men to create disorder. The bombs they made right in Canton itself, so that by March they had three hundred of them on hand. The day of reckoning was near, and there was general excitement. On March 10, still nearly three weeks before the appointed day, the government officials at Canton were out to view a flying exhibition of an airplane, then a novelty in China. One young man thought that it was too good an opportunity to miss and, concealing a bomb, he went to a teashop near which he thought the Manchu officials would pass. Soon he heard the sound of gongs announcing the approach of some important official who was being carried in a sedan chair to the airfield. Slowly the procession came, and just as it passed the teashop there was a terrific explosion. The young man had thrown his bomb! The official was dead. He was the Manchu defense commissioner. The culprit was apprehended on the spot and later, of course, decapitated.

True, one official had been killed, but it made matters worse for the general uprising on March 29. The government at once enforced all kinds of precautionary measures, and it appeared as if the revolution could not start off on the appointed day. One man, Huang Hsin, had the courage to say: "The date has been decided upon, and there will be no change. Even if no one follows me, I shall alone proceed with my plans to kill both the military and civil governors. I want to do this to show the world that we can be relied upon and that we are grateful to all our compatriots overseas who have such confidence in us. To tell you quite frankly, when I came here to Canton I had made up my mind to sacrifice my life. I have written these last words as a will for my comrades. Let us dissolve this meeting at once so that no disaster will come upon you."

Whereupon he produced a slip of paper upon which he had written:

> Please forgive me that I have had no time to reply to all of your letters. I am going to the battle line today with the oath that I shall sacrifice my life and kill our enemies.
>
> HUANG HSIN

The revolution had to go off on the appointed day, even with all the precautions which the authorities were taking, and there were still some three hundred Tungmenghui members in Hong Kong who had to proceed to Canton to join their comrades. Among them was Hu Han-min. The majority of them had cut off their queues and could therefore be easily spotted, so there was a mad scramble for the shops selling hair and artificial pigtails, which were put on and kept in place by the "watermelon-skin" caps.

The evening of March 29 came. The temple bells rang. Then suddenly the sound of a trumpet was heard. That was the signal for action. Huang Hsin, at the head of an army of forty people, rushed to the yamen of the Viceroy, where they were confronted by a bodyguard that naturally greatly outnumbered them. The forces were not equal, and so instead of an open fight the revolutionary army of forty made a passionate spiritual appeal to the soldiers.

"Brothers!" shouted Huang Hsin, "We are struggling for the freedom of our race. We are fighting for the glory of China. We are fellow countrymen, and surely we shall not murder one another. Please give way to us!"

The soldiers were not impressed, and as the revolutionaries advanced, firing broke out. Casualties on both sides were heavy. In the meantime the Viceroy escaped through the back door, and the revolutionaries actually managed to go so far as to set the building on fire. They then proceeded to the other centers of Manchu authority, but on their way they were met by the soldiers of the military governor and were overwhelmed. The other three groups which Huang Hsin expected would break out simultaneously fared even worse, and so by the next morning the revolution had been squashed with most of the troublemakers captured. Huang Hsin lost a few fingers through a bullet shot and was among the fortunate ones who escaped.

All told, seventy-two of the heroes were brought before the military court, and the verdict was, of course, the supreme penalty. Each of them gave his life nobly and without regret.

15

Going into Action

CHIANG KAI-SHEK HEARD the call in Japan, and six months later he left that country for Shanghai to continue the work which had been so heroically and tragically begun.

Chiang joined Chen Chi-mei, who was the first revolutionary to befriend him back in 1906, and who first introduced him to Sun Yat-sen and the Tungmenghui. Chen was now in Shanghai, having returned from Hong Kong, where he was staying when the revolution of March 29 broke out. On the day following the uprising the Manchu government issued an order that everyone not wearing a pigtail be seized and thrown into prison. Those who were unfortunate enough not to escape thus had no way of leaving Canton to go back to Hong Kong. Huang Hsin disguised himself as a poor farmer and got away through one of the less conspicuous gates. Others did the same thing, but there were still many in Canton who were in danger of being rounded up. The governor not only gave instructions that all ships leaving Canton for Hong Kong were to be carefully inspected, but that all houses within the city were also to be searched. He was determined to stamp out the movement completely. It was at this point that Chen Chi-mei rose to save the situation. He rushed from Hong Kong to Canton, pretending to be a newspaper correspondent, and demanded an audience with the deputy governor. He spoke so eloquently that the deputy governor thought it wise to introduce him to the governor himself. Chen pleaded that on the ground of self-protection it was best not to kill all of the revolutionaries, for he had knowledge that there were sympathizers everywhere and that once they began to take revenge the situation would get entirely out of control. The governor thought that this information from a "neutral source" tallied with what the revolutionaries themselves said during the trial, and so the restrictive measures were rescinded. Whereupon Chen immediately provided fares for his comrades and left for Hong Kong with them. By October Chen Chi-mei was in Shanghai, and Chiang Kai-shek came there to join him.

Chiang had been in Japan for over four years; the first two he spent in the Shinbo Gokyo, the preparatory military academy, and the remaining period as a cadet in the 13th Field Artillery Regiment of the Japanese Army. He had received not only military knowledge but also rigorous military training, more than most of the members of the Tungmenghui ever had, so when the revolution broke out again in October he was ready to go into action. He asked for a short leave of absence from the regiment, got in touch with two of his friends, borrowed some money with which they bought some civilian clothes, and slipped into Shanghai. He had neatly packed his uniform and the accessories of a cadet before he left Japan and had them sent back to the regiment by parcel post.

When Chiang Kai-shek decided upon this course of action he was entering upon a new chapter of his life. His period of formal training was over, and he was stepping into the world of realities and practical problems. This first step was attended with great danger to his personal life, for Shanghai, like other ports of entry along the coast, was being closely watched for all persons who were suspected of being sympathetic to the revolutionaries.

There were many reasons why, after the failure of the March 29 uprising, the center of Tungmenghui activities shifted to Shanghai and along the Yangtze River. First, the authorities were paying too much attention to Canton, and it was difficult to do anything there without being recognized. Second, the moving spirit of the October revolution was Chen Chi-mei, and he was familiar with Shanghai and its leading citizens. Third, the time had arrived when the movement could not be confined to a distant corner of China and so needed a larger base that would provide sufficient room for expansion. The Yangtze basin, occupying the central portion of the country, was an ideal location. And lastly, Shanghai had the facilities of the foreign settlements, which could offer asylum to the revolutionaries; it was, moreover, so important a city that, once it had been captured, the success of the revolution would be more or less assured.

The strategy of the outbreak was planned largely by Chen Chi-mei in collaboration with Chiang Kai-shek. The scheme decided upon was to fire the first shot at Wuchang, which is situated in the center of China, and then the other major cities along the Yangtze River would follow up with similar uprisings. Chen felt that the extension of the area of activity was fully justified by what he had been able to find out about the attitude of the people since the March 29 outbreak. Each failure had made the cause of the revolution better known to the people of China, and the last failure especially, which involved the sacrifice of more than seventy young people, had so emphasized the need of radical action that the majority of the people were willing, either openly or secretly, to render some assistance. The people as a whole, perhaps, would not revolt, but they were prepared to give support and sympathy to the revolutionaries as soon as action was taken. Chiang fully concurred with the views of Chen Chi-mei, which later proved to be correct. Between the two of them they were to be responsible for the revolution in the neighboring cities of Shanghai and Hangchow. Chen was to be in charge of operations in the

Shanghai area, and Chiang, who was then to all intents and purposes Chen's chief of staff, was to take care of Hangchow.

On October 10, 1911, as planned, the revolution broke out at Wuchang. For a time things went well, but it was apparent that the government troops were overwhelmingly superior both in numbers and in equipment. The revolutionary army did not collapse, yet it was not making much progress, and the revolutionaries in the other cities, fearing that defeat would again be their lot, hesitated to respond. The government dispatched Feng Kuo-chang, who subsequently became one of the presidents in the early years of the republic, to quell the insurrection in Wuchang, which he did with much credit to himself. It looked for a time as if the revolutionary cause had lost out again. It was then that Chen Chi-mei and Chiang Kai-shek went into action.

Chiang left Shanghai for Hangchow toward the end of October, after having made all final arrangements with Chen Chi-mei. Even though the revolution was not making any remarkable progress elsewhere, they decided to revolt simultaneously on November 3. What happened then was little short of miraculous. Chiang had only a superficial knowledge of the city of Hangchow, which he had acquired some six years previously, and a small brave band of intense patriots like himself. Their only equipment was a few crude bombs and some guns, a number of which were out of repair. A handful of sympathetic citizens were able to smuggle a few rounds of ammunition to the revolutionists. Against this ill-equipped and inadequate force were the government troops who, although their hearts might not have been in their work, nevertheless had everything in their favor.

What Chiang was facing in Hangchow was much like what had happened at Canton in March, and he knew what the consequences would be if he failed. At the appointed time, like Huang Hsin in Canton, Chiang at the head of a small group of "dare-to-die" revolutionists began storming the governor's yamen, the symbol of Manchu authority. There they came into immediate conflict with the guards of the yamen and exchanged fire with them; some of the bombs were effective. But instead of fighting back as did the guards at Canton, these guards at Hangchow actually gave way. The yamen was set on fire, and Chiang led his men on to the occupation of the other centers of Manchu authority within the city. Hangchow fell, and a provisional revolutionary government was established. This was the first time that a whole city had fallen to the followers of Sun Yat-sen.

In the meantime operations in Shanghai were also going ahead according to plan. The first object of attack was the arsenal, because its occupation meant an enormous increase in fighting power. Chen Chi-mei succeeded in winning over a portion of the defenders to his side, but the guards who really did the fighting were among those who had not been won over. Chen, after vainly trying to talk the government troops into laying down their arms, was captured and bound in chains. He was not held long, however, since the revolutionists captured the arsenal during the next day and released him. With the seizure of the arsenal, all of the surrounding areas of Shanghai fell like a house of cards to the revolutionary cause.

I was in Shanghai at that time myself, a boy of twelve, and I can clearly remember that exciting day, although I had no understanding of what the excitement was about. The shops in the areas adjoining the foreign settlements were closed, and a feeling of suspense was in the air. We children were kept at home, but actually nothing happened. I heard the newsboys selling extras announcing the fall of the arsenal to the revolutionaries, and quite soon the police and other officials were wearing white bands round their arms bearing the two words "*kwang fu,*" meaning "Restoration of the Han people." The immediate reaction of the people was one of unrelieved joy. Everybody was excited, waiting for some radical changes that would favorably affect their lives. It was then announced that we had to cut off our pigtails, which was a minor revolution in itself. This was gratifying news, and I remember that there was a rush to the barbershops. We returned from the shops proud of our new style of hairdressing, which used up a generous amount of vaseline to paste the short hair down, and in our hands was a small package containing our pigtails, which we brought home to our mothers to keep. To this day my mother keeps the coil of my hair which was cut off on that early morning in November thirty-two years ago.

That was how the Chinese Revolution took place. There was not much bloodshed, and the two key cities of Shanghai and Hangchow were, in a few days, in the hands of Sun Yat-sen's followers. When the new provisional government was set up in Hangchow, Chiang Kai-shek as one of the heroes of the uprising was naturally asked to take a leading part. But he declined the offer as he had to hurry back to Chen Chi-mei at Shanghai. That city was vastly more important to the cause of the revolution than any other city, and it was essential that Chiang assist Chen in consolidating their position. Chen became military commander of the Shanghai area and at once made Chiang the commander of the 5th Regiment, with power to train a new army. The recruits came in by the thousands. They were all primed for excitement, though they were mostly people who had no family attachments; in other words, they were a part of Shanghai's floating population. It was Chiang's duty to give them the required training, and results ultimately turned out much better than had been expected. The civilian and military headquarters of the Manchu officials fell one after another into the hands of this motley crowd, and quite soon the revolutionaries found themselves in possession of all the Shanghai area.

The organs of public opinion at Shanghai could now openly espouse the new cause, and all the government papers, including the post and telegraph offices, declared their independence. But the severest blow to the authority of the Manchu government was the revolt of its navy at Shanghai, which had announced its allegiance to the new regime. It was then obvious that the end of the Manchu rule was really near. The whole of the Yangtze Valley, from Wuhan (Wuchang, Hankow, and Hanyang) to Shanghai, had revolted. One stronghold still remained to be taken, and that was Nanking. If that could be taken the revolution would be completely successful.

Accordingly a combined expedition by the revolutionary forces of Kiangsu and Chekiang against Nanking was planned. Chen and Chiang remained at Shanghai to direct the operations. It was essential that they hold the base from which all reinforcements of men and equipment had to come. The campaign proved to be a difficult and costly one, for the city of Nanking not only had one of the most massive walls in the world, but it was also under the military control of the colorful reactionary Chang Hsun. He was a stanch loyalist, famous for his collection of ladies. He was also famous for an unusually thick pigtail which he wore as a symbol of great loyalty to the Manchu court.

It happened that the province of Chekiang, in which Chiang Kai-shek was born, and which he more than anyone else helped to conquer for the revolutionary cause through his triumphal occupation of its capital, Hangchow, dispatched, as a part of its military contribution against Nanking, a Women's Northern Expeditionary Force. When these women soldiers approached the city wall they displayed extraordinary bravery, but could make no headway against the pigtailed defenders, for whom they provided a good deal of mirth. The defenders had every advantage on their side—position, equipment, and strength—and had the sense of humor to treat the situation lightly. Instead of exchanging bullets there ensued a rapid exchange of strong words and curses followed by peals of laughter. But the women were in dead earnest. They had come to sacrifice their lives and were unafraid of what might happen. They brought tall ladders and began scaling the walls. The defenders had just enough sense of chivalry, however, not to shoot, but as the women neared the battlements, they tipped the ladders, and down fell the women, tumbling over one another.

A hearty peal of laughter ensued. But the leader of the Women's Expeditionary Force was undaunted. She got on her feet and said: "How can we face our elders again if we continue to be the butt of laughter of these pigtailed soldiers? We must honor the new women of China and wipe away our shame. We are fighting not only to overthrow the oppression of the Manchu house but also for a position of equality with the men, which we shall enjoy from now on. Sisters, let us be brave! For this is the day for which we have vowed to give up our lives. Let us pull together and fight for the eternal glory of our womanhood!"

With that speech there was a renewed attack, and some of the women actually succeeded in climbing up to the top of the wall. But their number was small, and they were soon captured and brought before pigtailed General Chang Hsun himself.

"As women, we have no weapons on us. We are simply performing a patriotic duty. You can kill us with your knives or with your guns—just as you will," said one young woman.

"Well, no. I have no desire to harm you. Do you think that we soldiers would have allowed you to climb up to the top of the wall if we really wanted to harm you?"

"Then who are you anyway?" the young woman wanted to know.

"Me? I am the old one,[1] famous for the massacre of the revolutionaries. I am widely known under all the heavens as the Great Executioner. The Supreme General and Commander, Chang Hsun. This is my name. Now aren't you afraid? And you girls of such tender age—why are you not at home learning to show devotion and love to your parents, and learning to be obedient to your husbands? See what a crime you have committed by joining the ranks of the revolutionaries. I do take pity on you and haven't the heart to 'lower my hand

[1] An expression of pride and haughtiness. To be a senior in China means a position of superiority.

of poison,' though revolutionaries must all die whenever I have them caught."

With cool courage the woman, knowing now to whom she was speaking, approached the general, pulled out her guns, and shot at him. But before she could harm him her own body was riddled with bullets from the guns of Chang's bodyguard.

While the women were performing this delaying action, and throwing the defenders off their guard, the regular force sent from Shanghai and Hangchow by Chen Chi-mei and Chiang Kai-shek was gathering in strength. The pigtailed general with his troops crossed the river and went northward, and the revolutionaries soon became the masters of the strategic city of Nanking. The occupation of that city was a symbol to the nation that the native Chinese had come back to the capital of the first Ming Emperor, and preparations were made at once to proclaim it the capital of the new China.

Thus at the age of twenty-four Chiang Kai-shek, in active military experience for the first time in his life, contributed to the final success of the revolution. It could be that the revolution would have been successful this time under any circumstances, after ten previous attempts and as many failures, but the fact remains that Chiang's emergence on the political scene was a factor in the successful outcome of the revolution.

In the Book of Prophecy, written as long ago as the Tang Dynasty, and discovered in 1859 when the British and French troops burned the Winter Palace of Yuan Ming Yuan, it is said that a general will one day rule China; he will be one with grass on his head. The Chinese words for "general" are *"chiang chun,"* and the *"chiang"* of Chiang Kai-shek is the same word with a few extra strokes on the top, which are the sign for grass.

16

Shifting Fortunes

WITH THE ENTIRE Yangtze Valley, including the important commerical port of Shanghai, within their control, the revolutionaries at once called for a national convention in which representatives from seventeen provinces participated. It was unanimously voted to ask Sun Yat-sen to return to his country and become the provisional President of the Republic of China. At that time he was in the United States, soliciting support as usual from his fellow countrymen. He took his time returning since he had the utmost confidence in his followers, in men like Chen Chi-mei and Chiang Kai-shek, under whose aegis the new regime was coming into being. Sun finally arrived at Shanghai on Christmas Day, 1911. With church bells ringing, Sun Yat-sen came home to see his dream of thirty years realized at last.

There had been little bloodshed during the whole course of the revolution, and yet an old and entrenched monarchy had given way to a republican regime. On January 1, 1912, with impressive ceremony Sun was installed as the first President of the republic. Offerings were given to the first Emperor of the Ming Dynasty (A.D. 1368–1644), whose tomb is located at Nanking in a colossal tumulus, as if to convey to him that the government of his country was again in the hands of his native Chinese.

If the bloodless revolution had its advantages, it soon was apparent that it had not gone very far. The people to the south of the Yangtze River had, it is true, been converted in varying degrees to the ideas upon which the new regime was founded, but north of that river they remained quite indifferent and seemed to be satisfied with the life to which they had been accustomed. There were many factors responsible for the differences between the north and the south in their receptivity to these ideas. In the south the big cities and centers of trade from Shanghai to Canton brought larger views of the world to the people, while the north remained conservative. Also, temperamentally the people in the south are more mercurial and expressive, while those in the north are much more inclined to be stolid and unyielding. Finally, under the Manchu government there was really no mechanism by which its will could be effectively enforced. The farther away the territory was from the center of authority in Peking, the less influence it felt. The people became conscious of the imperial rule in proportion to their nearness to the capital. Owing to a combination of these circumstances, the south was much freer to produce revolutionary leaders than the north. Sun Yat-sen, Chen Chi-mei, and Chiang Kai-shek were all southerners.

When the republican regime was established and Sun assumed the presidency on January 1, 1912, the revolutionaries soon found out that it was not the end of their troubles but the beginning. Within ten weeks, by March 10, the presidency passed into the hands of Yuan Shih-kai, who had been waiting for just such an opportunity to satisfy his personal ambitions. What happened in that short period to bring Yuan into the saddle, and how he managed to maintain that supremacy on the Chinese political scene till he died on June 6, 1916—a period of four and a half years—constitutes one of the most interesting episodes of modern Chinese history. The part that Chiang Kai-shek played in that episode had no importance, but the part that the episode played in developing his thought and personality was immense. It provided him with an opportunity to observe at close range, during the first days of his own active participation in practical politics, the unfolding of the inherent forces in the Chinese political scene, and gave him a knowledge that was to prove essential to his work in the future.

This is not the place to describe the changes which took place, but from them Chiang Kai-shek undoubtedly learned many valuable lessons. In the first place he realized that the people were not yet sufficiently indoctrinated with the new ideas of Sun Yat-sen. Second, in the game of practical politics, even though there was an adequately worked out program, there must be real power, and no power was more effective than military power. Third, in order to maintain that military power it was necessary that there should be strong financial backing. Fourth, the foreign powers were not, generally speaking, sympathetic toward a revolutionary program which they considered to be undermining the vested interests by which they maintained their grip on China. And lastly, Chiang Kai-shek realized that the Tungmenghui, which soon came to be known as the Kuomintang or the People's party, still lacked a strong central organization of its own.

What happened immediately after the inauguration of Sun Yat-sen as the provisional President at Nanking is simply told. The imperial throne, which was occupied by a baby Emperor upon the death, in 1908, of both the wily old Empress Dowager and the well-meaning but weak-kneed Emperor Kuang Hsu, was beginning to totter after more than half the country had gone over to the revolutionary cause. In order to bolster its waning prestige and to prevent any precipitate collapse, the court had no alternative but to call for the help of the one man whose satraps still had considerable military power in the various provinces. That man was Yuan Shih-kai, who had earlier reorganized the army with an eye to his own assumption of power. The Military Academy from which Chiang Kai-shek had graduated and received the scholarship to pursue further studies in Japan was a part of Yuan's ambitious scheme. Most of the graduates who received commissions from Yuan were stationed in the various provinces and became his supporters.

As a result of court intrigue Yuan was forced to retire from public life in 1908. He had been Emperor Kuang Hsu's military adviser, though it was he who checked the Reform Movement in 1898 sponsored by the same Emperor. But since he had managed to retain the actual military power, he was asked now by the court to come out of retirement and handle the emergency situation created by the revolutionaries. From that time on, for four and a half years, he was not only the dominant personality on the Chinese political stage, but he also strove earnestly to better his personal fortune. His ruling passion was ambition and a desire for personal glory, but the story of how he played the game, how he maneuvered and jockeyed for position, and then finally collapsed, provides great color to that short period of modern Chinese history. Ever since Chiang Kai-shek had attended the Military Academy at Paoting, he had had grave doubts about Yuan's integrity. He soon discovered that Yuan was no patriot and had little patience with ideals.

Yuan did not commit himself one way or the other in 1911. He knew that both the revolutionaries and the court needed his mediation. He held the trump card because of the military power he controlled. He could, if he wished, make use of the situation and step onto the throne himself, for no moment was more propitious. But if he did proclaim himself Emperor under those circumstances he would be regarded as a usurper by posterity, and so he could not consider ascending the Dragon Throne until he had time to prepare the mood of the people to the point where they would offer him the crown, rather than he should stretch out his hand for it himself. That moment had not yet arrived. Yuan reached Peking seventeen days after the revolution broke out at Wuchang. His first act was to have the baby Emperor give up the throne, without actually abdicating. In the meantime he sent representatives to establish friendly contact with the revolutionaries in the south. That move was calculated to split the ranks of the revolutionaries, and it did. Chen Chi-mei, and with him his young lieutenant Chiang Kai-shek, realized that any compromise with Yuan meant the end of the revolutionary effort, but the majority of the other revolutionaries urged moderation and insisted that they should face the problem realistically. They were in no position to conduct military operations as far north as Peking, they argued. Yuan had the upper hand there, since he was the commander of a much more powerful military force. Any further military activity on the part of the revolutionaries was certain to meet strong opposition from Yuan. It would also meet opposition from the foreign powers which still considered the government at Peking the legal government of China. Realism, the revolutionaries contended, necessitated that the offer for an understanding from Yuan should not be summarily rejected.

Six weeks after Sun Yat-sen was installed in Nanking, Yuan forced the court to issue a series of edicts which were meant to satisfy all parties. They provided in essence that Yuan should be entrusted with the power of government and the power to negotiate with Sun Yat-sen and his followers for the establishment of a republic. The court, in the meantime, was to remain within the confines of the Forbidden City, shorn of all its powers, and to be provided with an adequate stipend for its maintenance. These measures were an expression of the spirit of compromise which is characteristic of the Chinese as a race. The court was playing a losing game, but instead of being entirely eliminated as revolutions in other countries would have required, the new arrangement allowed for its continued existence and further gave it the opportunity to renounce itself in favor of a republican regime. The republicans, on the other hand, did not get all that they wanted, but then they were in no position to realize all of their aims anyway. The government under this new dispensation became republican, which was their primary aim, and the revolutionaries had to be satisfied for the moment. At least the first of the three major political doctrines of Sun Yat-sen was put into effect, for the Manchu rule had come to an end.

This new setup actually placed all the powers in the hands of Yuan. It was a supreme triumph of opportunism. The revolutionaries had no alternative but to agree to these measures. Having gone that far, Yuan went one step further and tried to re-establish the superficial unity which had become disrupted on October 10. But the revolutionaries had started and won a revolution: they had created a new capital at Nanking and had the right to call the representatives thither from other parts of the country to a convention. Yuan, of course, was in no mood to journey south to Nanking, for he knew that it was not only physically unsafe for him to make the trip, but that he would also place himself morally in an inferior position by leaving Peking. He readily assented to proceed to Nanking, but he also cleverly created a mutiny in Peking in order to justify his continued presence there. The result was that he asked the republicans to come north to him instead. Step by step the republicans were placed on the defensive. For them to send their representatives to the stronghold of monarchism was to make a concession to those very forces and institutions which it was their avowed purpose to demolish. However, there was little they could do about it. And when finally Sun Yat-sen, on March 10, only ten weeks after he became the provisional President, had to transfer his title to Yuan Shih-kai, it seemed that the revolution had been accomplished for the benefit of Yuan Shih-kai and his cohorts and not for the Chinese people for whom Sun had fought during thirty years of his life.

Although the defeat of the revolution was complete, Yuan wanted to create no such impression. He ostentatiously asked Sun Yat-sen to take charge of the railway development of the country. Sun had always been eloquent on the subjects of the development of the country along modern lines and the promotion of the economic well-being of the people. Was he not being given the opportunity to put his theories into practice on a national scale? In the new cabinet which he thus formed, Yuan also asked Chen Chi-mei to become his Minister of Commerce and Industry. If he could, he would keep all the revolutionary leaders right under his nose at Peking!

There was nothing that Sun Yat-sen and his followers could do, under the circumstances, except return to Japan and plan all over again. The revolution had been betrayed.

In the meantime the power of Yuan Shih-kai grew steadily. At first he proceeded cautiously. Though he was now master of the situation, he was not unaware of the fact that the moral victory still belonged to the revolutionaries. It was they who had placed him where he was. The people also knew this, and it was necessary to consider their feelings. The Kuomintang as a group could not yet be openly suppressed, but he did everything he could to curtail its power. He organized a group of his own men as the party of opposition which he called the Chinputang, or the Progressive party, so that, even though parliamentary rule was a mere fiction, he had a weapon with which to defeat the revolutionaries.

The most important force of Yuan's power was the army. This he proceeded to reorganize with the idea that his appointees must remain personally loyal to him, although they might enjoy the fullest freedom of action within their own localities. This was the origin of the tuchuns or war lords, in China, who in the next fifteen years brought the country to the verge of utter bankruptcy and demoralization. If the army had been reorganized for patriotic reasons and national defense, Yuan would have emphasized quality and rigid training. For a time he did make an attempt to show the country that he could create a model army. He chose the peasants with the best physiques from Shantung and Honan. They were all six-footers, and the army, though small in number, looked impressive and was well-disciplined, but he had no use for that kind of an army. What he wanted was vast numbers of soldiers placed in strategic positions throughout the country for garrison purposes against anyone within the country who dared challenge his authority. Inferior equipment and bad discipline gave Yuan no cause for concern so long as he was able to enforce a military dictatorship through which he could keep the country under his control.

The first thing he did was to appoint new commanders, especially in the southern provinces, to replace those who were sympathetic to the revolutionary cause. Having done this, he gave his appointees immense powers which virtually converted them into tyrants who held in their grip the military and civil administration of the provinces. Even in the decadent Manchu days an effort had been made to draw a line of demarcation between the Tartar general and the civilian viceroy or governor. But now China returned to days worse than those of the Contending States in the fifth century B.C. The country became a hunting ground for personal fortunes. Poverty, ignorance and wickedness rose like phantoms, and stalked through the towns and villages in one of the most degrading periods of modern Chinese history. Yuan himself lived through some four years of his own creation. It was after his death, in 1916, that pestilence in the wake of civil wars grew rampant and covered the country with ugly scars.

Among the few colorful personalities who grew out of this period of chaos was Wu Pei-fu, who was a man of honor and integrity. But with all his virtues he was like a feudal lord stepping into the twentieth century; and though he found it uncomfortable, he insisted upon applying his set of values from a world which no longer existed. He had no knowledge of the foreigner and desired to have as little as possible to do with him. Although his life was constantly in danger during that troubled time, he had to have his feet firmly planted on territory that was not only legally but also genuinely Chinese. He spent his last days in Peiping after having been defeated by Chiang Kai-shek in the early days of the Northern Expedition, but he maintained his character to the end. When the Japanese later entered that city they tried to make use of Wu who, in his own way, appealed strongly to his countrymen. After the fall of Hankow in 1938 the Japanese decided to make the old retired war lord the Chief Executive of China's occupied territory. Many overtures were conveyed to Wu, but all he wanted was to be left in peace. He became angry and spurned all Japanese emissaries. The Japanese then sent their archconspirator Doihara, but Wu Pei-fu, as usual, refused to see him. Doihara forced his way into Wu's presence. It was then that the old general spoke out. "To establish a nation on earth," Wu began, "you either follow the kingly way by being obedient to the moral law or the way of force through military pressure. When, as you Japanese have repeatedly done, you have violated our territorial and administrative integrity, it is obviously useless for me to talk to you about the moral law. But you have no qualifications even to warrant my speaking to you about the way of force. I am compelled to speak to you only about the way of robbers and highwaymen. But even they are guided by principles which I do not discover in you. What is the good of my talking to you at all?" Having thus delivered himself, the old general "waved his sleeves" (a Chinese expression meaning nonchalance) and went into his inner chambers. Doihara and his henchmen were red in the face and, having nothing to say, quietly sneaked away. Wu's death not long afterward was very probably due to poison.

Another personality was Feng Yu-hsiang, big, bulky, with fat chubby cheeks, and a rough, stubbly chin, unusual for a Chinese. He was the best actor of them all. He played the part of a latter-day Cromwell with telling effect. Crowned with a fur hat that Daniel Boone would have coveted, his tall figure was often seen bending over his soldiers, shaving them. Though banquets in China, especially among people of importance and wealth, are generally sixteen- or twenty-four-course affairs, the most elaborate feast at the headquarters of the "Christian general," as Feng was often called, consisted of a bowl of noodles and a plate of vegetables. He now lives quietly in Chungking with the title of Vice-Chairman of the Military Affairs Commission, keeping to his usual simple life, and attended by a handful of soldiers who are all that remain of the once powerful Kuominchun, or People's Army.

Two Chang war lords were also colorful figures of this period. Chang Tso-lin, the more powerful of the two, at one time ruler of the extensive domain of Manchuria, had delicate and gentle features. He looked every inch a scholar, and yet he struck terror to the heart of millions as the boldest and most successful of the *hunghutze,* the redbeards, who emerged from the darknesses of Manchuria's primeval forests for periodic forages on unwary travelers. His success might be explained by the fact that in China the tradition of letters is so strong that even a bandit chief must look like a scholar before he can accomplish anything in his field. He died when his train was blown up en route to Mukden from Peking in 1928.

But if Chang Tso-lin had the suavity and refinement of a scholar, Chang Chung-chang, the burly dog-meat general, six feet four inches tall, was a romantic embodiment of an oriental potentate. He would have been the delight of Hollywood. It used to be said of him that there were three things about which he had no knowledge. He did not know how much money he had, he did not know how many wives he had, and he did not know how many children he had. His array of ladies, collected from all parts of the world, used to trail behind him wherever he went, and on one occasion, at the Grand Hotel de Pekin, when the procession came in, he was seen distributing ruby, sapphire, and diamond rings and brooches, throwing them at the feet of his many wives.

These and other war lords were a part of the checkered career of republican China, which Chiang Kai-shek had helped to create. Chiang saw them rise and prosper but was wise enough to follow the example of patience which Sun Yat-sen displayed. Not until 1927 was the time ripe for Chiang to demand a new deal and sweep away the last vestiges of this modern feudalism.

17

The Revolution Continues

THE NEXT TEN YEARS of Chiang Kai-shek's life were uneventful—a period of blasted hopes, disappointment, and disillusionment. There were days when he was deeply despondent. It would have been better, he sometimes thought, had the revolution failed, for then the monarchy would still remain as something tangible to fight against. The revolution had succeeded in ushering in a republic, ostensibly an entirely new regime, and yet what a travesty of a republic it had turned out to be! It was a republic in which Sun Yat-sen, the leading proponent of republicanism, had no place, let alone his followers: the change had been a change in name only. In place of the old decadent Manchu monarchy the wily opportunist Yuan Shih-kai had established a virtual military dictatorship of which the motivating principle was the nourishing of his own overweening personal ambition. The ideas for which Sun Yat-sen had fought during a whole generation appeared to be as far from realization as ever.

If this was a period of darkness for Chiang Kai-shek, it was also one of self-analysis and quiet observation. After a few short months of remarkable achievement during which he had become a personality of importance both in his native province of Chekiang and in Shanghai, Chiang thought that he would induce his mother to leave her village of Chikow and stay with him at Shanghai under more comfortable circumstances. It was with some reluctance that she left her home for the city, and the visit lasted only a few days. She felt more at home in her village and insisted upon going back. She was happy over her son's success but felt that it was only the beginning, and she knew that there would be difficulties ahead on the long and arduous way. When she returned to Chikow she had only a single bit of advice to offer her son: he should redouble his efforts and continue the fight until the aims of the revolution were finally achieved. Chiang never forgot these parting words, and to this day refers to them not only as the advice of an enlightened mother but also as a source of continual encouragement in the uncertain life of a revolutionary.

Together with the others of the same political belief, Chiang left for Japan, demonstrating his faith in Sun Yat-sen. Their relationship now became much more personal. They had gone through the big experience together, which was the beginning of a spiritual bond that to this day has not been broken. Chiang Kai-shek came to love Sun for his selflessness, for the purity of his motives, and for the unflinching devotion to his ideals. A less worthy person than Sun would certainly have made virtue of necessity and accepted the offer of Yuan Shih-kai to join his cabinet. Having lived the life of a rebel for thirty years, in hourly danger of being hunted down and thrown into prison, Sun's return to China in 1911 as the provisional President of the republic must have given him considerable joy and satisfaction. However, he was ready to be a rebel again when the principles which he fought for were so summarily brushed aside by Yuan and his satraps. Personal interests meant nothing to Sun Yat-sen. Only a man with such qualities could merit Chiang Kai-shek's genuine admiration.

When Sun gave up the presidency of the Chinese Republic to Yuan Shih-kai, Chiang understood that it was not due to any moral weakness on Sun's part. There was no other choice when Yuan had all the military power in his hands. Not all the Kuomintang members approved of this move, for some of them thought that it was wrong policy to yield so easily. There were others also who perhaps gave prior consideration to their personal interests and wished that Sun would co-operate with Yuan, even if it involved a temporary suspension of his political and social program, for that co-operation would have meant for them the opening up of avenues of official emolument. These followers were not men from whom Sun could expect unwavering faith, but Chiang could not be counted among them. Sun knew it. It was for that reason that Sun said to Chen Chi-mei, then his principal lieutenant, that it was well worth watching Chiang, for it was people like him who would carry on and complete the revolution.

Chiang did not have much to do in Japan, but having developed the habit, like Sun Yat-sen himself, of taking a long-range view of things, he spent much of his time writing articles on military and international affairs. These articles were contributed to the magazine *The Military Voice,* and are valuable as indications of the trend of his thought in those days. They have since been collected and published as *A Record of Self-Analysis,* and are interesting in two respects. In the first place, as a student of military science, having had both theoretical training and some practical experience, Chiang's interest was very largely a military one. Secondly, he was convinced, even in those early days, that military power, in order to have any value, must be based on the fullest preparation.

While Yuan Shih-kai was extending his military control over the country by the appointment of military commanders in the provinces and by flooding them with vast numbers of soldiers without sufficient training or equipment, in order that no one might rise to challenge his power, Chiang Kai-shek was thinking of soldiers in terms of national defense and as a means of promoting national prestige. The point of departure was totally different, and the conclusions Chiang arrived at were therefore totally at variance with what was actually going on within the country.

In the first place, Chiang Kai-shek maintained that the army must be a national possession, organized for a national purpose and held directly responsible to the central authority of the government. He foresaw the great danger of the war lord system, which was growing under Yuan's patronage and encouragement. It was helping to develop a large measure of local authority with centers of rivalry, and was therefore sowing the seeds of conflict and disunity. In order to reinforce his argument he advanced the United States as an example. This was significant because Chiang's many years of sojourn and study in Japan had made him familiar with conditions there, and Japan could have been used as an example just as well, for there was no doubt that the Japanese Army was a very strong national army. But Chiang's thoughts, even during those early days, turned to the United States as the only country comparable to his own. He argued that the governors of the different states were equivalent to the tuchuns of the Chinese provinces, but their functions were purely of a civilian nature. They had nothing to do with the soldiers, who were of federal concern and were stationed in military districts where the limits were not identical with those of the states. He strongly urged that the same be done in his own country. A strong Ministry of War should be created and given the responsibility of training a national army with emphasis on quality, rigid training, and good equipment, even though it might be numerically unimpressive.

Secondly, for purposes of national defense, he maintained in those articles that, since the immediate international problems before China were Russia and Japan, soldiers should be trained for eventual service in Mongolia and Manchuria. Chiang realized that China, a big but weak country, was an invitation to continual threat from many foreign sources, but the threat from Europe was primarily a naval concern. Though he would not ignore the navy, the young Chiang was realist enough to know that the development of a strong army was more within the realm of immediate practical possibilities. It was the periphery of China that was in danger of falling apart—Manchuria, Mongolia, Sinkiang, and Tibet—as long as China was not sufficiently strong to defend herself.

Of these four outlying territories, the problem of Tibet appeared to be least complicated. Great Britain was concerned with it because it affected the protection of India, and only indirectly coveted the territory. The problem of Sinkiang was then comparatively dormant, but the danger to Mongolia and Manchuria was real and immediate. Russia until then had consistently played the part of the *enfant terrible* in Asiatic affairs. Her policy was direct and openly aggressive, and left no doubt that she meant to grab what she could. She had already acquired enormous slices of territory from China north of the Amur River, and her appetite was not assuaged. She had inveigled Li Hung-chang into accepting an invitation to visit Russia, and by fair means and foul—it was mostly foul because even bribery seemed to be openly resorted to—she succeeded in wresting concession after concession from the effete mandarins. The disastrous war which Russia waged with Japan did not permanently eliminate that threat to China, but brought on a new one which proved to be even more serious. The desire of Japan to occupy Manchuria received a sharp fillip after that war; it remained unsatisfied till September 18, 1931, when the Japanese started a series of acts of aggression which precipitated the war between China and Japan and led step by step to the present global conflict.

While Yuan was thinking of ways to consolidate his power, Chiang was worrying over China's international position. He urged full military preparedness in his articles. His plans were then still all on paper, of course, but they shed light on his subsequent activities. He calculated that there should be at least eight divisions of well-trained troops stationed in Manchuria in addition to five cavalry divisions, a total of a quarter of a million men. There should also be eight divisions for Mongolia and three divisions each for Sinkiang and Tibet. Six hundred thousand well-trained troops, he thought, would give China an entirely new outlook. To meet the expenses of such an army he would devote at least one third to one half of the national revenue. Chiang was of the opinion that in ten years China would have the strongest army of any power in the world. It is now easy to see that he was carried away by youthful enthusiasm, since a strong army depends upon many factors in the realm of science, industry, and technology for which China even today is not fully prepared. Nevertheless, it is important to note that then as now Chiang held long-range views and stood for thorough and adequate preparation before launching upon any plan of action. Ill-advised or ill-prepared activities served no useful purpose: they were a waste of time, energy, and strength.

THE REVOLUTION CONTINUES

In the meantime, Yuan Shih-kai was forging ahead with his own plans. Not only was he able, within six months after becoming President, to appoint his own men to the military commands in the key provinces south of the Yangtze River, thus placing virtually all of the country under his control, but he even began dickering successfully with foreign countries for a big international loan further to consolidate his powers. A consortium consisting of six powers—the United States, Britain, France, Germany, Russia, and Japan—was formed ostensibly to pool the Chinese loans for an eventual unified liquidation. It prevented any single power from making loans to China without the prior knowledge and consent of the others. What it actually meant was international control over China's finances, for the terms under which any loans could be made were so heavy as to compromise Chinese sovereignty. But Yuan was prepared to sign any document so long as it helped him to fortify his position.

Credit must be given to President Woodrow Wilson for not consenting to support the scheme, as he felt that the conditions were such as "to touch nearly on the independence of China." The American group, therefore, finally dropped out, but the other powers continued their discussions and negotiations. The Kuomintang, or the followers of Sun Yat-sen, were naturally furious. They saw in the consortium an insidious device to keep China permanently weak and crippled. It was the drama of Faust and Mephistopheles played on an international scale. They saw further that the consortium was a combined attempt on the part of the foreign powers to suppress republican tendencies and the honest efforts of the republicans to make China a strong and progressive country. A knowledge of this background is essential because it explains why Sun Yat-sen became completely disillusioned as regards the policy of the foreign powers which, as he saw it, was motivated only by the desire to exploit China to the utmost. It explains why he made himself an open enemy of imperialism and why he joined forces with Soviet Russia some ten years later when Soviet policy, both theoretically and practically, was founded on the principle of equality and mutual consideration.

But the Kuomintang was powerless to prevent the negotiations from being concluded with the consortium. There was just one vain hope that objections might be made on constitutional grounds. When Yuan became President, he gave the oath to support the provisional constitution upon which the republic was founded. That constitution included the establishment of a Parliament whose assent was essential for the validity of any loan such as the one under discussion. Since the Kuomintang still had a majority in that Parliament, it insisted upon having a cabinet form of government and hoped in that way to have its voice heard. The party, therefore, elected one of its most prominent members, Sung Chiao-jen, to proceed to Peking with a view to his eventually becoming Prime Minister as a check to Yuan's powers. Yuan made short work of this attempt by assassinating Sung in the railway station at Shanghai just as he was boarding the train. That was on March 21, 1913. There was no reason for Yuan to be afraid of the Kuomintang. He had the military strength, and he had the backing of the foreign powers. After this cold-blooded murder, which created a tremendous sensation and really began a whole series of assassinations in the checkered career of political China for the next fifteen years, Yuan proceeded with perfect insouciance for the conclusion of the consortium loan, known euphemistically as the Reorganization Loan. The agreement was signed on May 21, with the representatives of the six powers, including the United States, and Yuan was richer by $125,000,000, a portion of which he judiciously distributed to his henchmen in the various provinces in order that their loyalty might remain firmer on a "reorganized" basis.

At the same time Yuan had the impudence, even though the facts were so glaringly against him, to spread the rumor that the assassination of the Kuomintang leader was none of his business but was the climax of jealousy and internal feud within the ranks of the Kuomintang itself. That was too much for the Kuomintang to stomach. It was at this juncture that Chen Chi-mei and Chiang Kai-shek appeared in Shanghai again. They were just on the point of departing on a tour of the world, which would have taken them to Europe and America. That trip unfortunately never materialized, and to this day Chiang Kai-shek has not set foot on the soil of those continents.

The assassins were speedily caught. Both Chen and Chiang had been in military command of the Shanghai area before, and with the co-operation of the Settlement Police, they succeeded in getting hold of all the evidence to show that the assassins were directly instigated by Yuan Shih-kai. The indignation of the country against Yuan grew rapidly, and with it sympathy for the Kuomintang. Sun Yat-sen openly sent a wire to Yuan accusing him of betraying the country and assuring him that he would oppose him with all his force, in the same way that he had opposed the Manchu Dynasty.

Nor was this an empty threat. Four months later, in spite of inadequate preparations, movements declaring their independence from Yuan were started in various provinces to the south of the Yangtze River. This is what is known as the Second Revolution. The center of operations, as during the first revolution, was in Shanghai. Chen Chi-mei was immediately appointed commander of the anti-Yuan forces, and Chiang Kai-shek his chief of staff. The two of them had in the meantime made some contact with the soldiers, though they were in Yuan's pay. But Yuan was intelligent enough to see the importance of Shanghai and dispatched one of his most trusted men, Cheng Ju-chen, to head a naval force to go down to that port and maintain vigilance over the soldiers. Chen and Chiang directed their operations against the arsenal, the possession of which would, as usual, have made matters much easier for them. However, this time Yuan's gunboats were in the river to reinforce the soldiers defending the arsenal, so it was never captured. Shanghai did not fall, and the independence movements in the interior gradually petered out. The Second Revolution rose and fell, leaving Yuan Shih-kai stronger than ever before.

Once more Chiang Kai-shek went to Japan. By this time his devotion and loyalty to Sun Yat-sen had become so solid and indisputable that the relationship between the two men came to a new plane of understanding and friendship. Together they went through another period of self-analysis and examination. Yuan's position had indeed become unassailable, though there was still no cause for despair. Sun reorganized the party and called it the Chinese Revolutionary party. Some few of the followers began to fail in their devotion and perseverance. They asked for a period of rest, but Sun deprecated such an attitude.

"The Second Revolution has failed," he said later to his followers, "because there is no unity within the party. You have no belief, no faith in my principles. Your actions have become haphazard. No wonder nothing can be accomplished. If we resolve to defeat the enemy and really bring success to our revolution, it is essential that the party have a healthy and effective organization. I want all my followers to understand my principles clearly and to keep their motives absolutely pure. If you feel that you must have a rest you will find yourselves as far away from the objectives of the revolution ten, fifty, or even a hundred years from now. This is no time for rest. This is the time for self-analysis and for finding out the reasons why we have failed. This is the time, above all, for mustering our energy, to show that we have persistence and an abiding faith in our final success. Yuan Shih-kai may have power, but the people hate him; and as long as we have the sympathy and support of the nation the success of our revolution is assured."

Chiang's reaction to this stand by Sun was shown by his frequent statement: "I have implicit faith in Sun Yat-sen not because I am his blind follower but because he really arouses the deepest respect in everybody. I do not know of another person in China who has such a broad and international outlook, whose ideas are so constructive and who has such deep faith and confidence in his own mission. How can anyone help showing real reverence for a man with such ideals and such an indomitable personality? It is for these reasons that I am his faithful follower."

This was also consistently the attitude of Chen Chi-mei, who all through this period was Chiang's closest collaborator and confidant

18

Abiding Loyalty

IT WAS NOT UNTIL 1922, when Chen Chiung-ming, a follower of Sun Yat-sen, showed his treachery, that Chiang Kai-shek reached another important landmark in the development of his career.

Into the history of the ten years between the failure of the Second Revolution and 1922 we need not go. Chiang Kai-shek was on the stage in a minor way. Yuan Shih-kai's power steadily grew, and nothing could be done to stop it. The Kuomintang was overshadowed; it was even dissolved toward the end of 1913, and the members of the party had to flee for their lives. But while the history of this decade need not be related here, it is relevant to mention some of the high lights insofar as they bear upon the life of Chiang.

Yuan Shih-kai proceeded to make use of the political machinery which was installed after the fall of the imperial house and the establishment of the republic. Every step that he took had the semblance of legality. He presented a parliamentary façade, but behind it he was consolidating his power until it became plain that what he really wanted was to restore the monarchy and make himself Emperor. To that end he even had an American political adviser to lend weight to his action. A few months after Yuan dissolved the Kuomintang, he created, early in 1914, a Political Council and a Constitutional Council which drafted a new constitution to take the place of the one drafted by the Parliament when Sun Yat-sen was the provisional President at Nanking.

The first World War then broke out, and it was thought that with foreign pressure removed from China the country would have a chance to go through a period of reorganization. But the resources of the nation were being sapped by the personal cupidity of Yuan and his satraps. Instead, the situation offered an opportunity to Japan, for in 1915 she struck a terrific blow by presenting the infamous Twenty-one Demands, which sought to make China a vast dependency of the Japanese Empire.

The world was stunned, though naturally no one was more stunned than the people of China themselves. But even under those conditions Yuan continued to dream about wearing the imperial crown. At last, in December 1915, he actually declared himself Emperor! That was too much for the Chinese people, powerless as they were. Under the leadership of Tsai Ao a new uprising against Yuan quickly broke out in the southwest province of Yunnan, and other provinces, especially those in the south, joined the movement to eliminate an impossible situation. Even Yuan's own satraps deserted. He had taken a bold step that was to precipitate his downfall. On June 16, 1916, Yuan died an inglorious death, bearing the curse of the nation to his grave.

But prior to his death he battled with the Kuomintang, which he mortally feared. He put as many as possible of their leaders to death. Sung Chiao-jen he had murdered in 1913, and a few weeks before he himself passed into oblivion Yuan hired assassins to murder Chen Chi-mei, who had proved on more than one occasion to be a creative revolutionary of outstanding ability. He had been a pillar of the revolutionary movement since the time it broke out in 1911. His loyalty and integrity were unimpeachable, and Yuan was afraid of him. In 1915, when the strength of the Kuomintang was in eclipse, Chen looked about for funds to give it the necessary support. Yuan's intelligence officers got wind of it, arranged a snare into which Chen fell, and he was shot to death in cold blood. That death caused more grief to Chiang Kai-shek than any other single event up to that time.

There were similar attempts on Chiang's own life, but fortunately for China he always managed to escape. From that time on the burden of carrying on the revolutionary activities fell very largely on Chiang's shoulders.

For Chen Chi-mei, Chiang always had great love and respect. Only two years previously, as they studied their revolutionary plans, they had come to the conclusion that they had confined their efforts too much to the south and that vigorous activities should be pushed in the north, even in Manchuria. It was then that Chiang went on a secret mission that carried him as far north as Tsitsihar and Heilungkiang. The mission was a hazardous one, and Chiang had full knowledge of the extent of its dangers. The Kuomintang was down and out, and Yuan Shih-kai had an intelligence system that worked. Traveling in Manchuria was not like traveling in any of the southern provinces of China, where Chiang could find many sympathetic people. His speech and manners would instantly betray him as a man from the south, and with Russia steadily extending her influence along the then Trans-Siberian Railway, she would be only too glad to please Yuan Shih-kai and expose any revolutionary activities of the Kuomintang. In spite of all these difficulties, Chiang managed to cover a large part of his itinerary and succeeded in crossing over to Japan and making a report to Sun Yat-sen.

We now come to 1916. The much hated Yuan Shih-kai had died, leaving a legacy of utter chaos and confusion to the country. If Chen Chi-mei were alive, Chiang Kai-shek and he together could have perhaps accomplished much. But he was gone, and Chiang had to carry on alone. He looked over the political scene, and there was little to encourage him. Yuan was succeeded by Li Yuan-hung, who in turn was succeeded by Feng Kuo-chang and Hsu Shi-chang. But what difference did any of these personalities make to China as a whole? War lords were everywhere, each carving a sphere of influence for himself. There was no longer any supreme authority in the country. It had become a happy hunting ground for all who could afford to keep soldiers around them. Clearly the country had lapsed into a period much like the age of feudalism that had followed the collapse of the Chou Dynasty, some twenty-six hundred years before. There was only one person who had it in his power to liquidate this recrudescence of feudalism, and that was Sun Yat-sen, but the war lords were determined that nothing should curtail their life of pleasant adventure.

In September of 1917 Sun Yat-sen managed to entrench himself in Canton again, the city that had always symbolized the birth of a new life for China. It was in Canton that all of his revolutionary ideas and plans were conceived and first put into practice. So a new military government under Sun Yat-sen was established with the great revolutionary leader himself appointed as its Generalissimo. It was his declared purpose to begin the revolution all over again. But the revolutionists' mood had changed: it was different from the spirit that his followers had shown in 1911 and earlier. There was vacillation among the ranks. There were all shades of opinion, but it was clear that many were inclined to compromise with the existing state of affairs. The revolution in Russia had started in the meantime and had succeeded in establishing a Soviet regime. It was a stimulus to Sun and some of his followers, who thought there was no reason why they could not accomplish just as much for China. Chiang Kai-shek remained as loyal as ever to the ideals of his leader. He had become a mature man, being now in his thirty-fifth year, but the scene remained so uninspiring that he could look forward to little in the way of substantial accomplishment. He went to Fukien, to Canton to be with Sun Yat-sen, to Shanghai, to his home village of Chikow to visit his mother—he wandered like Ulysses, for just as long a period, gathering all kinds of new and unexpected experiences. It was during this period that Chiang is said to have speculated on the stock market at Shanghai. When Sun was again elected President at Canton, on May 5, 1921, it is also said, the loyal supporter left Shanghai and brought Sun large funds, which he had made on the stock market, with which to run the new government. For even though there were times when Chiang could not entirely agree with Sun and his policies there was nothing in the world that could shake his implicit faith and confidence in his leader.

Sun reciprocated that feeling, made good use of the money, which he spent in purchasing badly needed ammunition and supplies, and the government at Canton began to show signs of renewed vigor. On June 4 Chiang's mother died at Chikow. That was the saddest news of Chiang Kai-shek's life. He hurried back to his native village, remained there wrapped in mourning, and for a time secluded himself from the affairs of the nation.

One year later the revolt of a subordinate named Chen Chiung-ming took place in Canton. That episode was destined to bring Sun Yat-sen and Chiang Kai-shek, who for many long years had been closely associated with one another, into a relationship the like of which has been rarely seen.

In the period of general dislocation from about 1912-22 it was to be expected that some few of the followers of Sun Yat-sen would waver in their loyalty to their leader. Chen Chiung-ming was one of the most important of these weak characters. He had been in command of the Canton soldiers, but according to his way of looking at things the chances for another successful revolution were indeed small. He was therefore in constant touch with the war lords whom it was Sun's duty to eliminate. He entered into secret negotiations with Wu Pei-fu, who was then the most powerful figure in central China, but all the time he managed to maintain a semblance of loyalty to Sun Yat-sen. Time and again Sun was warned that he should be wary of his general, as there were clear indications that he was playing a game of duplicity. But Sun refused to believe that one of his own subordinates could be unfaithful. Chiang Kai-shek's contact with Chen Chiung-ming had been intermittent, but it was close nevertheless. He saw military service with him in Fukien in 1918, and for four years Chiang had held the belief that the time would come when Chen Chiung-ming would turn traitor and stab his leader in the back. Chiang was therefore among those who cautioned Sun Yat-sen, but Sun always replied, "There are many people who speak ill of Chen Chiung-ming, but after all he is an able soldier." Chiang was disappointed that Sun had not heeded his warning. Sun was a deeply sincere man and believed that his personal influence was sufficient to extract loyalty and devotion from his followers.

On June 16, 1922, Chen Chiung-ming, after having established contact with some of the northern war lords and feeling secure that he could carve a sphere for his own influence, broke out into open revolt.

Sun Yat-sen, as President of the new government at Canton, was then engaged in the Northern Expedition. His plan was to capture Kwangsi Province first and, after establishing his headquarters there, to proceed to take military measures against the provinces of Kiangsi, Hunan, Hupeh, and those on the lower reaches of the Yangtze River. He gave instructions to Chen Chiung-ming to proceed to Canton to take charge of the transportation of supplies and munitions. These Chen never sent, with the result that the soldiers at the front came near being cut off. Sun had to revise his plans as a consequence of Chen's action, and he returned immediately to Canton. Fearing that Sun might punish him for what he had done, Chen sent in his resignation on November 4, 1921, and retired with his soldiers to the city of Weichow in Kwangtung Province. In the meantime he had sent secret agents to establish contact with Wu Pei-fu. Sun Yat-sen would not believe even then that Chen Chiung-ming was a traitor. On May 2 of the following year, in the hope that Chen might still be won over, Sun placed him in charge of all military affairs in both Kwangtung and Kwangsi. Chen was frightened by the appointment, feeling that his plans had been discovered and that a snare was being prepared for him. He was in no position to accept, and on June 16, 1922, in the small hours of the morning, he attacked the residence of the President and sought the destruction of Sun Yat-sen.

What happened then was quite exciting. At about one o'clock on the morning of that day Sun Yat-sen, feeling perfectly safe in his residence in the Kuanyin Hill, heard bugle calls and the muffled noise of soldiers on the march. Two devoted followers rushed in to report that the soldiers of Chen Chiung-ming had received orders to surround his residence and murder him. Sun was astounded. "I cannot believe that anyone has the courage to do this sort of thing to me," was all that he replied. The noise outside was coming nearer and the followers begged Sun to leave the residence without a moment's delay. By that time the rebel soldiers had come so near that escape was almost impossible. Whereupon Sun, with great presence of mind, put on the clothing of an ordinary pedestrian, mingled with the crowd, and even talked with the soldiers who had come to take his life.

"Where are you going?" he calmly asked the soldiers.

"We are going to attack the President's residence," was the reply. Sun proceeded along with them fully conscious of the danger to which he was exposed. He watched the soldiers firing into his residence, then placidly left them and went on board a waiting gunboat. Safe on the boat's deck, Sun looked back at his residence on the Kuanyin Hill. It was a mass of flames, and his most treasured possessions were destroyed with it. He was then putting his Three Principles into final shape, and all his notes and books were reduced to ashes.

When the incident occurred Chiang Kai-shek was in Shanghai. On hearing the news, he rushed to Canton and for fifty-six days until he and Sun arrived back at Shanghai on August 13 he shared a life of suffering and privation with his chief. As Chiang said later, that was one of the most memorable experiences of his life.

For days and nights Chiang ministered to the comforts of a man who had been shocked by the knowledge that more than a generation of sacrifice to his country had brought him only treachery and faithlessness. Chiang well understood Sun's feelings and gave him the tender care that he needed. Because food on the gunboat was inadequate, Chiang made nocturnal forages for provisions. News coming to the gunboat was not consistently good, so Chiang had to choose for presentation to Sun only those bits of information that were pleasant to hear. There were moments when even the loyalty of the gunboat crew came into question, and Chiang, under those circumstances, had to decide what instructions to give. One false move and they might easily have been delivered to the enemy. The situation was delicate. They waited eagerly for news of the return to Canton of their own troops, who might possibly drive out Chen Chiung-ming. But on August 7 it was confirmed that Chen had the upper hand in Canton. It then became clear that the rebels, for the moment at any rate, had won out. Chen Chiung-ming even tried to have the gunboat on which Sun and Chiang had taken refuge torpedoed, but his men's aim was fortunately bad. Finally Sun and Chiang sailed in a British gunboat for Hong Kong, thence to Shanghai, arriving there on August 13. The two men had established a new understanding, a new relationship created out of the danger of their common experiences.

What does Chiang Kai-shek think of this episode? What lessons has he been able to draw from it? Twelve years afterward, in 1934, on the anniversary of this episode, Chiang delivered a speech to the students of the Central Military College at Nanking. He said: "The fact that the President [Sun Yat-sen] stayed in the residence to the very last, in spite of repeated warnings that his life was in danger—isn't this what we may call 'supreme courage'? But where does this courage come from? When he was surrounded by the confusion of a rebel army, he was yet able, with great presence of mind, to join the ranks of these rebel forces, and thereby evade the danger. This is an example of 'supreme courage,' as having come from 'supreme wisdom.' But the final question is, how has he been able to develop this 'supreme courage' and 'supreme wisdom'? My answer is they come from his 'supreme righteousness.' The President had only one desire, and that was to bring salvation to his nation, to his people, and to mankind as a whole. For that he was willing to sacrifice anything. And therefore he walked in the path of absolute justice and sincerity . . . in all that he did toward himself and toward others. There was

Generalissimo Chiang Kai-shek reviewing his troops. The medal which he wears is the highest that the Chinese Government can confer.

China Film, from Paul Guillumette, Inc.

only one word to describe him—truth. If you produce your labors with a motive that is true, sincere, just, there is absolutely no fear that your revolution will fail—it must succeed."

After arriving at Shanghai in August of 1922 Sun Yat-sen went through a period of deep agony and mortification. He had undertaken some forty years of revolutionary activity, and now he was tired and sick. He gathered what followers there were around him, told them what Chen Chiung-ming had done, and made them vow that the traitor would be eliminated. Canton, however, was still in the hands of the rebel, so there was nothing that could be done for the moment: they had to be patient and plan ahead. He made Shanghai his headquarters for the next two years until, in November of 1924, at the invitation of Tuan Chi-jui, he went north to Peking to join in peace talks in order to settle the differences between the two sections of the country. There was naturally some opposition to such a step, since it appeared to be a compromise with the war lords. But it seemed to be the only way that offered some hope for the country, so he met with Chang Tso-lin, Feng Yu-hsiang, Wu Pei-fu, and others of their kind to see if he could not win them over to his point of view.

Before proceeding north he did one thing which was to prove of far-reaching consequence. Contacts with Soviet Russia were becoming ever more frequent. Chiang could be spared for the moment, and Sun Yat-sen took the opportunity of sending him to Moscow to study the Russian situation at first hand and especially, as a military man, to study military conditions in the new Soviet state. Upon Chiang's return he was sent to Canton to continue the war against Chen Chiung-ming. There were times when Chen was perhaps struck by remorse. He even expressed his desire, in the early days of 1923, to retire altogether from the political scene. He knew that public opinion had branded him a rebel. But when Sun Yat-sen went north, his cupidity and lust for power got the better of him. He thought that Kwangtung lay in the palm of his hand. It was then that he discovered Chiang Kai-shek guarding the gates of Canton, for that city had been retaken by two loyal supporters of Sun Yat-sen on December 15, 1922. It was a new Chiang Kai-shek that he faced, for Chiang had not only been in Russia, but had returned and organized the Whampoa Military Academy. It was Sun Yat-sen's express wish that Chiang should train a truly revolutionary army, and he appointed him president of the academy. Fifteen years before Chiang had been a student at the Paoting Military Academy created by Yuan Shih-kai to further his personal ambitions. Chiang was now placed at the head of a similar academy that had been created to serve an entirely different purpose.

Chen Chiung-ming struck at Canton with all his forces. He had soldiers, ammunition, and equipment. His opponent had only two thousand graduates of the newly established academy. The odds were much against Chiang. In fact a rumor spread fast that Chiang had been killed. When Sun heard it in Peking he exclaimed: "I had rather lose a hundred thousand soldiers than the life of one Kai-shek."

But Chiang Kai-shek was not killed. On January 1, 1925, he received official orders to send an expeditionary force against Chen Chiung-ming. It was a small force, but they were out to kill the rebel so that they might save the life of their leader who was ill at Peking; and in saving their leader, they felt that they were saving their country. For the first time in modern Chinese military history soldiers became aware that they were dedicating their lives to a national cause. As they continued to advance it was reported that Sun Yat-sen was actually improving in Peking. With fervor and simplicity bordering upon naïveté, Chiang said to his soldiers: "I must let you know that upon receiving news of our onward march, the Generalissimo has actually made considerable improvement. If we clean up the East River, he is sure to recover. Whether he will regain his health or not depends therefore entirely on us. It is by saving his life that we save the life of our nation and the life of our people. We would rather sacrifice our own lives in order that they may live."

But unfortunately Sun Yat-sen grew worse. On March 12, 1925, he passed away in Peking in the home of Dr. V. K. Wellington Koo, the present Chinese Ambassador to the Court of St. James's.

Even as the soldiers of Chiang Kai-shek received the sad news they continued to advance with little opposition. Seven months later, on October 14, the strongest fortress of the enemy, Weichow, a city completely surrounded by water, not successfully besieged by an invading force for over a thousand years, gave way to the revolutionary soldiers of Chiang Kai-shek. The position of this small band of resolute youths in southern China became undisputed. Within the year they were destined to carry out the Northern Expedition that was to unite the country under the supreme command of Chiang Kai-shek.

19

Genius for Military Organization

THERE IS a double significance to the Chen Chiung-ming episode. In the first place it showed the undying loyalty of Chiang Kai-shek to Sun Yat-sen and his ideals. Secondly, it showed that Chiang Kai-shek had the ability to organize and train the army which was to write a new chapter in the history of modern China. How did he manage to create such an army?

In the early days of his own military training Chiang had observed that the individual Chinese soldier was as good a fighter as one could find anywhere. He had perseverance, physical courage, the ability to endure hardships; he was obedient to orders and above all intelligent and quick to learn. All that he needed was adequate leadership. Someday, Chiang had decided, he was going to provide that leadership himself. That opportunity came in the early days of 1924.

The treachery of Chen Chiung-ming taught Sun Yat-sen a great lesson—that unless he had an army of soldiers, albeit small in number, who were thoroughly indoctrinated with his ideas and loyal to his cause, there was no hope of a successful revolution. He had spent some forty years in revolutionary activities trying to win people to his doctrines, but he never possessed any real military power that would give the necessary support to his ideas. However successfully he might negotiate with the Chang Tso-lins and Wu Pei-fus, they possessed the actual control of the country through the military power they wielded, and all that Sun could do was to watch and wait. The Chen Chiung-ming rebellion convinced him that he must have an effective army of his own, and no one was better qualified to provide it than this young man, Chiang Kai-shek, whose loyalty and devotion to his cause had been tried and found to be absolutely firm.

It was at this juncture, while Sun Yat-sen was languishing in Shanghai in the winter of 1922, that a new influence came into his life. Adolf Joffe, a Soviet emissary who had arrived in China to negotiate an agreement in behalf of his new government, met Sun and came to an instant understanding with him. The Soviet Government had been established in 1917, and in July of 1919 and later, in September 1920, Leo Karakhan, Acting People's Commissar for Foreign Affairs, who later became the first Soviet Ambassador to China, was already able to announce to an astonished world that Russia was prepared to give up all the special privileges in China, including the right of consular jurisdiction, and that thenceforth she would enforce the principle of equality in her relations with China as well as with the other nations of the world. That was a diplomatic thunderbolt. It shook the chancelleries of the legations of the imperialist powers in Peking. Sun Yat-sen was naturally overjoyed that, with a stroke of the pen, all that he had fought for in his lifetime was going to be given to China by the new government of Soviet Russia. When Joffe arrived at Peking he was considered a bitter enemy by the Diplomatic Quarter. Joffe fully expected that, but he did not expect that the men who were supposed to be running the government at Peking would be so timid about accepting the generous offer of the Soviet Government. Behind these men were the money and power of the same imperialist powers. Joffe soon came to understand this and immediately went to Shanghai to see Sun Yat-sen.

Meanwhile the people of China were pleased by the friendly gestures of this new state. The intelligentsia especially began lecturing to the people, pointing out to them how China was entering a new era of international relations. Students spoke from improvised platforms. Newspapers and magazines turned out articles by the thousands extolling the virtues of the new Soviet regime. The chancellor of the Peking National University, Tsai Yuan-pei, an old Hanlin scholar and a member of the Kuomintang of long standing, declared at a banquet of welcome to Joffe that "since the penetration of European thought into China a process of social, economic, and political change had developed in the country. The Chinese Revolution was a political one. Now we are heading toward a social revolution. Russia furnished a good example to China, who thinks it advisable to learn the lessons of the Russian Revolution, which started also as a political movement and later assumed the nature of a social revolution." In the midst of this excitement the man who had issued this statement of equality in behalf of the Soviet Government, Leo Karakhan, arrived in Peking, in June 1924, as the first Soviet Ambassador. His face was pallid and tense with emotion; he wore a goatee; and as he stood on the platform surrounded by a surging crowd of cheering and admiring students and citizens of Peking, he looked like a martyr to a great and noble cause. He won immense popularity

GENIUS FOR MILITARY ORGANIZATION

through a series of brilliant speeches. On one occasion he said, "Only the Soviet Republics, only the Russian people, desire to see China strong, powerful, possessing a strong army, and capable of defending the interest and sovereignty of its people." At these words, of course, the people rose and clapped their hands. On another occasion he declared, "The great Chinese people, with its culture, peacefulness, and exceptional diligence, is the best ally of the Russian people in Asia. The friendship of Russia and China is a pledge of the peace of the Far East." Again there was a great ovation. But Karakhan was careful not to refer to Outer Mongolia, where conditions were steadily growing worse. Soviet troops had entered this integral part of China and had started an independence movement. To this day the question has not been completely settled. However, the atmosphere was in the main most friendly. On January 26, 1923, Joffe had signed a joint statement with Sun Yat-sen. Sun was willing to give this new rapprochement a trial. There was no question that the Russian Revolution had exceeded all expectations. It was in this frame of mind that he decided to send Chiang Kai-shek to Moscow.

What was it that had made the Russian Revolution so successful? Why was it that Sun's own revolutionary activities had been so slow in yielding the desired result? The answers to these grave questions had to be found. Sun Yat-sen dispatched Chiang to Russia at once and commissioned him to study the situation in that country at first hand.

In August 1923 Chiang Kai-shek, as chief of staff in the headquarters of the commander in chief of the Canton government, was on his way to the north to take the Trans-Siberian train bound for Moscow. He bore letters of introduction to Lenin, Trotsky, and Chicherin. Lenin was then already too ill to receive Chiang, but with Trotsky and Chicherin it is said that he had lengthy talks and was well received by them. He was given an opportunity to visit military establishments in Soviet Russia and to see the organization of the new party. After a sojourn of some four months Chiang returned to Canton in December and rendered a report to Sun.

There was no doubt that Chiang was impressed by the efficiency of the Soviet organization. Whether he showed much sympathy with the social and political theories upon which the Soviet system was founded was another question. But at any rate he warmly admired the methods which the Soviets used in furthering their cause. "When, in 1923," Chiang said later, "we were unable to clear up the small rebel army of Chen Chiung-ming so that the people of Canton suffered terribly, I used to suggest to Generalissimo Sun that we reorganize our army completely. We also used to study the reasons why the Soviet Army showed such bravery and was willing to sacrifice for the welfare of the people. The result was that he sent me to Russia to study the situation at first hand. I saw there that the Soviet Army had wonderful discipline. Not only did they give no cause for complaint to the people, but they were always promoting the welfare of the people. The soldiers and the people were on friendly terms with one another. If an army and the people can live so peacefully together and can be so united, that army can know no defeat. That is the reason why, when I returned to China, I resolved that if we want our army now to fight for the freedom and happiness of our people so that they will put the Three Principles into practice, we must reorganize our army and adopt the Soviet system."[1]

The establishment of the Whampoa Military Academy in 1924 was the result of that conviction. Preparations were made as soon as Chiang returned, toward the end of 1923, but it was not till June 16 the following year that the academy was formally established. It is not too much to say that it was the most momentous decision in the history of the Kuomintang. It provided a channel through which the genius of Chiang Kai-shek could have full and unhampered expression. Without the formation of this basic army the Northern Expedition would have a different story to tell. Nor would the position of China in the present world struggle be what it is today.

Following the Russian model, the academy's work was divided into two categories—military and political. Chiang Kai-shek was appointed president of the academy, with Liao Chung-kai, another stanch follower of Sun Yat-sen who not long afterward died at the hands of an assassin, in charge of the political department. There was a panel of distinguished lecturers, including Hu Han-min, Wang Ching-wei (now puppet in Nanking), and Tai Chi-tao, the present incumbent at the Examination Yuan, as well as a few Russian advisers such as Borodin and Galen, the last of whom Chiang met on the train while returning to China. From the very start Chiang put his whole heart into the undertaking, and before Sun went north to Peking from Shanghai in November, he made a trip to the south and to his deep satisfaction found the institute working successfully. There was a conversation on this subject between the president of the academy

---

[1] Address before the representatives of the merchants when Chiang was appointed garrison commander of Canton in 1925.

and the dying revolutionary leader which is worthy of reproduction.

"I am going to the north," said Sun to Chiang. "Whether I can return or not is a question. But I am going there to continue my fight, and even if I die, I shall be contented and happy."

"Why do you say such things?" queried Chiang.

"The Three Principles I hope to see fully put into practice," Sun replied. "It will depend entirely upon the students of the Military Academy of which you are now the president. We all must die someday, but we should die with a meaning. When I see today what you and your students and soldiers are doing, when I realize the spirit you are showing, I know that I can depend upon you to continue the work that I have begun. That is why I say that, even though I shall die, I shall rest peacefully. After all, I am a man of fifty-nine years, and I shall not live long. Two or three years ago I would have felt that I should not die, but now I know you will all continue to fight for my ideals."

When the gates of the academy were first opened it was planned to admit only some three hundred students. The number of candidates who applied for admission was much higher than was expected, so it was decided to take in 470 students. With this increase in enrollment, the academy went through some financial difficulties. When the second batch of candidates was admitted these difficulties became so real that it was difficult to carry on the work. The ranks of the students had swollen to over 1000. There were even attempts from the outside to cause embarrassment to the academy; but Chiang's resolve was firm: he was going to carry the scheme through, whatever the difficulties might be. Within one and a half years the number of students rose to 5540! The equipment was shabby, but it was a tribute to the man with the iron will that the students stood the test superbly. They continued in excellent spirits, and Chiang frequently encouraged them: "We are all going to live the lives of soldiers, and we know what kind of lives they lead. Day and night they spend their lives in the open. They are not allowed to occupy the premises of the civilians. They have no definite times for their meals. There are times when for a complete day they do not have one square meal. 'They sleep in the dew and swallow wind as their food,' as we say. It is all a question of discipline. With discipline we can do wonders. Without it there is no use talking about soldiery."

It is in discipline that we find the key to the success of Chiang Kai-shek's soldiery. Chiang did not find a moment of relaxation. He lived in the academy and shared everything with his students. The food which they ate, he ate. At five in the morning he was already up and about preparing for the day's work. He was always studying the lives of the great military heroes of antiquity. With Sun Tse's military classic he was familiar when he was himself a student, and the life of Yo Fei was a constant source of inspiration to him and to his students. Among modern men he had great admiration for Tseng Kuo-fan, a scholar and a civilian who for twelve long years lived a life of exemplary discipline and self-denial, raising an army which succeeded finally in quelling the Taiping Rebellion. From these and many other sources he derived valuable lessons for the training of the cadets of the academy.

He created a few slogans to help bolster the spirit of the academy. Do not fear death. Do not covet money. Love your country, love your people. Abide by the law of *lien-tso* (standing and falling together).

It was Chiang's conviction that he could put Chinese society on a completely new basis—give it a "new deal," as it were—by inculcating in the people a spirit of intense purposefulness. It was his favorite theme that Chinese society had grown decadent owing to a combination of causes. A large number of the people were more dead than alive. It were better that they were dead, for then he could make a new start. But just because they were not dead, their spirit of degeneracy contaminated the youth of the nation. Chiang desired that his students should live and be thrilled with life, or else they must learn to die honorably. As a matter of fact, to die honorably was one of the great glories of life. Hence the slogan: Do not fear death. When the second commencement exercises for the graduating class were held, this is what he said:

"Tsung-li [Sun Yat-sen] used to say, 'When a man lives to see his own accomplishments as a revolutionary, we call this success. When a man does not live long enough to see the fruits of his revolutionary labor and sacrifices his life first, we call this the establishment of virtue.' My own impression is that it is difficult for anyone, who really fights for the good of humanity, who fights for principles, to achieve success during his lifetime. These people are not real revolutionaries. The real revolutionary invariably loses his life before his ideals are actually realized. . . . I will cite you a few examples in our history. Wen Tien-hsiang, Lu Hsiu-fu, Yo Fei, Shih Ko-fa[2]—all these men

---

[2] The first three were great patriots of the Southern Sung Dynasty (A.D. 1127-1280) and the last an outstanding patriot of the Ming Dynasty (A.D. 1368-1644).

gave their very best for the glory of their race. Some of them saw success during their lifetime, but they were all enormously successful in having established their virtues by creating a noble tradition. It is these people whom we must worship and emulate."

Not to love money but to love your country and people are obvious virtues and can be easily understood. But the law of *lien-tso* needs some explanation. In order to create a solid front of his cadets, Chiang said that they must learn either to live or to perish together. If they were capable of that, then even though their number might be small they would be able to defeat an enemy ten times their size. By *lien-tso* is meant that the officers in charge and the soldiers are united in a solid block. If the commander in chief has not issued the order and the brigade commander retreats, that brigade commander has disobeyed the law and must be put to death. If the brigade commander has not retreated, and the commander of the regiment begins to do so, then the commander of the regiment has disobeyed the law and must be put to death. If the commander of the regiment has not retreated and the commander of the battalion begins to do so, then the commander of the battalion has disobeyed the law and must be put to death. And so it goes on until you reach the smallest unit of the army, which is the private. In all engagements, therefore, it is imperative that the Chinese soldier follow his superior officer and that he do nothing unless his officer expressly desires that it be done. This law was not created by Chiang Kai-shek but was used in the 1860s when Tseng Kuo-fan was in command of soldiers opposing the Taiping rebels. When carried out effectively, it is clear that no army adhering to it can be beaten. It was put into effective operation by Chiang Kai-shek. His war against Chen Chiung-ming, whom he finally eliminated, even though that unfortunately had to take place after Sun Yat-sen passed away, was merely an experiment. True, he routed an army more than ten times the size of his own. The real test came, however, when he launched out on his Northern Expedition, which carried his soldiers into the very heart of China thousands of miles away from their base.

No wonder the Whampoa cadets have now established a tradition in China, one of which they have every reason to be proud. People in China speak of the Whampoa spirit as something of a novelty. It is new in the sense that a group of boys recruited from the rank and file of the people of China should be transformed after a few years of discipline into sturdy young men who are not only good soldiers, ardent revolutionaries fighting for a worthy cause, but are also fine examples of young manhood. They have been indoctrinated with ideals. They are followers of the *San-min chu-i* (the Three Principles of the People) and believe in them implicitly.

The first batch of 470 graduates was reduced to only a little more than 100 soon after their engagements with the rebel Chen Chiungming. But the enrollment, instead of diminishing, kept on increasing until the number became too large to be comfortably handled. The Chinese soldier from that time on really came of age. To compare him with the bandit soldiers of the war lord period is to insult him. The bandit soldiers were a nuisance to the nation, while the Whampoa cadet is a lover of his people and a defender of the rights of his country. They were drawn in many cases from the same stock, but the alchemy of discipline, proper instruction, and leadership provided by Chiang Kai-shek effected a change so radical that comparison between the two groups was out of the question. The present war unfortunately requires soldiers who must be chosen by the millions instead of by the thousands, and in many cases there is not the necessary time to submit them to the crucible of adequate training; but the spirit has affected all of them, and those who have had contact with the Chinese soldier can bear witness to his quality.

The boys admitted into the Whampoa Academy are recruited from high schools all over the country. As soon as they enter the academy's gate they begin a new life. They go through a sort of physical and spiritual catharsis. In the early days of the academy Chiang Kai-shek lived with them and had almost hourly contact with them. The atmosphere was tense, and one could not blame them if they now and then desired a breath of outside air, especially when they had just been graduated. Then Chiang Kai-shek would give one of his characteristic talks, for he was always lecturing to them.

"Fellow students! You have now lived in the academy for some time. I wonder what impression you have gained. As president of the academy, I hope you will remain here, for the longer you stay the more chance there is for me to speak to you. Every time that I see you brings me joy and happiness. And yet I know that you desire to leave here as early as possible. I wonder what the reason is. I feel that you students should have a deeper attachment to the academy even than to your families, especially as you are now being graduated and the chances of your meeting each other will in the future be much fewer. The more I see you and speak to you, the more I feel I can help you to increase your knowledge and strengthen your character. That is the reason why, although I am very busy with my other duties, I come to live with you in the academy. You are, after all, young and have limited experience. Your knowledge also is not wide, and frankly I sometimes worry that, when you go outside, you may do things which will not uphold the good name of the academy. I want you all, when you do go out, to be models of good character so that other young men will emulate you and not submit you to ridicule and slander."

Most of the graduates elected to stay on. One day a cadet came to Chiang Kai-shek and said that he wanted to go home to get married. He said that he had seen the commander of his battalion and requested that he be given traveling expenses. The commander would not give it to him. He thought that it was best to approach Chiang directly on the subject. Chiang told him, however, that for certain classes of officers it was true that there was a holiday of two months in the year, but that no traveling expenses were allowed.

"This order has to be strictly enforced or else everybody would come and ask for holidays. Having been refused by your superior officer," Chiang continued to reproach him, "you now come to me with the request that I pay you $180. Your salary as a cadet lieutenant colonel is $70 monthly. If you were economical, you could have saved $30 to $40 a month. Why then do you need any traveling expenses? I can, however, advance you, according to rule, two months' salary, which is $140 and sufficient for your purposes. I hope you will save in the future."

Chiang found out later that the advance on the salary for the two months had been given already and that the commander also knew the cadet to be a weak character. To go to Chiang after having been refused by the commander was a serious misdemeanor. If Chiang overruled the commander, how would the commander take it? Besides, there were over 2500 cadets in the academy, and if everyone felt free to ask for $180, how could Chiang run the academy? Chiang gave orders that the cadet be severely disciplined.

The academy was transferred to Nanking when the capital moved there in 1927 and is now located in Chungking. It is obvious that, since Chiang's duties have increased a hundredfold with the enormous responsibilities of the war, he does not give the Whampoa Academy quite the amount of personal attention that he did in the early years of its inception. But it remains his pet project, and students still fondly address him as president of the academy rather than as the Generalissimo or the President of the Republic of China.

20

The Russian Interlude—I[1]

THE WHAMPOA MILITARY ACADEMY was among the first of the revolutionary institutions to be built on Soviet models. It was a concrete expression of co-operation between the Soviet Government and Sun Yat-sen's party. But it is important to inquire into the nature and extent of that co-operation, because even to this day there seems to be some confusion about it in the minds of many people.

It is essential to recall that the first of the four articles in the joint statement issued by Sun and Joffe had this to say:

Dr. Sun Yat-sen holds that the Communist order or even the Soviet system cannot actually be introduced into China, because there do not exist here the conditions for the successful establishment of either Communism or Sovietism. This view is entirely shared by Mr. Joffe, who is further of opinion that China's paramount and most pressing problem is to achieve national unification and attain full national independence; and regarding this first task, he has assured Dr. Sun Yat-sen that China has the warmest sympathy of the Russian people and can count on the support of Russia.[2]

The wording is sufficiently clear to show that while China was glad to receive the support of Russia for the attainment of certain very definite ends, among other things the learning of Soviet technique and methods for China's war against imperialism so as to regain her complete national independence, still the two countries will be run on completely different principles. It is necessary to understand this distinction because it will help to make intelligible subsequent developments in China, especially at the close of the Northern Expedition in 1927 and the present stand of the Chinese Government. Chiang

---

[1] I owe some information on this subject to a series of four articles contributed by Mr. Tsui Shu-chin to the *Chinese Social and Political Science Review* and dealing with the influence of the Canton-Moscow Entente upon Sun Yat-sen. See Vols. 18 and 20.

[2] *The China Year Book*, 1924, p. 863.

Kai-shek's position from then until now has been a consistent one and is in entire agreement with that of Sun Yat-sen.

In the first days of the contact between the two countries there was naturally a manifestation of enthusiasm on both sides. Russia offered Sun Yat-sen everything that he had been fighting for in his lifetime. No wonder both he and Chiang Kai-shek, in many of their speeches and statements during this period, expressed opinions which gave the impression that they had embraced the Soviet ideology. But it was really not so. We must never forget that Sun's Three Principles grew specifically out of peculiar Chinese conditions. The vast background of forty-five centuries of Chinese history is where these principles have their roots. Here and there Sun Yat-sen might have incorporated ideas from foreign sources—from Henry George, for instance, or from Maurice William—and that has led one writer to say with more wit than understanding that "as a social and economic philosophy they [the Three Principles] can be described only as chop suey." But, regarded in their entirety, there is no question that there is remarkable consistency in all of Sun's writings because they are an amplification and development of traditional Chinese thought. As such there is nothing in common between his system of thinking and the Marxist ideology. It is important to show where the two widely differ. But before we do that it is only fair to point out in what way the Soviets influenced the development of the Kuomintang.

In the first place, the whole of the Kuomintang party went through a radical reorganization near the end of 1923. Chiang Kai-shek was about to return to Canton from Moscow. Borodin, who for the next three or four years had so much to do with Chinese political development, had arrived in October of that year. In December 1923 Sun Yat-sen, after a series of conferences with him, was already able to say, "The Russian Revolution succeeded because the Communists carried on a hard and bitter struggle. If we want to accomplish as much in our revolution, we must learn from the Russians their method, organization, and training. So I have asked Mr. Borodin to come and teach us these things. He is a man with wide experience in party organization. It is my hope that my associates will give up their prejudices and faithfully learn what he has to teach. Mr. Borodin tells us that, given six months of good solid training, Canton will be a strong base for our party."

Borodin proceeded to reorganize the Kuomintang. He lifted the party from a group of almost moribund members who had become cynical and hesitant as a result of repeated failures and disappointments in the past, and put it on a completely popular basis where students, peasants, workers, and other people from the nation at large might all come in and join. The organization immediately came to life, especially as the thoughts and feelings of the members were unified by the effective propaganda in which the Soviets were past masters and which was among the new forces that helped galvanize the Kuomintang into action.

By the first month of 1924, when Chiang Kai-shek had returned from Moscow and was entrusted with the task of organizing the Whampoa Military Academy on the Russian model, Sun Yat-sen was able to call a National Congress of the revived party which, he said, would create "a new epoch" in the history of the Chinese Revolution. Three important results which proved to be of far-reaching consequences were announced by the Congress: namely, the adoption of a new constitution which was largely the brain child of Borodin, the admission of Chinese Communists (undoubtedly a significant step in Soviet penetration, which has since caused so much disturbance in the Chinese social and political scene), and the publication of a manifesto. Sun Yat-sen was so completely satisfied with Borodin's co-operation and assistance that he said in his opening speech: "The Russians decided to revolt and hoped to succeed within one hundred years, but in about ten years they have completely achieved their aims. On the other hand, I expected to succeed within a few years, but in thirty years' time I have not accomplished much. This is because our methods are inferior as compared with those of the Russians. . . . They are firm in their purpose and farsighted. They made plans for their nation a hundred years in advance that are thorough and exhaustive. Their success has been one of good methods."

In nearly all important details the reorganized Kuomintang is a reproduction of the Soviet system. There are "vertical organizations," party cells, control committees, and all the paraphernalia of Bolshevism. There was a new emphasis on party discipline, and the principle of "democratic centralism" was adopted, which means that party members may have the freedom of discussion on all vital issues, but once a vote has been taken, all the members including those who originally opposed the measures must strictly abide by them. Above all, there was increased recognition of the value of propaganda. In one important respect the two party organizations differed, and that was in relationship to membership. The Communist party in Russia is open to workers, peasants, soldiers, and officeholders, while the Kuomintang remains open to all classes of people in the country. The difference is an important one and implies that there is no class struggle in China.

Along with the reorganization of the Kuomintang party, the government at Canton itself was submitted to a series of changes. That government was established in 1917 as a protest against Yuan Shih-kai's attempt to consolidate his autocratic rule. Its sphere of operation was limited only to the south, and it was never officially recognized by a foreign government. Sun Yat-sen, as head of the government, was known as its Generalissimo. Sun was forced by Chen Chiung-ming to leave for Shanghai in the summer of 1922, but his contact with the government was re-established as soon as Canton fell into the hands of his loyal supporters toward the end of that year. Upon the advice of Borodin Sun thought the moment had arrived to put his government on a new basis. It was going to be called the "National Government," and its rupture with Peking had to be complete. But the Chen Chiung-ming episode continued to harass him and to cause delay in the carrying out of these reforms. It was then that the Whampoa Military Academy was established under the presidency of Chiang Kai-shek.

It was primarily a military institute, but it was at the same time a center for the training of the Kuomintang party members. In other words, it was specifically a party organization, created with the idea of propagating the principles upon which the Kuomintang was founded. The influence of the Soviet advisers was therefore extensive. The Red Army itself served as a model for the academy. The system of political commissars which, until the early days of the present war, was a special feature of the Soviet Army also became a part of the academy's organization, so that the cadets not only received military training but were also thoroughly indoctrinated in the Kuomintang ideology. In this regard General Galen or Bluecher, as he was otherwise known, held a strategically important position. All through this period Chiang Kai-shek spoke of him in the most glowing terms. It was clearly and unequivocally a period of co-operation with Russia. There was no reason why Chiang should not be eloquent in the praise of the Soviets as Sun Yat-sen was himself. During a speech which he delivered at Swatow in 1925, on the anniversary of the Soviet Government, Chiang attributed the rapid advance of his soldiers to the assistance and influence of the Soviets. "I can say that we have achieved such military success because our Tsung-li [Sun Yat-sen] has carried out a policy of Sino-Soviet co-operation. . . . If our party had not gone through a radical reorganization, if our Russian comrades had not come to guide us and teach us the technique of revolution, I am afraid that our revolutionary army would not be where it is today. We have been able now to defeat our enemies and achieve our aim. This is largely because our Soviet friends, on the strength of their remarkable spirit, of their international position, and of their revolutionary fervor, have come to offer us their sincere co-operation."

Every true Kuomintang member, from Sun Yat-sen down, would have admitted as much in those days, but in their anxiety to model the Kuomintang after the Bolshevist party one thing was done which has caused an immense amount of complication and brought indescribable woe to the Kuomintang and the Chinese nation.

In spite of the understanding between Sun Yat-sen and Joffe that Communism was not suited to Chinese conditions, the Communists were admitted into the Kuomintang and "tolerated." That was the first instance in which the Third International succeeded in burrowing its way into the heart of Chinese society. The Canton-Moscow understanding was obviously an opportunity for the Communist party to get China in its grip, and it did not allow that opportunity to slip by. The fact has now been historically established that it was the Communists themselves who insisted upon their being admitted into the Kuomintang. Borodin, on June 25, 1924, granted that "it [the Third International] ordered both the Chinese Communist party and a young socialist group to join the Kuomintang. Anyone who does not follow this order must be considered disobedient." That fact was later borne out by Sun Yat-sen himself, who, in his letters to Chiang Kai-shek, freely gave him to understand that the Bolshevists urged the Chinese Communist party to join the Kuomintang "in order to act in harmony with us."

That there was going to be trouble ahead was felt by a large number of Kuomintang people. Chiang Kai-shek was among those who had that premonition, and he was among the first to oppose the measure of admitting the Communists into the Kuomintang. In a speech delivered before the people of Hunan after that province was cleared of Communist influence in 1929 Chiang said:

"In the early days of the Russian Revolution in 1917, I was completely in sympathy with it. I felt that it established a new era in the history of the modern world. I was so overwhelmed by it that, if people made any unfriendly comment, I would vigorously defend it. If people condemned the Communist party, I would speak in its defense. I admired, in those days, the whole revolutionary attitude of the Communists. I had no personal prejudice. When an opinion is expressed with the deepest sincerity there can be no bias, no ulterior motive. That was the reason why I decided to proceed to Russia and see for myself what the conditions were. But the internal situation at home then was such that I could not leave the country. When the Chen Chiung-ming rebellion broke out in 1922 I had to hurry to Canton. It was on the steamer coming back from Canton to Shanghai that I had the opportunity of speaking with the Tsung-li [Sun Yat-sen] for a whole night. He agreed that in the revolutionary work there was a good deal which we could learn from Russia, and so he gave me permission to proceed to Russia according to our prescribed plans....

"When I arrived in Russia, after making a careful investigation of conditions there, I must admit that all my hopes about the revolution then became blasted. I was convinced that the aims which the Communists struggled for could not be attained through the methods which they used. That was why I was of the opinion that the Russian Revolution was not really a success. Or let us perhaps retrace one step. Even if we considered that revolution as being successful, I said then it could not be followed in China. Upon my return to China therefore I raised serious objections to allowing the Communists to be admitted into the Kuomintang. I said so to the Tsung-li, and our party members knew that.

"My impressions of the Russian Revolution can be divided into two periods. The first period was when I showed deep sympathy. My second period is one of disappointment. This change was the result of close observation on the spot."

I think this passage makes it quite clear that Chiang Kai-shek was against the admission of the Communists into the ranks of the Kuomintang, but that Sun Yat-sen was on the horns of a dilemma. He was not unaware of the troubles that were likely to follow if he opened the Kuomintang gates wide for the Communists. But on the other hand, if the Communists stayed outside of the Kuomintang they would still grow strong under Russian influence, and a strong and independent Communist party would be an even greater threat to his own party. Sun thought that if the Communist party was to grow at all it was best to have it grow under the wings of the Kuomintang.

So the Communist party was officially admitted into the Kuomintang. Borodin, of course, sat behind the scenes placidly as the king of conspirators. At one time the Communists requested admission as a "cell" rather than as individuals of the Communist party. At another time they wished to be considered as individuals and not as a "cell." Whichever way best suited their purposes at the moment they clamored for. No sooner were they admitted into the Kuomintang than they began to criticize its policy. The Chinese Communist party, in the manifesto of its Third Congress, criticized the Kuomintang for having been too much inclined to seek foreign aid from capitalist countries and for having neglected propaganda work among the masses. They urged radical reorganization "so as to make it a real party." They vowed that they would adhere to the rules of the Kuomintang, but how was that possible when they enjoyed dual membership, just as some of the Japanese in the United States enjoyed dual nationality? Yet when any conflict between the two parties arose their allegiance was always for the Communist party and not for the Kuomintang. Finally the day came when the Communists plotted to wreck the Kuomintang. The situation was becoming, as Alice said, "curiouser and curiouser." And when the atmosphere was smothered with Communism, it was just like Alice seeing a grin without a cat. The grin of Communism was seen everywhere; and when two prominent members of the Kuomintang party approached Borodin to ask for an explanation the Russian adviser announced, "The Kuomintang has died, and it is no longer a party. We can only say that there are members of the party, but we cannot say that there is a Kuomintang. If we add some new element, such as the Communists, and organize them as a cell, then the old members will be aroused to compete with them and consequently the party will be revived."

Such then, in brief, was the relationship between the Kuomintang and the Communist party during the early days of their contact. Why, then, one might ask, was there this contact at all, fraught as it was with such unhappy consequences? The answer was that Russia did issue those two statements of 1919 and 1920, in which she "gave back to the Chinese people all the power and authority which was obtained by the government of the Czar by tricks or by entering into understanding with Japan and the allies." The Soviet Government gave up "all the conquests made by the government of the czars which took away Manchuria and other territories from China." The Soviet Government returned "to the Chinese people, without demanding any kind of compensation, the Chinese Eastern Railway, as well as all the mining concessions, forestry, gold mines, and all the other things which were seized from them by the government of the czars." The Soviet Government gave up "the indemnities payable by China for the Boxer Insurrection of 1900." These were all substantial concessions which a revolutionary leader like Sun Yat-sen could not help but regard as expressions of a friendly policy. What did the United States and Britain do to help in those days? Very little. Whether it is apocryphal or not, this is what Sun Yat-sen was reported to have said when England and America criticized him for extending his hand of welcome to Joffe: "The republic is my child. It is in danger of drowning. I am trying to keep it afloat and we are being swept down the river. I call to England and America for help. They stand on the bank and jeer at me. Then comes a Russian straw. Drowning, I clutch at it. England and America, on the bank, shout at me on no account to clutch at that straw. But do they help me? No. I know it is a straw; better that than nothing."

21

The Russian Interlude—II

IT IS BEST to admit that the understanding between Canton and Moscow was made for mutual benefit. The Soviet plan was one of world revolution, and the entente thus reached with the Chinese revolutionary movement was one of the best opportunities, so Moscow thought, of merging the activities of the two countries into the great war against capitalism. The results would have staggered the world if the scheme had been successfully carried out. The prospects were altogether too tempting, and so even if there was an admission by Russia that Communism should not be introduced into China, it was part of the Soviet technique to infiltrate Communist ideas into the Kuomintang with the view of getting control of the party and eventually of the entire country. It was clear from the beginning that this *mariage de convenance* was going to give rise to unpleasantness, but the risk had to be taken by Sun Yat-sen both because Soviet Russia had offered something tangible to restore the integrity of the Chinese nation and because the other powers did nothing to arouse the same confidence in the Chinese people.

It was at this juncture that Sun Yat-sen proclaimed his anti-imperialist platform. So far as principles are concerned, there are practically none in the Sun Yat-sen system of thinking which can be traced back to Soviet influence. They were all sufficiently crystallized by nearly forty years of labor, and contact with Joffe, Borodin, and their associates made no change in his basic concepts. But the anti-imperialist slant was a new idea and might conceivably not have developed were it not for some incidents which gave Sun Yat-sen considerable reason to be irritated. Among other things there was the squabble over the Canton customs revenue; if Britain, the United States, and the other powers had seen their way clear to being a little more flexible than they were in this situation, they could perhaps have counterbalanced the offers of Moscow. But those powers were adamant, and ill feeling was unavoidable. Sun Yat-sen, as Generalissimo of the Canton government, asked the diplomatic corps in Peking, on September 5, 1923, to reconsider its claim to the customs surplus of the southwestern provinces, over which Canton had extended its influence. There was no reply in three months. Sun grew impatient and decided to take such measures as he saw fit. The foreign governments thereupon ordered their gunboats to proceed to Canton to forestall Sun's action. It was a pathetic situation as described by Wu Chao-chu, who was then Canton's Foreign Minister. The customs revenue in the provinces under Canton's jurisdiction, after the foreign loan obligations were met, was turned over to the northern militarists to finance the war against Sun's followers, who consequently suffered a double loss: "loss of funds which should be used for constructive purposes and which, turned over to the northern militarists, are actually used to institute war against them, and loss in that, for every one of these dollars employed against them, they have to raise one or more dollars in self-defense. Such a situation is not only impossible but also insufferable. It has been tolerated so long already; it obviously cannot be endured any longer." (Wu's note to Sir James W. Jamieson, then British Consul General at Canton.)

The last sentence showed the mood of Sun Yat-sen's government. Sun was on the warpath. From that time on the word "anti-imperialism" was constantly on his lips. It remained there to the end of his days. It was taken up by Chiang Kai-shek and became a formal part of Kuomintang policy. But anti-imperialism has never meant anti-foreignism. The two are entirely separate issues. Sun heartily welcomed all forms of co-operation with foreign capitalists, or else all his enthusiasm for "the international development of China" would have been meaningless. What he wanted was co-operation only to the extent that it would not compromise China as a fully independent nation. This ideal remains as an integral part of Kuomintang policy today as visualized by Chiang Kai-shek and his government. In this respect the anti-imperialism of Sun Yat-sen was something quite at variance with the anti-imperialism in the Soviet vocabulary. Imperialism, according to Marxist interpretation, is the latest stage in the development of capitalism, and to overthrow the whole of the capitalist system was the very essence of the Bolshevik movement.

Soviet policy in the 1920s called for the union of all the proletariat and oppressed peoples wherever they might be. There was no national boundary. It was a class struggle, and Lenin wanted to create a "united states of the world," in which the power would be lodged exclusively in the oppressed classes. Sun Yat-sen nursed no such ambition. On every point, therefore, even though he and Lenin used the same word "anti-imperialism," the two schools of thought faced in different directions.

Marxist cosmology with its historical materialism and its Hegelian dialectic was much too esoteric a form of thinking for the Chinese mind to digest. It does not feel at home in these vague generalities; nor does it show much interest in them. Sun Yat-sen knew that mind and sedulously avoided confusing his own simple desire to make his country strong and independent without the pressure of alien rule, be it Manchu or from the imperialist powers, with the ideology of Moscow. He was not concerned with any theory of class war; he was interested only in welding all the classes in China into a solid and united front for the purpose of regaining their right as a self-respecting nation. That having been accomplished, Sun would then launch a larger and more embracing platform. As a realist he wanted to put the Chinese house in order first. And that sense of realism has never deserted Chiang Kai-shek. As Sun said to Joffe in those early days of their contact, the Soviet system of thinking was founded on hatred while all Chinese thinking was based on harmony. That distinction has had a profound appeal to the leader of present-day China.

There is another aspect of Sun Yat-sen's Three Principles which seems to suggest the Soviet theory of revolution and yet is entirely different. The second of these principles concerns democracy or, to use the original Chinese words "the power of the people"; that is, the political power should be in the hands of the people. But the question arises: Do the political conditions of the immediate past under the regime of Kuomintang warrant any assertion that China is being trained for a democracy? An adequate answer to this question would dissipate a good deal of the doubt that seems to exist in the minds of many. Isn't it true, as critics say, that there is now a mild form of dictatorship in China? It may be mild today, but will it not grow stronger if the tendency is not checked? Even if it is mild, isn't it a dictatorship all the same? These questions have arisen because the period of what is known as political tutelage provided for in Sun's revolutionary scheme has been prolonged, and its end is not in immediate sight. Sun allowed some six years for this period, and that time has long since run out. The answer to this question of time is simply given. The present war has created a state of emergency, and the large amount of time and energy which would normally be devoted to the political training of the people has been directed to military considerations and necessities.

But the more serious criticism is that "political tutelage" is itself a form of dictatorship and seems to be akin to the Soviet conception of the "dictatorship of the proletariat." There is, in fact, no relationship between the two. It is true that, both in Marxist ideology and in Sun's system of thinking, there are three stages in the realization of the political ideal, but this is as far as their agreement goes. We should not, in fact, be surprised by the agreement in the number of stages, for after all this is a convenient division for most revolutionary activities. You have the first stage, when you struggle for the actual possession of power. That is followed by the next stage, when you try to consolidate that power, preparing for the third stage, when what you fought for, your political ideal, is gradually put into practice. George Washington in his revolutionary activities had to pass through practically the same stages. The first stage was his war against the British, culminating in the success of his movement after the bitter days of Valley Forge. The republic was not and could not be a strong entity immediately after Washington's military success. There was a period of chaos and confusion which was dissolved only after the assertion of his strong character and personality. Some of the people even wanted him to be a king, which desire he repudiated in short order. But it was not until after the Convention of 1787 at Philadelphia that a new and vigorous government came into existence. Then it was that the thirteen colonies saw the birth of a puissant nation, when great figures like Hamilton, Jefferson, Adams, and Randolph could each place his talent at the service of the country.

China's remaining in the present period of political tutelage, albeit it has lasted longer than it was originally intended, does not mean that a dictatorship will be established as a permanent system. That period was provided for by Sun Yat-sen as a period of concentration of power. The present government has so far developed strictly according to Sun's scheme, and there is no reason to believe that the constitutional period, which is the last stage when political power will be invested in the hands of the people, will be purposely submerged. In fact the Eleventh Plenary Session of the Central Executive Committee of the Kuomintang in September 1943 passed the resolution that a people's assembly will meet one year after the present war ends to usher in the constitutional period. In spite of the military exigencies of the present moment, a large amount of spadework is now continually being done for the last of the three stages. Sun Yat-sen emphasized the need of training and education for the period of political tutelage, training which must not be confined to any particular class but to all the Chinese people. He was even anxious that Western parliamentary methods be widely understood and appreciated in China. For while he was deeply conscious that democracy as an ideal needs no special effort of cultivation because it is the very essence of Chinese political thought, still there is ample room for improvement in the organization of political machinery through which that democratic spirit of long historic standing may be expressed. Sun Yat-sen had no sympathy with any theory of a dictatorship of the proletariat, even though it might lead to an era of Communism when the apparently worthy ideal "from each according to his capacity, to each according to his need" would be realized.

The important difference, in any case, between the dictatorship of the proletariat and Sun's political message lies in the fact that while Communism works toward the aim that the state may ultimately "wither away," in the colorful language of Marxism, Sun worked toward a social democracy in which the constitutional powers will, according to old Chinese conceptions, reside in the people and thereby create the perfect state. Sun's only interest, which was shared by Chiang Kai-shek and his associates, was to restore China's complete liberty as a nation, and that required revolutionary measures. He desired to see the average person's loyalty to the family enlarged so as to cover the state and be made coextensive with it. That is now being done, and to a large extent has been done in the past by the government under Chiang Kai-shek. Their concern is not with the future of the world—not, at any rate, for the time being—but specifically with their own countrymen of 450,000,000.

There is another consideration into which we need to inquire. Having shown how the first two of Sun's Three Principles have nothing to do with Marxist philosophy, it now remains for us to point out that his last principle, that of social welfare or the people's livelihood, known as *min-sheng* in Chinese, is again something specifically his own.

The principle of social welfare, which is the cornerstone of Sun's whole ideological edifice, was crystallized in his mind as early as the Sino-Japanese War of 1894. When the effete mandarinate of those days was appalled by the efficacy of the Western means of destruction and murder and thought that all that China needed was the same weapons, Sun had a different point of view. It was his conviction that in the Western nations "every man has a chance to use his ability; all land is cultivated to the full extent of its fertility; all goods are fully utilized; and all commodities freely circulated." Instead of just buying guns and building up a strong army and navy, it was essential to learn the secrets of Western industry and commerce, of agriculture and education. People must have an adequate livelihood, their social welfare must be fully promoted before it is possible to have a strong nation. This is the early pattern of Sun's thought that ultimately led to the formulation of the principle. By 1905 the first of the two measures covered by that principle—namely, "equalization of land and ownership"—was already being freely discussed, and by 1912 the second measure, that of "limitation of private capital," was included in the Kuomintang platform. Between the adoption of these measures and the outbreak of the Russian Revolution there was a long period, so that the meeting with Joffe and Borodin could have had no bearing on their development.

In a way it was unusual that Sun should insist upon land ownership being controlled when large landowners have never really existed in China. The peasants who till the soil have been virtually its owners. Even in early feudal times, over three thousand years ago, a piece of land was supposed to have been divided into nine lots, with the cultivators enjoying the fruits of their labor from eight lots and contributing their energy to tilling the soil of the central or ninth lot for the feudal lord. Under such a system it was practically impossible to become a large landowner, and an unusual phenomenon that strikes a traveler in China is that, considering the enormous size of the country, the land lots for agriculture are very small even compared with those in small European countries. It has been possible in Europe—in Poland, for example—to be invited by a rich landowner to visit his estate, get into his wagon driven by horses, and drive for two or three days without being able to cover all of the owner's property, which may extend to a hundred thousand acres or more. That is not possible in China, where no one owns any land that extends farther than the eye can reach. A man who owns three thousand *mow* of land, the equivalent of five hundred acres, would be considered a rich landowner in China. When he dies the land is subdivided into equal lots for the children, so that the chances of any single man owning large tracts of land do not exist. The fabulously rich man never existed in China until he was able to put his money in foreign banks. Why, then, did Sun devise such a measure? He was visualizing a period when social conditions would improve, land value would rise, and rich people might conceivably use their wealth for the acquisition of land. His measure was to forestall any such eventuality and protect the peasants, who even now are frequently oppressed by the small landowners. But unlike the Russian Revolution, under no circumstances would Sun allow any confiscation of property. The measure for the "limitation of private capital" was devised with the same aim. Powerful individual capitalists are still few, but they will multiply with the improvement of social conditions, and preventive steps should be taken. Certain enterprises should, at the very outset, according to Sun, be state-owned and -operated. Among these are means of communication, mining, and manufacturing, which should be hastened in their development through the investment of foreign capital and the employment of foreign technical assistants. Sun's desire for foreign cooperation goes back to an early date and has been consistently maintained.

The last thing that Sun wanted was any kind of radical social revolution. He urged the steady improvement in the social welfare of his people and an increase in the national wealth so that all might have a share in it. He had no sympathy with Marx, whom he described as a "social pathologist rather than a social psychologist," nor with his theory, "from each according to his capacity and to each according to his need." If that theory were applied now when the moral standard of the people was still not sufficiently high, then, Sun thought, those who should contribute would not do so strictly according to their ability, while those who merely took would take more than they actually needed. If, on the other hand, the theory was going to be applied in the future after the moral standard of the people had been raised, then why should anyone in the present state of moral inadequacy prescribe anything for those who would later be much more competent? "Since the people then would have higher moral development and superior knowledge than ourselves and would be able to practice the theory themselves, what is the use for us to waste our time and spend our mental efforts speculating for an eventuality which will not emerge until thousands of years later?"

Least of all did Sun Yat-sen have any sympathy with the Marxist view of the collapse or downfall of capitalism, or believe in the inevitability of class struggle. He maintained that capitalism was essential to the realization of his *min-sheng* principle. That was another reason why he invited foreign capital which would facilitate and quicken the industrial development of China and, when properly handled, would prevent class warfare. Sun was adverse to any theory of conflict or struggle; he wanted co-operation and went even to the post-Darwinians for support. "As it has been discovered by the post-Darwinian philosophy," he said, "the primary force of human evolution is co-operation and not struggle as in the animal world, so the fighting nature, a residue of the animal instinct in man, must be eliminated from mankind, and the sooner the better."

It is essential that we discuss Sun Yat-sen's thinking in relation to Marxist views because it should not be believed that he embraced Marxist ideology and then later deserted it. He never was a Marxist; he had been consistent in his own way. In the statement with Joffe, as the first official indication of Sino-Soviet collaboration, Sun insisted upon making it quite definite and explicit that such collaboration did not mean he had any use for Communism as a social or political theory. The significance of what happened in China between the Kuomintang and the Communists after the success of the Northern Expedition three years later should also be understood. The Communists obviously had a motive in working their way into the Kuomintang, and they completely ignored the joint statement of January 26, 1923. All the developments in China from that time to this, a period of twenty years, which have taken place with Chiang Kai-shek as the dominating personality on the political scene thus become intelligible. They were not haphazard; they follow a consistent plan; they are part of a large program based on the Three Principles which Sun Yat-sen conceived and which Chiang Kai-shek has been putting into actual practice.

After Sun Yat-sen passed away in March 1925 it fell upon Chiang to make Sun's ideals work. Whether there is room for improvement in the way that his government tries to realize these ideals is another question, but that Chiang is absolutely loyal there is not the slightest doubt.

Fulfillment

22

The Legacy of Inequality

AT THE TIME of Sun Yat-sen's death he left a will which has since been read aloud at the opening of all meetings of the Chinese Government or of the Kuomintang party. It begins by saying that he spent some forty years in revolutionary activities, "the aim of which is to win freedom and equality for China." In order, however, to achieve this aim it is necessary to awaken the entire nation and unite it into a solid entity and "ally ourselves with those countries which treat us on the basis of equality."

Both the purpose and method of Sun's efforts were thus clearly defined. It was necessary to define the purpose because for a period of eighty years, at the time of Sun's death, China had been subject to the rule of the unequal treaties. It was necessary to define the method because, unless the efforts of the nation were canalized and controlled, the aim would not be realized. This document was drawn up at a time when the Kuomintang members were most vocal on the subject of co-operation with Soviet Russia, and yet that country was not singled out nor even mentioned. Sun's instruction was that China must ally herself with any country so long as it was prepared to treat her as an equal. If Soviet Russia was the first one to renounce the inequalities, she was first to come as a friend. But the Kuomintang waited to see if the other countries would follow suit. The only criterion as to whether another country was a friend or foe was whether or not it was going to relieve the burden of inequalities that China had borne since 1842. That was the only issue worth considering. Nearly twenty years elapsed before that weight was lifted. Those twenty years constitute the period of maturity of Chiang Kai-shek, the period of the fulfillment of an historic mission. Through his efforts the aim of the Chinese Revolution is at last being achieved: a chapter of exactly one hundred years is being closed in the history of China. One century in a national lifetime of forty-five centuries is a short period, but the destruction and ravages wrought in so brief a time can sometimes be

devastating enough to keep a nation in permanent bondage. That was the supreme test for the character of Chiang Kai-shek, for by the sheer exertion of the efforts of a single person China has become a new entity. Chiang was able in the space of twenty years to lead his country from bondage to liberty, from virtual slavery to freedom. He has changed the entire course of Chinese history. The future historian will give him his appropriate position in that history; but that he has become the eternal benefactor of his race is unquestioned. Chiang was fully aware of the deep significance of the announcement made by America and Britain on October 10, 1942, to the effect that they were "prepared promptly to negotiate a treaty providing for the immediate relinquishment of extraterritorial rights" in China and the other unequal treaties. Chiang knows better than anyone else what tremendous inroads the unequal treaties have made, especially into the soul and mentality of his people, and the dangers to China which the treaties brought about.

The chapter is now closed, and it serves no useful purpose to discuss the unfair treaties. But Chiang's concern, in the year 1925, was not so much with the actual loss of China's national rights which these treaties entailed, great as that was, as with the general state of national demoralization and the disintegration of the national soul as a consequence of this unequal regime, which was all the more dangerous because its progress had been imperceptible. The stipulations in the treaties from 1842 on were links of a chain by which the Chinese body was so securely bound that no freedom of movement was possible. There were extraterritoriality; customs restrictions; settlements, concessions, and leased territories; rights of foreign war vessels to sail into the innermost part of the country, of foreign merchantmen to trade along its coast and in its rivers; railway and mining concessions; the right to station foreign troops on Chinese soil; control of the salt and postal administrations—there was not one vital part of Chinese life that was not compromised and hampered by foreign intrusion. These were tangible and explicit, and the people could point to them and enumerate them. It remained for Chiang Kai-shek to see that, serious as these embarrassments were, there was something even more serious. If the state of the national ego was healthy, then disabilities would in time disappear. But it was abundantly clear that after eighty years of wear that ego was weakening. It was Chiang's duty first of all to restore the Chinese soul to its normal state of health.

THE LEGACY OF INEQUALITY

Chiang looked at the economic situation of the country as it was then and compared it with what it had been in past history. The center of China's economic life in the early Tsin and Han periods was in the Yellow River valley. It shifted to the Yangtze River valley from the period of the Three Kingdoms to the Tang Dynasty. From the Tang Dynasty until the Ming Ching period it again moved to the southeastern corner, where its rich resources began to be fully exploited. Harmony was established within the country so that the riches of the southeast contributed to national defense in the northwestern area. The country was self-sufficient. No wonder Marco Polo could go back and describe to an astonished Europe that there were cities in Manzi (southern China) richer by far than anything Europe could show. And Marco Polo himself hailed from rich Venice, the queen of the Adriatic. No wonder also that as late as the end of the eighteenth century Emperor Chien Lung could with just pride convey to George III the remark, "As your Ambassador can see for himself, we possess all things."

Such was the economic situation in China before the advent of the unequal treaties. What happened afterward? The treaty ports grew on the coast and along the rivers. They grew up as industrial centers away from the means which make industry possible, away from the coal and iron mines, and created an anomalous situation. They were only a convenient arrangement for the exclusive benefit of the foreigners who imposed the treaties upon China. They became centers of exploitation through which the wealth of the land was drained away. They were not a part of the country's economic scheme. The crafts of old became bankrupt, agriculture was abandoned, and the people as a whole began to suffer while the treaty ports remained as emporia for the trade of foreign merchandise. The glittering prosperity of a few isolated spots set a false standard for the rest of the country. It was an empty façade behind which there was no productive labor. It offered manifold temptations to the people of the interior who are the backbone of the country. They lost their old virtues, were left without honest work. They were converted into bandits, into mercenary soldiers. The people in the treaty ports themselves likewise rapidly degenerated. There was little in the way of productive enterprise, and people turned to speculation, thereby precipitating crises in the stock market and bringing ruin in its wake.

The whole of the social structure built up by thousands of years of patient work began to totter under the impact of this abnormal situa-

tion. That structure was completely indigenous to China, and it had meant security, orderly development, and happiness to the people. It was a structure built on moral concepts with the family as the primary unit and the relationship of its different members conducted on the basis of love, devotion, and consideration for the feelings of others. From the family the influences radiated to the clan and the village, and between them everything that pertained to social welfare, ranging from education of the young to the protection of the old, was properly provided for. There was no need for the Emperor or the central government to be at all concerned with these problems. The Chinese view was that the best government was one that had least to do with the people. "Heaven is high and the Emperor is far off"—this was the ideal of peace, security, and happiness, and Chinese classics are full of descriptions of such conditions. It was under such circumstances that it was possible to speak of the development of personal virtues, for the criterion of the success of society was its ability to foster the growth of the largest number of virtuous people, not spectacular personalities who attract public attention, but solid, down-to-earth, good, honest, trustworthy, and loyal people who worship virtue for its own sake. It was a society in which human desires were reduced to the minimum. There was thus no room for selfishness, for a selfish person could not maintain himself for long in a milieu in which other people were always contending for the recognition of nobler qualities, art, scholarship, culture, courtesy, and the refinements of civilized life.

Then came the unequal treaties with Europe and America that completely upset the simple life of this social structure. They introduced a new set of values with emphasis no longer on virtue and moral probity of an unimpeachable personal life, but upon gain and acquisition, even though that might be obtained at the expense of others. Life in the countryside and the village grew unstable. The peasants began forsaking the land to disgorge themselves into the big cities where they hoped to amass wealth but, once there, became more impecunious than ever. Having gained nothing, they lost their former virtues, which were the source of social stability. Many of them even lost their civility of manners, and in a country that is known proverbially for this kind of refinement it is disturbing to see people, especially those who are the products of the treaty ports, show so little of it.

The differences in the psychology of the people that Chiang Kai-

THE LEGACY OF INEQUALITY 155

shek has taken pains to analyze[1] and discuss are patent enough to those who are familiar with Chinese conditions. Chinese society, before and after the introduction of the unequal treaties, differed widely. Vestiges of the old society can still be found today, of course, sometimes in large measure among the common people, for it has frequently been observed that a mere ricksha coolie has often more charm of manners than the socially elite.

The task, as Chiang Kai-shek sees it, is an enormous one. Only the most superficial of observers can feel that the modernization of China means only the importation of machines and all their accessories. The Chinese have sufficient sense to realize that there is no meaning in the worship of the machine. The beauty of life lies in its poise and quiet dignity, the result of sustained and continual effort to uphold and cultivate the humanistic values. It is Chiang Kai-shek's ambition to effect a moral rehabilitation of his people upon the basis of their traditional virtues, along with modernization in industry. Are the two things compatible? He thinks they are.

The whole subject of the unequal treaties, considered from this special angle by Chiang Kai-shek, assumes a new importance. Other Chinese see only the impairment of their national sovereignty; but Chiang goes much deeper than that. He also brings the people to a realization of the grave dangers in Chinese society brought in by the unhealthy changes in China's national soul since the Opium War. They are ordinarily not perceptible to the untrained eye, which is all the more reason why they are so treacherous. They have more to do with the mind and the spirit of the nation than with its wealth or possessions. I do not believe that the average foreign observer is ever in a position to analyze and dissect these social evils. He does not have the necessary feeling or sympathy with the subject. He may sometimes have a sentimental attachment to the old order without asking how its charm was fostered or managed to grow. But in the majority of cases the average treaty-port foreigner, with his narrow and frankly materialistic point of view, simply brushes aside anything that is unfamiliar to him as being irrelevant and unworthy of study. To the Chinese themselves, to men like Chiang Kai-shek and others of his generation, who still have vital contacts with the old China, the changes are not only palpably disturbing but are also portents for a future that re-

---

[1] In his recent book, *China's Destiny*, which is in Chinese and will eventually be available, I hope, in an English version, Chiang Kai-shek goes into an exhaustive discussion of this important subject.

quires a firm and determined way of approach. Chiang Kai-shek considers the question of moral rehabilitation much more pressing than any other single problem.

The period between the death of Sun Yat-sen and the Northern Expedition was one in which Chiang Kai-shek made the most rigorous attack on imperialism. Before him lay the immense task of having to bring the whole country into his unified control, but there was a group of militarists who were an obstacle to his plans. The militarists were able to survive because they continued to receive support from foreign imperialists.

In a speech delivered before the newly formed Military Council at this period we have, I think, one of the clearest analyses by Chiang of the way in which imperialism worked in China. He asked why it was that the revolution in China had been so prolonged. It was because there was no adequate recognition of its purposes, and further, there was no clear understanding as to who the real enemy was. The problem could not be solved by directing attention toward any one particular war lord, because as soon as he was put down another would rise in his place. It was important to understand that behind these war lords were the imperialists in whose hands the war lords were mere marionettes. "It is the imperialists who are, therefore, our real enemies," and as long as their power remained, the war lords would continue to be an effective obstacle.

Then Chiang went on to expose the methods which the imperialists used. "It is their policy to keep on fomenting troubles within China so that we will annihilate each other. They want to keep our country so divided that progress and constructive work will be impossible. To them the Chinese political scene is a dramatic performance which they have put on after having sunk so much money in the militarists, who thus become the principal performers of the drama. But the most vicious of the imperialist practices in China is that, even when they themselves are in conflict with us, they never call out their own troops to settle the difference with us, but spend their money on those ignorant people who come out to be sacrifices for them. . . . It is the classic formula of the imperialists to make the Chinese themselves fight against the Chinese." There was only one conclusion that he could draw: "If imperialism is not banished from the country China will perish as a nation. If China does not perish, then imperialism cannot remain." There is no compromise, no middle ground between the two.

THE LEGACY OF INEQUALITY

The utter folly of the militarists in willingly making themselves the tools of the imperialists was illustrated by the way in which they made use of their money. It was the same from Yuan Shih-kai down to the least important of the war lords. Having obtained their money, they would deposit it in foreign banks where they felt it would be secure. But wasn't this equivalent, as far as the foreigners were concerned, to sending the money back to where it came from? There were those like Feng Kuo-chang, Tsao Kun, or Chang Tso-lin, who believed they were more intelligent than the rest and who, instead of depositing all their money in the foreign banks, kept a portion of it and sought to establish banks or factories themselves with the money. That they considered the best kind of security. If the foreign banks should go out of business, they thought, there would still be their own enterprises to depend on. But it was not so simple as all that. Any form of enterprise would fail if the imperialists wished to have it so, since they possessed more capital. Nor was there any way to protect native enterprises. In this manner the British-American Tobacco Company exercised a virtual monopoly over the cigarette market in China, against which no Chinese cigarette company was able to compete.

"The means by which the imperialists oppress China," said Chiang, "are not only military, but also financial. We all know that their alliance with the militarists is made through ammunition and money. The militarists, in order to satisfy their personal cupidity, are willing to make themselves the 'walking dogs'[2] of these imperialists. But actually what the militarists acquire has never lasted long. When the country perishes completely, they will not, of course, have the freedom to withdraw from the foreign banks any amount they like. Granted that the country continues to exist, how many war lords are there since the revolution broke out who can still claim their ill-gotten money as their personal property?"

That speech of Chiang Kai-shek's was not only an effective attack on imperialism as being the source of all of China's ills but was also meant to be an appeal to the war lords who, at the time of Sun Yat-sen's death and afterward, were still creating confusion in the country. After pointing out to them their utter folly in depending upon the imperialists, Chiang tried to arouse their patriotic feelings. After all, a deep love for the country did not seem to be confined to any

[2] A widely used Chinese expression meaning anyone who is servile and always willing to do another's bidding.

particular part of China. It should have been as strong in the north as it was in the south. If only the militarists would realize the importance of forgetting their selfishness and stand together as the common enemy of imperialism, Chiang was sure that in three years the revolution would be a complete success. Those were the days when the attainments of the Russian Revolution were followed by the victory of Mustapha Kemal in Turkey. Chiang grew impatient and vowed that he would do at least as much for his own country. In 1926 he was prepared to stake everything on the Northern Expedition. Upon that one move depended the entire future of his own life as well as the existence of his country.

23

The Northern Expedition

WHILE Chiang Kai-shek was directing the attack on imperialism it is useless to deny that Soviet Russia exerted some influence over him. The entire Kuomintang was under that spell, and Sun Yat-sen himself was thought to have been converted to the Marxist view. So long as Sun lived the Bolshevists hoped to spread their doctrines through him and were prepared to recognize him as the leader of the party. Now that he was dead, all pretense of respecting the Kuomintang as a separate entity disappeared. Borodin stepped into Sun's place and virtually made himself dictator in Canton. He was, in fact, more than a successor to Sun Yat-sen, for he had enormous power over the Kuomintang and quickly placed Communists in all the key positions. The death of Sun Yat-sen left the party without a leader. Although Chiang Kai-shek had become intimately attached to Sun, especially since the revolt of Chen Chiung-ming, Chiang was in no position to assume the leadership yet. His claim would be hotly contested by others who had a longer and closer relationship with the party. In the midst of all this controversy as to who should be elected to the chairmanship of the Central Executive Committee or the Political Council of the party, Borodin, being the one man who was instrumental in creating the reorganized Kuomintang along Russian lines, was naturally the person to be relied upon to understand and direct

THE NORTHERN EXPEDITION 159

the intricate workings of the organization. The opportunity of securing a firm grip on the party had arrived, and Borodin was not going to let it go by.

His was a mind that had been meticulously trained and disciplined in the revolutionary method of Moscow. He had clarity of vision, intelligence, unbounded ambition, and the ability, as one journalist puts it, "to disentangle a principle from the confusion of external events." He was just the sort of person that intelligent young radicals would worship. "Borodin, a large, calm man with the natural dignity of a lion or a panther," as the same admiring journalist described him, "had the special quality of not being in, but above, the battle ... the quality that seems to me to deserve, in itself and without regard to the judgment of the world, the name of greatness. His slow, resolute way of talking, his refusal to be hurried or to get excited, his insistence upon the five fundamental lines of action that determined detailed events, gave a spacious, deliberate character to his conversation, lifting it far above the shallowness of journalism and the hysteria of politics."[1] He could well have added that Borodin's fundamental line of action was to convert the Kuomintang into an effective Communist machine and nullify the solemn pledge which Joffe, as the first official representative of Soviet Russia, gave to Sun Yat-sen in January of 1923.

Borodin at once proceeded to form numerous auxiliary organizations of the Kuomintang. One such organization was called the "League for the Freedom of the Race," another was called the "Order of the Students"; still another was formed under the noble appellation of the "Federation of Farmers, Workers, Soldiers, and Students to Promote the Revolutionary Movement." It was Borodin's purpose to create a Bolshevist movement in China. It was in Borodin's power, as adviser to the Kuomintang, to appoint young men to these new organizations who had been baptized at the Bolshevist font. The Soviet Embassy in Peking was the clearinghouse for new Communist agents who were either recruited from openly professed Bolshevist groups in China or brought over specifically from Russia.

Two months after the death of Sun Yat-sen another opportunity for strengthening the Bolshevist grip on China presented itself. The Shanghai police, under the control of the Municipal Council which was in effect a British organization, opened fire on the students during a patriotic demonstration and precipitated the May 30 incident.

[1] Vincent Sheean, *Personal History*. (Doubleday, Doran & Co., 1935), p. 203.

The Chinese were naturally outraged by the unprecedented cruelty of the British on Chinese territory, and Borodin further strengthened his power and prestige by making capital of the Chinese feeling. All the popular anger and animosity became centered on Great Britain as being the main support of imperialism in China. If Britain fell, so Borodin thought, the whole structure would necessarily collapse. The people were given a popular issue in which their feelings were united; this was precisely what the Communists wanted, for it was an important part of their technique to grow strong through the support of the masses.

Even in that particular sphere in which Chiang Kai-shek had carved for himself an unquestioned position of importance, Borodin allowed his influence to be felt. For the Whampoa Military Academy, of which Chiang was president, had its political department modeled after the Red Army. Into that political department Borodin brought all his competent political aides. There was a department in each army, and its secretary was a Communist, so that any possible Kuomintang opposition would be immediately detected and checked through ruthless methods. Each army also had a Russian military adviser so that, between the two of them, they could render a full report to Borodin regarding conditions in the army and the academy.

Such was the situation in which Chiang Kai-shek found himself after the death of Sun Yat-sen and before he launched the Northern Expedition. He thoroughly understood the position of the dead leader; he knew where his own sympathies were. Yet what was there to be done under these trying circumstances? It was a delicate situation, and Chiang had to muster all his tact and energy to steer a careful course. A weaker person would have been swamped in this sea of Bolshevism; a headstrong and petulant man, on the other hand, might have had the satisfaction of declaring his opposition, but he would not have lasted long. Chiang Kai-shek could not afford, in those days, to be put out of the game. He did not yet possess enough prestige to make him absolutely indispensable. Both for his own future and for the welfare of his country he could not allow himself to be submerged. So he stayed on, observed the momentous changes that were going on around him, and devoted all his time and energy to the training of his military cadets. There were times when he even had to simulate sympathy and co-operation with the Communists. Some of the addresses that he delivered in those days, when they are read today, convey a completely different impression of the man. He too could speak about world revolution. One would think that he was hand in glove with Borodin and his cohorts. That he could never be. But the tide was then rising high, and it was much the better part of wisdom to rise with it until such time as he could ride on the crest of another wave bound in another direction. In the meantime he had to work hard and be unusually patient, for didn't Trotsky himself advise him back in 1923, when Chiang took leave of him in Moscow, "Patience and activity are the two essential factors for a revolutionary party, and the one complements the other"? It was a sound piece of advice that he was trying out on the Bolsheviks themselves. If he could only be patient, Chiang knew that he would ultimately win out. For there were three factors upon which he could depend for support, and the strength of these factors would grow with time. The first was that there were elements within the Kuomintang party that could never approve of Bolshevism with its un-Chinese sentiments. In time a strong reaction would set in and give Bolshevism a stubborn fight. The second factor was even more important: the Chinese masses, the Chinese nation as a whole, could and would not permit a group of Russians with their hotheaded Chinese accomplices to dominate the Chinese political scene. That would be worse than being under the rule of imperialism, for imperialism was at least indirect, but Bolshevist control was open, frank, and to the point. There was no sense in substituting one foreign control for another when what they really wanted was to put their house in order in their own Chinese way. The third factor was that the excesses of Bolshevism were incompatible with the rational instincts of the race. It could stand them for a limited period, perhaps, but a tyranny of extravagance would strike terror into the people's hearts. These factors, in Chiang Kai-shek's estimation, were powerful, but their effectiveness would only grow with the passing of time. He must, above everything else, first accomplish something that would rivet the nation's attention upon him. He must carry out the Northern Expedition.

The idea of the Northern Expedition was conceived by Sun Yat-sen back in 1921 when he was elected President by a special parliament. But nothing serious was done during the succeeding years because Chen Chiung-ming's revolt held up the schedule. Sun himself had to leave Canton, and the expedition was suspended until Chiang Kai-shek, in 1924 and 1925, liquidated the Chen Chiung-ming incident and re-established Kuomintang supremacy in the Canton region. Sun Yat-sen did, however, issue an effective statement, in September 1924, which placed all the responsibility for the chaos in the country since 1911 on the shoulders of the militarists and on those who made it possible for the militarists to continue their careers as freebooters, namely, the foreign imperialists.

When the expedition was launched in earnest early in 1926, the soldiers knew what they were fighting for. They had been trained and disciplined; they had been taught their duties to the nation; they joined the war as crusaders; they were ardent young men who were willing to sacrifice their lives for the ideals of the Kuomintang; and, thanks to Soviet influence, they had been galvanized into action through cleverly manipulated propaganda. Pitted against them were the soldiers of Wu Pei-fu and the other war lords—rabble troops that were haphazardly picked up to swell the numbers and who were kept on the go simply because they were assured two meals a day and given a promise of loot if things went well. The differences between these fighting forces were great.

When the Chen Chiung-ming episode had been settled, there were still things to be done in the province of Kwangtung before the expedition could start. The issue of the relationship between the Kuomintang members and the Communists continued to rankle Chiang. He knew that the number of Communists in the Military Academy continued to increase and that there was growing friction between the two elements. On one occasion he took the opportunity of making himself clear. During a meeting of the executive committee of the special party headquarters affiliated with the academy, held on September 13, 1925, Chiang was very explicit: "I hope that the Communist members will bear in mind that they have joined the ranks of the Kuomintang in order that they may help to carry out the Three Principles. This is the only political faith that we uphold in the Chinese Revolution. If they understand the significance of the Chinese Revolution at all, then they must know that they are followers of the Three Principles. ... You have not brought Communism into our ranks to substitute for these principles. I wish to warn you especially that you must show the greatest respect to the personality of Tsung-li [Sun Yat-sen]. ... If the Communists are willing to consider him as their leader also, then I believe that the members of the Kuomintang will not try to eliminate the Communists from their ranks. I hope, therefore, that from now on there will be no discrimination between the two groups. ... My own view is that within the Kuomintang there are those who are more conservative (the Rightists) and those who are more liberal (the Leftists). There is no division between Communists and non-Communists, and more particularly there shall be no division between Kuomintang members and Communist members."

By November of the same year he had made a few preliminary military moves. He reached Swatow, some two hundred miles to the east of Canton. That was the first major city to fall into his hands. During a reception held in his honor by the Swatow Chamber of Commerce on November 16 he dealt with the question of Communism again. "The enemy," he said, "has been spreading counter-propaganda by calling us Communists. Gentlemen, here we are now in Swatow. Have we shown ourselves to be Communists? But I have a word of explanation to give you. It is true that the organization of our Kuomintang Army is modeled after the Red Army. The soldiers are not allowed to loot or to rape and they are not allowed to cause any destruction among innocent people. You must not, on that account, call us Communists. And I can further assure you that our Chinese merchants are not considered capitalists. Each of them may have a few thousand dollars [Chinese dollars], the richest are not worth over a million. That amount is enough to maintain a decent living, but it is certainly not so large as to make others want to share it. Therefore I say that there is no possibility of Communism in China today. . . . As regards the reasons why we have Russian Communists among our ranks, it is because our Tsung-li [Sun Yat-sen] wanted us to ally ourselves with those countries that treat us as equals. We have joined hands with Russia in the hope that together we may contribute to a world peace. The Russians are also willing to join hands with us because they too desire to defeat the forces of imperialism. They do not maintain that China must be converted to Communism." Chiang Kai-shek had too strong a sense of responsibility to break away from the scene of activities, but it was imperative for him to give his views on this vital subject every now and then.

As he continued to grow stronger every day and to proceed further from Canton, where obviously the Communists under the direction of Borodin would not be too well disposed toward him, Chiang took a characteristic step. It was as commander of the First Army Corps that he conquered Swatow and unified Kwangtung. From that position he resigned. He knew that his military successes had made him more or less indispensable. Yet his political enemies might turn around and accuse him of being a militarist himself. He made, therefore, a strategic retreat: he made a recommendation to the Military Council to the effect that a division should be the largest unit under a single commander, who was to be directly responsible to the Council and not to the commander of the army corps. For the moment an army corps, he thought, was not necessary. That could wait until the Northern Expedition was under way. Chiang proposed also that there should be a standing army of some eighteen divisions and a reserve army of some one hundred thousand men composed largely of students and farmers. With these men properly trained, they could start the drive to the north. There were other recommendations—on the pay of the soldiers, their education, morale, and discipline—all of which were favorably considered by the loyal Kuomintang members.

When the year 1926 began, the Communists were as strong as ever in Canton. The Kuomintang held a congress of the Central Executive Committee from January 1-20, and the close alliance with Soviet Russia was reaffirmed. But Borodin felt that he was not entirely master of the situation, and on February 4 he suddenly left Canton and proceeded to Mongolia, where he visited Feng Yu-hsiang (the "Christian general") in order that he might prepare a new base of operations in case things came to a showdown at Canton.

During Borodin's absence Chiang Kai-shek frankly stepped in and effected an anti-Communist coup, eliminating all the Communists from Canton. On March 15 warrants of arrest were issued for a number of people, including the Russians. There was considerable satisfaction in Canton itself that the step had been taken, and everybody wondered whether it was to be the end of Communist control of the Kuomintang and whether Borodin would ever be able to come back to Canton. The Communists in Russia were aroused, and Zinoviev openly expressed pessimism over the situation in a speech in Moscow. "I cannot pass over the question of China," he said. "I have not yet told you that the strategical position of the Chinese Revolution is at the present time getting worse. . . . The position of the enemy forces is getting stronger and the enemy is becoming more impertinent. Yet in spite of all this we are assured that a not very distant future will bring more amelioration, and that obliges us to follow most fixedly the events in China." Naturally there were bitter attacks on Chiang, but even in those attacks we can see that the Russian Communists had deep respect for him. A typical example is the following by Comrade Stepanoff, who said:

"To me and to our Chinese comrades, Chiang appears as a brilliant figure with clearly expressed features. His prominent attributes are ambition and lust of power. He longs to become a hero in the eyes of all China. . . . His purposes are power and money. I emphasize, as having observed it myself, that he wants money not to enrich himself but to effect some grand liberal gesture. He is exceedingly lavish as regards rewards and pecuniary recompenses. . . . Besides, he is rather clever. He understands pretty well political questions, not only of a local Chinese but of a world-wide nature. . . . He uses us and the Chinese Communists, but only as long as we assist him and are useful to him."

But to show that Communism still had a strong footing in Canton Borodin returned to that city as suddenly as he had left. He came back on August 5, after having been away for three months. He was again face to face with Chiang Kai-shek. But neither of them desired an open rupture at this point. Both played for time in order to consolidate their respective positions. Chiang's main task of spreading his military power to the north had not yet been performed, and any situation that might prove to be an obstacle would be disconcerting. It is said, therefore, that the two worked out a plan of compromise and called for a truce. Borodin even promised that he would help Chiang by supplying him with Soviet ammunition.

Chiang Kai-shek's position was clearly getting stronger every day. On June 4, 1926, he called for an extraordinary session of the Central Executive Committee and urged that the Northern Expedition be undertaken at once. The government appointed him commander in chief of the expeditionary forces, which position he assumed on July 9. He had altogether some one hundred thousand soldiers on the historic march which has since placed all of China under the unified military command of the National Government. A brief résumé of the military events will show what a spectacular conquest it was.

In the early days of August the National troops were already in Hunan Province. The important city of Changsha, which in the current war the Japanese have tried and failed to capture on four successive occasions, was occupied by Chiang's troops on the twelfth. Then followed one of the most decisive battles with the last and most redoubtable of the militarists, Wu Pei-fu. Wu, in his own way, was an outstanding character. He too had deep respect for China's ancient lore and wisdom. He had great personal integrity and was on a much higher level than all the other militarists. But he had no feeling whatever for the modern world. He could well appear in the pages of the novel of the Three Kingdoms, for he was an impressive feudal lord, but he was out of place in a country that was anxious to become a great and modern power. He had the utmost contempt for the Nationalist Army under Chiang Kai-shek, but by the end of August he realized that the army for which he had scant respect, though much inferior in numbers, had a driving power that was irresistible. Wu collapsed and retreated from his headquarters at Wuchang in the heart of China.

By September Chiang Kai-shek was the master of the Yangtze Valley around Hankow and immediately directed his attention to Kiangsi Province to the southeast. The capital of that province, Nanchang, was captured on the nineteenth. Kiukiang, to the north, followed suit.

This series of victories surprised the world. They completely upset the foreign communities in the treaty ports: it was the most uncomfortable news they had received for a long time. But the impossible had been done, and they thought it wise to find out who this military wizard was who in two months could bring his soldiers from the base at Canton seven hundred miles away to the banks of the Yangtze River. Journalists from the treaty ports hastened to interview Chiang. "A pleasant-looking young man," said Lewis S. Gannett somewhat patronizingly,[2] "in an officer's uniform without distinguishing marks of rank." He noticed the bare and simple room which this man occupied as his office.

Most of the time he sat erect, his folded arms on the table before him. There was no bombast about him, hardly any gesture, but he had a quiet dignity—a quality rare in Chinese, rare enough anywhere—and he smiled as he spoke. A tall, slight man under forty, there was nothing in his appearance to mark him as a leader of men; his high forehead, which seemed higher because of his close-cropped head, his delicate features and small-boned hands seemed rather to indicate the scholar type.

Mr. Gannett wrote another article for the New York *Times* for November 14, 1926, from which the following quotations will show the attitude of many people toward Chiang Kai-shek in those days.

There was no questioning the sincerity and intensity of the man as a Chinese patriot. But can he work with other men? Is he really a party man, a co-operator, or just another personal dictator? Strong men have

[2] "China's New Strong Man" by Lewis Gannett, *Literary Digest*, December 25, 1926.

THE NORTHERN EXPEDITION 167

risen and fallen interminably in China since the revolution. Will Chiang go the way of the rest or is he a strong man come to stay—a man who understands how to work with a national party and move from military dictatorship toward a measure of democracy? I do not know; but his prophecies of military successes which seemed so swollen last winter have proved uncannily accurate.

It was about Christmas time. Normally at Christmas the journalists would remain in their comfortably heated apartments in Shanghai, Tientsin, and Hong Kong, for their turkey and cranberry sauce, and for the time being try to forget that they were in China. But this was an exceptional time. The interests of the imperialists were at stake. Chiang Kai-shek, the headstrong young man who so often had pointed out the dangers of imperialism to his country, really meant business, and it was important that the newspapers inform their readers as to what he proposed to do next. They took their valises and journeyed upriver to meet and talk with the man of the hour. Chiang gave them the interview they wanted. In a prepared statement he reiterated what he had so often said before: that the two sources of evil for China—militarism and imperialism—were intimately related to one another. "The only aim of the National Revolution is to crush all that pertains to imperialism and militarism and at the same time to establish an independent and free nation so as to improve the standing of both the nation and the people." He repeated also what Sun Yat-sen had said, that, "when he had won the day he would utilize all the power and influence the revolutionary government might possess, first to put an end to all the opposing forces within the national boundaries so that the people could enjoy true liberty and have a government 'of the people, by the people, and for the people.'" When the unequal treaties were abolished, he went on to say, a six-point program concerning the development of industry and agriculture would be carried out. He then proposed that a series of eight measures be immediately put into effect—calling a national convention, negotiation of fair and equal treaties, withdrawal of foreign armies, abolition of consular jurisdiction, the retrocession of treaty ports and leased territories, customs autonomy, the control of all missionary institutions, the control of all property in China by Chinese except as otherwise sanctioned by the government. There were other lists that he mentioned. A program of nineteen items touching every phase of Chinese national life was also given to the journalists which among other points included liberty of assembly, of speech, of the press, of residence, and of creed; training for self-government; and improvement in the conditions of peasants and workers. It was a comprehensive program amplifying the Three Principles which Sun Yat-sen had laid as the cornerstone of his revolution.

At the same time that he was consolidating his position in the Wuhan area, Chiang Kai-shek proposed to the government at Canton that it should be transferred to where his soldiers were. That was a brave and astute move. It was difficult not to permit the transfer because with the government moved into central China it could more easily direct its military activities against the northern provinces, but it was a blow to the Communists. Borodin and the government, including Sun Fo (Sun Yat-sen's only son), T. V. Soong, Eugene Chen, Mme. Sun Yat-sen, and the other important members, moved to Wuchang in November.

The new year of 1927 found Chiang Kai-shek busy liquidating another of the remaining redoubtable war lords, Sun Chuan-fang, who was then master of two of the most strategic and important provinces of China: Chekiang and Kiangsu. By the middle of February Hangchow had fallen to the Nationalist Army under Pai Chung-hsi, and in the course of the next month Soochow, Nanking, and Shanghai all flew the Nationalist banner.

From July 1926 to March 1927 half of China to the south of the Yangtze River had been conquered by Chiang Kai-shek's armies. Nothing like it had ever happened before in modern Chinese history, and it was all because Chinese nationalism had at last become articulate and found a leader to undertake its aims. Sun Yat-sen, had he lived, would have been overjoyed, for his ideas were at last being vindicated by the man whom he most trusted. Chiang Kai-shek had become the acknowledged leader of his people.

24

The Split

COMMUNISM IN CHINA has played one of the most significant and spectacular roles in modern times. Like a Shakespearean drama, it falls into five acts.

THE SPLIT

The first act was when Leo Karakhan gave a promise to China. It was a new message of deliverance which he brought to a people then struggling for independence and a free status of nationhood under the leadership of Sun Yat-sen. The arrival of Joffe and Borodin, and later of Karakhan himself, brought the principal Russian actors to the Chinese stage. While he was conscious of the benefits which this close association with these Soviets conferred on him, Sun was aware also that Sovietism, as a way of life, was foreign to his people. In order, therefore, to forestall any possibility of his own political and social doctrines being overshadowed by this alien creed, he was wise enough to conclude an agreement with Joffe to the effect that Communism was not suited to Chinese purposes. But that still left the problem of the relationship between his own Kuomintang and the new Communist party unsolved, for the Communists were clamoring for admission into the ranks of the Kuomintang. Some of the old and respected members were frankly afraid of these new friends and cautioned their leader to be wary of them. But the doctor gave one of his characteristic answers. He was accustomed to a large and generous view of life, and he was not going to cast suspicion on people with whom an understanding and a *modus vivendi* had been reached; if they wanted to join with him and become co-workers in the same camp, he believed that his own personality would be sufficient to exercise a wholesome influence on them. It was unquestionably a worthy attitude to show confidence in your friends rather than doubt and suspicion, although it was then already being proven to his dismay that such a policy did not always work; for in spite of all the trust that Sun had placed in Chen Chiung-ming, Chen turned out to be a traitor. Nevertheless, Sun maintained the same attitude toward the Soviets, because he thought it would be dangerous to allow the Communists to form a party by themselves.

Where did Chiang Kai-shek stand during this first act? Although Chiang believed that his leader always had great vision and was therefore correct in his diagnosis of the situation, he suspended his judgment, especially after returning from Moscow at the end of 1923. He felt that there was danger ahead.

When the second act began Sun Yat-sen was a dying man in the hospital at Peking. By that time the Communist party had become an organic part of the Kuomintang, and its growing strength left no doubt as to the direction in which it was moving. Borodin became the principal actor, and his base of operations was Canton, with the Soviet

Embassy in Peking and the Soviet consulates in other parts of China supplying all the necessary equipment in the form of ammunition and propaganda material to carry on the activities of the Communist party. The Kuomintang, as the parent party, began to lose its grip, and Chiang Kai-shek as one of the few bulwarks that could stem the tide had to present a friendly side as a matter of tactics and expediency. Apparently even that did not satisfy his enemies, for they saw that he was going to prove a stumbling block to their plans. They resorted to conspiracy, tried to lure him to a waiting gunboat in Canton, and had designs on his life. Fortunately the plot was discovered in time, and, acting with rapidity and decision, Chiang managed to effect a coup and rounded up the Communists in March of 1926. When Borodin came back to Canton from his trip to the north the differences were patched up for the moment, but it was clear that an open rupture was only a question of time. In the meantime, Chiang concentrated all his energy on the Northern Expedition. When, within six months, he brought one half of China under his military control, his prestige with the people and with his party was immeasurably increased. He was now the national hero and had become the principal actor in the third act of the Communist drama. The third act is usually the climax; so also was the drama enacted in the Wuhan area (Wuchang, Hankow, and Hanyang). It remains for us to see the fourth act when Chiang Kai-shek was engaged in cleaning up the Communist mess after his victory over the Communist party, which led to the party's official disappearance from China and the departure of Borodin. The fifth and last act is being played out today while the nation is engaged in another and a larger conflict. It continues to be generally known as the conflict with the Communists, although it has changed greatly since the earlier days.

By the early months of 1927 Chiang Kai-shek's soldiers had reached the Yangtze delta and the port of Shanghai. This series of victories was unprecedented, but there was a reason for it. In the first place, the soldiers, having gone through a course of training at the Whampoa Military Academy, were different from the soldiers of the war lords. They had certain ideals. They were the servants of their nation, and their behavior toward the people, as they marched northward, was unique. Many people, among them foreign correspondents, were skeptical. They went to see for themselves and were surprised. A typical reaction is that of Herbert Owen Chapman, who wrote in his *The Chinese Revolution 1926–27:*

It was found that the Nationalist soldiers never looted. . . . The villagers and townspeople rubbed their eyes in amazement; the propaganda was true after all that these men were one with the common people. The people reciprocated this attitude with open cordiality, and it was not uncommon to see, a few hours after the occupation of a town or village, the soldiers fraternizing and chatting in a most friendly way with the shopkeepers and families on the street front.

Chapman went on to describe how the heart of the people was conquered even before the arrival of the soldiers.

An indigenous intelligence service was thus ready waiting to assist the incoming army; reliable guides were available whenever wanted: in some cases, days before the army arrived, towns and cities were taken possession of by little groups of enthusiasts, perhaps with the aid of a handful of local militia, in the name of the Nationalist Government.

This, as it is now understood, was fifth column activity or, as Sun Tse long ago described it in his *Art of War* with which Chiang Kai-shek was thoroughly familiar, "the employment of local spies." There is no doubt that Chiang's association with the Communists contributed to the perfection of that technique, since the effectiveness of their revolutionary methods was one reason for that association. Before the army advanced, its agents would be in close touch with the students and workers of the areas to be attacked, and these would so weaken the morale of the opposing soldiers that they sometimes refused to fight. That happened time and again in the case of the soldiers in Sun Chuan-fang's army in the Shanghai-Hangchow-Nanking area. Also the army of Chiang Kai-shek formed a solid front through their *lien tso* discipline; yet the battles fought in the area between Chinkiang and Nanking were among the bloodiest on record.

It is true that the propaganda arm of the revolutionary forces, under expert management, was an enormous contribution. As soon as the army entered a city, the agitation which had been underground before would come out openly with its slogans, strikes, and intimidations so that organized resistance to Chiang's army became all but impossible. But the Kuomintang army had to be wary of those war lords who would seemingly swear allegiance to the Kuomintang because they couldn't help themselves, but who really were bent on securing every benefit for themselves. That had happened before. With the Kuomintang technique now in use, this type of conversion could be resorted to only with great personal danger to the war lord himself. The

Kuomintang army allowed its political commissars to mingle with the "converted" army so freely that the actual control of that army virtually passed into Kuomintang hands, and the war lord had little chance of exacting the revenue from his territory which he sought by his "conversion." The control of the National Army over the situation, from both the military and popular point of view, was therefore quite complete. However, much more serious problems within the Kuomintang's own ranks had, in the meantime, come out into the open. The conflict with the Communists could no longer be concealed. Chiang Kai-shek, having won the necessary prestige, was prepared for it.

When Borodin and his accomplices arrived at the Wuhan area, where the new government was established, they were certain that the time had come for them to play their cards. It was useless for them to pretend that they could live side by side with the loyal Kuomintang members. They had their own purposes to serve, and these had to be realized as quickly as possible. They came out openly to establish a Red regime, with instructions from Moscow to do what had been done in Russia. In order to do that the power of Chiang Kai-shek had to be ruthlessly crippled.

When Borodin secured virtual control of Hankow, the first thing that he did was to gain a firm grip on the masses, including the students and workers of the area, whom he shrewdly utilized. The work was entrusted to Chen Kung-po (now serving the Japanese as an official of the puppet government of Nanking), who soon struck terror into the hearts of the merchant and banking classes because, as representatives of the bourgeois classes, these obviously could not exist in the new regime. A general strike was called for November 27. The foreign population, who were classed among the imperialists, fared just as badly. The attack was concentrated on the British as being the most important of the imperialists, and the fact that there were British concessions both at Hankow and at Kiukiang (less than a hundred and fifty miles down the Yangtze River) was sufficient incentive to give rise to popular demonstrations. The areas were entered on January 3, 1927. The British Minister, Sir Miles Lampson (now Lord Lampson, British Ambassador in Cairo), who proved later on to be one of the most popular diplomats in Nanking, was then only a new arrival, and the British Government immediately dispatched the counselor, Owen O'Malley, who left for Hankow from Peking on January 6.

On his arrival at Hankow O'Malley at once entered into negotiations with the fiery Minister of Foreign Affairs of the Hankow government, Eugene Chen. They lasted for some time, but by the end of the month a general agreement was ready for signature. On January 24, however, the decision of the British Government to dispatch troops to Shanghai in order to prevent any repetition of the Hankow situation became known in Hankow, and Eugene Chen immediately took this as reason for breaking off the negotiations. He issued a statement in which he declared that "the continued concentration of the British forces . . . as well as certain military information relating to the British plan of war operation in China, which has now come to the knowledge of the Nationalist Government, make it impossible for the Nationalist Government to continue to view the British concentrations at Shanghai except as an act of coercion directed against Chinese nationalism. To sign any agreement in these circumstances would be tantamount to signing under duress of force."

Negotiations were resumed after some delay, and on February 19 and March 2 agreements were signed whereby the administration of the British Concessions at Hankow and Kiukiang was handed over to the Chinese authorities. While the retrocession was carried out under pressure from the Communists, news about the signing of the agreements was favorably received by the populace.

Another form of activity to which the Communists directed a large part of their energy was toward the suppression of the Christian movement in China. The anti-Christian movement began as part of the emergence of nationalism after the May 4 incident of 1919. In 1922 the World's Students Christian Federation was held at Peking. That was an occasion for a general movement against Christianity. Among the reasons advanced as to why the spread of Christianity must be checked were that it "is the forerunner of imperialism and foreign exploitation" and that it "develops a servile attitude toward foreigners." Unfortunately there was some historical truth behind that attitude, and the visit of John Dewey and Bertrand Russell helped to spread the anti-Christian movement. When the Communists came along to preach their gospel against Christianity, which they considered as "opium for the people," they found fertile ground in which the seeds had already been sown. When the Hankow government was established, the Communists had complete freedom in their war against religion.

Control of the masses, war against imperialism, war against religion—the program was complete for the establishment of the Communist regime. For the days near the end of 1926 and the beginning of 1927 were critical not only for China but for the whole of the Trotsky movement. As an eyewitness expressed it: "In its spirit, at least, if not in its accomplishment, it [Hankow] was the world of Lenin."[1]

The city of Hankow was then the mecca of men and women of all nationalities whose hopes rested on the outcome of the Third Internationale. French, German, American, British, Hindu, Turkish—everyone ranging from pink to crimson was interested in the outcome of the exciting experiment that was being tried on Chinese soil. It had been tried elsewhere and had failed. Whether in Germany, Austria, Hungary, or England, the results had all been the same. Owing to a combination of circumstances, the Communist revolutions in those countries made no headway. China was going to be the last experiment on an impressive scale. As Lenin said himself: "Today China is seething, and it is our duty to keep the pot boiling." His followers had already put in four years of unremitting labor, and the results were encouraging. Their influence extended all the way from Canton to the heart of China. If they succeeded it meant not only a new Soviet state but also a triumph for the followers of the Third Internationale in Moscow, who desired a world revolution, and a triumph over Joseph Stalin, whose primary interest was in concentrating power in Soviet Russia itself. They did not succeed, however, because foreign gunboats were in the river to protect foreign interests as soon as they were threatened, and more particularly because Chiang Kai-shek was ready to challenge the Communists.

The excesses in which the Bolsheviks indulged were causing unfavorable reaction everywhere. The Kuomintang was rapidly swinging to the support of Chiang Kai-shek. The people could no longer tolerate the tyranny of a foreigner, be he Bolshevik or otherwise. Reason and the national instincts of the Chinese race were beginning to assert themselves in support of Chiang Kai-shek.

Leon Trotsky's testimony at that time is quite revealing:

> The epigone's leadership in China trampled on all the traditions of Bolshevism. The Chinese Communist party was forced against its will to join the bourgeois Kuomintang party and submit to its military discipline. The creating of Soviets was forbidden. The Communists were advised to hold the agrarian revolution in check, and to abstain from arousing the workers without the permission of the bourgeoisie. Long before Chiang

[1] Vincent Sheean, *Personal History*, p. 231.

Kai-shek crushed the Shanghai workers and concentrated the power in the hands of a military clique, we issued warnings that such a consequence was inevitable. Since 1925, I had demanded the withdrawal of the Communists from the Kuomintang. The policy of Stalin and Bukharin not only prepared for and facilitated the crushing of the revolution but, with the help of reprisals by the state apparatus, shielded the counter-revolutionary work of Chiang Kai-shek from our criticisms. In April 1927, at the party meeting in the Hall of Columns, Stalin defended the policy of coalition with Chiang Kai-shek and called for confidence in him. Five or six days later, Chiang Kai-shek drowned the Shanghai workers and the Communist party in blood.

A wave of excitement swept over the party. The opposition raised its head, and disregarding all rules of "conspiratzia"—and at the same time, in Moscow, we were already obliged to defend the Chinese workers against Chiang Kai-shek by using the methods of "conspiratzia"—the oppositionists came to me by scores in the offices of the Chief Concessions Committee. Many younger comrades thought the patent bankruptcy of Stalin's policy was bound to bring the triumph of the opposition nearer. During the first days of the coup d'état by Chiang Kai-shek, I was obliged to pour many a bucket of cold water over the hot heads of my young friends—and over some not so young. I tried to show them that the opposition could not rise on the defeat of the Chinese revolution. The fact that our forecast had proved correct might attract one thousand, five thousand, or even ten thousand new supporters to us. But for the millions, the significant thing was not our forecast, but the fact of the crushing of the Chinese proletariat. After the defeat of the German revolution in 1923, after the breakdown of the English general strike in 1925, the new disaster in China would only intensify the disappointment of the masses in the international revolution. *And it was this disappointment that served as the chief psychological source for Stalin's policy of national reformism.*

In a very short time, it was apparent that as a faction we had undoubtedly gained in strength—that is to say, we had grown more united intellectually, and stronger in numbers. But the umbilical cord that connected us with power was cut by the sword of Chiang Kai-shek. *His finally discredited Russian ally, Stalin, now had only to complete the crushing of the Shanghai workers by routing the opposition within the party.*[2] (Italics mine.)

I wonder if one is warranted in drawing the conclusion from this account that there is something like a causal relationship between the vigorous policy of Chiang Kai-shek then and the position of Joseph Stalin today?

[2] Leon Trotsky, *My Life* (Charles Scribner's Sons, 1930), pp. 529–30.

In the meantime, while the Communists, under the dictatorship of Borodin, were busy consolidating their position in the Yangtze area and attempting to establish a Red regime in China, Chiang was going straight ahead with his military campaigns down the river. He had moved his headquarters to Nanchang, some two hundred miles to the southeast of Hankow. If he had been surrounded in Hankow, there is no telling what would have happened to him. It is probable that some attempt on his life would have been made, as it was in March of 1926. But as it happened, all that the Communists could do was to cause him embarrassment and discredit the work which he was doing. They called him names: he was "counter-revolutionary," "traitor," "a new militarist," "worse than the worst type of war lord." They "expelled" him from their Kuomintang and drew up a lengthy document charging him with twelve unpardonable sins and ending with the grandiloquent epilogue that "whereas Chiang Kai-shek is found guilty of massacre of the people and oppression of the party, and whereas he deliberately engages himself in reactionary acts and his crimes and outrages are so obvious, the mandate is hereby issued that the Central Executive Committee has adopted a resolution that Chiang shall be expelled from the party and dismissed from all his posts," etc.

Chiang Kai-shek pushed on with his military schemes as vigorously as ever. By the first three months of 1927 he had occupied all of the important cities within the triangle of Shanghai, Nanking, and Hangchow. But far as these cities were from the Wuhan area, the Communists had spread their influence in them, so that Chiang could occupy them only under the most trying circumstances.

For the capture of these cities in Kiangsu and Chekiang provinces Chiang had to rely on two loyal supporters in the persons of Ho Ying-chin and Pai Chung-hsi, both of whom remain today among his most important military aides. Marching along with the soldiers of these two men were Cheng Chien and his soldiers. Cheng was a man of pronounced Communist sympathies who was intensely jealous of Chiang's rapid rise to power. While the troops of Ho Ying-chin and Pai Chung-hsi were coming up from Chekiang, Chang Chien rushed into Nanking with his men, arriving on March 24. With a thoroughness that had every indication of being a well-conceived plot he systematically looted and plundered the city. He received instructions from his Communist masters to commit outrages against the foreign communities, with the result that a number of foreigners were killed, among them some Americans. This has become known as the Nanking Incident. Subsequent investigations fully established that the plot was engineered to cause serious international complications for Chiang Kai-shek.

Chiang immediately rushed down to Shanghai in his gunboat and prevented the same thing from taking place in that city where the consequences would, of course, have been far more serious. There the foreign population was nervous, excited, and irritable. Without anyone knowing of his whereabouts Chiang suddenly appeared on the scene. Though he had only some three thousand soldiers, he had the situation completely under control. What was so impressive was that he could have co-operated with the foreign forces, but did not. He had to be consistent: the stationing of foreign forces on Chinese soil was against the policy of the Kuomintang. But the most unusual thing Chiang did was to declare openly that he assumed full responsibility for what had happened in Nanking and that he was having an investigation made so that those who committed the crime would be punished. He then made a statement in which he assured the foreign population that it was the settled policy of his government not to use force or violence in any form to effect changes in the foreign settlement, though he was determined to secure international equality for China. "Any nation," he added, "that is prepared and willing to treat us as an equal is our friend, and as such we are willing to work with it and associate ourselves with it even though it has been previously a source of oppression for us."

Chiang Kai-shek then went ahead, with the co-operation of Shanghai's secret societies, to suppress all Communist activities in the city and to dissolve the labor unions.

Hangchow, the last of the big cities within that area, was likewise ripe for Communist agitation, but when the Shanghai situation was settled so quickly, order in Hangchow was also soon established.

To give an example of what was then being done by the Communists to create disturbances, I can tell the following story. It was my father's habit to make periodic visits from Shanghai to the small village of Haiyen, not far from Hangchow. The tombs of my ancestors are all there, and it was my father's duty to "sweep" these tombs and to donate money for the upkeep of roads and bridges in the village. He went there in the early part of March when the Nationalist troops were just advancing toward the Shanghai area. I was myself spending my honeymoon among the hills and temples of Hangchow. One day, after our return to Shanghai, my mother told me that my father had been captured by the local riffraff. She had no political interest and knew nothing about Communism. All she said was that my father was branded as a member of the gentry and had been thrown into prison!

The difficulties were immediately apparent to me, and I knew I would have no easy time solving them. The train services were disrupted, so I hired a motorboat and hurried down to see what I could do. Upon my arrival I contacted the members of the family of a relative. They were all harmless scholars, but pallid with fear. I spoke with them, but they were afraid to describe to me what had happened. All they could say was that a group of irresponsible young men were in control of the village, and that they were going to imprison my father permanently for being a rich man. The word "rich" was, I thought, inappropriate to describe my father, but it is true that he had more wealth than the average villager through long years of honorable devotion to a worthy industry. So I concluded immediately that the youngsters were holding him for ransom. The knowledge of my presence was soon spread to them, and representatives were sent to negotiate with me for fantastic sums of money. I promised a small amount, and that brought me into the presence of my father, who was incarcerated in a temple. More demands came from various quarters, and I knew that it was impossible to satisfy all of them. In a fit of anger I had a few harsh words to say, and toward evening I was given to understand that they were preparing reprisals against me, that, like my father, I would be thrown into the prison. There was nothing that could be done about it then, so before daybreak I went aboard the motorboat and moved to another village some distance away and continued negotiations from there. It was only when the situation at Shanghai eased up that my father was released, none the worse for the experience.

The Shanghai-Hangchow area having been restored to normal conditions by Chiang Kai-shek, the militarists in the north began also to tighten their grip on the Communists. On April 6 the Peking police, under instructions from Chang Tso-lin, raided the Soviet Embassy, which, since its inception, had been known to be the center of Bolshevist activities. A number of Communists were captured and subsequently shot. From the material which was confiscated during the raid it was definitely established that Borodin had complete control of the Kuomintang in Hankow and proved "beyond all ques-

THE SPLIT

tion the complicity of the Soviet Government in the anti-foreign agitation and its continuous interference in China's civil war."[8] This material is most illuminating. There is excessive use of words like "repressive measures," "looting," "massacre," "agitation," "mob violence," etc. The effect of the publication of these documents was instantaneous. The people came to have full knowledge of the Soviet conspiracy, and the Kuomintang members who were supporting Borodin in Hankow became disillusioned.

As if these documents were not enough to incriminate the Communists, another incident occurred, this time in Hankow itself, which showed the hand of the Third Internationale in China and precipitated the downfall of Borodin. Sometime in June an Indian Communist, Manabendra Nath Roy, head of the Far Eastern Section of the Comintern, revealed in a casual conversation that the Third Internationale had a new program for China. It was contained in a series of instructions secretly sent to Borodin. They were:

1. Land in Hunan and Hupeh was to be confiscated by the peasants without any reference to the government, the peasants acting through the Communist party.

2. A new leadership was to be created within the Kuomintang, consisting entirely of Communist party members; the left wing of the Kuomintang was to be eliminated.

3. The Kuomintang organization was to be reconstructed along more radical lines so that, in due course, the Kuomintang as a party would disappear and the Communist party of China take its place.

4. A court was to be created consisting of persons with known reputations which was to judge counter-revolutionary military men and punish them for their opposition to the revolutionary activities of the Communist party.

5. Finally, an army was to be organized, drilled, and armed. This army was to consist of twenty thousand armed Communists and fifty thousand laborers and peasants of Hunan and Hupeh.

So the Kuomintang members in Hankow were in danger of being liquidated. Borodin was asked to explain himself and could not. Whereupon a meeting was held on July 13, 1927, declaring that Communism and the Communist party were outlawed from China. The days of Borodin became numbered. Movements were started for his expulsion from China, but before they could be put into effect Borodin fled overland to Russia. A year later, Professor Arthur W. Hol-

[8] *China Year Book*, 1928, p. 793.

combe of Harvard, saw Borodin in Moscow, "unhonored and without employment, a virtual prisoner in the Soviet capital." He is now the editor of a small paper in English, the Moscow *Daily News*.

Negotiations for a compromise between the members of the Kuomintang in Hankow and those in Nanking, where Chiang had established the government, were instantly opened, and it was thought that, since Borodin had left, Chiang Kai-shek should also resign. This idea was entirely agreeable to Chiang. He knew that his triumph was so complete that he had become indispensable to the country and that he would soon be called back. In the meantime, he saw the Communist edifice collapse like a house of cards. Everyone hastened to declare himself against Borodin and the Communists. Even so pronounced a sympathizer as Hsu Chien, who had been Borodin's principal associate, lost little time in joining the anti-Communist camp.

Chiang Kai-shek resigned as commander in chief of the Nationalist Army on August 12, 1927, to go back to the quiet, rustic scenes of his boyhood at Chikow. Like Washington, who wanted to be "a private citizen on the banks of the Potomac... free from the bustle of a camp and the busy scenes of public life," Chiang retired to his mountain home surrounded by the peace and tranquillity of the Buddhist temples. But before he left, he issued a statement that summarized the issues so clearly that parts of it should be quoted:

As a servant of the Kuomintang party and the republic I have been in command of the Northern Punitive Expedition launched over a year ago. Not being able to achieve as yet my object of subjugating the northern stronghold of the military autocrats, I am aggrieved to see around me signs of a split, endangering both the party and the nation. The people are overwhelmed with sorrow because in the territory brought under the revolutionary banner there has been dissension and because, while all professed devotion to the San Min Principles, the followers of the Great Leader appear to separate themselves into two camps. To what shall we attribute the sufferings of the people and the delayed execution of our great plans if not to the sinister designs of the Communists who have indulged in the intrigues of causing dissension in the Kuomintang fold? ... I, therefore, appeal to all my fellow countrymen, my fellow members of the Kuomintang, and my colleagues to give heed to the reasons for my retirement as set forth in the present manifesto.

Being a man of no scholarly attainments, but fortunate enough to have been taught by Dr. Sun Yat-sen, I have made two resolutions which I will never abandon, namely: 1. I acknowledge that the party is above everything, and when the interests of the party are at stake each and every member of the party should follow the principles of the party without heeding his personal feelings and private interests. 2. I hold that the highest duty of a member of the party is to consolidate the foundation of the party at all costs, and for this reason I shall mobilize all available resources for the purpose of suppressing all who resort to clever ruses and hypocritical methods to shake the foundation of our party and pollute our party principles—in a word, all those who attempt to make the Kuomintang a dead party without a soul.... If I find that China's sovereignty is impaired and that the party is being ruined as had been done by the Communists, I expect every member, in spite of minor differences of opinion, to live up to his duty of defending the party. This is why I have been unyielding on one point, namely, I would not rest until I saw effected the suppression of the Communists who were scheming to ruin our party.

The manifesto went on to describe the revolt of Chen Chiung-ming and Chiang's success in bringing Kwangtung, "the original cradle of the revolution," back to normal conditions.

Contrary to expectations, the Communists were exceedingly crafty. When they perceived that the unification of Kwangtung would pave the way for the success of the revolution they wanted to give the first knockout blow in order to fulfill their plunderous desires. This tells why they attempted the coup d'état on March 20, 1926. While seeking to promote the welfare of the party and country, I felt that I was obliged to disclose the evil plot, and by sheer quick action the incident passed off with smoothness. I admitted my sense of neglect and accused myself before the Central Executive Committee, which passed a resolution of confidence in me. It was under these circumstances that I was appointed to the dual post of commander in chief of the revolutionary army and the commander of the Northern Punitive Expedition. I received the appointments with diffidence, although I felt that my duty was to obey the party. If the revolution did not make any headway, so I reasoned, the danger of falling into the snares of the Communists was imminent, and the people might get confused over the San Min Principles. I went ahead, regardless of the consequences.

Thanks to the uplifting influence of our principles, and thanks to the loyalty of our comrades, we succeeded in the brief space of several months to bring into the Kuomintang fold the whole provinces of Hunan, Hupeh, Kiangsi, and Fukien.... But the Communists, getting jealous of the rapid progress of the people's revolution and acting under the secret orders of Borodin, took advantage of my absence in Nanchang and manufactured for the Wuhan district a number of slogans, including those of "military dictatorship" and "tyranny," all seeking to overthrow me directly and to undermine the people's revolution indirectly. There are certain fellow members in the party and army who have been misled by these falsehoods and have attached credence to them owing to the deceptive view created for them.

Chiang then went on to explain the reasons why he was anti-Communist.

For several years I have been credited with advocating the policy of befriending Russia and admitting the Communists. When I came back from Russia after a tour of inspection, I had very clear-cut views as to the essential differences between the two policies. . . . I was unable to convert the learned doctor to these views, but I was anxious to know his. He said, "China has no room for the coexistence of Communism and the Kuomintang. We have to admit the Communists and convert them, and the San Min Principles will serve as a good melting pot." This is more than enough to show that in admitting the Communists into the Kuomintang fold Dr. Sun never intended to do so at the expense of injuring his party. Moreover, the Chinese Communists tried to outdo the Russians in their plots and conspiracies. What was the result? By professing to be Kuomintang members in a halfhearted fashion and adopting deceptive methods they have tried to disorganize our military and party affairs besides calling a halt to the whole expedition. The intriguers would not rest until they could sap the vitality of our party. The fact that I am a Kuomintang man makes it impossible for me to look on, and I am firmly resolved to wage war on the Communists. . . . From first to last, all I demand is: 1. The expulsion of Borodin from China; and, 2, non-cooperation with the Communists. Since Borodin has been expelled from China and is now on his way to his country, and since the Wuhan authorities as well as those in Kiangsi and Hunan have undertaken on their own accord to oust the Communists, there need be no further proof that the execution of my views is vital to the existence of our party and nation. . . .

All that I request of my fellow party members is that they should present a united front and accomplish the twofold aim of the revolution. Do not for a moment let the tottering militarists and intriguing Communists take advantage of our own weaknesses and survive through them. And it is with the utmost sincerity that I hereby state what I expect of all my comrades:

1. I wish that members of both factions would hereafter turn a deaf ear to all ill-prompted words, that they would sink their differences and cast away their spirit of mutual suspicion. I wish that the Wuhan comrades would come to Nanking and jointly direct the future of our party. If I have been looked upon as the cause of the split in the party, I am willing, as I have repeatedly stated here, to make any sacrifices for the

sake of the Kuomintang; and if any punishment is needed for my crime in order to add to the solidarity of our party, I will regard whatever punishment is meted out to me as a mark of unusual honor.

2. I wish that all my comrades under arms who are now stationed in Hunan, Hupeh, and Kiangsi would immediately advance northward and concentrate along the Tsinpu Railway in our drive toward Peking. Such has always been our aim since the beginning of the expedition, and I believe that we would have reached our goal had it not been for the intrigue of the Communists. . . .

3. I hope that the authorities in Hunan, Hupeh, and Kiangsi will effect a thorough "cleansing" of the party. The intrigues of the Communists are well known to us. The fact that those who have been under their influences are now alive to their danger is an indication that the mind of our nation is still sound. Though I do not believe the report that the present anti-Communist campaign in Wuhan is not made in sincerity, nevertheless, in view of the unheard-of sufferings the people in Wuhan have gone through under the Communist regime, it is not uncalled for that a pledge should be given by the authorities that no effort will be spared to prevent Communism from being revived in the region where it once reigned supreme.

These are the three things I have piously prayed for and upon which I have placed my hopes. . . . Though I do not know of any better remedy for the situation, I sincerely believe that if the three points mentioned above are carried out, nothing will be able to threaten our unity. And if all the Nationalist forces are united, the northern militarists will not be our equals on the field; and when the entire nation is united, imperialism will fall because of its very nature. The overthrow of imperialism and militarism has always been my aim. There is nothing more that I seek. I take upon myself all the blame for what has happened and hereby tender my resignation. But I shall still, as a member of the party, do all I can for its interests and, as an ordinary citizen, do all I can to promote the welfare of my country. . . .

And so Chiang Kai-shek retired to a Buddhist temple perched on one of the loveliest mountains in the neighborhood of his village. He was tired, and he needed a rest. And there is nothing in the world that can offer so effective a cure to the soul and body of a tired person as one of those ancient Chinese temples, surrounded by the tall pines and the sparkling waterfalls. In the meantime, the news of his resignation and retirement was received with dismay by his people. How could he leave the country in this predicament? There were still grave dangers ahead, and Chiang had now become the only man in the country who could establish order and bring peace.

A constant stream of visitors came up the slopes of the mountain to the temple. These were trusted friends who saw in Chiang the symbol of the orderly development of a great and unified China. Among them was T. V. Soong who later was to become Chiang's brother-in-law. Newspapermen and journalists, especially those from abroad, journeyed to see Chiang, wanting to know what he was thinking about and doing in a secluded Buddhist temple. In his simple, affable way Chiang received them all, appearing before them in the traditional gown of the Chinese scholar. He was straight and gaunt, his eyes bright and stern, his features clear-cut and finely chiseled. He welcomed them with a friendly smile and invited them to take their seats before a tray of luscious grapes, with the gorgeous panorama of the mountains in front of them.

"Are you planning to take a trip abroad, General?" queried the journalists.

"Yes, I should like to observe the customs of the great nations among which China must one day take her rightful place."

"And where do you propose to go?" was the next query.

"I should like very much to go to America. I have heard so much of the great industrial and economic development of that great land and I wish to see things for myself."

"And what is going to be the future of China—a republic, or is she likely to be socialistic?"

"Why, of course, China must develop along republican lines," Chiang replied.

There was a moment's relaxation while the journalists smoked and talked leisurely. But the general didn't smoke; neither did he drink. When the conversation was resumed, the subject drifted to America again.

"The Chinese people have turned from the conservative friendship of America and accepted the offers from Russia. There were reasons, of course, which you all know. But Russia has now betrayed us, and we must look to America as our only real friend among the nations. I hope that America will reciprocate that friendship." At which the journalists assured him that she would.

"Yes," continued the general, "to America first, as the people there are so sympathetic, and then to Europe and elsewhere. But it is all so indefinite, of course." Much as he wanted to go abroad, however, Chiang knew that he was too deeply involved with the revolution. As he admitted to the journalists: "I am too much a part of it, it is too much a part of me, for me to get out for all time." No, he could not get out even for a short time.

25

Marriage

IT WAS NOT YET TIME for a man of forty, already the undoubted strong man of China, to withdraw from public life. Chiang's life up in the Buddhist temple in Ningpo was anything but mild and peaceful. There were letters, telegrams, and a constant stream of callers to discuss the political situation with him. But it was just as well that he had resigned, for it gave him the opportunity to concentrate on another matter, more personal and nearer to his heart. He was, in fact, planning the greatest conquest of his life. He must finish this job before he went back to the turmoils of the political scene.

The beauty and charm of Mme. Chiang Kai-shek have now become so real and close to the American public, as the result of her recent trip to the United States (November 1942–June 1943), that it is superfluous to describe them. At any rate, we can quite understand why Chiang Kai-shek, during this short period of retirement from public life, wanted to complete the work which he had begun in 1922. It was five years before that he had met Miss Soong Mei-ling at Canton, and then and there a resolution had been born. But there were obstacles, as there are obstacles in the realization of every great human desire. The two people were brought up in different environments, and there were prejudices among the members of the families. It took time to dissolve these prejudices. If, as it was said, Trotsky gave him the advice that patience and activity were essential to a revolutionist, Chiang must have assumed that they were equally essential for matters of the heart. One of the most difficult obstacles to overcome was the old mother of Miss Soong, who could not regard with equanimity the intentions of her youngest daughter to marry a man who did not hold her Christian beliefs. In order to allow the matter to rest and perhaps be forgotten, Mrs. Soong went off to Japan to pass the summer. So August and September of 1927 were two busy months for Chiang. There was a good deal to be done, and before the month of September had expired Miss Soong was able to announce, at a dinner that she gave for some of her intimate friends, that she was going to marry the hero of the day, that she was determined to go ahead with the plans even though all the obstacles had not been overcome. "I sincerely love the great general," she was reported to have said, and the words were immediately flashed ten thousand miles to the office of the Associated Press in New York. The New York *Times* correspondent was not going to be outdone and followed four days later with a colorful message: "The retired Nationalist leader returned to Shanghai from Ningpo yesterday with Cupid, not Mars, as the patron deity."

One stumbling block that Chiang had to remove was the gossip that he was already married and that he had been friendly with other women. One young lady who sailed from Shanghai at about that time, on arriving at San Francisco, let it be known that she was Chiang's wife. That was, as it was soon learned, a trick played on Chiang by his political enemies. It was true that he had been married, according to the custom of his village, when he was quite young, but a divorce had been secured in 1921. As regards the other women, the gossip was spread merely to embarrass Chiang and Miss Soong.

Not so easy to overcome was the objection of Miss Soong's mother. She had gone to Japan, so the only thing the lovers could do was to go there too and see her. They went separately. Chiang explained to the old lady and promised her that, since the matter of religious belief was a vital question, he would consider it carefully. Mrs. Soong's heart finally softened, and by the time they all returned to Shanghai the last obstacle had been removed.

The marriage took place on December 1, 1927. The place was the Majestic Hotel, one of the famous landmarks of Shanghai, which has since disappeared. The ceremony was divided into two parts, apparently one of the conditions decided upon in Japan with the old lady. The first part was Christian and took place in the private residence of the Soong family. It was an intimate affair and attended only by members of the families and their very close friends. The second part was open to more than a thousand invited guests and conformed with the usual type of wedding in present-day China. Marriage in China is not a religious affair. It would be fantastic to think of it taking place in a Buddhist temple. It has never been done, though there is no reason why it shouldn't. It is a purely civil ceremony, although not infrequently the departed ancestors would be informed that a new member had come into the family. The old elaborate customs have now been generally discarded. The modern wedding is much simpler, with the master of ceremonies announcing the items from a prepared program. During the Chiang-Soong marriage the gentleman who officiated was Tsai Yuan-pei, an old and much respected Kuomintang member, Hanlin scholar, and chancellor for many years of the Peking National University, which had been the center of all kinds of social, political, and intellectual movements since 1919. Standing on a platform and surrounded by the best man and the bridesmaids, the old scholar read the formal wedding address. When that was done, the master of ceremonies again read from the prepared program: "Now the bridegroom and the bride will bow once to one another"—which was accordingly done. "Now the bridegroom and the bride will bow once to the guests." Another part of the program was the placing of the seals on the marriage certificate.

The hall was profusely decorated with flowers and scrolls in red with golden characters wishing the newly wedded couple the best things in life. "A hundred years of happy union" was one of the most popular sentiments, and they will "live like a pair of mandarin ducks" —birds which are proverbially known to be absolutely devoted and inseparable. In addition to these good wishes and floral decorations there was a portrait of Sun Yat-sen flanked by the flags of the Kuomintang party and the government. To the portrait the bride and groom bowed three times as a mark of deep respect.

It is customary also, during these modern marriage ceremonies, to have the bride and bridegroom make speeches and to have the guests respond. The guests usually take this opportunity to display their sense of humor, for a Chinese wedding is frequently a hilarious affair, with humor sometimes as broad as that of Rabelais. The bridegroom, when the guests insist upon his making a speech, probably mumbles a few words. But it all depends upon his oratorical talents. I have known bridegrooms to stand up and speak for half an hour and solemnly tell the audience that, if he didn't marry, the country would all but perish! He would give reasons for his marriage, "politically, economically, socially, educationally, psychologically," etc. If the bridegroom, as in the case of Chiang Kai-shek, was the most powerful man in China, such an address would indeed be appropriate, but to have all bridegrooms do that would mean giving China more saviors than she could ever use.

Chiang Kai-shek did not speak during the wedding. But he gave out a statement called "Our Day" which was published the next morning in the papers. It was an expression of their deep joy. Indeed it was the happiest day of his life. It was a pledge that through their devotion to one another they would contribute all they had to the cause of the revolution.

They did not have much of a honeymoon. During the months when the marriage was being planned and Chiang had been away from the government, the continuation of the military expedition against the war lords of the north had, of course, been impossible. More than that, the militarists took that opportunity to fight back and tried to regain the position they had lost. The situation grew critical, and since Chiang was the only person who could handle it successfully, requests came to him thick and fast that he resume his work as commander in chief of the revolutionary army to complete the work which he had so well begun. Chiang had planned to go abroad as soon as he resigned in August. He had even said that he would stay away for five years, but it now became clear that he could not stay away for even five weeks, and preparations were made at once for the newly married couple to proceed to Nanking, where the new capital of the government had just been established and important decisions were waiting to be made.

For the bride to go along would ordinarily have been the most natural thing for her to do. But it was not so in that case because Nanking, though it had become the capital of the new China according to Sun Yat-sen's wishes, was in those days a medieval village without any of the comforts of modern life to which the modern woman in China had become accustomed. Sun chose this city as the new capital for very good reasons. It was an expression of nationalism, for Nanking was the capital of the first Emperor of the Ming Dynasty, which was exclusively a Chinese dynasty. The removal to Peking took place later, in the time of Yung Lu. Sun always thought that he was continuing the work of that great Emperor whose tomb today remains one of the interesting landmarks just outside of the city. Nanking must have known days of great glory and splendor. Its city wall is an impressive structure, longer and higher than any city wall in the world. But all that did not make it a comfortable city to live in for those accustomed to modern conveniences. The bride had spent many long years of her early girlhood in the United States, especially in the Southern states. Her college days were spent in Wellesley, Massachusetts. Upon her return to China, as a mature young lady, she spent most of her time in large cities like Shanghai, Tientsin, Hong Kong, or Canton, where she first met Chiang Kai-shek. That was why residing in Nanking after her marriage was a novelty in those days, but Mei-ling loved every moment of her new life.

There are different types of people in China, as there are different types of cities in this great period of transformation from a medieval to a modern country. These differences are, in fact, sometimes even more marked in the women than in the men. Consider for a moment the Chinese woman whose mind has been shaped and molded by the old exclusively Chinese influences and the woman who is the product of modern training, and you have two types who are as wide apart from one another as, let us say, Peiping and New York. There are these two extreme types, and in between there are any number of nuances as a result of an interplay of various influences.

The old type of Chinese women, of whom there are still many, have a poise and quiet dignity all their own. Their minds have developed along classical lines. The best of Chinese art, poetry, literature, with their accompanying attitude toward life—and the best is of exquisite beauty and refinement—has been woven into the texture of their every movement and speech. These women speak no foreign languages and know little or nothing about foreign ways. They have, therefore, a harmony of their own, complete, self-contained, and definite.

Then there is the modern type of Chinese women who have become quite common within the last generation. They have naturally grown with the increasing influence of Western thought and ways of living. They are largely confined to the treaty ports, they go to schools which are mostly run by missionaries who, in days past, though not so much now, were interested in making the young ladies realize that to become modern meant to discard everything Chinese and adopt foreign ways as foreign ways could be learned in Shanghai and the other treaty ports.

Between these two extreme types there are other kinds of Chinese women who are nearer to one type or the other, depending upon the training they have received and the influences that have molded their minds. But there is one specific type that is yet rare, but which will probably grow in numbers when national consciousness and pride of race re-establish themselves. Chiang Kai-shek's program of national reconstruction includes psychological reconstruction as its most important factor, without which other kinds of reconstruction are of little value. And the more the present generation of women become conscious of the value of their own cultural legacy, while at the same time absorbing the best of modern life and enlarging the sphere of their contacts, the more this type of womanhood will blossom forth with beauty and value to their country. It is fair to say that Mme. Chiang Kai-shek, by being what she is and doing the work she is doing, is helping to evolve this type of womanhood more effectively than all other factors combined.

If to be modern means "knowing the best that has been said and thought" in European and American culture, itself a difficult task, it is clearly not enough for the Chinese woman. For she must integrate that acquisition with her own cultural background. There must be a synthesis and a harmony from which a rich and varied personality can develop. The charm of Mme. Chiang Kai-shek, of a quality that will "charm the birds off the trees," as Martha Gellhorn so aptly said, but above all, her supreme vitality and sense of devotion to her husband and to the nation are all attributes of a rich personality that has been observed by people everywhere.

There is, of course, such a thing as a personality *sui generis* which is part of one's natural endowments and cannot be easily accounted for by any specific influences. Nevertheless, in the case of Mme. Chiang, her variety has become accentuated through a number of circumstances. Identity with the life of an extraordinary man, as in the case of her own sister, Mme. Sun Yat-sen, has undoubtedly brought radical changes. Her own exalted position has brought great responsibilities and contacts with all manner of people whom she must try to understand. That has brought sympathy, a breadth of view, and a generous attitude toward life which other women, less privileged, can develop only with difficulty. But more than anything else, she has steeped herself in the lore of ancient Chinese wisdom from which she has constantly drawn abundant resources.

This is one aspect of her life which has not been stressed and which, of course, is not likely to be known fully by foreign journalists. When, as Miss Soong Mei-ling, she came back to China, a full-grown young lady, after a prolonged stay in the United States, her mental equipment was almost completely American. The average Chinese girl would be contented with that and stop there. But Miss Soong was not an average girl. She knew that as a Chinese girl she had deficiencies in not knowing her own country as well as she knew America. She was determined to remove these deficiencies. And for the next few years she hired a tutor to guide her through the riches of Chinese literature. She found a new world of beauty. Her soul began to grow roots into her true milieu. The universe began to expand in front of her, and in that universe was a harmonious blending of the knowledge of two cultures.

That was why, when she went to Nanking as a bride, she had no difficulty in adapting herself to the new environment, even though she was denied the comforts she had known in her daily life in Shanghai and elsewhere. For, after all, personal habits are a matter of adaptation. They were much too unimportant to hamper her in her work as wife and companion to the unifier and creator of a new China. She took personal interest in every step which was being taken to convert Nanking into a modern metropolis.

Chiang Kai-shek was busy planning the details of the new government and directing his attention to the completion of the Northern Expedition, which had been suspended since the autumn of 1927. His bride was his chief adviser and counselor, but she had also her own work to perform. There were orphans and widows left behind by the soldiers who had sacrificed their lives for the ideals of Sun Yat-sen. They had to be taken care of, and very soon outside of the walls of Nanking, with the Sun Yat-sen mausoleum overlooking it, there grew up a school covering acres of ground which was devoted to the education of these youngsters. Clean, orderly, and efficiently managed, the school was the first expression, on a reasonably large scale, of Mme. Chiang's ability as an administrator. She took an interest also in the cadets who came to Nanking to await instructions for their next assignment. For these she provided wholesome amusements. Her duties were many and heavy, and there was but little relaxation. An occasional trip to Shanghai, walks among the new pines that were rapidly covering the hillside outside of Nanking, and sulphur baths in the Tangshan hot springs which were an hour's drive from the city—these were about all the relaxation there was. Nevertheless, the marriage of Chiang Kai-shek and Soong Mei-ling has been a happy union in which the qualities of the one complement those of the other.

There is nothing that they do not share together. Even when, a few years later, Chiang Kai-shek was called upon to quell a rebellion in Fukien Province and suppress Communist activities in Kiangsi

Province, tasks which were most exacting and called for great physical endurance in the face of personal danger and hardships, Mme. Chiang accompanied her husband wherever he went. She has been capable of doing this not only because she has an abiding love for her soldier husband, but also because, though she knows its strength as well as its weaknesses, she has a deep love for her country.

As ample proof of the danger that has often been a part of her life when accompanying Chiang Kai-shek, Mme. Chiang describes "an incident which occurred at field headquarters in Kiangsi in the dead of night. Suddenly, we heard crack, crack, crack of several hundred shots from the direction of the city wall. What had happened? The general was up instantly, calling me to dress hurriedly. He ordered the secret service men to investigate. The shots became more frequent, more insistent. Shivering with cold, in the feeble candlelight I threw on my clothes and sorted out certain papers which must not fall into enemy hands. I kept these within reach to be burned if we had to leave the house. Then I took my revolver and sat down to wait for what might come. I heard my husband giving orders for all available guards to form a cordon so that we could shoot our way out if we were actually surrounded by the Communists. . . .

"After an hour reports came back that a portion of the enemy troops had staged a surprise attack under cover of darkness, knowing that only a few hundred sentries guarded the city wall. While we were in apparent danger I was not frightened. I had two things on my mind: the paper giving information of our troop movements and positions, and the determination, should I be taken captive, to shoot myself. I would prefer death to the fate of women who fall into the hands of bandits. But, fortunately, the attack was repelled, and we went back to sleep."

With all these hazards she was still able to enjoy life. Walking on New Year's Eve with her husband, they discovered a tree laden with white plum blossoms. "In Chinese literature the five petals of the winter plum portend the five blessings of joy, good luck, longevity, prosperity, and, (to us most desired of all), peace! The general carefully plucked a few branches and carried them home. When our evening candles were lighted, he presented them to me in a little bamboo basket—a New Year's gift. The plum blossoms had looked graceful and lovely on the tree, but massed in the basket by candlelight they took on an indescribable beauty, their shadows on the wall making clear, bold strokes like those of the great Ming artist, Pa-Ta Shan-Jen.

Generalissimo and Mme. Chiang Kai-shek emerging from their dugout in Chungking.

Perhaps you can see why I am willing to share the rigors of life at the front with my husband. He has the courage of the soldier and the sensitive soul of the poet."

In this beautiful passage we see the full expression of Mme. Chiang's Chinese instincts. Her training and education were in every sense modern and occidental, but her soul is anchored to the spiritual foundations of her own race. In her we have one of the finest expressions of the blending of cultures. We can understand why Wendell Willkie said that Mme. Chiang "is the only international celebrity whose personal attractiveness far exceeds her advance notices."

26

The Peking Drive and After

FROM THE TIME that the Yangtze delta was captured by Chiang Kai-shek in his Northern Expedition until the present day, the history of the Kuomintang becomes the history of China. But the history of the Kuomintang evolved from the personality of Chiang; so that one may well say that the history of Chiang is the modern history of China. The two become inseparable, and the biographer must resist the temptation to become a historian.

The principal events in the resumption of the military drive toward Peking in 1928, and what happened afterward in 1929-30 and immediately before Japan's attack on Manchuria must, however, be given. When Chiang Kai-shek returned to Nanking on January 6, 1928, a month and four days after his marriage with Miss Soong Mei-ling, he had three immediate problems to face. First, he must conclude the Northern Expedition. That meant that he must bring his soldiers into Peking.[1] Secondly, although the Communist party had been officially dissolved and Borodin had left China, Chiang was to learn that there was still much to be done before its poison could be entirely eliminated. The Communist movement went underground and spread first into central and afterward into northern China. In the course of its de-

[1] Peking, after the conclusion of the Northern Expedition, was restored to its old name, Peiping.

velopment it went through a number of changes itself, but it is nonetheless Communism, and as such it must be held in check by the Chinese Government. The problem remains to this day. Thirdly, the newly established government at Nanking had to be strengthened so that it would lose no time in carrying out Sun Yat-sen's political platform, especially in the field of foreign policy.

When Chiang Kai-shek resigned in August 1927, military activities under the Kuomintang could make no further progress. That was, as we saw, the best time for the northern militarists to stage a comeback. Sun Chuan-fang immediately made the most of the opportunity and regained his lost territory as far south as Pukow, which is just across the river from Nanking. In time he even crossed the river and threatened Nanking itself. Fortunately he was driven back, and with the help of Feng Yu-hsiang, the well-known "Christian general," Sun Chuan-fang continued to retreat northward. The military position of Feng was a curious one at the time. He knew that it was strategically sound. His movements one way or the other were bound to have important results. He personally led his army across the Gobi Desert through some of the poorest and most barren parts of northwest China—Kansu, Shensi, and then down into Honan, where he came into control of the only railway that runs from the west on the south side of the Yellow River to connect with the trunk line that goes up north to Peking. He could have come to some agreement with the Hankow Communists, but chose to throw in his lot with Chiang Kai-shek and the right-wing Kuomintang at Nanking. At that juncture his assistance to Nanking against Sun Chuan-fang became an important factor.

But there were other difficulties. In October, when Chiang was in Japan visiting his prospective mother-in-law, Tang Sheng-chih, whom the Communists once tried to build up to take the place of Chiang, caused trouble in the neighborhood of Hankow. The uprising was of short duration, and Tang ultimately left the country. He was defeated by Pai Chung-hsi and Li Tsung-jen, powerful Kwangsi leaders who today continue to co-operate closely with the government at Chungking. There was also trouble at Canton, where an attempt was made to set up an independent government. It was made by the present puppet in Nanking, Wang Ching-wei, with the military assistance of Chang Fa-kwei.

Within the Kuomintang party itself, after the expulsion of the Communists, all the elements made an honest effort to come together.

The so-called Western Hills Conference group, which was implacably opposed to the Communists even when Sun Yat-sen was close to them, also came in. But the fact remained that it was difficult to harmonize the different shades of opinion, and to that end one conference after another was held. The names of these conferences are many and are confusing to those unfamiliar with Chinese history. There were plenary sessions, conferences of the Central Executive Committee, conferences of the Central Supervisory Committee, and party congresses, each of which issued statements and manifestoes that were important, but into which we need not go.

When Chiang Kai-shek returned to Shanghai from Japan on November 10, 1927, the atmosphere immediately changed. He was now the recognized leader of the party and was the only person who could attempt the task of reconciling the differences within the party. His residence in Shanghai became the headquarters of parleys and meetings which came to be considered the Preliminary Conference of the Fourth Plenary Session of the Central Executive Committee.

When Chiang Kai-shek arrived in Nanking on January 4, 1928, he was at once elected commander in chief of the Nationalist forces and concurrently chairman of the Military Council. This was a significant move. It combined all the military power in one person and overruled the motion that had previously been adopted that the two posts should be kept separate. That motion was, of course, speedily abolished. On the acceptance of these responsibilities, Chiang issued a statement in which he said that he would personally resume and direct the Northern Expedition and suppress all Communist activities. "When the Northern Expedition shall have been completed, I shall immediately tender my resignation with the central authorities so as to make amends for any evasion of duty last year"—that is, since August of the previous year when he was making preparations for his marriage.

It is customary in Chinese statements of this sort to speak of one's shortcomings and of resignation. It is not only being necessarily humble and modest, but it is also a good policy to speak much less of what one anticipates and to "allow room for retreat." If one comes out with very sanguine expectations and makes them public, one is liable to be ridiculed if the actual accomplishments do not measure up to these expectations. It is best to speak less and accomplish more.

By the early days of February the Fourth Plenary Session, though much delayed, was in session, and a manifesto was issued on its conclusion. For the first time since Sun Yat-sen's contact with the Russians, it was openly stated that China had no use for Soviet co-operation, and all arrangements and understandings previously made with the Soviet regime were considered null and void. China's foreign policy was to be based exclusively on Sun Yat-sen's own principles of friendly co-operation with foreign powers for treaty adjustments. An invitation was extended to those powers to revise the out-of-date treaties.

The powers responded with alacrity. After the terrific manifestations of the Hankow regime the reasonableness of the new Nanking government was a welcome relief. On March 14, 1928, the government issued two state papers on the Nanking Incident of the previous year, the first important contact with the foreign powers that was carried through on a friendly basis. Communist implications in the Nanking Incident were openly recognized and also acknowledged by the foreign powers. The United States Government was the first to sign an agreement with China on that regrettable incident. That was on March 24. The British followed suit in August, and the other powers soon afterward. The relations with the outside world then became normal again. The value of such a move cannot be overestimated. It paved the way for what was to take place in July and all through the next year, the long-awaited period of treaty revision.

The Northern Expedition could now be resumed in earnest. That began on April 10 when Chiang Kai-shek crossed the Yangtze River to assume command of his forces. Everywhere along the Tsinpu Railway, at the stations and on the trains themselves, there were slogans: "Down with the Militarists," "Down with the Imperialists," "Abolish the Unequal Treaties"—all of which were parts of the Soviet legacy that had come to stay. But the meaning of these slogans was not quite the same then as they had been when displayed in Hankow under Borodin. On one occasion, some of the accompanying foreign correspondents showed their heads above a "Down with the Imperialists" slogan to the delight and amusement of everyone. Chiang laughed along with them. War against imperialism never meant in Kuomintang ideology war against everything foreign.

Before the month of April was out, the Sun Chuan-fang forces were defeated in Shantung. It remained to tackle Chang Chung-chang and the Manchurian war lord Chang Tso-lin, who with his son, Chang Hsueh-liang, were the only remaining militarists of any strength. Chang Chung-chang, with the overpopulated harem, and famous for his three negatives—not knowing how much money he had, how many women he had, and how many children he had—was not an opponent worthy of Chiang's steel. Chang Tso-lin was, however, a different matter. As the Nationalist troops moved northward along the Tsinpu Railway, sooner or later they had to pass through an area in which the Japanese considered they had a prior interest. It was with much reluctance that they were compelled to give up all official claim to the province of Shantung during the Washington Conference of 1921-22, but they could never keep their eyes away from that rich province. Into Tsingtao and all along the railway leading westward to Tsinan, which is on the junction with the Tsinpu Railway, the Japanese poured men and capital, built factories, and established commercial firms. Tsinan was now being threatened by the Nationalist troops, and the Japanese immediately landed troops and dispatched them to that city. Having occupied Tsinan on May 3, they declared an area of twenty *li* (about seven miles) on both sides of the railway a neutral zone. That was obviously meant to block the northern advance of the Nationalist armies. Chiang Kai-shek immediately recognized the danger of the situation and showed for the first time that extraordinary patience and sense of control in dealing with the Japanese which have been such great assets in the present war against the same invaders. He could not afford to be embroiled with a foreign enemy when he had his biggest tasks ahead of him within his own country. But conflicts of a sort were inevitable and had taken place, involving the murder of the Chinese Commissioner of Foreign Affairs by the Japanese. The Japanese meant to find a *casus belli* at all costs. That was the reason for the presence of their troops. China addressed a note of protest to the League of Nations. That was the first time the troubles between China and Japan really began to plague the genial but ineffectual angels of peace at Geneva.

However, on May 5, Chiang Kai-shek notified the Japanese commander that his troops had been ordered to evacuate the area which had been declared neutral and that they were resuming the Northern Expedition along another route. The assistance rendered by Yen Hsi-shan, the governor of Shansi, and of Feng Yu-hsiang at this stage of the Northern Expedition was valuable. At a conference held at Kaifeng earlier in the year, in February, Yen and Feng had been won over to help in the northern drive toward Peking. As the armies of the three military leaders gradually converged on Peking, the Japanese realized that if Shantung could not be retrieved, the menace must at all costs be prevented from reaching Manchuria, which they considered their special preserve.

Even though the Nationalist troops were still hundreds of miles from Peking, to say nothing of the distance from Manchuria, the Japanese addressed a note to the Chinese Foreign Minister as early as May 18 warning him that, if the disturbances should spread into Manchuria, "the Japanese Government, in order to maintain the peace in Manchuria, will be compelled to adopt appropriate and effective measures." It was an impudence which the new Nationalist Government could not overlook, and a reply was sent to the Japanese: "The Three Eastern Provinces [Manchuria] are where a large number of foreign merchants congregate for trade. The maintenance of peace in that area is the special responsibility of the Nationalist Government, which will see to it that all residents, Chinese as well as foreign, are adequately protected. In declaring that the Japanese Government will be compelled to adopt appropriate and effective measures in the Three Eastern Provinces, it must be pointed out that it is clearly a step in the interference with China's domestic problems and that it contravenes all principles of international law relating to mutual respect of territorial integrity. The Nationalist Government cannot recognize such a declaration." Three years of smoldering were still required before the northeastern parts of China were to burst into flames. That, at any rate, was the prelude to the Japanese attack on Manchuria on September 18, 1931.

In the meantime, the Manchurian war lord Chang Tso-lin, who was then in Peking, which he included within his domain, was advised by the Japanese to leave for Mukden. He left June 4, 1928, but was killed when his train was dynamited just outside of the Mukden station. The Japanese then decided to take matters into their own hands. They were going to assume the responsibility of maintaining peace in Manchuria now that its ruler was dead.

Meanwhile the northern opponents of Chiang's army crumbled before the advance of the Nationalist forces. Sun Chuan-fang escaped to the north of the Great Wall, and Wu Pei-fu went into hiding in Szechuan. Chang Chung-chang was disarmed. On June 8 Yen Hsi-shan's troops first entered Peking, and the Nationalist flag was hoisted on the palaces of the imperial city. By that act the Northern Expedition was successfully terminated.

Chiang Kai-shek did not arrive in Peiping till the first days of July 1928. He entered the city, however, when the soldiers of occupation were not his own but those of Yen Hsi-shan. Superficially they were all a part of the Nationalist forces, but actually Feng and Yen were both jockeying for power. Feng was very much chagrined that he had lagged behind, but his points of concentration were farther away from Peiping than Yen's, and there was nothing that he could do about it. In the case of Chiang, he had no actual military power in Peiping, and yet he remained the unquestioned leader of all the Nationalist troops. Chiang acted with a quickness and precision that were remarkable. He was the commander in chief, vested with all the power and authority by the government in Nanking to which officially, at any rate, all the military commanders owed allegiance. That government was the creation of the father of the revolution, whose body was lying in state in a temple outside of Peiping. Chiang, therefore, immediately arranged a memorial service so that the great news of the completion of the Northern Expedition might be conveyed to the departed spirit of Sun Yat-sen. The effect on the imagination of the nation was instantaneous. Chiang Kai-shek was the central figure of the drama. His prestige and influence increased immeasurably. Beyond any question of a doubt he was now China's unifier. The fact that he entered the city of Peiping with or without his own soldiers was of no importance.

It has been said that the British crown has no practical value in the actual government of the country. But it has another value that is even more real. It rules the imagination of the people. It is a symbol of unity. So also with Sun Yat-sen. Sun, after his death, became a greater and nobler personality. To the Chinese people, he embraces all the ideals worth fighting for; he is one with the aspirations of the Chinese race. Chiang Kai-shek's memorial service to Sun Yat-sen, on his entry into Peiping, gave life to the legend, and the memory of Sun Yat-sen in Chinese minds assumed enormous proportions. Chiang, as the devoted follower, became his logical successor and the executor of his wishes. His own position, with his noteworthy military record behind him, was proportionately enhanced.

The government at Nanking was entirely different from what it had been a year previously. It could now speak on behalf of the whole country. It could really represent the country in its international dealings. It was on friendly relations with the foreign powers. With the capture of Peiping it further strengthened its position by a series of intelligent measures.

In the first place, it won to itself the most respected and the oldest members of the Kuomintang, men who again were more valuable as symbols than as able administrators or governors of men. Tsai Yuan-pei especially was a man who combined in his person all the mellowness and wisdom of both the old and the new. I had a personal attachment for Tsai since he did me the honor of placing me, when I was twenty-three years old, on the faculty of the Peking National University, of which he was then, in 1922, its distinguished chancelor. From that time on my contact with him was frequent, and never did I fail to feel that I was in the presence of a compelling personality, rich and warm in human appeal. Tsai Yuan-pei's inclusion would add prestige to any government in China. He had a large following and was always pleasant, radiant with smiles, considerate, accommodating, and as mellow as the fine Shaoshing wine to which he was deeply attached. He was once asked to become the chairman of the Executive Yuan which is equivalent to being the premier, but he decided that it was then not to the best interest of the nation for him to assume the post, so he simply disappeared into seclusion until the offer had been withdrawn.

There were other senior Kuomintang members, not as great as Tsai Yuan-pei, who nevertheless fell in the same category. There were Wu Tse-hui, Li Shih-tseng, and Chang Ching-kiang, who are all still alive, the first in Chungking and the other two now in the United States. Chiang Kai-shek in an astute way included all these nestors in his government at Nanking. They acted as ballast to the ship that was only newly launched and still sailing among the shoals of an uncertain sea. Wu Tse-hui, with the face of a cherub and a merry twinkle in his eyes, is full of charming humor. He is one of the few men whom Chiang Kai-shek, however busy he may be, visits now and then. It was said that one day when Chiang called at Wu's home, a servant who was new did not recognize the visitor and, in order that Wu would not be disturbed, told the visitor that his master was not at home. Chiang gave his name, but the servant did not believe him, so Chiang gave his name again. "Please do not bother me, Mr. Wu is not at home," replied the servant. Then, suddenly feeling that the man might be who he said he was, the servant ran to his room, took out a picture of Chiang Kai-shek which he had clipped from a newspaper, held it before the visitor and, in a state of great excitement, said, "Yes, you didn't tell me any lie. You are Chairman Chiang. Yes, yes, you are. . . ." Wu Tse-hui is now eighty-one years old, but twelve years ago when hiking in the Nanking hills he left a group of us younger people down in the valley gasping for breath while he was already halfway up the slope. No Chinese is more democratic than Wu. He looks and acts like one of the village gentry. He is a typical Chinese product, the kind that makes Chinese culture so unique and vital.

The first constructive act of the government in the sphere of public administration was the convocation of the Economic Conference held at the end of June 1928, the same month that Peking fell. That was due to the efforts of T. V. Soong, who is at present China's Foreign Minister. A statement that he issued on the aim of the conference had far-reaching effect in all quarters in creating confidence and trust in the government.

No government [said Soong] can enjoy the confidence of the people unless the people share in formulating its policy. We have asked the Chinese people to make large sacrifices to pay for the success of our armies during the recent war. In time of war we have perhaps been forced to resort to extraordinary measures to raise funds. Now that the war is over we shall have to raise enormous funds to rehabilitate the country, to restore peace and order, to disband the surplus troops, to restore the dilapidated railways, to care for famine-stricken areas which have served as a battlefield. In this work of rehabilitation the people must have a voice. . . . We have called together responsible non-political persons, representatives of the taxpayers, to criticize us, to help us, and to guide us. This is, so far as I know, the first conference of its nature to be held in China. Its success will be a step forward in the democratic institutions in China.

This announcement marked the ascendancy of the bourgeoisie. The last nail had been struck into the coffin of Communism.

The conference was attended by the leading financiers, bankers, economists, and merchants in the country. Most of them came from Shanghai. At the end of a ten-day session resolutions of five different kinds were passed, regarding the disbandment of surplus troops, the promotion of economic prosperity, the liquidation of the national indebtedness, taxation, and finally banking and currency. The Economic Conference was immediately followed by the National Financial Conference, attended by financial officials of the country, and its purpose was the carrying out of the resolutions adopted by the earlier conference. However, while it was all very well to pass these resolutions, it was obvious that the country had not yet come to a point where they could be effectively put into practice. The most difficult problem was the disbandment of troops. That involved the power and position of the military commanders, who were not yet ready to give over. This was especially true of Feng Yu-hsiang and Yen Hsi-shan, who were not originally Kuomintang members. The first disbandment conference was held in July and did not prove a success.

Yen, with his drooping mustache so typical of old China, cleverly made it appear that he suffered from one ailment after another and confined himself to his own province. But Feng Yu-hsiang, who sang "Onward, Christian Soldiers" with his troops, to the intense satisfaction of the missionaries, was always more spectacular. He could not forget the importance of his part in the Northern Expedition and saw to it that others did not forget it either. Chiang had returned from Peiping to Nanking at the end of July and was busy calling another conference, known as the Fifth Plenary Session. Feng would not be Feng if he stayed away; he came and let everyone know that he had arrived.

Feng is a tall person, big and solid. There has been no better actor on the Chinese political stage. He was determined to let Nanking know that, while it was all right to have a government of the bourgeoisie, he could not allow luxury to spread without saying a few words. The wife of the city mayor was reputed to have paid twenty-five dollars for a pair of silk hose. Scandalous, said Feng, when people in northwest China were feeding on grass and the bark of trees. When he stalked into Nanking, he paraded himself on the streets dressed in the plain uniform of a private, wearing a crumpled straw hat that was too small for his head, and began calling on the leading members of the government at early hours of the morning. Walking was his favorite exercise, but he would quite often appear in a truck seated next to the chauffeur, while his bodyguards would be riding in brand-new limousines following behind him. His food was the simplest in the world. When other officials had meals with numerous courses, his would be plain noodles and Chinese bread. People used to malign him by saying that he had his own banquets behind the curtain. He gave many addresses to the youth of the country against the extravagance and luxury of the new governing class.

The final act to complete the triumph of the Kuomintang over all of China was the hoisting of the Nationalist flag above the government buildings in Mukden. Manchuria thus came within the fold. The date was December 29, 1928.

27

The Road to Manchuria

ALTHOUGH China was now united under the Kuomintang flag and militarism was at an end, it did not mean that all troubles had disappeared. True to his word, the first thing that Chiang Kai-shek did on the completion of his Northern Expedition was to resign his military command. The government did not accept his resignation, and instead asked him to proceed with the plans for disbandment of the surplus soldiers and the unification of military control under the Central Government. This was one of Chiang's pet schemes with which he had toyed in the early days of the revolution. A preliminary trial had been made six months before, and a second conference met in earnest on January 15, 1929. Chiang submitted a plan whereby the country was to be divided into twelve military areas to be garrisoned by forty to fifty thousand soldiers each. All the surplus soldiers were to be converted into labor battalions, to be employed for the constructions of dikes and highways, for river control, forestation, irrigation, and colonization. He proposed also that the government float a loan of some fifty million dollars to meet the expenses. Ho Ying-chin, Chiang's principal aide, who remains today as Minister of War at Chungking, warned the conference that the country was spending some eight hundred million dollars a year for military expenses while the national revenue was only three hundred million.

The situation was admittedly serious. The militarists themselves conceded that it was serious. Some forty members of the conference, most of whom were militarists, then sat assembled in Nanking. To gather them all under one roof was an immensely difficult thing to do. And they must express their views on their own destruction! They were expected to suppress all their selfishness, jealousy, and suspicion, and become meek, trusting, and sincere. Even Chiang Kai-shek couldn't persuade them to do that. For the militarists, while they sat at the conference table, could not help thinking that if they were to carry out that plan, they would be contributing to the power and glory of Chiang at their own expense. The day had not yet arrived for such drastic reforms.

Feng Yu-hsiang was among the first to ask to be excused from the conference. He went back to Shantung and soon was strong enough to threaten the authority of the Central Government. He amassed a formidable army of fifteen divisions, and Chiang had just as many troops to oppose him. The story went that after figuring that each division of from ten to twelve thousand men would cost over a million dollars in training, equipment, and transportation and that he had to sacrifice at least some three divisions of his own costing well over three million dollars, Chiang decided that it was a much wiser policy to spend a million dollars to win over some of Feng's generals than to fight. At any rate, Feng's army suddenly collapsed, the government's authority was maintained, and money and lives were saved. This may or may not be true, but I would subscribe that it was at least a sensible arrangement. Having achieved unity, it was Chiang's policy to consolidate it by all possible means and avoid as far as possible any actual fighting.

The Kwangsi group led by Pai Chung-hsi, Li Chung-jen, and Li Chi-sen created further troubles in Hunan. Those were suppressed in short order. There were also troubles in Shantung and other parts of China. But they were all brought to an end, and the authority of Chiang Kai-shek, as representing the Central Government, was questioned less and less. When we realize that all of these militarists have either been defeated or are now offering their fullest co-operation to the government in Chungking, the tact, the astuteness, and the firmness which Chiang used to bring them into line must have been extraordinary. There were still troubles, both great and small, that lasted until 1937, but when Japan attacked China all groups agreed to drop their differences and present a united front against the foreign invader. That they were able to do this spoke eloquently of the success of Chiang's policy. Today they still have their differences, but these differences are being handled in the same way as differences in any other country. The Communists are the only exception. When we realize the long and difficult road through which the government has passed in order to arrive at its present state of development, it is safe to say that whoever threatens its unity after it has been so painfully established will meet the strongest opposition from all ranks of Chinese society. Regarded from this point of view, the present Communist attempt to embarrass the government, no matter how plausible their reasons may be, is destined to fail.

One act of far-reaching importance at this time was the promulgation of the Organic Law on October 4, 1928, the fundamental law of China down to the present day. It is not the constitution of China, because the country is officially still in the period of political tutelage, the second of the three periods through which Sun Yat-sen thought China must pass in order to attain full constitutionalism. Constitutionalism is the third and last period. But the law is the basic law and is known in full as the Organic Law of the National Government of the Republic of China.

The central structure of this law is the five-power system. In addition to the familiar executive, legislative, and judicial functions of the government, there were added the control and examination functions. Each of these five functions is entrusted to a yuan or council. Each yuan has a number of ministries, or departments as they are called in the United States. The Executive Yuan has the largest and, for all practical purposes, the most important ministries. There is a president and a vice-president to each yuan, and the president of the Executive Yuan is in effect the prime minister. The Organic Law also created a state or government council consisting of a specific number of high officials who meet periodically to discuss state policy. Presiding over the State Council is the chairman or president, who in those days was Chiang Kai-shek himself, having been inducted into office on October 10, 1928. He was later succeeded by Lin Sen, who remained as the president until he died on August 1, 1943. Chiang was again elected on September 11, 1943, to succeed Lin Sen after important changes in the basic law had been made. One of these changes made the president concurrently the commander in chief of the nation's armed forces as in the United States.

From the middle of 1928 until the Manchurian crisis in 1931 Nanking enjoyed a brief three years of cheer and hopefulness unparalleled in modern Chinese history. The authority of the newly established government under Chiang Kai-shek, in spite of inevitable faint rumblings of discontent in distant corners of the country, remained firm and unquestioned. People began to pursue the arts of peace on a scale unknown before. Officials were busy studying the ideas of Sun Yat-sen so that for the first time they might in truth be put into practice. Carpenters, contractors, builders, and architects were coming to Nanking from Shanghai by the hundreds. Shanghai, as the clearinghouse for imports from abroad as well as from home, became the great provider. People of importance in the government, bankers, capitalists, engineers constantly shuttled between Shanghai and Nanking. The single highway that went from the depot through the heart of the city to the Sun Yat-sen mausoleum was lined with impressive office buildings in old-style Chinese architecture, though their interiors were fitted with modern appointments.

The atmosphere of Nanking was electrified with new hope, and everyone was putting his best into the building of the new capital. Peiping, with its magnificent palaces and tombs of the emperors and Buddhist temples nestled among the ancient trees in the hills, was of course a hallowed place in the history of Chinese culture and civilization, but there was something retrospective about it. People were happy in contemplating the glories of the past but did not look for anything in the future.

But Nanking, in those days, was young, energetic, and forward-looking. It was a young city and yet it was much older than Peiping itself, for it was the capital of China in the time of the Sui Emperors, earlier than the Tang Dynasty. Its monuments date back over fifteen hundred years. From the spacious view looking toward the Sun mausoleum which was then being completed, one could see the peak of the towering Purple Mountain, not a high mountain—of perhaps some thirteen hundred feet—but a beautiful one. The mountainsides were formerly somewhat barren, but they had been covered by millions of pine trees. It was the favorite spot for hikes by government officials and diplomats who were then beginning to pour in from Peiping. Chiang Kai-shek and his bride also found in this spot the peace and quiet they love so much. The American Minister, Nelson Johnson, later Ambassador, was then one of the most energetic of these hikers. We used to have breakfast in the American Consulate where he had his quarters, and a party of ten or a dozen would drive out to the foot of the mountain and scale it. And as we came down the mountain, we used to stop at Sun Fo's retreat, panting and perspiring and anxious for drinks and food. Sun Fo knows how to make life comfortable and enjoy it. When lunch was over, those of us who still felt like seeing a little of the surrounding country would go to the tomb of the first Ming Emperor through a long spirit path flanked on both sides by gigantic sculptures of horses, camels, and officials in both civilian and military garb. The tomb itself is a huge tumulus, of a type that is seen in the Scandinavian countries and in Poland. The raised mound as a tomb probably came into China from the first Chou Emperors of thirty-five centuries ago.

However, the Ming tomb, impressive as it is, is now overshadowed by the Sun Yat-sen mausoleum, where later, upon its completion, a state funeral took place and the remains of the revolutionary leader were transferred from the Temple of the Jade Clouds in Peiping to their permanent resting place in Nanking. There are numerous other ancient monuments in the vicinity that are also interesting. Lying about in the fields in those days were old sculptures of winged lions or chimeras that make up one of the most interesting chapters of Chinese art. They should certainly be preserved in museums. But there they were, lying in the rice fields for over fifteen centuries with their heads inclined toward the heavens and their tongues hanging from gaping mouths, laughing, as it were, at all the vanities and frailties of mankind. These sculptures were impressive examples of a great period of Chinese art under Sassanian influences and were completely secular in the sense that the artists enjoyed and tried to express the rhythm and movement of the animal body for its own sake. The Buddhist influence came in later and created a new artistic style.

Coming back into the city, one would pass the ancient wall of Nanking again, truly one of the glories of all time. But in the enthusiasm attendant on building a new capital this old relic was almost lost. The city mayor, who thought modernization consisted of a total elimination of the old, wanted to have the wall dismantled to make room for his highways, as if there was not enough space for those in the vast stretches of Nanking. The task of taking down the bricks began, and for a time one portion of the wall lay littered on the ground. Those of us who loved this grandeur of the old would pass that spot and actually weep. We used to take up a broken slab, caressingly wipe off the dirt, and find to our amazement the names of the kilns in which the bricks were made and the names of those who donated the bricks. Those names were from all parts of China, showing that the whole country contributed to the building of that magnificent wall. And this mayor had the heart to desecrate it!

It was finally saved for two reasons. It was found that the labor of taking down the wall was too costly. And then an American architect to whom we owe our eternal gratitude was clever enough to propose to the august official that the wall was so wide that a highway could be built right on the top of it, so that the people driving on it would have a wonderful view of the country. The mayor wanted highways, and here was one on an elevation! The ruse worked. The dismantling was suspended.

Such was Nanking in those days, a new capital being built by Chiang Kai-shek on the basis of a glorious past. Always the new on the basis of the old. It is the key to the understanding of Chiang's lifework in every sphere of activity. New trees must be grafted, but the roots are deep down in an ancient but still fertile soil.

With the new government in proper working order, its first duty was in the international sphere: the adjustment of the old treaties from 1842 on. Chiang had promised, although the promise was scarcely necessary, that his first task after the completion of the Northern Expedition would be to begin negotiations for the abolition of those anachronistic treaties. "The completion of the Northern Expedition," he had said, "is the closing of a chapter, but it also begins a new chapter. The earlier chapter is not the real revolutionary work; it is preparatory to the real revolution that starts with the new chapter." He had also said in the same address, which he gave to the Kuomintang party members shortly after the Northern Expedition, "The occupation of Peking concludes our military drive. Whether our revolution is accomplished or not depends entirely upon diplomatic activities, upon whether or not the unequal treaties can be abolished." The address was, in fact, a warning to those young men in the Kuomintang who had the mistaken notion that, once Peking was occupied, the revolution was over and they could begin to enjoy the fruits of that success. They actually did begin to assume an arrogant attitude, to be noisy, domineering, and obstreperous; and Chiang constantly had to remind them that there were immense duties ahead for everyone.

The Foreign Minister was then C. T. Wang, an energetic and able diplomat, who had received copious training as a speaker during his student days at Yale. For three years previous to the Manchurian crisis, when students stormed the Foreign Office and threw bottles of red ink at him, he was at the helm of the Waichiaopu, or Chinese Foreign Office. Those were hectic days. As one of the counselors, the equivalent of the assistant undersecretary of state in the State Department of the United States, it was my pleasant duty to work together with my colleagues under the direction of C.T. There were notes which we had to draft and dispatch to diplomatic representatives of the different countries. We used to work until late in the evening, and the official residence of the Foreign Minister at the Bend of the Sah family, a piece of property which belonged to a rich merchant, was a beehive of activity. The first diplomatic document that we presented to the powers through their representatives, most of whom then still resided at Peiping, was a bombshell which disturbed the quietness and sanctity of the Diplomatic Quarter of the old capital. It concluded with a three-point declaration:

1. All the unequal treaties between the Republic of China and other countries, which have already expired, shall be *ipso facto* abrogated, and new treaties shall be concluded. 2. The Nationalist Government will immediately take steps to terminate, in accordance with proper procedure, those unequal treaties that have not yet expired, and conclude new treaties. 3. In the case of old treaties that have already expired, but which have not yet been replaced by new treaties, the Nationalist Government will promulgate appropriate interim regulations to meet the exigencies of such situations.

Seven countries were affected by the first of these declarations, and there was brisk correspondence suggesting that the representatives come to Nanking to open negotiations. The situation was exciting and interesting. The Chinese Foreign Office under the Peking administration could scarcely take any initiative. It was always confronted by the diplomatic corps as a group. The legations—there was no embassy except the one of Soviet Russia, which never fell in line with the rest—were physically near one another, being enclosed within the charmed circle of the Diplomatic Quarter, a unique creation not to be found in other parts of the world. Whenever a problem concerning the international situation of China arose, the Diplomatic Quarter would be busy with meetings and parleys, and the diplomatic corps would present itself in a body to the Chinese Government. The Chinese Government would then be paralyzed and nothing would happen. Union has always meant strength. But the opposite—to divide and rule—has also worked like magic. It is still the basis of all colonial policy, whatever the combinations may be. So we decided at the Waichiaopu that we would use this formula on the imperialists themselves. It worked. The diplomats, who were separately invited to Nanking, tumbled into their seats of the railroad cars at the Chienmen station of Peiping and vied with one another as to who would see C.T. first, and for every diplomatic guest who arrived, C.T. would give a sumptuous Chinese dinner.

The hilarity and bonhomie of those diplomatic functions were unbelievable. The foreign diplomats were practically all career diplomats who had been *en poste* in various capitals of the world where a diplomatic function was never complete without a swallow-tailed coat and orders and decorations on the breast. But in China's new capital all that stiffness had been left behind and forgotten. The diplomats enjoyed a freedom that upset all conventions. From the moment they sat down at the round tables where Chinese food was served till the end of the function, it was one great round of mirth and good-fellowship. The amount of Chinese Shaoshing wine that was drunk was enough to float the new ship of state. C.T. was a capacious drinker, and the guests had to follow him. He would begin the Chinese finger game, and the one who lost had to pay the penalty of drinking wine. But C. T. Wang converted a plain finger game into something fanciful. It went something like this: "There is an old man who is seventy-seven years of age. He can play a flute and he can also play on the guitar. And now let us play . . ." One was supposed to say all this in Chinese every time that one threw out one's fingers to play the game. Being a Chinese game, C.T. always won, and the foreign diplomats always lost, which meant that they had to drink more wine. Before the dinner was half over we found those austere, dignified diplomats doing the strangest things imaginable. One of them found a gong and began striking it as if he were leading a circus parade. Another fell on his knees, and the next day when he was sober he confessed that, if the news was brought to the attention of his home government, he would certainly be sacked. Sir Miles Lampson (now Lord Lampson, British Ambassador at Cairo) was then an impressive and towering figure. He was very well liked by everybody. He had a large body, being at least six feet six, and held his wine well, but at the same time he had a large heart, and Sino-British relations had everything to gain in that congenial atmosphere. The newly arrived Portuguese Minister, a mere pygmy compared with Lampson, used to gaze at those functions, utterly speechless, and then exclaim to the delight of everybody: "Look! They are like children." After that he would again shut his mouth as tight as a clam. He had been long in his country's diplomatic service, but it was the first time that he had attended such strange diplomatic functions!

In the atmosphere of geniality and friendliness some twelve to eighteen new treaties were signed, placing China at last on the path to complete international equality. The first treaty was signed with the United States on July 24, 1928. "The Chinese people rejoice in the fact," said C.T. in one of his notes, "that the United States is yet the first power to make a response, in a spirit of sincerity and good will, to the policy of treaty revision maintained by the Nationalist Government." This group of new treaties re-established China's right to tariff autonomy and affirmed acceptance of the principle that consular jurisdiction or extraterritoriality should be abolished. The actual abolition took place in a series of agreements signed on October 10, 1942.

During all this period of negotiation Chiang Kai-shek watched with keen interest. C. T. Wang made numerous reports of its progress, and there was no doubt that Chiang was immensely satisfied that one of the most important aims of the revolution was being steadily accomplished.

There was more progress made during those three or four years by China, whether in the field of international relations or in reconstruction within the nation itself, than in any previous century. No one could doubt that a new China was rapidly emerging under the leadership of Chiang Kai-shek. But a new China, so the Japanese believed, was a dangerous threat to Japan. It was time to stop China. Japan struck on the night of September 18, 1931.

The details of the Mukden incident and the occupation of Manchuria by Japanese troops are too well known to be described in detail here. The trouble later spread to Shanghai in January of the following year. The principles involved in the conflict are clear and definite. A nation that was on friendly relations with its neighbor adopted a policy of aggression and, in contravention of all existing treaties, invaded the territory of that neighbor, which today it still occupies. The American Secretary of State then was Henry L. Stimson, whose statesmanship, wisdom, and foresight—all so clearly expressed in his book, *The Far Eastern Crisis*, published in 1936—have won for him the admiration of the world.

The American Government deems it to be its duty to notify the Government of the Chinese Republic and the Imperial Japanese Government [said Stimson in his note of January 7, 1932] that it cannot admit the legality of any situation de facto nor does it intend to recognize any treaty or agreement entered into between those Governments, or agents thereof, which may impair the treaty rights of the United States or its citizens in China, including those which relate to the sovereignty, the independence or the territorial and administrative integrity of the Republic of China, or to the international policy relative to China, commonly known as the open door policy; neither does it intend to recognize any situation, treaty, or agreement, which may be brought about by means contrary to the covenants and obligations of the Pact of Paris of August 27, 1928, to which treaty both China and Japan, as well as the United States, are parties.

This is the famous non-recognition principle. With that in view, Stimson tried every possible means to bring pressure to bear upon Japan to observe the treaties. But America was not a member of the League of Nations, and a combination of other circumstances made it difficult for Stimson to do anything effective. The road from Manchuria to Ethiopia in 1935, thence to the Rhineland, Austria, Czechoslovakia, and Poland finally precipitated the war in which we are still engaged. It is clear that Manchuria, in those fateful days of 1931 and 1932, was the turning point in the world's history. As Mr. Cordell Hull very correctly observed during the 1942 anniversary of the Manchurian incident: "September 18, as the world knows, marks the eleventh anniversary of a fateful step of aggression in Manchuria by the Japanese war lords.... The course of aggression then embarked upon was followed by successive aggressions in Asia, Africa, and Europe, and has led step by step to the present world conflict." Failure to solve that problem, we should have known then, would mean the triumph of aggression and the defeat of collective security everywhere in the world.

The position of Stimson as Secretary of State was unequivocal; that of Sir John Simon (now Lord Simon) was not so clear. What took place between those two Foreign Secretaries was so important that it is best to allow Mr. Stimson to speak for himself. On February 11, when the situation in Shanghai was getting more tense every moment, Stimson called Simon directly on the telephone at Geneva. He was thinking of a joint démarche by America and Britain and other powers under the terms of the Nine-Power Treaty.

I suggested [to quote Stimson's own words] that our two Governments, together with any other signatories, who might be willing to follow us, might act under Article VII of that treaty in a joint statement as to the attack then made on the policy of the Nine Power Treaty, and make it clear that we, as such signatories, did not propose to acquiesce in any of the suggestions for the abandonment of that treaty which were emanating from Tokyo. The following day, February 12th, I talked with him again at Geneva after he had had an opportunity to reflect upon the suggestion, and on that day, at his request, I cabled him a proposed draft of such a joint statement. . . . I made it clear to him that this statement was, in form, merely a tentative draft open for the fullest discussion and amendment. The proposal was obviously a matter of importance which should be passed upon by the Cabinet and Prime Minister. Sir John Simon was returning to London the following day, February 13th, and the draft statement was sent at his suggestion to enable him to consider and reflect upon it on his journey. There were complications, obvious to anyone, arising out of the fact that Great Britain was not only a signatory of the Nine Power Treaty, but also a member of the League of Nations, which was engaged in considering the same controversy. The League had already shown its readiness to seek the support of the Pact of Paris in the earlier negotiations during the autumn, and members of the League had already discussed in informal talks with our minister in Geneva the possibility of also falling back on the Nine Power Treaty. Therefore, such obstacles did not seem insuperable. In the light of them, however, the draft which I sent him was expressly drawn so as not to prejudice the question of responsibility for the present situation as between China and Japan, which was pending for adjudication before the League of Nations. As I explained to the British Foreign Minister, its main purpose was to make clear our faith in, and intention to live up to, the covenants of the Nine Power Treaty—respecting the future sovereignty and integrity of China.

I talked with the Foreign Minister again on the same subject at London on February 13th and February 15th and, while no explicit refusal to my suggestion was ever made, I finally became convinced from his attitude in those conversations that for reasons satisfactory to it, and which I certainly had no desire to inquire into or criticize, the British government felt reluctant to join in such a démarche. I, therefore, pressed it no further.

The British non-joinder obviously killed the possibility of any such démarche. The American government, in the circumstances, could not act alone in sending such a communication to the other signatories of the Nine Power Treaty without inviting the danger of receiving replies from some of them of such a nature as to destroy the effect of the démarche. My plan was therefore blocked.[1]

It would be idle to speculate how Mussolini and Hitler would have behaved if Japanese aggression had been curbed in 1931 and 1932. It was possible that Japan might have gone ahead with her dreams of world conquest anyhow. The world depression which began in 1928 was still finding everyone in a dejected mood. Shidehara, who for ten years between 1921 and 1931 tried to hold back the Japanese militarists, had fallen, and Japan was being ruled by the military swashbucklers who are responsible only to the Emperor and not to the

[1] Henry L. Stimson, *The Far Eastern Crisis*, pp. 162–64.

government. Even so, a joint démarche from the world's great powers would have made Japan pause and reflect. Hitler had not appeared prominently on the scene yet, and Italy was only a third-rate military power. Their rise might have been checked.

28

The Communists Again

WHEN the Manchurian incident occurred and nothing effective was done internationally, the feeling was general that aggression had won the day and that Chinese territorial integrity would continue to be violated. Exactly what the British Foreign Minister was thinking no one can tell. But what was more natural than that he should have only the interests of Britain uppermost in his mind? If Japan expanded at the expense of China in the north, would that not aid in preserving and maintaining British interests in the south and the other parts of China? If Japan should grow too strong in Manchuria, wasn't there a possibility that she might come headlong into conflict with Russia and thus relieve pressure on Britain somewhere else in the world? There can be many speculations, of course. Nor is the Foreign Secretary to be blamed for thinking strictly in terms of his own national interests. But sometimes those national interests are better served by a solicitude for the interests of others or for ideals which transcend national interests. It is clear that Sir John Simon did not have that solicitude. It is the absence of such solicitude in British statesmanship generally that does not instill in the world at large the confidence to which Britain's position and prestige would seem to be entitled.

When the attack on Manchuria occurred it was evident to all close observers that it was likely to develop into a grave issue. Chiang Kai-shek naturally also saw that very clearly. The Japanese effort to create obstacles for him at Tsinan four years before during the Northern Expedition was at that time a prologue and portent to more serious developments in the future. Chiang showed great forbearance then. He was determined to finish his drive to Peking. Now the situation was different. The whole country had been brought under his control, but it was still a long way from enjoying the unity and peace which Chiang had sought for it. The Communists had taken on a different course of development, but they were nonetheless a canker that was still eating into the very heart of the nation. Borodin and the other Russians had been driven out long before, but the Communist menace had recently become even more real than it was before. It was spreading in the provinces of Kiangsi, Anhwei, Hunan, and Hupeh, which straddle the Yangtze River right in its central portion, and the problem for Chiang was more difficult of solution than had been the Northern Expedition of 1928. Then the problem was largely a military one. It was a matter of pushing from his own base into the camp of the militarists and defeating them. Now the menace was right in the territory under his own direct control; and unless he could remove this threat it was impossible for him to face the great international issue in which a formidable enemy bent on conquest and aggression was involved. He would have been inviting disaster to himself and to the nation if he had tried to deal with the two major issues simultaneously. Clearly the situation called for the utmost circumspection and even greater forbearance. It is an old classical Chinese observation that "in order to fight against external aggression it is essential that a country must first have internal peace." Besides, China was not prepared, in either a military sense or in any other way, to cross swords with the Japanese. The only way was to present the Manchurian issue for adjudication by the enlightened opinion of the world. It must be presented before the League of Nations even though that organization was powerless to settle it. In the meantime, Chiang directed all his energy to the solution of the internal problem and the strengthening of his military forces, which, it was patent to Chiang as to all intelligent Chinese, must one day be deployed for service against the Japanese invaders.

The initial struggle against the Communists was over when they, as a party, were suppressed in Hankow in the middle of 1927, and likewise in Shanghai through the application of stern measures against the labor unions in April of the same year. But their strength, it was all too evident, still remained. Soviet influence and organization continued to spread. Local Soviet governments were formed in hundreds of *hsien* districts, and the peasants, not knowing any better, were beginning to be won over to them.

Shortly after the Manchurian incident occurred, the Chinese Soviets managed to hold a national conference in Kiangsi Province, where they formally established the Provisional Chinese Soviet Republic. That was in November 1931. Mao Tse-tung was elected chairman, and a government with ten commissaries was established. By the spring of 1932 that government had spread its influence over an area having a population of some fifty million, probably the largest and most populous area outside of Soviet Russia itself.

It was imperative that the campaign against the Communists be started at once. In the meantime, Japanese aggression was likewise spreading. All of Manchuria had been lost, and the invaders were pressing down into Jehol with a view to reaching ultimately the Peiping-Tientsin area. Those were days of great anxiety for China's new leader. The fight was long and difficult. The ever-victorious general who could conquer all of China in a year's time was still winning battles, but at a tremendous sacrifice. The nature of the fighting had changed entirely. The Communists developed the art of guerrilla warfare to a high degree of excellence, and if it had not been for the discipline and morale of the government troops it might have been impossible to drive them out of Kiangsi and capture the city of Juiking, which the Soviets had established as their capital. That was done, but not, however, before November 10, 1934. I went out to Kiangsi to see the Generalissimo before embarking on my diplomatic mission in Europe, and going through the neighborhood of Nanchang in the rear of the Communist-infested areas, I realized for the first time how arduous and difficult a task it was to carry on war against the elusive guerrilla. We passed through villages that had been recaptured from the Communists, but soldiers were still stationed there, ever on the lookout for the guerrillas. The government troops under Chiang Kai-shek were in pursuit of the Communists always during the day and sometimes at night. They had to cross valleys and mountains, but as they penetrated farther into the territory of the enemy they could find no trace of him. That condition did not exist very long, since Chiang soon learned how to deal with the situation. The Communists left Kiangsi for Hunan, thence to Kueichow and Szechuan, and finally they withdrew into the barren northwest.

To what then can we attribute Chiang's success in this difficult war? An adequate answer to this question will shed much light on Chiang Kai-shek as a leader of men. All through these years Chiang must have thought deeply. Although he knew the past well, his many speeches during this period show that he must have studied Chinese history all over again and from a new approach. This is a characteristic Chinese undertaking. No person who carries the weight of national responsibilities on his shoulders in China can afford to neglect the pursuit of Chinese history. It is a mirror of the past and a prologue of things to come. The Chinese as a race are pre-eminently humanistic and deeply interested in human affairs. Hence their preoccupation with history as a record of past events in which the key to an understanding of human motives may be found. As Chiang's responsibilities grow, we find him reverting more and more to the type of the great Chinese rulers.

On June 2, 1932, speaking before a gathering of civil and military officials of Honan, Hupeh, Anhwei, Hunan, and Kiangsi provinces, Chiang began describing the extreme seriousness of the Communist situation. It meant no less than a question of life and death for the whole nation. Then, emphasizing the fact that to suppress Communism was not exclusively a military operation, he brought out the formula that "it is seventy per cent political administration and only thirty per cent military activity." In other words, it was futile to speak of cleaning up the Communist menace, which was itself an expression of popular discontent, if the country was not properly administered. And it was likewise futile to speak of facing a national emergency if internally the country was not in a healthy condition.

Chiang was fully aware of his country's ills. Evading responsibility, indifference, the lack of courage to face issues—these and similar weaknesses were the result of hundreds of years of political ineptitude; and until these were removed there was little hope for any improvement. He then recounted his experiences, gained during the previous year of warfare against the Communists, and his conclusion was that the campaign was only partially successful, because "we were thinking of defeating the Communists first and then introducing political reforms so that the emphasis was still a military one. We now realize that before any military operation can be effective we must go through radical reforms in our own hearts and cultivate healthy habits." He went on to say that there were too many Chinese people with no sense of honor, no sense of shame; as a result they were dishonest and selfish in regard to the national interest. The lack of feeling of responsibility in public life had long been characteristic of Chinese officialdom. As if it had not been bad enough before, the committee system was introduced and made matters even worse. In the committee system which came in when the Kuomintang was reorganized according to the Soviet model, everyone tried to "pass the buck" and as it were, gave official approval to a defect which should be the first thing a revolutionary regime would remove. Chiang, therefore, abolished this system and made each official responsible for his own specific duties. "During all the periods of dynastic change in China," Chiang said, "we observe that there has always been banditry in one form or another. The present is no exception. What the Communists are doing is merely a re-enactment of what was done during the Taiping Rebellion. The rebels then were well organized; even so, they were defeated by Tseng Kuo-fan and Hu Lin-yi." From this moment on, we find in Chiang's speeches more and more frequent references to the lifework of these two outstanding personalities of the middle nineteenth century in the Ching Dynasty. "We must first learn to be severe with ourselves before we can impose severity upon others. Tseng Kuo-fan, Hu Lin-yi, Tso Tsung-tang, and Peng Yu-lin succeeded in their duties because they were able to promote that atmosphere of being stern, just, and honorable; and the only way we can save our situation is to have the same discipline." Chiang freely acknowledged that Communism was able to spread because there was discontent among the people and that it was his duty and that of the government to see that the discontent was removed. "In the whole of the land area in China, only twenty-seven per cent is tillable. Out of that only seven per cent has been actually cultivated. In other words, two or three per cent of the land is under cultivation." Chiang's task of agrarian reform was going to be a large one.

In a speech delivered on January 30, 1933, at Nanchang, before the Memorial Service of the Provisional Kuomintang, the same sentiments were again emphasized. "The success or failure of any undertaking depends upon ourselves and not upon our enemy. Our enemy is only the Red bandits. There are also the combined land and naval forces of a powerful neighbor which are even more formidable. But we need not be afraid if we are healthy ourselves and have a strong determination. Otherwise we shall find no way to defeat the bandits, let alone resist foreign aggression."

The comparison of Communism to an evil spirit in another part of that same speech was one of those interesting light touches which on the whole are rare in Chiang's stern and severe tone. "Suppose we live next door to a haunted house. All kinds of rumors begin to float around, and people become terribly afraid. Well, the only thing to do under the circumstances is to push open one of its doors and see for ourselves what the ghost inside looks like. As soon as we see the courage to do that, I am sure the ghost will disappear. The same is true of the Communists. If we are only courageous, forthright, willing to shoulder responsibilities and really act, there will be no difficulty in suppressing them. The trouble with us is that we beat about the bush too much, we are selfish and take care 'only of the snow in front of our own doors.'"

Two years later, on March 25, 1935, in Kueichow, after having driven the Communists out of Kiangsi, the emphasis on Chinese ancient virtues as the only road to salvation became more insistent. The promotion of these virtues became a panacea to all the existing evils. "The Communists murder and pillage wherever they go. They want to destroy all that Chinese culture stands for. They want to wipe out our ancient virtues of loyalty, filial devotion, benevolence, love, fidelity, courage, peace, and justice toward others as well as those of discipline and courtesy, sense of public duty, purity, and sense of honor."

This ideal of moral uplift supported Chiang all through this period when the Communists were being pursued into Szechuan and far western China. In July 1935, having fought all the way to Chengtu, Chiang assembled his military leaders and spoke to them. Those leaders had accompanied their soldiers through some of the most inaccessible parts of China's west and southwest, and had covered a distance of some six thousand miles. As Chiang truly observed at that time, although Chinese history is full of epic undertakings, nothing like the campaign against the Communists had ever taken place before. As a result of discipline and rigid training the government soldiers everywhere received the welcome of the local inhabitants. Chiang was pleased. The Communists had lost heavily. Out of the seventy thousand Communists who had precipitately left Kiangsi, there were only some five thousand who finally reached Szechuan. That was the period which the Communists called the fourth stage of their revolution. It was the Long March that had begun in October 1934.

"One supreme duty in coming to Szechuan," Chiang said to his troops shortly after their arrival in that province, "is to become examples of good conduct to the people of this province. Remember there are seventy millions of them, and their eyes are on you. If you, as soldiers of the Central Government, can really prove that you love your country and people, that you do not covet wealth, that you are not afraid of death, that you are not seeking power, that you can endure all kinds of hardships, and that you are willing to sacrifice, then you can be sure that the people will warmly welcome you. They will love you, respect you, and do everything to help you. But if you are not true revolutionary soldiers, then the people will loathe you, and the effect not only on the suppression of the Communists but also on the nation as a whole will be serious." Toward the end of this speech Chiang reminded the soldiers that they must each keep a diary recording events and the things that they saw every day, including the nature of the terrain they passed through, the social habits and customs of the local population, and their impressions and observations. Few soldiers anywhere are subjected to so rigid a discipline and are called upon to show such moral earnestness as are the government troops serving under Chiang Kai-shek.

This habit of keeping a diary is now being widely encouraged among all ranks of the Chinese fighting forces. For many years Chiang Kai-shek has religiously kept one himself. Diaries are sometimes distributed to high Chinese officers when they visit Chiang before they leave on a long trip. They are specially printed and have a page at the end of each week where the keeper of the diary is supposed to make a strict moral analysis of himself. This is followed by another page where he is supposed to set down a plan of his activities for the next week. There is also a sheet at the end of each month where the owner of the diary is supposed to make a final examination of himself for that period. If the diary is kept as it should be, the task is an exacting one.

29

The Sustaining Power of the Past

IT IS ONLY LOGICAL that people in Europe and America should judge Chiang Kai-shek according to the standards which they themselves know best, but any attempt to do so will not result in a complete understanding of the man. He is completely friendly to foreign visitors, and his mind is receptive to all constructive ideas wherever they may come from. In fact he keeps a secretarial staff busy bringing him information about new books and publications about which he de-

sires to know something. But the fact remains that Chiang's whole background and training are so thoroughly Chinese, and he draws so heavily on Chinese learning and scholarship, that it is impossible to conceive of him apart from this Chinese milieu.

No great leader in Chinese history can have a permanent influence on his people without himself being an example of the virtues and qualities which are traditionally considered by the Chinese as being indispensable to such a person. In spite of busy days that begin early in the morning and last until around eleven in the evening, interspersed with brief periods of rest, Chiang still reads constantly and absorbs what he reads into his daily life. He does not crave novelties. There are a number of basic works which he reads over and over again. As the successor of Sun Yat-sen, Chiang periodically reads through the works of the great leader in a mood of almost religious reverence. He is systematic in his reading and makes notes and comments in the margins of his books. The following are standard works that Chiang reads often: the Four Books, Tso Chuan, Chan Kuo, a group of military classics including Sun Tse and Wu Tse, the philosopher Chuan Tse, the philosopher Han Fei, the great history of Ssu Ma Chien, the *Mirror of History,* and historical accounts of the Ching Dynasty, of World War I, of the Franco-Prussian War, of the Napoleonic Wars, and of the Russo-Japanese War. He also includes in his list books on the geography of China and the world. He concludes with selections from the lives of China's national heroes of both ancient and modern times: Chu-ko Liang, Yo Fei, Wen Tien-hsiang, Tsieh Chi-kuang, Shi Ko-fa, Hu Lin-yi, and more particularly the great Ming philosopher Wang Yang-ming and the Ching statesman Tseng Kuo-fan. The lives of Wang Yang-ming and Tseng Kuo-fan were a constant source of inspiration to Chiang, especially during the period when he waged war against the Communists.

Chiang long ago learned that conquest over oneself is the greatest of all conquests. That is the only way to influence other people. That is why he is a taskmaster to himself before he is taskmaster to others. He does not drink, nor does he smoke. These may be minor details to which people normally attach little importance, but to Chiang they are all part of having control over oneself. Chiang rises early in the morning at around five-thirty, goes through his morning exercises, and has a simple breakfast by himself. It is a characteristically Chinese breakfast with perhaps a couple of dumplings one day and a small bowl of noodles the next. There is nothing very unusual about the simplicity of this repast. There are millions of Chinese who eat the same way. After breakfast Chiang takes out his diary and records what happened to him the previous day. This is not merely a record of events; he also sets down his reflections, his thoughts, and his observations on men and on the life of the nation. He has done this for many years. It is all part of a rigid self-discipline. Confucius also habitually submitted himself to a careful scrutiny of his own conduct: "I examine myself daily on three points; whether in transacting business for others I may not have been faithful, whether, in relationships with friends, I may not have been sincere, and whether I may not have thoroughly assimilated and put into practice the instructions of my teacher." In another Confucian classic it is said that "the gentleman, the man of supreme moral virtues, examines his heart to see that there is nothing wrong so that he may have no cause for dissatisfaction with himself." It is entirely with those aims in view that Chiang Kai-shek keeps his own diary.

The diary over, Chiang follows another procedure along similar lines. It takes him some fifteen minutes, but it is probably the most important quarter of an hour of the day. He sits quietly with his eyes closed and meditates. At the end of the period he feels that his spiritual vitality has been enormously increased. This is an old Chinese practice probably later deepened by Buddhist influences. The principal thing is that the body is completely relaxed so that all vital and nervous energy flows unhampered. In ordinary consciousness one's attention is directed to the outside world and one's energy and resources are conditioned by these experiences from without. During this short period of meditation contact with the outside world is reduced to a minimum; with practice it almost becomes non-existent. One's thoughts are also directed to the pure and divine so that the soul attains to a state of perfect tranquillity. It develops poise and serenity.

Then he works on a stack of documents which, although it has been carefully sorted, is still about two feet high. Chiang goes through every one of them carefully, makes appropriate comments, and in two hours, by about ten o'clock, he is through with the task. Next comes the time for conferences and meetings, and for personal contact with military officers with whom he discusses the situation at the front. Lunch is a private affair on most days and it is reserved for his immediate family and his wife, although exceptions are occasionally made. Then a nap, and at four o'clock he is up again, receiving official guests. At six o'clock he drives out with Mme. Chiang and takes his daily walk among the hills. And then dinner, which is frequently attended by cabinet ministers and important members of the government. He may be thinking of a particular national problem and invites those who have most to do with that problem to have dinner with him. He tries to hear as many points of view as possible and then finally decides for himself the line of action to be pursued. These dinner discussions may sometimes last till eleven o'clock when he retires. There is no special brain trust. He draws from all and sundry and makes his decisions accordingly. During those earlier days of the war with Japan when China was fighting alone he used to have weekly luncheons to which he invited men who were well informed on foreign affairs. He would listen intensely (for he has enormous powers of absorption), weigh in his own mind the conflicting points of view, and then determine his course of action.

Later, during his confinement at Sian, Chiang's normal pattern of life was naturally upset. But it had its compensation; for instead of snatching a few short minutes from a busy day for introspection and self-analysis he had a great deal of time at his disposal. His spiritual experiences grew deeper. All people, for that matter, draw heavily on their spiritual resources during a great crisis in their lives. Chiang Kai-shek thought and read, and his mind roamed in all the realms of spiritual richness. No doubt his belief in Christianity received a stimulus and an impetus that it had not known before. As he confessed himself, in an address at Nanking, on March 26, 1937, "The crisis in Sian last winter arose suddenly. Imprisoned in solitude for a week by the rebelling regiment, I read the Bible aloud to my jailers and found it much more meaningful and delightful than ever before."

How, then, can one reconcile the one fact of Chiang's devout Christianity with the other fact that his roots are still deep in the past of China's history? The answer, I think, is quite simple. And it should act as a deterrent to anyone who desires to capitalize on his Christianity for purposes of proselyting. To grow spiritually is to expand and enlarge the richness of one's soul. An ordinary act of conversion to Christianity involves two processes: the acceptance of the new faith and the renunciation of the old. Most missionaries' version of Christianity is essentially a militant one. It cannot exist alongside of other beliefs. It is not for me to criticize whether this should or should not be. I am merely stating a fact and consider the fact an obstacle in the spreading of the Gospel. Most Chinese are too intelligent for that, and Chiang Kai-shek is no exception. It is a great credit to the man that he has no prejudices whatever; it is a credit to all the faiths in China that none of them have prejudices. Neither the Confucianist nor the Buddhist nor the Taoist will say to you that once you embrace his religion you are his exclusive property, for each of them has learned that the spirit, the true spirit, is one and that the secret of spiritual greatness lies in its elasticity and its capacity to absorb all profound truths into a larger unity no matter what origin they may have. It is as mighty as the sea which maintains its identity though all the rivers contribute their water to it. Chiang Kai-shek's spiritual foundation will forever remain in the greatness of China's historical past. His belief in Christianity is no conversion; it is enlargement, development, and expansion. If, conversely, Christians are also willing to regard Confucianism, Buddhism, and Taoism in the spirit of a dispassionate search for truth, then we are on the way to a real universal brotherhood of men for which we have been groping but have failed to reach. We are too much confined to institutions which are not an essential part of the spirit and become therefore circumscribed in our outlook. But the true life of the spirit is full and all-embracing and welcomes other kindred truths. Chiang Kai-shek's life is a demonstration of this eternal principle.

To the members of his family Chiang Kai-shek is austere. When Wei-kuo, Chiang's second son, was in America a few years ago, he received a good many letters from his father. His own letters back to China would almost without exception be properly corrected by his father and returned to him to be carefully studied. When Wei-kuo went back to China and saw his father, there was no expression of the usual easy fellowship and no patting on the back. He had to stand waiting to receive moral commands and injunctions!

The result is that Chiang's two sons and one nephew, the son of Chiang's only surviving sister who died but recently, are all fine young men whom it is impossible to distinguish from any other self-respecting and hard-working young men in China. Ching-kuo, Chiang's oldest son, is now serving as a magistrate in Kiangsi Province and as a member of the provincial government, and is as exemplary an official in a small area as his father is on a national scale. He has a Russian wife whom he married in the earlier days when he spent much of his time in Soviet Russia. That was when he was greatly interested in Bolshevism and was supposed to have violently disagreed with the father. Now he has come to understand that the father's ways are

Thomas Kwang—Chungking, Paul Guillumette, Inc.

Generalissimo Chiang Kai-shek taking a walk with the venerable President Lin Sen who passed away on August 1, 1943, and whom the Generalissimo was elected on September 11 to succeed.

the best for his country. Wei-kuo is in military service somewhere in the Yellow River Valley and escorted Wendell L. Willkie when he visited the front lines. When he was in the United States, Wei-kuo was liked everywhere for his simple and lovable ways. He would instinctively click his heels and salute a senior military officer wherever he met one. The nephew is now in the United States, has studied aeronautical engineering, and is learning to be a pilot in Arizona. Living in a simple boardinghouse just as any other student would do, he was much given to sports when his day of work was over. None of the boys have any of the mannerisms or objectionable habits so common among the children of many of the wealthy and influential families in China. The influence of the great statesman Tseng Kuo-fan is clearly discernible in the development of this family discipline.

30

They Start a Movement

THE YEARS immediately before and after the Japanese attack on Manchuria were an extremely difficult period for China and gave Chiang Kai-shek much worry and anxiety. The government, during the first years that it had been in existence, had accomplished much both in its international relations and in its domestic policy. It had at least some stability. But it was, after all, young and had been called upon to stand up under an enormous strain.

That was also the time when the Roosevelt Administration in the United States came into office. Its first act was to relieve the great depression of 1929–33. It mustered all its energy to avert an economic crisis, and in a series of bold measures it decided ultimately to abandon the gold standard and move toward a revaluation of the dollar. An embargo was placed on silver with a consequent rise in the price of that metal all over the world. That was a blow to the Chinese economy, which was built on a silver basis. There was only a small amount of silver being produced in China. Every year large amounts of silver bullion had to be imported. But with the situation what it was in the United States, there was instead a steady outflow of that metal. The prices of commodities began a downward plunge. The country's productive capacity likewise suffered and the international trade balance became so unfavorable that there were serious economic disturbances throughout China. America's headache had become China's headache also.

It was then that Chiang Kai-shek sought some formula of national financial regeneration. Some measure of economic rehabilitation was obviously imperative. But the important thing was that the morale of the people should also be sustained. It was essential to have material prosperity, but Chiang felt that, in the presence of so many national disasters, as long as the spirit of the people could be bolstered and their moral strength increased, the danger could in some way be averted, and then material prosperity would follow. It was under these circumstances that he promoted what has now come to be called the New Life Movement.

The immediate stimulus was undoubtedly the ravages of the Communists. In the many years of warfare against them he had come to the conclusion that the problem was very largely a social and political one and only in a minor way a military one. The Communists had been able to intimidate and oppress the people because the people lacked the inner strength to resist them. The oppressors were organized, while the people were ignorant, superstitious, indifferent, callous, and had no sense of social responsibility. The differences between the two were great, and the people possessed nothing that would enable them to resist the oppression. As Mme. Chiang Kai-shek observed: "The Generalissimo saw that the way to prevent Communist teachings from taking root was to beat the Communists at their own game—to institute better administration and to give the people, in the former Communist-infested areas and elsewhere, the chance to improve their conditions of life in all respects." That was the spirit behind the New Life Movement.

The New Life Movement may be said to have been officially launched on February 19, 1934, in Nanchang in the province of Kiangsi. That was where Communism was strongest. But a good deal of preliminary work had been done before that official date. As soon as the Communists were driven out of a certain area it was Chiang's task to make the people so contented and strong that, even if there was a recrudescence of the same menace, they would have the strength to cope with it. For every area reconquered and reclaimed from the Communists he organized what was known as a special movement corps to help the people in the work of rehabilitation. The members of the corps were young men who had received proper training at the central military headquarters. They were taught to be kind, courteous, and helpful to the peasants and villagers. It was essential to win their confidence. The members would study the extent of the damage that the Communists had done and would then form co-operatives for the people so that they could secure the tools with which to rebuild their rural life. Things that were missing had to be replaced. Implements that were damaged had to be repaired. Pigs, sheep, cows, and other livestock had to be bought and bred. Cottages which had been burned down had to be rebuilt, and all able-bodied villagers above sixteen years of age had to be trained to use adequate weapons so that, if the Communists should come again after the government troops had gone on ahead, the village people could defend themselves. It was clear that a program of this sort, of first winning the confidence of the people and then giving them constructive assistance, involved hard and patient work, but it was touching to see how the villagers showed their appreciation when the Chiangs toured through those devastated areas. They also personally attended to the education of the children, established schools, saw to it that there was proper sanitation, that the village industries were reconstructed on a sound basis, and that the rural economy regained its health.

With all that done, Chiang still felt that something more was needed. It was all very well to help the people in this material way, but it was still more important that their spirit be fortified. Tseng Kuo-fan and many other great leaders in their time had similar problems, but Chiang realized that his problems were much wider in scope. China was now striving to be a modern nation, an equal of the other nations of the world, and that meant that it imposed more than the usual responsibility on Chiang. However, the basic moral problem was the same—how to make the people develop in their daily habits those cardinal virtues that had been the mainstay of the Chinese race.

There are four such virtues which, when they were universally practiced, Chiang observed, always meant a period of great prosperity for the nation. If they were neglected, disorder and confusion were the results. Those virtues are *li, yi, lien, chih,* all of which involve a high degree of moral and mental discipline.

Li means respect and courtesy, the ability to abide by the law and to observe regulations, to be cautious and circumspect in the transaction of business, to be firm and yet kindly in relation with other people, to be devoted to one's parents and respectful to elders, and to possess a scrupulous regard for social order and harmony. It means, in a word, discipline.

Yi means service to mankind, being generous and magnanimous to others, but strict and abstemious with oneself, having no desire to struggle for power or wealth, showing devotion to public welfare and having a willingness to work hard for others, helping the good and suppressing the evil so that justice may prevail. It means in short moral courage.

Lien means cleanness and purity of thought, meticulous care in giving and taking, conducting oneself with a high sense of honor, ability to discriminate right from wrong, suppression of all falsehood and avoidance of waste in the practice of economy.

Chih means instinctive hatred of all evil, avoidance of the morally low and improper, conducting oneself with a high sense of self-respect, constant struggle to achieve progress and moral advancement, and cultivation of the sense of shame.

As they stand, they seem to be rather abstract virtues, but virtues are of no value unless they are lived and practiced every hour and every day of one's life. Chiang gave instructions that these virtues should find visible expression in the four principal elements of life, namely, in food, clothing, shelter, and conduct. These instructions may sound simple, and a good many of them are taken for granted in an organized society, but the plain people of China had not been taught them; and after many years of Communist oppression they had become so demoralized that a "new life" indeed became necessary.

In the matter of food the New Life Movement urges the people to have regular hours of eating, to seek cleanliness both in the food and in the manner of cooking, to be moderate in their desires especially as regards drinking, not to waste food, to observe mutual consideration while eating, to abstain completely from opium and other narcotics and even, if possible, not to smoke cigarettes. Chiang once saw a boy smoking a cigarette on the street. He immediately stopped and asked for the parents of the boy and had them thoroughly reprimanded.

In the matter of clothing the New Life Movement teaches the people to dress simply. This is naturally somewhat harder on Chinese women than it is on the men. The women's time should be employed in doing household duties, in washing and sewing. While walking on the streets a person should see to it that he is properly shod and buttoned and that his hat is adjusted at a proper angle. Clothes should not be worn in a sloppy fashion, for sloppiness in dress reflects an untidy mind.

In the matter of shelter the movement teaches the people to understand that family joys are the most solid and substantial of joys. The house should therefore be kept immaculately clean. One should get out of bed at the rise of dawn and instantly go for a bath. On the subject of the morning toilet Chiang recommends as a matter of discipline that one should daily wash one's face with cold water. He still practices this himself. At one of his young people's lectures he asked how many of the audience had that habit and was provoked when he learned that many of the youngsters would rather leave their faces unwashed than to use cold water. Providing proper home ventilation, keeping the kitchen clean, swatting the flies, exterminating vermin—these and many bits of advice are included in the instructions to the people.

While walking and appearing in public the people are asked to be orderly in their conduct. While boarding a train or going on a boat there should be no pushing; rather everyone should patiently stand in line. The old and the weak should always be given help. There should be no spitting. While sneezing, see that one does it away from other people. If they should meet a funeral procession on the street a proper expression of sympathy should be given. Chiang himself came on such a procession one day in Nanchang. On one side a band was playing foreign music, and on the other another band was playing Chinese classical music. The mourners were dressed in the raw hemp costumes of antiquity and yet they were riding in automobiles. It was sheer confusion. Ancient and modern, Chinese and foreign customs, were hopelessly mixed up. Chiang did not say what he did about the procession, but the chances are that he instructed the mayor to have proper regulations drawn up for such occasions. Chiang can be a superpoliceman when he goes out for a stroll, which he often does without so much as a bodyguard near him. He makes mental notes of what goes on around him. On the streets of Nanchang he one day observed that, while the ricksha men had their clothes properly buttoned, the policemen did not. He was furious and gave the chief of police a thorough scolding.

Chiang's point of view is that these minor details of life may appear to be insignificant in themselves, but that they express an attitude, and it depends upon what that attitude is before we can say whether or not the people are able to form a great and progressive nation. The people must show an unrelenting effort to improve upon themselves.

The Chinese national flag is red with a blue corner in which there is a white sun with twelve rays. The idea for the flag came from Sun Yat-sen and is based on the concept of universal justice and the brotherhood of man. It is the duty of every Chinese to apply himself rigidly to self-improvement in order that these concepts and the historic mission of Chinese culture may spread to the far corners of the world. The twelve rays are the twelve time periods, each consisting of two hours according to the Chinese way of calculating, and also the twelve months of the year, the idea being that the work of the people should be one with the universe and know no rest. It is an idea adapted from the Yi-King that the man of superior virtues increases his moral power through unceasing labor. The Chinese national flag is thus a symbol that the nation will last as long as the blue sky and the white sun, that it remains permanently in the universe. The rays of that sun will bring light to every part of the universe so that there will be eternal justice, freedom, and equality for all.

If that is what the Chinese national flag aims at, how can we relax, Chiang asks, in our efforts for unceasing progress and self-improvement which are the basis of the New Life Movement?

31

He Starts Another Movement

THERE IS an old Chinese saying that a person must have destroyed himself first before others can destroy him and that a nation must have attacked itself first before others can attack it. When anything unfortunate happens it is best not to lay the blame on others so much as on oneself. "That," said Chiang Kai-shek in one of his Kuling addresses in the summer of 1934, "was the secret of Tseng Kuo-fan's success." That should be the secret of anybody's success. For unless one adopts this attitude there is little hope of self-improvement; and unless there is constant moral enlargement there is no hope of success.

Chiang Kai-shek's art of government is really as simple as that. He is always calling upon the people to exert themselves, to apply themselves seriously to their work. In those days when the nation was trying to rid itself of the unequal treaties he insisted upon having the people realize that, onerous as those treaties were, the important thing was to make the nation so strong that those treaties would naturally lose their grip. But if the country remained weak, even though they were abolished, they would come back, perhaps in another form.

The two movements which Chiang Kai-shek started were designed to build up both the moral and material strength of the Chinese nation. The New Life Movement grew out of his experiences in fighting the Communists in Kiangsi. It was a local affair which developed into national proportions. Mme. Chiang was an ardent and enthusiastic cosponsor from the very beginning, and with her were a number of missionary friends who found that this work of raising the level of public morality fitted into their programs, though they learned that the spiritual basis was constructed on the four cardinal virtues of traditional Chinese morality. It was a new approach. It became clear that modernization did not necessitate the imposition of new and alien values but rather the adaptation of old values which only waited to be strengthened. Moreover, no nation, least of all a nation like China, can be regenerated except from its own roots implanted deep in the past.

But moral rebirth should be accompanied by material growth. In fact the one cannot exist for long without the other. On October 10, 1935, the twenty-fourth anniversary of the Republic of China, Chiang Kai-shek therefore started a second movement for the economic reconstruction of the nation with the declared purpose of "opening up the national resources of the country so that all the people will enjoy an equal share in their development and thereby establish a healthy national economy." He explained how this movement and the New Life Movement were closely related and were in fact two aspects of a single movement for the realization of the third of Sun Yàt-sen's principles, which is the improvement of the social and economic welfare of the people.

Chiang announced an eight-point program. The first point had to do with the promotion of agriculture. Inasmuch as the whole of Chinese culture is constructed on a land economy, Chiang explained that this should be the nation's primary concern. There should be co-operatives among the farmers and facilities for the study and spread of improved methods of cultivation. Not only production should be increased, but also transportation, to make these products accessible, should be multiplied so that there will be an even distribution for the entire country and a growing independence from imported foodstuff. What is locally produced should at least supply local needs or even create a surplus for those localities that are devoted to industry.

The second point provided for the increase in the acreage of arable land and the breeding of cattle. The land must be made to give its maximum output for the welfare of the nation. Areas which were not being cultivated, whether they were public or private, should be opened up. A program for colonization of border regions that were sparsely populated would be set up, and cattle breeding on a large scale would be carried out. Labor would be recruited for these ends from demobilized soldiers, so that all the branches of agricultural life including fruit growing, fishing, and forestation would receive equal emphasis.

The third item regarded the exploitation of mines. Chiang pointed out that the national industries could not develop because, owing to political and other reasons, mining had not been fostered. The government would, henceforth, assume the responsibility of giving the industry every encouragement and support. Thorough geological surveys would be made to determine the extent of mineral resources, and laws would be passed to remove all restrictions. Taxes would be reduced to a minimum, and every inducement given the people to invest capital in the mines so that industry would have its own independent growth and freedom. If the local authorities tried to cause embarrassment in order to claim priority over the mines, they would be punished. Also, in view of the fact that Chinese national strength is limited, Chiang repeated that he would warmly welcome any foreign capital for use in the joint operation of the mines. All this should not only absorb a tremendous amount of labor, thus solving the problem of unemployment, but should also multiply the riches of the nation.

The fourth item concerned the mobilization of labor. Chiang wanted to impress upon the people that, although the other resources of the nation are low, there is a large reservoir of human labor which should give the necessary compensation. It is the nation's greatest asset. So long as that asset is properly organized and used, it should be adequate to create a new economic foundation for the nation. China, Chiang reminded the country, has gone through similar periods in her history. "Enrichment through Labor" and "The Mobilization of Human Energy to Make a Nation Strong" are slogans that have been used in the past, and he appealed to the people to contribute their labor freely to the improvement of transportation, irrigation, the building of dikes, the planting of trees, and other similar undertakings which need the application of organized labor on a large scale.

Next came industrial development, on which the whole of the national economy and prosperity would ultimately have to depend. Chiang deplored the fact that the old handicrafts had dwindled in importance, and yet modern industry, owing to foreign economic pressure, had hardly begun to grow. The immediate problem was the encouragement of basic industries on a small scale in rural areas in co-operation with agricultural interest while the government would give increasing attention to the protection of the large industries. Organizations would be created to solve differences between capital and labor; they would be given effective power so that they would work in harmony and contribute to their mutual interest.

The sixth item was the enforcement of national saving. Chiang constantly bears in mind the fact that China is a poor country and that she has to depend very largely upon imported commodities to maintain the daily life of her people. Rural capital began to accumulate in the cities to be ultimately transferred abroad. Rural economy thus became bankrupt, creating even greater poverty for the nation. It was imperative, therefore, that, while production in every field should be multiplied, the people should cultivate the habit of saving and avoid waste. This should be much easier to accomplish than to increase production, but both served the same end.

The seventh point which Chiang emphasized was the improvement of transportation. The building of national highways, of railways, and of all the other means of communication by land, sea, and air would all receive the careful attention of the government so that agricultural products like cotton, tea, silk, rice, and wheat could be transported freely from one part of the country to another.

The last point dealt with the improvement of currency.

This eight-point program was explained by Chiang Kai-shek on a radio broadcast that he made to the nation on January 1, 1936. His concluding remarks were: "I want every one of you to exert your energy in the direction I have indicated, from today on. We should all know that our ability and intelligence are as great as those of any other nation, but we have an additional advantage in a large population. What other countries take ten or fifty years to build should not take us one year if we are really united and work in harmony. There is no reason to be afraid that we are poor. What we should really be afraid of is that we shall not use our ability and intelligence for the best interest of the nation, that we still have no consciousness of the importance of the nation and race over the individual, that we do not work together and submit ourselves to discipline. We must work, create, and perform. With that spirit, nothing is impossible to accomplish. But if we fold our arms, then what can we accomplish? Through the New Life Movement and now through this movement for national economic reconstruction it is my hope to lay a new foundation for the people and to create a modern and progressive nation. I lay equal emphasis on moral and material improvement, for it is only in this way that we can carry out the San Min Principles and bring salvation to the nation."

32

Half a Century

IT IS IMPORTANT to know that when the Japanese attacked Mukden on the night of September 18, 1931, Chiang Kai-shek was in the midst of a political quarrel with several members of the Kuomintang who felt that Chiang's great prestige was overshadowing them. Hu Han-min, who had been one of Sun Yat-sen's most trusted followers, began criticizing the Nanking government for its foreign and financial policies. He also openly disagreed with Chiang on the question of the provisional constitution. He was a very able person but not an especially tolerant one. There was a narrowness about him which did not allow him to enter into full co-operation with others. He insisted upon absolute control of the nation by the Kuomintang while Chiang thought that to work for a wider popular basis even during the period of political tutelage, which was officially a period of only six years ending in 1935, would prepare for an earlier democratic and constitutional government.

Behind these political differences were personal differences, always a potent factor in politics anywhere, but perhaps especially so in China. The quarrels ultimately reached a climax, and out of sheer necessity to preserve a unified government Hu had to be kept in Nanking in what is known in Chinese as "soft detainment." Chiang called a People's Convention which opened on May 5, 1931, in a newly erected building on the campus of the Central University at Nanking. In a frank address Chiang appealed to the nation to establish national unity and to proceed with the plans for reconstruction.

But just as Chiang was pleading for unity and peace, troubles started in Canton under the banner of Chen Chi-tang. Canton was always a favorite city in which to start a major political move, because it was associated with the rise of all revolutionary activities. Chen Chi-tang thought that by thus revolting against Chiang he would win the sympathy of the nation. He won over a group from Kwangsi and started to establish a new government. In the meantime, taking advantage of the split within the ranks of the Kuomintang, Shih Yu-shan, one of the few remaining minor war lords, thought that he would try his fortunes by starting another rebellion in Shantung. With the help of Chang Hsueh-liang, that local incident was put down in short order.

The Canton troubles, however, were not yet over by the time the Japanese presented the country with a major international issue. Four days after the Mukden incident Chiang made another appeal that all political differences be shelved, at least until the national crisis was over. But the people in the south were adamant and claimed that Chiang was himself the obstacle to the unified government for which he spoke and that, if he resigned, all troubles would cease. By December, as a result of long and tedious parleys, Chiang agreed to accept the southern demands and see how events would turn out. He resigned from all his posts on December 15, 1931. With him resigned all the important members of the Nanking government.

But Chiang could not resign from the government until another significant event had occurred. As in 1919, the students all over the country were again on the warpath as a result of the Japanese invasion. The students form the only articulate expression of popular will in a country where most of the population have not been accustomed to show any active interest in political matters. Their voice cannot, therefore, be ignored. All that they knew was that the country was in grave peril at the hands of an implacable foe, and all they wanted was that the government adopt some strong measures to cope with the situation. With a formula as simple as that they marched into Nanking by the thousands. In November some twelve thousand students surrounded the government buildings and demanded an explanation from the head of the government. Chiang allowed them to remain in the bleak air for twenty-four hours so that their heads might become a little cooler, and it took effect. When he spoke to them the next day and asked them to go back to their colleges and resume their studies, leaving national affairs to be handled by the government, they willingly obeyed and departed. But when these were dispersed new batches began pouring in from all directions. The trains refused to carry them. Whereupon the students slept on the rails and challenged the locomotive drivers to run over them. They won, as students have always won in these patriotic demonstrations. By December there was a furious group of some seventy thousand students in Nanking, which became almost an armed camp, and garrison troops had to be called out to maintain order.

In the meantime, Chiang had gone away with Mme. Chiang to the Chekiang hills to resume the life of solitude that he so deeply loved, and the new government was doing its best to carry on. It soon became clear that Chiang had become all but indispensable. By the end of January the new government under Sun Fo fell, and Chiang Kai-shek came back with infinitely enhanced prestige. Wang Ching-wei, the present puppet Prime Minister at Nanking, became president of the Executive Yuan of the new government.

Simultaneously with the return of Chiang Kai-shek to Nanking, the Japanese extended the scope of their hostilities to Shanghai. That was an episode in which the commander of the Nineteenth Route Army, Tsai Ting-kai, shone like a meteor in the skies. He gave a brilliant performance and demonstrated for the first time that, if the Chinese soldiers were determined to resist, they could hold the Japanese invaders at bay. Chiang gave all possible encouragement to Tsai and sacrificed two of his most modern and best-equipped divisions, the 87th and the 88th. All through the year the Communists tried to capitalize on the situation and rise again. The Japanese, by the early part of 1933, had penetrated some distance south of the Great Wall and were in the Peiping-Tientsin area. On May 31 the so-called Tangku truce was signed. The Chinese Government had no choice but to retreat temporarily before the foreign invaders. There was renewed discontent in the country. Feng Yu-hsiang appointed himself commander in chief of the People's Anti-Japanese Army and declared that he could tolerate the situation no longer. Chiang assured him, however, that while the government was following a policy of extreme forbearance and patience it would never sign any treaty recognizing the fruits of Japanese aggression. That would be impossible. The government was willing to retreat, but only up to a certain limit beyond which it would never go.

In the meantime, another attempt to discredit Chiang was made in November 1933 in the province of Fukien. This time Chen Ming-shu, who had figured in the earlier Sun Fo government, was the ringleader. Some of the political enemies of Chiang's 1927 Hankow regime joined hands with Chen. But the most deplorable fact was that Tsai Ting-kai, the general who led the Nineteenth Route Army against the Japanese at Shanghai and who had been acclaimed a national hero, should join the Fukien revolt. Chiang was ready for the insurrectionists. He made full use of his air force, and in two weeks the Fukien revolt was over. During the whole episode Mme. Chiang was of great help. She was with Chiang during the campaigns against the Communists, and when the Fukien troubles began she was instrumental in winning over some of the generals of the Nineteenth Route Army under Tsai and thus redeemed some of their reputations as patriots for their brilliant fight against the Japanese invaders.

All through 1934 and 1935 Mme. Chiang accompanied her husband through most of the Communist-infested provinces that he was then in the process of cleaning up. From Kiangsi they went to Kueichow and Szechuan. They then visited China's northwest together. They were in Loyang at the inaugural ceremony of a military academy. From there they took to the air and covered all of the area between southern Mongolia and central China. There was little rest for the couple during this extended tour of the historic provinces from which Chinese culture had arisen and which then seemed to be so neglected.

Without the airplane such a journey would have been impossible. It was the first time in the history of China that a ruler and his consort had covered so large an area of the land over which he ruled. It was nevertheless done in the best historic tradition. Chinese rulers from the earliest times felt the need of national itineraries in order personally to learn the condition of the people and to seek means of improving their lot.

That journey was indeed a historic performance. It had its effect in two ways. The people of China had heard a great deal about the country's leading man, and now they had made his personal acquaintance. At the same time it had brought unity between the different sections of the country, something that had not been entirely done before. But more than that, the journey symbolized the direction of China's future development and expansion. China's growth had historically been from north to south, from west to east. Chiang, in this journey, indicated his intense interest and preoccupation with the development of the country from east to west. Everywhere he went with Mme. Chiang they were warmly received. It was also an opportunity to spread the New Life Movement to the out-of-the-way provinces. Chiang brought out the significant fact that the movement was no more than the construction of a new society on the basis of old values and that his own journey had a similar purpose in another sphere. If the people would recall the past glories of the cities and provinces through which Chiang passed, they would understand the meaning of his journey. What greater names are there in Chinese history than those of Sian, Loyang, and Kaifeng, all of which at one time or another had been glorious capitals in days long past? It was from these cities that some of the great explorers, like Chang Chien and Pan Chao of the Han Dynasty started out on their long journeys that brought Central Asia within the realm of the Chinese Empire. It was from these cities that the silk routes across the Gobi Desert to Khotan, Yarkand, and Fergana and to Hami and Kashgar through Sinkiang were opened up. That was two thousand years ago. Ladies of the Roman Empire thus began to wear luxurious silks, and China came into contact not only with Rome but also with Persia, Bactria, Parthia, and with all the intervening lands and peoples. It was from these capitals also that the initiative for an intercourse of cultures was made. Devout religious pilgrims made their way into the heart of India and brought Buddhism into China, and with Buddhism came the glories of the Gandhara art which evolved into the sheer beauty of the sculpture that can still be seen in the grottoes in Shansi and outside of Loyang. The whole romance of the expansion of China rose from the area which Chiang and Mme. Chiang covered, and Chiang took every opportunity to remind the people of these past glories so that their constructive efforts might be directed to an even greater goal in the future. No Chinese can pass through the northwestern areas without feeling a deep sense of pride and patriotism and at the same time a sense of shame that so much desecration has been allowed to ravage those territories. The journey covered a distance of over five thousand miles and brought Chiang and his wife into contact with millions of their countrymen.

On October 31, 1936, Chiang Kai-shek, according to the orthodox

Chinese way of calculating age, reached his fiftieth year. The celebration of that birthday was one of the most magnificent expressions of popular love for a leader in modern Chinese history. At nine o'clock in the morning, surrounding the spacious airfield outside the ancient walls of Nanking and in front of the tombs of the first Ming Emperor and Sun Yat-sen, a throng of a quarter of a million people had assembled, anxious to pay their respects to their national hero. Chiang's own sense of modesty could not allow such adulation. He went away to Loyang on some pretext. But the crowd grew larger, and on the airfield were seventy airplanes that the people had bought with their own money and which they wanted to present to Chiang Kai-shek. There was a brief ceremony. Representatives from the government, the party, and from different walks of life were seated on a platform around the bearded and distinguished President Lin Sen. Ho Ying-chin received the planes on behalf of the absent Chiang and turned them over to the president amid wild and thunderous applause. The significance of the airplane to the new China was tellingly brought home to the people. Then came music, and one of the songs was a commemoration ode eulogizing the extraordinary accomplishments of the man whose birthday they were celebrating that day.

While the ceremony was still going on, planes were heard overhead. The huge crowd all looked up and saw displayed in the sky the two characters of Chiang's name 中 正 (Chung-cheng) in perfect formation. A few minutes later the formation changed into the characters 五 十 (fifty), signifying Chiang's fiftieth birthday. Never in contemporary China had the people seen so grand and so touching a display of devotion to one man.

As the planes flew away Wu Te-cheng, then the mayor of Shanghai, delivered the principal speech. This was what he said: "In the ten years of a bitter war which began in 1926, Mr. Chiang, as the devoted follower of Sun Yat-sen, has banished militarism from China and suppressed the Communist menace. The country has at last become united. But these are still anxious days. For now we are faced with an even greater national calamity [the Japanese]. There is not one moment when Mr. Chiang is not going through some bitter struggle and accomplishing great deeds beyond the ability of ordinary men. He has shown extraordinary patience and solicitude. In the midst of these deep sorrows, both within and without the country, with what unusual strength has he been able to lay the firm foundations of our race. Today, on the fiftieth anniversary of his birth, it is fitting and proper that the nation should present him with a gift of these airplanes as a mark of respect and appreciation of his noble deeds.

"Mr. Chiang under the guidance of the president of the republic is exerting all his effort for the revival of our race and for the regeneration of our national soul. In thus building a new and more powerful nation there is no need for me to say that we all consider him as our leader whom we are willing to follow. But in expressing our respect for this leader it is essential that we realize the great spirit of sacrifice behind all that he has accomplished and that we give him every assistance in what he still has to accomplish. Fellow citizens, I enjoin all of you, wherever you may be, in the heart of the country or on its borderland, to contribute generously to a fund for the purchase of airplanes as a part of his plans for national defense. If we believe Mr. Chiang to be a great patriot and a tower of strength, this should be the way of showing our appreciation, for in this manner we all help to build up a new nation."

When the ceremony was over there were pageants and processions throughout the city. A festive mood was everywhere. On the doors of the homes of citizens were inscribed the words "Happy Birthday." The streets were crowded. A monster lantern procession that night ended the all-day celebration.

In a nation where the people obstinately refuse to idolize its heroes or to worship them until after they are dead, where a good sense of proportion is always more highly valued than emotionalism, Chiang Kai-shek had been uniquely honored.

Then, in a characteristically Chinese way, Chiang gave a message to the nation which was partly an expression of his gratitude but largely an encouragement to everyone to exert his utmost for the advancement of the nation. Perhaps the most touching part of the message was where he described his life after the death of his father when he was only nine years old and "widow and orphan took pity on each other as the body and its shadow." The difficulties that mother and son had to go through, the humiliations to which they were subjected, were great. It was the mother who redeemed the situation. For she was no ordinary woman, and the lessons that he learned from her were those of rigid self-application, self-discipline, and self-denial in order to build up moral force and character. He divided his life of fifty years into two well-defined parts. The first, before he was twenty-five, and the other after that age. The first period was completely dominated by his mother. That was when he watched his mother fight the battle of life and learned the lesson of abiding value that "no crops can be harvested without due share of labor, and no labor is ever denied its just reward." It was his hope that his countrymen would apply the same lesson to the building of the nation. During the second part of his life his mother's influence still prevailed, though gradually yielding its place to that of Sun Yat-sen. But the principle of life was the same. All moral development must begin with the word *hsiao,* devotion to one's parents. That was why Sun Yat-sen impressed upon his countrymen the truth that Chinese civilization had its own foundation to stand upon, and that it was imperative that there should be no imitation of Western superficialities, especially in regard to the worship of might as the guiding principle of national or international life.

The message was presented in the best classical tradition, the language was beautiful, and the tone was modest and humble, but it was Chiang Kai-shek's earnest hope that great and noble achievements were in store for the nation if everyone would work hard and develop his own source of inner strength.

33

Sian Incident

EXACTLY SIX WEEKS after the celebration of Chiang Kai-shek's fiftieth birthday came the startling news that he was being detained by force in Sian, the ancient historic capital of China that he had visited only a few months before.

The news came as a great shock to all the world. I was then in Warsaw, in a country where, since the historic days of Genghis Khan, the people had little interest in so distant a nation as China. And yet even there the people seemed to be greatly aroused. The news of this dramatic event was brought to me first not through the usual official channels but through the bold headlines of the Polish morning newspapers. There was a long account of the incident in all these papers. While I was stirred with deep anxiety for the safety of the great leader, I blamed myself for being unable to understand even a small fraction of what was printed in the papers. I had to ring up my Polish secretary and ask her to come to me at once before the usual office hour. When she came the official information had arrived, but it was not adequate, and as she read to me from the papers the picture began to assume more definite outlines. Chang Hsueh-liang and Yang Hu-cheng were the two principal agents responsible for this rash act.

Telephone calls now began to pour in from my diplomatic colleagues and from friends in the Polish Government. They were all anxious to know what had happened, but I was in no position to offer more than a general explanation of the relationship between Chiang Kai-shek and his captors. I did not realize till then what a great hold the man evidently had over people of all nationalities and in every corner of the world. Chang Hsueh-liang, popularly known as the "Young Marshal," succeeded his father, the refined and almost delicate Chang Tso-lin, who had been killed on his train outside of Mukden in 1928. The Young Marshal has a great deal of native intelligence, but as the son of a powerful ruler of so rich and extensive an area as Manchuria, he had everything he wanted and was considerably spoiled. He never had the spiritual discipline or the education that would make him a good successor to his father. But he had the enlightenment and the good sense to realize that it was a much wiser policy to declare his allegiance to the Kuomintang, then rising in power, than to remain independent and throw in his fortunes with the Japanese. It was both an intelligent and patriotic move when he hoisted the National flag in Mukden on December 29, 1929. He did that against opposition from many of his friends and subordinates. Also he was waiting an opportunity to avenge his father's death. When Chiang later came to know him, he liked the young man and gave him every encouragement to improve himself and made him realize the great responsibilities he was shouldering. He had been a drug addict, but after coming under Chiang's influence he grew sufficiently strong within to see the error of his ways and to submit himself to drastic reforms. He took to playing golf, rid himself of all his bad habits, and grew to be a healthy young man.

In 1930, when Yen Hsi-shan and Feng Yu-hsiang were creating trouble for Chiang Kai-shek and planning to seize the Peiping-Tientsin area, Chang Hsueh-liang watched them and then acted with a decisiveness that did him much credit. He moved his troops to the rear of Yen and Feng, and the rebellion quickly fell to pieces. Chiang was grateful for what he did. In the following year, when the Japanese attacked Mukden and the soldiers of Chang Hsueh-liang gave up large areas without firing a shot, there was wide-spread antagonism against him in the country, but Chiang stepped in and shouldered the responsibility. Chiang simply took the matter over and made it a national issue, which it was. Chang Hsueh-liang ultimately lost all he had in Manchuria and came down south.

In 1933 Chang decided to take a trip abroad. He traveled on one of the Italian liners, then the best steamers going to Europe from China, and tipped the stewards so very generously that it was terribly hard on other Chinese passengers who traveled after him. I happen to be one of them, and I know. The Young Marshal stayed in Italy for some time, saw a great deal of Ciano, whom he knew well and with whom he had spent a good deal of time in Peiping, and he came to admire the Fascist regime of Mussolini. When he went back to China, he tried to persuade Chiang to embrace Fascism, but to no avail. Even so Chiang liked him personally, saw much improvement in his physical health since he left China, and thought that his European experiences had at least broadened his views, and began giving him responsible positions. He made him vice-commander of the anti-Communist troops and stationed him in the Wuhan area.

When, in 1935, there was the unveiling ceremony of the statue of Chiang Kai-shek at Hankow, Chang Hsueh-liang delivered a warm and enthusiastic speech praising the great qualities of the national leader. "Chiang Kai-shek has taken upon himself the task," he said, "of putting the Three Principles of Sun Yat-sen into practice. He is the epitome of Chinese civilization. The entire destiny of the nation depends upon the work of this our national leader. He is the hope of the entire Chinese race." And so he went on, pouring out words that were perhaps sincere and genuine.

In 1936, when the Communists were driven out of Szechuan and moved to the northwestern area, Chang Hsueh-liang received instructions from Chiang moving him to Sian in Shensi Province and was told to be ready to continue the fight against the Communists in that district. A large portion of the soldiers under his command had come down with him from Manchuria. They now came into contact with the Communist troops. The provinces in which they were stationed were poor and barren. Life was difficult, and they began to think of their homes back in Manchuria. The Communists, past masters in the art of propaganda, capitalized on the opportunity to exhort the soldiers. "Why don't you fight against the foreign invader? For the sooner they are gone, the earlier you can go back to your homes and villages. After all we are all Chinese. Why should you be fighting us instead of fighting the Japanese?" The words took effect. Chang Hsueh-liang's soldiers became restive and desired more to join the Communists than to fight against them. Representatives called upon the Young Marshal and persuaded him to follow the popular demand for a united front against the Japanese invaders. That was a critical moment for him. In the meantime, Chiang dispatched an able soldier from Fukien to head the command against the Communists; he was also to be stationed in Shensi Province. Chang Hsueh-liang took this as an indication of Chiang's waning confidence in him. Funds were not reaching him, although they were being sent regularly but were detained by a subordinate. Another factor was Yang Hu-cheng, then Pacification Commissioner in Sian, who had some divisions of soldiers under him and whose loyalty to the Central Government was none too pronounced. Besides, Chiang's own trusted general, Hu Tsung-nan, of the early Whampoa days had suffered reverses at the hands of the Communists. These and other factors combined to work on the unstable Chang Hsueh-liang. The stage was set for the unfortunate drama which for thirteen days held the entire nation in breathless anxiety.

It was Mencius who said: "When Heaven decides to impose tremendous responsibilities on a man, he first submits him to the severest tests so that his body may endure the greatest of hardships and his spirit may grow strong and powerful. He makes him go through a rigid discipline so as to enable him to attain enormous power of will and accomplish the impossible." Not all the details of what happened in Sian have been revealed. But we do know that it was one of the great crises in Chinese history. The fate of an entire race hung in the balance. Chiang was called upon to use all the spiritual resources at his command. It was an episode which for sheer courage, fortitude, sacrifice, and high patriotism cannot be equaled. Anything less than that would have produced fatal results. The whole situation was Chinese and was difficult for Europeans and Americans to understand. The London *Times* described it as a "strange affair," "a theme for a new Gilbert," "a strange brief interlude in Chinese history." That is true enough. But the more we study the episode, the more we must be impressed by the human qualities of its participants. Chiang undoubtedly came out of this incident a stronger person and a nobler soul. With him was his wife, whose devotion, courage, and spirit of sacrifice were likewise examples that will not easily be forgotten.

Out of it all was created a more beautiful harmony of man and wife through the sharing of a harrowing common experience.

On receiving reports that Chang Hsueh-liang was wavering, Chiang Kai-shek flew from Loyang to Sian. There was no other alternative for him. It was all very well to say that the entire resources of the country should be pooled to fight against the foreign invader, but Chiang first had to be sure that there was no trouble within. So he took the bold step of meeting Yang Hu-cheng and Chang Hsueh-liang in person. He wanted them to proceed with the anti-Communist campaign as originally planned. Chang was on the horns of a dilemma. If he obeyed Chiang's orders his own soldiers would probably create trouble for him: they would refuse to fight. If he disobeyed he had no idea what Chiang would do with him. The wave of popular disapproval of the government's apathy toward Japan was then strong, and Chang decided to ride it and see how far it would carry him.

Chiang left Loyang on December 4, and on arriving first at Tungkwan he summoned the commanders of the anti-Communist troops from Shensi and Kansu for conferences with him. He asked about conditions at the front and told his listeners that the campaign which had been going on for eight long years was close to being successfully concluded. The activities at Suiyuan to the north were to be the final effort. If they would only carry out his orders and fight on with determination and courage, all would be over in a few days, and the nation could then direct its attention to the Japanese.

On December 8 Chiang arrived at Sian and continued the conferences with the same commanders in the presence of Chang Hsueh-liang. He spoke at great length about the proposed campaign, and Chang displayed unquestioned obedience and loyalty. Three days later, after having given all the necessary instructions and dispatched a few wires to Yen Hsi-shan and Fu Tso-yi in Shensi, Chiang retired to a celebrated bath at Lintung, some fifteen miles outside of Sian, for a rest. That was a favorite spot as it commands a beautiful view, and the air is refreshing. In the evening he gave a dinner to which he invited Chang Hsueh-liang, Yang Hu-cheng and another former Manchurian general, General Yu Hsueh-chung. Only Chang turned up, excusing the other two by saying that they were themselves hosts at a dinner in Sian to which they had invited the high civil and military officials who had accompanied Chiang on this trip. Chang added that he himself had to join them as soon as the dinner with

Chiang was over. All through the dinner, however, Chiang noticed Chang Hsueh-liang's uneasy manner and restlessness. He did not pay much attention to it, as he thought that Chang was probably unhappy over the severity of his attitude during the last few days of discussion. In the meanwhile, Chang brought into Chiang's presence a young colonel, whom he properly introduced, saying that a few words of encouragement from the Generalissimo would do the officer some good. Early next morning the house where Chiang stayed for the night was surrounded by the soldiers of this young colonel.

Chiang rose as usual at five-thirty, and while he was dressing and going through his daily morning exercises he heard gunshots just outside his headquarters. He had brought with him only his personal bodyguards and some twenty uniformed soldiers. He sent one of his lieutenants out to see what was going on. The lieutenant dispatched a messenger back to report that the troops had mutinied and that they were soldiers of Chang Hsueh-liang. The messenger said that there was no time to lose and that Chiang must leave at once. Finding some of the doors securely locked, Chiang then scaled the wall, which was only about ten feet high, but just outside the wall there was a deep moat about thirty feet below the top of the wall. To quote from his own diary:

As it was still dark, I missed my footing and fell into the moat. I had a bad pain and was unable to rise. About three minutes later I managed to stand up and walk with difficulty. After having walked several tens of paces we reached a small temple, where some of my bodyguards were on duty. They helped me climb the mountain.

Chiang was then still under the impression that the mutiny was a local affair.

After about half an hour we reached the mountain top and sat down on a piece of level ground for a short rest. I sent a bodyguard to a cliff before us to reconnoiter. Presently gunfire was heard on all sides. Bullets whizzed by quite close to my body. Some of the bodyguards were hit and dropped dead. I then realized that I was surrounded, that the mutiny was not local but the whole of the northeastern troops took part in it. So I decided not to take shelter but to go back to my headquarters and see what could be done. I walked down the mountain as quickly as I could. Halfway down the mountain I fell into a cave which was overgrown with thorny shrubs and with barely enough space to admit me. I was exhausted. Twice I struggled to my feet but fell down again. I was compelled to remain and rest and to wait further developments.

The day was then beginning to dawn, and Chiang could now see that the mountain was surrounded by mutinous troops. He heard machine guns and hand grenades going off near his headquarters. His small bodyguard was trying to fight the rebels, but of course most of them were killed. The rebels approached where Chiang was sitting and, seeing him, wondered if he was the person they were after. It was then that he raised his voice and said, "I am the Generalissimo. Don't be disrespectful. If you regard me as your prisoner, kill me, but don't subject me to indignities." The rebels dared not kill him but fired into the air and shouted, "The Generalissimo is here."

It was then nine o'clock, and the colonel who had been introduced to Chiang the previous night by Chang Hsueh-liang came in and requested that Chiang enter a car to be taken into the city of Sian, where, he was told, Chang Hsueh-liang was waiting to see him. Actually Chiang was taken not to Chang's headquarters but to those of Yang Hu-cheng.

At the same time, while Chang Hsueh-liang's troops were surrounding Chiang at Lintung, Yang Hu-cheng's troops placed all the civilian and military officials who had come to Sian with Chiang and whom he had invited to his party the previous evening under detention in the Reception Hostel where they were being quartered. They were all important people and included Chiang Po-li, who had arrived the previous day to render a report on his recent travels in Europe to Chiang Kai-shek. Chiang Po-li was not then holding any responsible post in the government, but he had been president of the Paoting Military Academy, and a large number of his students were scattered through the different government armies. He was a man of great charm, and although a military man and thoroughly Chinese, he was also deeply interested in European art and culture.

Chiang Po-li and the others were not molested during the detention. They were completely cut off from the outside world, except that now and then young colonels who held them under guard would enter the hostel and exchange a few words with them. One of them sighed deeply as he was questioned for some information, and said, "You gentlemen are all getting on in years, but you don't realize what sorrows we of the younger generation are going through. However, there is nothing important. Just rest yourselves and nothing will happen." The news that something serious had occurred did not reach them until the afternoon, when newsboys began yelling on the streets. They were later assigned to a separate room with an orderly my husband if such a sacrifice could be of the least benefit to the nation. . . . Place the armies in position if you so desire, but do not fire a single shot. Meanwhile let us use every effort to secure his release. If peaceful means fail, then it is not too late to use force." But the people would not listen to her. She suggested that she fly to Sian to see the actual situation for herself. The "suggestion was received with stern disapproval." She was told that her going would be entirely futile, that she was exposing herself to unnecessary risks, and that she might be held as a hostage and tortured in order to make her husband submit to the demands of the rebels. She ultimately succeeded in having William Henry Donald, an Australian friend long associated with the Chiangs, who incidentally also knows the "Young Marshal" well (having taught him years before how to play golf and enjoy the pleasures of outdoor life), to proceed to Sian and establish contact with Chiang. On December 14 came word from Donald that all was well with the Generalissimo, and he urged H. H. Kung and Mme. Chiang to fly to Sian at once. But some of the people in Nanking still would not believe it. They insisted that the Donald telegram was sent by someone else to lure her and Kung to Sian, where they would be captured.

Then followed more agonizing and bitter days during which time planes were kept busy flying between Sian, Loyang, and Nanking, and Mme. Chiang continued her battle of wits with the people in Nanking so that punitive measures against Chang Hsueh-liang might be delayed. She was convinced that in the ensuing confusion which would certainly accompany any active military measures no one could tell what would happen to Chiang Kai-shek. On December 19, Mme. Chiang's brother, T. V. Soong, arrived in Sian and sent her a wire saying that Chiang was in good health. Her confidence began to grow. She was now sure that, if only she could see Chang Hsueh-liang and talk with him herself, the situation might be saved. For "Mr. Donald had laid the foundation, T.V. had built the walls, and it would be I who would have to put on the roof." So she thought, and on December 22, accompanied by General Chiang Ting-wen and Donald, she boarded a plane and flew to her husband. Shortly before she landed, she handed Donald a pistol and made him promise that, in case the troops were hostile and got out of control, he was to shoot her without hesitation.

Mme. Chiang's meeting with the captors, Chang Hsueh-liang and Yang Hu-cheng, was dramatic. There was tremendous tension which had to be held under control. She shook hands with them as if nothing had happened. And then she met her husband. The joy, the comfort, the consolation of again being together during the greatest crisis of their life and in the life of the nation, and the bitterness and resentment against those who were the cause of it all—these and many other feelings were theirs when they saw each other again. Chiang began to sob after saying to his wife, "Why have you come? You have walked into a tiger's lair." But he was supremely happy, for in turning over the pages of the Bible that morning his gaze had fallen on the words: "Jehovah will now do a new thing, and that is, He will make a woman protect a man." The prophecy had become true.

He was thin and pale; it was pathetic to see him. But now with the arrival of the woman whom he so deeply loved the crisis passed into a new phase. He was more confident and his spirit was more cheerful, although no one knew what his fate was going to be. Sian might still turn out to be a death trap.

Repeated talks with Chang Hsueh-liang convinced Mme. Chiang that he at least had no malicious designs. "This would never have happened at all had you been here, madame," he said to her once, which was a great surprise to her. "We did wrong in seizing the Generalissimo, but we tried to do something which we thought was for the good of the country. But the Generalissimo would not discuss things with us. He was so angry after we detained him that he would not talk at all. Please, you try to make the Generalissimo less angry and tell him we really do not want anything, not even for him to sign anything. We do not want money, nor do we want territory."

What had happened to make Chang Hsueh-liang repent his rash action? There were many reasons, but the principal one was that he had been tremendously impressed by the strength of Chiang's personality during the days of captivity. Chiang steadfastly declined to consider, much less accept, any demands that were presented to him while he was being detained. "Do you think," he once said to Chang Hsueh-liang, "that by using force you can compel me to surrender to you rebels? Today you are in possession of deadly weapons. I have none, but I am armed with the principles of righteousness. These are my weapons of defense. With these I must defend the honor of the people whom I represent and remain a faithful follower of Sun Yat-sen. I shall do nothing to betray the trust placed in me by the martyrs of the revolution. I shall not bring shame and dishonor to this world, to the memory of my parents and to the nation. You, young man, do you think you can make me submissive by force? You mistake my stand on the principles of law and order for obstinacy. If you are a brave man, kill me; if not, confess your sins and let me go. If you do neither, you will be in a dangerous position. Why don't you kill me now?"

A man who could take a stand so unflinching, who could regard death so lightly, was the sort of person Chang Hsueh-liang did not think existed any more. It was a credit to the young man that he did recognize it. For unstable as he was, Chang Hsueh-liang was still an intelligent person and had the capacity to know greatness when he encountered it.

There was another thing. The Young Marshal's views on Chiang were fortified by the diary which he had seized and read. That established beyond any doubt that Chiang was a thoroughly sincere man. Chang confessed to Chiang himself: "We have read your diary and other documents and from them have learned the greatness of your personality. Your loyalty to the revolutionary cause and your determination to bear the responsibility of saving the country far exceed anything we could have imagined. You have blamed me in your diary for having no character. I now really feel that this may be so. Your great fault is that you have always spoken too little of your mind to your subordinates. If I had known one tenth of what is recorded in your diary I would certainly not have done this rash act." The ability to admit one's fault implies moral courage and is the beginning of all moral development. It is the mark of a superior man, as Confucius used to say; and it was a credit which must not be denied to Chang Hsueh-liang.

Chang Hsueh-liang never understood how that elevation of character in Chiang came about. That part of the conversation between captor and captive which Chiang preserved was one of the most illuminating chapters of the diary which Chiang has kept for the world. Chang complained to Chiang, "You always have in your head such men as Yo Fei, Wen Tien-hsiang and Sze Ko-fa and are therefore behind time in your thinking. Why do you insist upon sacrificing yourself for the sake of principles and not think of the possibility of achievement? I think you are the only great man of this age, but won't you yield a little, comply with our request, and lead us on in this revolution so that we may achieve something instead of merely sacrificing your life? In our opinion, to sacrifice one's life is certainly not a good plan, nor the real object of a revolutionary."

These remarks are interesting not only because they show the dif-

completely wrong in doing what he did. He had been won over to
Chiang Kai-shek and could no longer work together with Yang Hu-
cheng. It soon became certain that Chiang was in no immediate
danger. But a rash act of such magnitude, especially when it involved
an accomplice, could not be so rapidly terminated. A certain length
of time was needed for the plot to unravel itself. The problem of
Yang Hu-cheng had still to be handled with tact, though with firmness. He must be made to feel how isolated his position was, yet certainly nothing should be done to provoke him. The psychology of a
desperado is a peculiar one. It is not enough for him to acknowledge
his own moral turpitude; he may sometimes even go to the extent of
carrying an act of desperation to its logical end simply because he
feels that the situation is irretrievable. Hence it was important that
the Nanking military officers refrained from giving the orders to
assume the offensive against the rebels. Mme. Chiang had the correct
instincts from the very beginning. Chiang himself was ready to die
at any moment, for, as he said, his own sacrifice would be his supreme
accomplishment. But for the entire country it was clearly not his
death but his life that was important.

Fortunately Chiang Po-li was allowed to call on Chiang and, taking
the same side as Mme. Chiang though without knowing it, he urged
over and over again that the military authorities at Nanking must be
given to understand that the punitive expedition should be called
off and the contemplated bombing of the rebel area stopped at once.
Chiang Po-li came in again the next day and urged Chiang to issue
the orders, as actual fighting was reported to have broken out. Chiang
finally agreed and dispatched a note to Ho Ying-chin to suspend
hostilities for at least three days.

In the meantime, Chang Hsueh-liang, having already read Chiang's
diary and wanting now to do everything to protect his captive rather
than harm him, strongly urged Chiang to move to another house.
Chiang was at first confined in the headquarters of the Pacification
Commissioner, which meant that the guards were Yang Hu-cheng's
men. Chiang could not understand the meaning of this request and
refused to consider it. His reply was that if he had to die it was only
proper that he should die in the headquarters that was directly under
the jurisdiction of the Executive Yuan, of which Chiang was then
president, rather than in the private residence to which Chang Hsueh-
liang wanted to move him. It was not until Donald came to Sian
that Chang Hsueh-liang managed to get across his meaning, and

through joint pressure they finally succeeded in having Chiang move into the Kao residence, where he stayed for the remaining period of his confinement.

With the arrival of Mme. Chiang and her brother, T. V. Soong, Chang Hsueh-liang's anxiety to bring the whole episode to a happy close became more pronounced. But as he admitted to Mme. Chiang, "Others were implicated in the affair," and he could not make any move without their approval and consent. He agreed, however, to talk the matter over with them without delay, and the next three or four days he spent in protracted negotiations with Yang Hu-cheng and the other accomplices.

Yang Hu-cheng knew that the game was up, but he insisted on having guarantees of his own personal safety. Chang Hsueh-liang talked with him until the early hours of the morning while Mme. Chiang kept vigil over her injured husband. Chang gave her this report: "Yang and his men are not willing to release the Generalissimo. They say that since T.V. and Madame are friendly toward me my head would be safe, but what about theirs? They now blame me for getting them into this affair and say that since none of our conditions are granted they would be in a worse fix than ever if they now released the Generalissimo. There will be another meeting tomorrow."

The days dragged on with no tangible results in sight. The suspense continued and with suspense an atmosphere of gloom. Christmas was drawing near, and the great leader of the nation was still under detention, though happily his wife was near him. "Merry Christmas," he said to her on that early Christmas morning of 1936. "Merry Christmas to you," she replied. And their hearts warmed and they felt strong, although their fate was still a matter of uncertainty. Then two servants came in, walking slowly as if on parade, each holding in his hands a stocking—yes, a golf stocking, one with a typewriter tied to it bearing a message of greeting for her, and the other with a steamer rug suspended with a similar message of greeting for him. Donald had done it. One can always depend upon him to do the unusual but wise thing. Chiang laughed his first laugh in Sian, saying, "That's just like the old gentleman." Often Donald has done something similar to cheer the hearts of people when they most needed it. He flew in an airplane once from Peiping to Shanghai with T. V. Soong, my wife, and myself. We were all feeling rather unwell until he began writing doggerel on a copy of Shelley and sent us into fits of laughter.

Christmas Day dragged on. Every hour was an hour of anguish. Ten o'clock, ten-thirty, eleven—and so it went on with hopes rising and then falling again. It was not till two in the afternoon that T. V. Soong rushed in with the great news that those who were in command of the city had agreed that the Generalissimo and his party were free and could leave. The gloom was lifted. Chang Hsueh-liang also came in, and asked, "But why leave so late? Would it not be better to wait till the morning and go direct to Nanking?"

Replied Mme. Chiang, always alert and supremely intelligent: "Wait! The quicker we clear out of here, the better. Wait! Till these people change their minds again? Give them another night in which to vacillate, to develop more fears, perhaps to run amuck—and this is Christmas Day! No indeed! We leave while the leaving is good!"

The information was conveyed to Chiang Kai-shek. He heard the news calmly and requested that Chang Hsueh-liang and Yang Hucheng be brought to him for a few words before he terminated his fortnight's residence at Sian.

When they had come before him he spoke quietly but earnestly. "This coup d'état," he said, "is an act that gravely affects the continuity of Chinese history of five thousand years. Upon it depended also the life and death of the nation. It is a criterion according to which the entire character of the Chinese race will be judged. Since you have today shown due regard for the welfare of the nation and have decided to send me back to Nanking without again making any special demands on me or forcing me to give any promise or orders, it marks a turning point in the life of the nation and is also an indication of the high moral and cultural achievements of the Chinese race. It is an old saying with us that a perfect gentleman is one who admits his faults and rectifies them. If, during the present crisis, we have arrived at the present conclusion it is because you have the moral courage to admit your faults. You have, through this admission, also immeasurably enhanced the integrity of the race. If you have been convinced by my sincerity and your character has thus become elevated there is no need for you to feel ashamed of being my subordinates. Besides, if you have been so readily converted it will set a good example to others.

"You have been deceived once by reactionary elements and believed that I did not treat people fairly and that I was not loyal to the revolutionary cause. You have now read my entire private diary for the past year, amounting to over sixty thousand words, and the documents

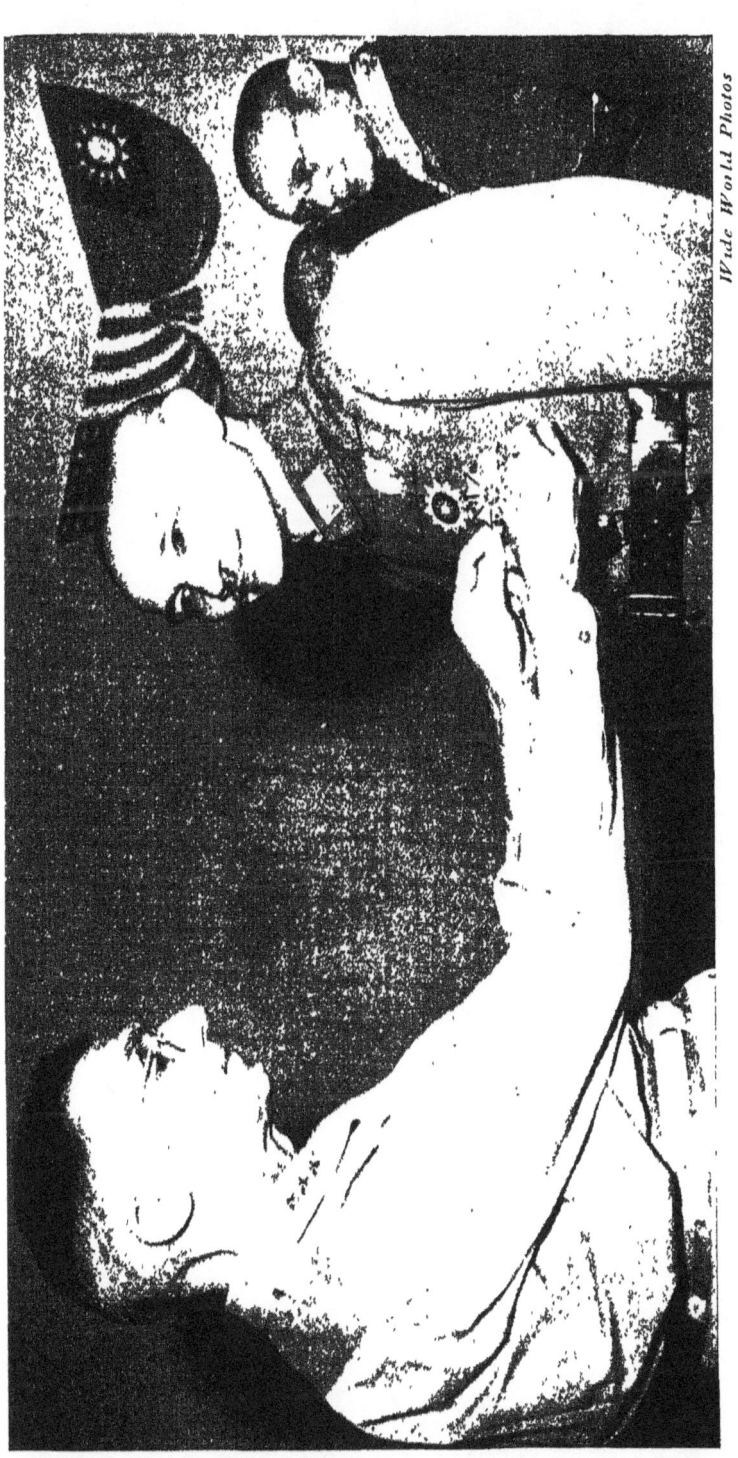

Wide World Photos

Generalissimo Chiang Kai-shek being decorated with the Legion of Merit Order by Lt. Gen. Joseph W. Stilwell, Commander of American forces in China, Burma, and India. The order was in the degree of Chief Commander, and award made on behalf of President Roosevelt.

and telegrams for the last two months, amounting to over fifty thousand words. You have also read my plans for the salvation of the country relating to internal administration, foreign policy, military affairs, economic and educational reorganization, all of which runs to more than one hundred thousand words. I should like to know if in all this material you have discovered one word or one statement which could condemn me of self-interest or of insincerity. . . . I can say in all confidence that I have done nothing of which I need be ashamed. . . .

"I have always told my subordinates that when they commit any mistakes the blame must be laid on the superior officers. As I am in supreme command of the army, it must be because I have not given you good instruction that the present episode could happen. For that I should shoulder the responsibility and ask for punishment by the Central authorities. At the same time, I shall explain to them that you sincerely regret what you have done. You realized your faults at an early stage of the crisis, so that it has been not prolonged, and for that I believe the authorities will show a lenient attitude.

"At the same time, you should let your subordinates know how you were deceived by the reactionary elements in the present crisis and how I always have the welfare of the nation at heart. In that way they will feel comforted and not be disturbed by thoughts of what the government will do to punish them. I have always impressed upon others the importance of high moral principles, of having a sense of honor, a sense of responsibility, and submission to discipline. . . . Moreover we must realize that the life of a nation is above every other consideration. A nation must live even at the expense of the individual. But it is only when we preserve a high character that the foundations of a nation can be laid. Our personal lives may be sacrificed, but the law and discipline of the nation must be upheld. Our bodies may be confined, but our spirit must be free.

"You have repeatedly tried to make me sign or give you written promises. I have always refused. This is because I value character and moral principles more than I do life or death. . . . If I had agreed to sign anything under duress at Sian, then the integrity of the entire nation which I represent would have perished. Whether it be an individual or a nation, the loss of integrity is equivalent to death itself. . . .

"Dr. Sun Yat-sen used to instruct us that in order to effect a national revival we must first rebuild and strengthen the moral fiber of the race. Honesty, sense of duty and public service, love of peace and justice—these are all great virtues for any nation. For over a decade I have devoted my life to the unification of the country and I have laid special emphasis on honor and duty. I have tried to do everything for the country in total disregard of any personal interest. It has been the policy of the government during the last few years to promote as speedily as possible a real unification, to establish peace, and to build up the resources and energy of the people. You have, in precipitating the present crisis, been responsible for breaking the law of the land and bringing on warfare. But you have now repented, and I can recommend the government to have the matter settled in a way that will not be prejudicial to the interests of the nation. . . . This is the way to save the nation from the dangers which it is facing; it is also the way to turn a national calamity into a national blessing."

Chiang left Sian with his party at about three o'clock in the afternoon and arrived at Loyang two and a half hours later. There he passed the night, and the next morning continued the flight to Nanking. The day he arrived at the capital marked a new epoch in his life and in the life of China. The spontaneous joy of the people was unbounded. The feeling that in the safe return of this one man a national crisis had been averted and the belief that all was going to be well, was so genuine and wide-spread that when Chiang's plane arrived at the airdrome shortly after noon, there was a throng of nearly half a million people waiting to give him a rousing welcome. The entire government turned out, shouting, "Long live the Generalissimo," "Long live the Kuomintang," "Long live the Chinese Republic," as Chiang took off his hat in the plane in recognition of the enthusiasm. When he stepped out of the plane with his wife at his side, his head clean-shaven, and dressed in the traditional Chinese long gown and jacket, he looked more like a scholar and a recluse than a military man ruling a nation of four hundred and fifty million people. He went up to President Lin Sen and respectfully bowed. To all the other officials he nodded his head as an expression of his appreciation. He then drove slowly through the streets where the people had assembled to give him a tumultuous ovation, greater, warmer, and more touching than he had received on his birthday less than two months before. The houses and stores were all beflagged and bannered, and the cheering was drowned in the din of thousands of bursting firecrackers. The whole of Nanking was on the streets to take part in the demonstration and parade. The theaters and amusement places, which had been closed for three days as a token of sorrow for Chiang's plight, all opened again for the most unrestrained and uncontrolled expression of joy and merrymaking that Nanking had ever known.

It was a solid testimonial that Chiang had won his way to the hearts of the most populous nation in the world. The people were now completely behind him.

Even the London *Times,* which continued to be bewildered by an episode that it could not understand, came out with an editorial that "General Chiang Kai-shek's escape from a strange and dangerous predicament has been hailed with immense relief by vast numbers of his fellow countrymen and will be welcomed by all Europeans who realize how much his sane and prudent leadership has contributed to the unification and development of the new China."

The first official act of Chiang Kai-shek upon his return to Nanking was to send a petition to the government asking that he be relieved of all his posts and that he be punished for his neglect in the performance of his duties. The supreme organ of the Kuomintang called a special meeting to deliberate over the matter, and it was unanimously decided that these requests need not be considered. The members of the meeting all stood when the motion was passed, which was an unusual mark of appreciation. An official reply to the request was given, which stated:

... During a period of great difficulty and danger you were able to maintain the spirit of grandeur and Olympian calm, you were able to show a large and magnanimous personality so that those who created the trouble became deeply and sincerely moved and at last repented. What is there about the episode to make you desire to resign from your posts, much less to ask for punishment?

Chang Hsueh-liang, who flew in another plane and came to Nanking with Chiang Kai-shek, likewise asked for punishment. He addressed a letter to Chiang in which he said that his nature was "crude, coarse, and wild," admitted responsibility for the entire episode, and asked for the severest punishment so that law and discipline in the country might be maintained. This letter was duly transmitted to the supreme organ of the Kuomintang with the recommendation from Chiang that "in view of his [Chang Hsueh-liang's] admission of guilt and repentance, the government be lenient with him and show a forgiving attitude so that he may lead a new life."

The military tribunal of the Military Council subsequently conducted a court-martial and decided upon a ten-year imprisonment and a suspension of his civil rights for five years. Whereupon Chiang requested a special pardon for Chang Hsueh-liang from the government, which was granted.

The attitude of Soviet Russia and Japan during the episode is worth examining. To what extent the Chinese Communists were then attached to the apron strings of Soviet Russia is a moot question. But when Chang Hsueh-liang precipitated the crisis he issued a statement saying that he was in favor of an understanding with Soviet Russia and with the Chinese Communists. The impression spread rapidly that if he had the courage to do as he did he must have received support or connivance from either or both of those quarters. The Moscow government, by a frank answer, at once disclaimed any knowledge of the plot and deprecated the action as being destructive of Chinese national unity. The Soviet chargé d'affaires was expressly instructed by his government to make clear to Nanking that it had nothing whatever to do with the Sian revolt and that, in fact, ever since Manchuria had been attacked by the Japanese in September 1931, the Soviet Government had not directly or indirectly established any contact with Chang Hsueh-liang. He further stated that the Soviet Government had not been in contact with the Chinese Reds either, so that it in no way could be responsible for anything that they might have done or might do in the future.

But the position of the Chinese Communists was different. By word and by deed Chang Hsueh-liang gave the world to understand that he was in close touch with them. When the government gave him instructions to push into the last stronghold of the Communists with the hope that the whole problem of Communism might be liquidated in a few short weeks, he sent back wires to Nanking giving all kinds of excuses. His troops were, in fact, fraternizing with the Reds. Exactly what understanding he made with them is still open to question, but the fact that the Communists took no advantage of Chiang's detention made a deep and lasting impression on everyone. It was natural to think that if the Reds were implicated in the plot, and if they nursed a personal hatred against Chiang Kai-shek as an enemy who had pursued them over thousands of miles for eight solid years, they would have made full use of the opportunity and taken revenge on him. Nothing of the sort happened. Not only that, the Communists helped in effecting the release of Chiang. Mme. Chiang herself testified in her account of the Sian incident that the Communists "were not interested in detaining the Generalissimo."

That was, in fact, a wonderful manifestation. Throughout the Sian incident, unhappy as it was, there was on all sides a deep solicitude for the national welfare. How much that was an advancement in the political morality of the people can be judged by the fact that the personal element has admittedly always been a strong and often decisive factor in Chinese politics. The temptation for the Communists to take revenge was strong, but they yielded, which was an eloquent tribute to their group discipline. They insisted that what they wanted was a "united front" against a foreign foe. They hoped that in the face of this grave danger all differences within the country should be put aside and forgotten, and they made it clear that they recognized Chiang Kai-shek as the logical and only leader under whose banner they were willing to fight against the Japanese. Chang Hsueh-liang was inspired by the same motives.

These are, I think, important considerations, for the Communist question remains a serious one and must be settled someday. If, as the Soviet diplomatic representative declared to the Chinese Government then, the Moscow government had nothing to do with the Chinese Communists—a belief which should be reinforced by the dissolution of the Comintern—then the question becomes largely a domestic issue and should be effectively and peacefully settled. The predominant factor to remember in the present political life of China is that Chiang Kai-shek has created and maintained a unified government for so long that no one, for purely practical reasons, would have the courage to disrupt that unity on pain of receiving unqualified condemnation. No group, least of all the Communists, who certainly have consistently displayed intelligence, would wish to bear the opprobrium of wrecking that unity. All talk, therefore, of renewed civil war in China as soon as the present war is over is, to say the least, irresponsible gossip. It has been Chiang Kai-shek's practice for some years now to solve all internal differences by political means and not by military force. As Mme. Chiang observed, "That had been the policy of the Generalissimo and was so even in the case of the Communists. How often had he ordered airplanes to drop leaflets telling the Communists that if they would repent and behave like law-abiding citizens they would be forgiven and could do China material good?" Perhaps the problem is not as simple as Mme. Chiang put it. But granting that the Communists have just grievances, the fact remains that there can be and will be no future civil war, particularly if foreign support of one kind or another is not permitted to complicate matters. As long as the issue is a domestic one, I believe that it is only a question of working out a *modus vivendi,* and that in the course of time it will be worked out. The Communists to this day give warm support to Chiang Kai-shek, and as George Uhlmann observed in an article published in the *New Masses* (August 31, 1943) there is "not one anti-Kuomintang slogan to be seen throughout the so-called Communist areas. The Generalissimo," he continued, "is held in high esteem, and it must not be forgotten that when he was kidnaped at Sian it was guerrilla leaders, through Chow En-lai, who interceded and secured his release." And in one of the pictures which he produced for the article, a slogan inscribed on a wall was clearly visible: "Let's support Generalissimo Chiang Kai-shek for his resistance to the end."

But what was the attitude of Japan during the Sian incident? There was no question that the incident concerned her more than any other foreign power. She was then already at war with China. She had occupied Manchuria, penetrated to south of the Great Wall, signed the Tangku agreement, while the incident was, furthermore, fomented on a pro-Soviet and anti-Japanese platform. Clearly it was an event of paramount interest to the Japanese. Which side were they going to take? Clearly they could not be sympathetic to Chang Hsueh-liang. They would very much like to show sympathy to Chiang Kai-shek, which in a way they did, but they were beset with doubts, for, after all, was not Chiang the person who created Chinese national unity and had stood as its symbol? And a strong and unified China in the long run could not, so the Japanese thought, be a blessing to Japan. Had not General Hayao Tada, on September 24, 1935, then in command of the Japanese forces in north China, said very clearly that Japan and Chiang Kai-shek's Nationalist party could not exist alongside each other? Every obstacle which the Japanese had met in their attempted conquest of north China could be traced back to Chiang Kai-shek. Should not, therefore, his detention be an occasion for rejoicing?

The Japanese were clearly torn by conflicting points of view. The Foreign Office at Tokyo called an urgent meeting and communicated its decision to remain calm to the army and navy, which in turn held a joint meeting and decided upon two principles: 1. To be prepared to adopt measures for self-protection. 2. To remain quiet and to be on the alert. The newspapers went in for all kinds of comment. The more liberal-minded Japanese suggested that use should be made of the opportunity to show friendship to China and establish Sino-Japanese relations on a new basis. Other Japanese were not unmindful of the fact that Chiang was the center of the anti-Communist movement and could not, therefore, support the pro-Soviet platform of Chang Hsueh-liang. Doihara, the so-called Lawrence of north China, was of the opinion that the hand of Soviet Russia was all too clearly visible and that Japan should assume a positive attitude toward China. Still others, following the same line of thought, were of the opinion that China had reverted to chaos, and it was Japan's responsibility to preserve the peace of east Asia. The result was that these different observations neutralized one another, and Japan followed a policy of non-action. It was well for China that they did so, for only six months afterward Chiang Kai-shek was called upon to play a major part in the conflict that has now become world-wide.

35

The General Surveys the Field

IT WAS on January 2, 1937, a week after his return from Sian, that Chiang Kai-shek left Nanking with Mme. Chiang for his native village of Chikow. He needed a rest, a long rest, after the suffering he had gone through during his detention. He had taken a bad fall and it was necessary that he seek medical advice. He had an X-ray made which fortunately showed that there was no serious damage. Even so he consulted a bone specialist in Shanghai, and a long rest away from the cares of state affairs was prescribed. That, however, was prescribing something impossible to fulfill.

The Sian incident, though it had been concluded, pursued Chiang even to Chikow. While the Young Marshal had the intelligence to realize the folly of an ill-considered and unpatriotic move, Yang Hucheng still retained his truculence. He seemed to be deeply penitent when called in for the valedictory address which Chiang gave before he left Sian, but when left alone to himself Yang's old plans came back with renewed vigor. He persisted in his contact with the Communists, with whom he thought he had made a fruitful alliance. He was far away from Nanking, for his headquarters were in Shensi and Kansu provinces, close to the Mongolian border, and he believed that if he continued to be defiant, particularly since he had maintained friendly relations with the Communists, there was nothing that the Central authorities could do. He even sent his personal representatives to Chikow to negotiate for terms favorable to himself. Chiang replied by sending him a letter written in a friendly tone, reminding him of the great responsibilities which he had and advising him not to disrupt the national unity that had been created through years of unremitting labor. Yang thought that this message was an expression of weakness. He then composed four demands which he sent to Nanking and requested that they be accepted as a condition for his continued allegiance to the Central Government. They included: 1. The granting of a proper legal status to the Communist army and the withdrawal of the punitive expedition against it. 2. The elimination of all internal wars and conflicts in order to pool the nation's resources for a war against Japan. 3. The power to appoint their own commanders for the Communist armies without having to apply to the Central Government. 4. Subsidy by the Central Government in the way of funds and equipment.

These and similar demands continued to pour in and annoy Chiang while he was resting at Chikow. He ignored them all and gave instructions that measures be taken against Yang. In the meantime, while he was seemingly relaxing among the hills and mountains of his childhood home, his mind was absorbed with the grave issues by which the country was confronted. His experience at Sian had enabled him to take stock of the situation. He had been able to ask himself a few basic questions. It had been his ambition, through ten years of persistent labor, to create a unified government for the country. Had he succeeded? Had all the vestiges of the war-lord regime been eliminated? Yang Hu-cheng was the last of a long line of medieval-minded swashbucklers who refused to see the nation as a political entity. The fact that although he had been under detention at Sian, yet the country remained peaceful and its government continued to function normally, convinced Chiang that at last the unity which he had sought had indeed become a reality. The Sian episode, unfortunate as it was, therefore came to have a new significance for Chiang. That no one had been bold enough to take advantage of the opportunity to expand his military power was indeed an indication that from now on he could think of launching upon a larger policy more in keeping with the nation's needs. Those who normally would have been expected to take advantage of the situation actually heartily disapproved of Yang Hu-cheng's reckless action and remained loyal to the Central Government.

The problem of Japan could not be solved except by the sword. Chiang, who had studied in Japan, understood the Japanese well, and, knowing what their national policy consisted of, he was under no illusions whatever that the Manchurian incident of September 18, 1931, was the beginning of a life-and-death struggle between the two nations. Surrounded by the peace and quiet of his native Chikow, Chiang could now reassess the entire situation. He had won unity, and that was an important factor in his new policy. But the Communists were still a menace to that unity. They had their own troops, which were not an integral part of the Central Government's military organization. That was a most serious obstacle. But the Communists had repeatedly declared that in a war of resistance against Japanese aggression they would support the idea of placing all the Chinese armies under the unified command of the Central Government, and that they would not take advantage of the situation to increase their own power. Whether these declarations were sincere remained to be seen, but at least they had been made.

Aside from an occasional trip to Nanking to attend a plenary session of the Kuomintang, Chiang Kai-shek spent five months in Chikow, perhaps the longest period that he was actually away from the center of politics since he became actively engaged in them. At no previous time, however, had he been called upon to make such grave decisions affecting the destiny of the country. The avalanche of the Japanese military machine was inexorable. There was nothing to stop it, although by proper maneuvering it might be delayed. The broad lines of Japanese policy were unmistakable. Chiang had stayed in Japan long enough to know that it was a nation of fanatics who had been nurtured on the ideals of Hideyoshi of three hundred years ago and on the dream of world conquest. The militarists had always been in power, and although there was a semblance of constitutional reform and parliamentary government, the Minister of War and the Minister of the Navy were still directly responsible only to the Emperor; therefore they were above Parliament and could at any time wreck the government. The desire to conquer China had showed itself in various ways ever since the war of 1894. The most outspoken expression of that intention was in 1915, when Japan tried to enslave China with the Twenty-one Demands. Another was the Tanaka Memorial, which was a plan for future Japanese aggression. There was no question of its authenticity because its tone and purport agreed perfectly with Japanese aspirations. The Manchurian incident of 1931 was the practical application of that memorial. First the northeastern provinces, then Peiping and Tientsin—what was there to prevent the Japanese from taking Nanking?

How could anybody—how could Chiang Kai-shek of all people—fail to see that the inevitable development of such a policy would affect the national destiny of China? It would indeed give Chiang profound satisfaction if he could call upon the Chinese people to rise at once against the threat. But were they prepared? Would it be a lasting satisfaction? From 1931-36 Chiang therefore had no other alternative than to be supremely patient. The immediate result of Chiang's inaction was that the whole nation seethed with anger against his policy of procrastination. There was a time when Chiang's reputation as a leader, especially in 1933, sank very low, but what did he do? He remained calm. As a responsible leader of a great nation he had to think of the destiny of four hundred and fifty million souls and their history of five thousand years. Every single thought in his mind, every action as a result of that thought, would affect that history and those people. It is only now that the people understand him. As a guerrilla fighter addressing himself "To the Generalissimo" said:

> *You are old! How the ephemeral daily prints*
> *Reveal your frosted looks. It pains*
> *The heart, as if the lateness of the year*
> *Is suddenly betrayed by the sight of red autumnal leaves.*
>
> *No wonder. You are the end of all labors and toil,*
> *Five thousand years' tradition, four hundred million minds*
> *Seek vent in you as water does behind a fountainhead.*
> *Each year you live through more than twelve moons wax and wane.*
> *But your eyes are shining bright,*
> *And midnight when you open the window*
> *The Northern Stars are outshone.*
>
> *"Meet all changes with no change," the papers quote you again.*
> *You persevere to the bitter end,*
> *And in the historic mold you steadily cast yourself.*

If the Chinese people did not know what Chiang's plans were, neither did the Japanese. They thought that by continually trying to stall them he was showing anything but strength. When he was detained at Sian they conveniently took a neutral attitude. They thought that in him they would have a focus of opposition against Communist forces. They little realized that in those later months at Chikow Chiang had reassessed the whole situation and had made up his mind in a way that was to change the whole course of events in Asia. But the Japanese continued to push on, since they felt that they had nothing to fear from a man who for five years had seemingly done everything to placate their feelings.

Into the details of what took place between China and Japan during those years we need not go, because they have been widely recorded as part of the Sino-Japanese War. In the main, the positions of the two countries were expressed in two formulas. The Japanese position as defined by Foreign Minister Hirota was: 1. The cessation of anti-Japanese movements in China and the abandonment by China of a pro-European and pro-American policy as a basis for Sino-Japanese co-operation. 2. The recognition by China of "Manchukuo" and the proper regulation of the relations between China, Japan, and "Manchukuo," particularly as regards north China. 3. China's co-operation with Japan and a decision upon a joint policy with her for the prevention of the spread of Communism. As against this position, the Chinese policy, as decided upon by the Fifth Plenary Session of the Central Executive Committee of the Kuomintang, included: 1. The upholding of China's territorial integrity and sovereignty. 2. The preservation of China's administrative independence. 3. The recognition of the principle of equality in the relations between the two countries. The differences are too wide to admit any reconciliation.

In the mountain fortress of his Chikow home, Chiang now pondered over the preparations he had made. In the event of any armed conflict with Japan Chiang realized that China's communication with the outside world would be immediately disrupted. The coast line of China, which is only slightly more than two thousand miles long, would be completely blockaded in the absence of a protecting navy, and China had no navy. So when the Manchurian incident started, Chiang began systematically to channel the nation's energy into the construction of a system of highways and railways all over the country, particularly in the area south of the Yangtze River. Territory north of that river would be difficult to hold, since the mechanized power of the Japanese army of penetration would rapidly move to occupy it. Near the coast line and along the Yangtze he expected that delaying actions would have to be undertaken. Behind the principal ports of Shanghai and Hankow he had built some thirteen hundred miles of highways, all leading into the interior. In the southwest, in the west, and in the northwest similar highways were built, using millions of laborers. That was the first effort to shift the center of gravity from the coast to the interior. China's development has historically been from the west and northwest to the east and southeast, and to the sea. Chiang realized that for strategic and military reasons the movement must now be reversed. By the time the war began in earnest in 1937 Chiang, in a general way, had solved the problem of communication. The highways were practically all completed, so that a traveler could go by car from the big ports along the coast to the hinterland and from there to Indo-China, Siam, and Singapore, to Burma through the famous Burma Road and down to Rangoon; and through the northwestern provinces of Kansu and Sinkiang to Russia and Europe. For the last highway the famous explorer and archaeologist, Sven Hedin, rendered valuable help. As early as the spring of 1937, when the Lytton Commission was busy in Peiping and Manchuria, I remember we began having informal discussions about the possibility of opening up this 2800-mile highway. The military road which Tso Tsung-tang constructed during the Taiping Rebellion served as an excellent roadbed; the country was flat and construction was easy.

The problem of munitions supply was not so easily solved, and with the exception of rifles and machine guns, which could be produced in none too great quantities in China herself, other equipment had to come from abroad. Even so one would have thought that the construction of the highways before 1937 alone would have made the Japanese feel somewhat uneasy, but evidently all along they considered Chiang an unworthy opponent. It was not until the war had begun that they discovered that Chiang had told his officers back in 1934 that war with Japan was inevitable and that it would be fought to the bitter end.

Although the transportation problem was more or less solved, what about Chiang's soldiers, who after all had to carry the principal burden of the war? What were their numbers? And were they in a position to fight a national war? To this question the Japanese seemed to have paid some attention. The Japanese War Office, shortly before it precipitated the Lukouchiao incident, issued a pamphlet called *Military Preparedness,* which said:

> The Chinese soldiers have been the private soldiers of the war lords and were therefore not unified. Outer Mongolia, Sinkiang, and Tibet are almost self-autonomous territories. In other areas also the war lords have been against the Central Government and seek the expansion of their own power. Chinese soldiers cannot, therefore, be compared to the national defense armies of modern and well-organized countries. But since Chiang Kai-shek succeeded in unifying the country, war lords have either been eliminated or absorbed, and the soldiers also have been incorporated into the armies of the Central Government. The present indications are that a national defense army is gradually taking shape.
>
> There are about two hundred divisions or over two million soldiers in China. Those who have come under the control of the Central Government are now competent enough to wage a foreign war. This is a subject which deserves our consideration. Moreover, these troops have been submitted recently to training by foreign staff officers and have been much improved, and therefore conditions have been very much changed. This has an important bearing on Nanking's policy toward Japan, and for our national defense it is a subject which we cannot ignore.

What precisely had Chiang Kai-shek done to make the Japanese feel uneasy? As early as 1924 Chiang had organized the Whampoa Military Academy, the equivalent of West Point, in which he trained young military officers who achieved such spectacular success in the Northern Expedition. Since then it had been a part of Chiang's policy to keep on enlarging that nucleus until he had a national army directly under the control of the Central Government. The training also was gradually spread over a longer period. It was only a matter of half a year in 1924. Later on training was extended to two years and finally to three. As for equipment, Chiang himself confessed that the five hundred rifles that he managed to get hold of for the cadets during the early years were all taken from the Canton arsenal, then under the control of the northern militarists. When the government was transferred to Nanking it was in a position to establish a number of these academies in various parts of the country with reasonably good equipment.

Chiang tried to keep these specially trained troops of his intact, and when the Northern Expedition was completed he decided to absorb as many soldiers as possible from the outside. For a time, although they were all nominally under the Central Government, the soldiers were of different qualities. Those that Chiang himself had trained constituted a class by themselves, then came the soldiers of the former war lords like Feng Yu-hsiang and Yen Hsi-shan, and finally soldiers from the various provinces who knew only personal loyalty to their chiefs. The fight with the Communists from 1928 on and the engagement with the Japanese around Shanghai in 1932 had some effect on the strength and size of the army, but Chiang early decided that at least sixty divisions should be given the best possible training with officers supplied from the different military academies. These officers numbered some one hundred and seventy thousand. He also established an officers' staff school for training officers of the higher ranks from which some two thousand men were graduated. When the Lukouchiao incident occurred thirty divisions had been trained.

In the training of this army Chiang employed a number of German officers. These were engaged entirely on a professional basis and had nothing to do with the international relations between China and Germany or with China's national policy. German military efficiency was recognized everywhere and the advisers were simply called in to give the training. In November 1928 Max Bauer, the first of these German military advisers, arrived accompanied by a number of assistants. To him was given much credit for defeating Li Tsung-jen when he created trouble for Chiang in the following year. Bauer, however, soon died, after having contracted smallpox. Then came Kriebel, and after him Wetzell, and finally Von Falkenhausen. The man behind the Reichswehr, General von Seeckt, was also in China for a short period and stimulated interest among the Chinese officers for German military methods. At one time there were two hundred of these German officers of one rank or another in China. They were recalled as a group by the German Government in the summer of 1938. On the whole, the relationship between the German officers and the Chinese was friendly, but the Germans' services were entirely of a technical nature, and not only did they exercise no influence on national policy, but even in regard to small matters Von Falkenhausen used to say: "I talk and talk and nobody listens to me." He once made a trip to Shansi, and wherever he went he was entertained with sumptuous dinners. The Chinese army officers were most friendly to him, but they never got around to doing any serious business with him. It was reported that he finally flared up and said: "What have I come for, to eat all these dinners or to train the Chinese Army?" When Japan attacked Pearl Harbor the then Chinese Foreign Minister, Quo Tai-chi, at once declared war on all the Axis powers. China can engage experts from all nations but her national policy remains her own.

The German advisers did indeed provide excellent military training but, after all, a Chinese soldier is Chinese and must receive Chinese discipline. Chiang Kai-shek did not think that mere military training was enough to make a good soldier. A Chinese soldier must be disciplined according to Chinese ideals and Chinese conceptions of life. Lieutenant General Joseph W. Stilwell once paid tribute to the Chinese soldier which is well worth repeating. "To me," said Stilwell, "the Chinese soldier best exemplifies the greatness of the Chinese people, their indomitable spirit, their uncomplaining loyalty, their honesty of purpose, their steadfast perseverance. He endures untold privations, and it never occurs to his simple and straightforward mind that he is doing something heroic. He asks for little and always stands ready to give all."

This is high tribute from a seasoned soldier. Many of these qualities which Stilwell observed are not the result of military training. They are just an integral part of being the plain common man of China.

But to become a really good soldier the common man has to go through the crucible of mental and spiritual discipline, and Chiang Kai-shek has been able to supply that. The following titles of lectures that officers, cadets, and soldiers constantly hear from the Generalissimo indicate the kind of training they receive: "What Are the Qualities of a Revolutionary Soldier?" "The Revolutionary Soldier's Moral Improvement." "The Revolutionary Soldier Sacrifices His Life for the Country and the Kuomintang Party." "Character and the Revolution." "Military Rule and Self-Discipline." "The Secret of Success of the Revolutionary Soldier." "The Fighting Spirit, Endurance, and Perseverance of the Soldier." "The Soldier Must Walk on the Road of High Moral Purpose." "What Is Military Discipline?" "The Responsibilities of the Soldier." "The Soldier and National Salvation." "The Soldier's View of Life."

Every soldier is provided with a set of four books which he must read and reread until they have made an indelible impression on his mind. The first is *Observations Supplementary to Military Discipline Compiled by Tseng Kuo-fan and Hu Lin-yi;* the emphasis is entirely on "discipline of the heart," which includes all the instructions for the building of character and personality. The second is *What the Soldier Should Know,* a compendium of Chiang's personal experiences as a soldier since 1926. The third is *The Spiritual Education of the Soldier*, a series of lectures delivered by Sun Yat-sen on the responsibilities and the aims of the military life. The last is *The Philosophical Basis of the Sun Yat-sen Principles*, which explains the soldier's relationship to the state and the race.

For five months, as the Japanese military machine rolled over the north China plains, Chiang Kai-shek stayed in Chikow. He finally came down from the hills, and on May 27 he went aboard a gunboat and sailed for Nanking to announce that he would resume his office in the government. On July 7, less than six weeks afterward, the Japanese struck at Lukouchiao, the Marco Polo Bridge outside of Peiping, and brought on the present war.

36

The Sword Is Unsheathed

A FEW STATEMENTS made by Chiang Kai-shek immediately after Japan's attack at Lukouchiao have become historic. It is essential that we bear them in mind in our estimate of his policy and strategy.

As late as ten days after the incident, Chiang was still saying to a group of Chinese leaders in the summer resort at Kuling that as a weak nation China should have a true estimate of her strength and, if possible, avoid any armed conflict. He reminded them that the aim of the revolution started by Sun Yat-sen was the reconstruction of the nation along sound democratic lines and that peace must be maintained even though it meant suffering and injustice. "While there was the slightest hope for peace we would not abandon it; so long as we had not reached the limit of endurance, we would not talk lightly of sacrifice," he had said. But it was now obvious the showdown was approaching. The Lukouchiao incident was that limit. So he said to the national leaders: "There is only one thing which we can do as a weak nation when we reach the limit of endurance: we must throw every ounce of our energy into the struggle for national existence and independence. Once we have thus begun, neither time nor any other circumstance will permit us to stop until victory is achieved. There will be then no peace. The only possible peace would be complete and abject surrender, which would mean the extinction of our race. I should like, therefore, the whole nation to know the full implication of the words, 'the limit of endurance,' and the extent of the sacrifice it would entail. For once that stage is reached, we can only fight to the bitter end. Only a determined will to sacrifice ourselves to the utmost will bring victory."

Chiang was fully aware that the Lukouchiao incident "raises problems which involve the existence of the Chinese nation as a whole." But even though the Japanese military machine was moving down from the north, he remained calm and gave a last, albeit hopeless, warning to the Japanese. "Whether the Lukouchiao incident will grow into a war between China and Japan depends entirely upon the attitude of the Japanese Government. Whether or not there is any hope for peace between China and Japan depends entirely upon the actions of the Japanese Army. We shall continue to hope for a peaceful solution through diplomatic means until that hope of peace must finally be given up." But he was under no delusions. His final words to these leaders were: "The government is exercising extreme caution as it approaches the grave crisis. Let the whole nation prepare for defense with calmness and rigid discipline. At this great moment when the issue for war or peace hangs in the balance, the nation can be saved only through our united efforts to maintain discipline and order."

No words were more considered. They could have come only from a man fully conscious of the limitations of his country, but conscious also of its strength and power. The Japanese took no heed. They did not think it necessary. They had never thought China a worthy foe. By the end of July the Japanese were in full occupation of Peiping and Tientsin. They moved also in the direction of Inner Mongolia, advancing into Chahar and Suiyuan, cutting the caravan route which was China's principal trade route with Soviet Russia. The whole of north China was in imminent danger.

Chiang Kai-shek reviewed the whole Sino-Japanese relationship from the time of the Mukden incident. In a message to all the armed forces of the nation he said: "Since the Japanese attacked Manchuria on September 18, 1931, every time that we have yielded and borne the indignities, every time have the Japanese considered us weak and given us more oppression. Now we have reached the point where we can endure it no longer: we will give way no more. The whole nation must rise as one man and fight these Japanese bandits until we have completely destroyed them and our life is made secure. Soldiers! The supreme moment has come. With one heart and purpose advance! Never retreat! Drive out the invaders so that our nation may be born anew!"

At last Chiang had given the orders for war. The nation had been clamoring for a showdown ever since 1931. The students and other more vociferous elements were for immediate war with Japan after the Mukden incident, just as if China had been already a well-organized, first-class military power. There was a time when Chiang's popularity and leadership were called into question. There was even active opposition against him from quarters that should have known better. But in spite of all this feverish agitation, Chiang did not waver.

Chiang was himself present when Tanaka, later the author of the infamous memorial which was presented to the Japanese Emperor on July 25, 1927, had an interview with Sun Yat-sen in 1914 at the outbreak of the first European War. Tanaka proposed that China and Japan should make full use of the Europeans' preoccupation in order to advance their mutual interests, which really meant, of course, Japanese interests. He suggested to Sun Yat-sen that China and Japan denounce their treaty relations with the foreign countries and construct "a new order in east Asia." Sun Yat-sen then asked if that step would involve the breaking of treaties which had solemnly been entered into. To which Tanaka replied: "Would not the denunciation of these international treaties and the termination of the unequal obligations be beneficial to China?" Sun solemnly said: "Yes, the unequal treaties should be terminated, but only through proper and legitimate procedure. China is not prepared to become a party to any illegal suspension of the treaties even though there might be advantages."

This episode which Chiang remembers is significant in revealing two completely different points of view toward human behavior. For the Japanese the end justifies the means, and the end is national expansion at all costs. He is never concerned with scruples about the propriety or the justice of the measures which he resorts to for the attainment of the end. The Chinese, on the other hand, is primarily concerned with the moral issue in anything that he does. Even though the end may be highly desirable, as, for instance, the abolition of the unequal treaties, if the procedure is open to question he would rather not have it. It is disconcerting to reflect how this bifurcation between the two peoples originated, for, after all, the basic ideals of Japanese life have been in the main of Chinese origin, and it is possible to

THE SWORD IS UNSHEATHED

establish the case that there is some identity of cultural background between them. But a Chinese conception, once it crosses over to the Japanese islands, somehow becomes different. Take, for example, the Chinese conception of *wang-tao,* as distinguished from *pah-tao.* The former means the kingly way or the way of moral persuasion while the latter means the way of force. The Chinese do not try to make an issue of the two: it is implied that in human conduct, whether it be between individuals or nations, the moral way should and must prevail. But the Japanese publicize their *kodo,* which is supposed to be their version of the *wang-tao,* and the result is that it is something even cruder than the *pah-tao,* which the Chinese deprecate. They have murdered, killed, plundered, raped, and poisoned the Chinese population wherever their soldiers have appeared on Chinese soil, and they still describe all this in terms of their *kodo.* The kidnaping of Henry Puyi and making him the puppet Emperor of Manchuria is *kodo.* The creation of the puppet Prime Minister, Wang Ching-wei, at Nanking is *kodo.* What a travesty of the original Chinese conception!

The same is true of the Japanese cult of *bushido.* What do people hear about *wu-shi-tao* in China, from which *bushido* is derived? They are three identical characters that are pronounced differently in Japanese. The original Chinese *wu-shi-tao* is a cult of gentlemanly conduct based upon the virtues of the Confucian moral hierarchy. It is in the true and highest sense a code of chivalrous conduct. But the Japanese in Guadalcanal, and for that matter in China, where reports about their behavior were not believed by the outside world until confirmed by what they have recently done in the Southwestern Pacific islands, shot down and brutally tortured helpless victims of war, and they called that *bushido!*

The Japanese make use of every worthy Chinese conception and distort it out of all recognition. Now and then it is refreshing to find an isolated Japanese who feels somewhat ashamed of this perversion. The *Art of War* by Sun Tse is itself founded upon moral conceptions, but the Japanese have also completely misconstrued its meaning. Ishimaru Tota, who wrote about Chiang, must be given credit for being the only member of his race to realize how the basic ideas of this book have been completely misinterpreted in his country. One of the famous sayings in that book is: "If in a hundred battles you win a hundred victories, that is still not the best strategy. It is when you succeed in conquering your enemy without having to engage him in war that you show the highest and best strategy." In other words, you conquer the enemy's heart by showing that you are a man of integrity and moral probity and that you really mean to promote his interest along with your own when he accepts your point of view and submits himself to you. This is completely over the head of the Japanese, who, as Ishimaru Tota pointed out, believe that it is all vague idealism which is out of keeping with modern warfare and has, therefore, absolutely no practical value. Tota quotes another saying from Sun Tse which the Japanese have also deliberately twisted. "The art of war is a serious national concern. Upon it the nation depends for its life or death. It is imperative that it should receive the most careful consideration." Without reading this in connection with the general spirit of the book, the Japanese take this saying as being a justification that war is inevitable and that militarism must be maintained at all costs.

As a close observer of Japanese life and thought, Chiang Kai-shek knew that to follow a rational policy with these people was impossible. He knew that from the Japanese point of view China and Japan could not live together as two strong nations. In the eyes of Japan the work that Chiang was doing for China was erecting a barrier to the expansion of the Japanese Empire. He had his first experience with Japanese obstructionist policy at Tsinan during the Northern Expedition. Chiang parried it. Then came the Mukden incident. Chiang again resorted to a delaying action and concentrated on putting his own house in order first. But the stronger he grew, the faster became the momentum of Japanese aggression.

The Tanaka Memorial of 1927 made matters all too clear. The first step must be the conquest of China, for "what is most to be feared is the awakening of China; if China were to become united the consequences would be industrial development; it is necessary to control Manchuria and Mongolia and then to use them as a base for the seizure of all China's wealth and resources." Tanaka further declared: "If China be completely conquered by us, Central Asia and Asia Minor, India and the South Seas, with their heterogeneous peoples, will certainly fear and yield to us. The world will be given to understand that east Asia is in our possession. The rich resources of China will become instrumental in the conquest of India, the South Seas, Central Asia, and Asia Minor and Europe."

By July 1937 the Japanese felt that the zero hour had arrived. There were three reasons why they believed that they must now strike at China and, as they thought, bring her to her knees in a few months.

The first was the resignation of the Hayashi government and the appointment of Prince Konoye as Prime Minister. The change of cabinet did not imply any change of policy, for the different groups in Japan all subscribed to the policy of continental expansion. There were only minor differences of opinion as to procedure in the carrying out of the policy. Konoye made certain concessions to the businessmen and capitalists in his country and brought them into still closer co-operation with the militarists than did his predecessor. The military party felt all the more strongly that the nation was solidly behind it in the big game that it had in mind.

The second reason was the situation in Europe, where the policy of continuous appeasement followed by the Western powers was considered as a sign of weakness by the Fascist powers. The Ethiopian conquest strengthened Fascist Italy, which in turn encouraged Hitler in his relationship with his neighbors. "Each act of Fascist aggression in Europe," as a Soviet writer observed, "has been made easier by the provocative advances of Japanese imperialism in the Far East, and vice versa."

The third factor was the increasing realization on the part of the Japanese that Chinese national solidarity was an ugly and unpleasant fact that was becoming only too real. By 1936, the year before the Japanese attacked at Lukouchiao, it had become abundantly clear that isolated cases of anti-Japanese feeling had swollen into a mighty volume. The Japanese had consistently underestimated Chinese strength until it became too late for them to do anything about it. The tide had now become irresistible.

37

Planning a Strategy

I THINK it was Edgar Snow who described Chiang Kai-shek as a weak strategist. It was Snow who observed that "among the world's men of power there has seldom been one so rich in contradictions, so ripe with paradox."[1] It just shows how difficult it is for one who is unfamiliar with Chinese psychology and history to pass judgment upon a man

[1] Edgar Snow, "China's Fighting Generalissimo," *Foreign Affairs*, July 1938, p. 616.

whose entire intellectual and spiritual make-up is so thoroughly Chinese. For Chiang is the very opposite of Snow's description. He is a master strategist if ever there was one. And he is one of the most consistent men that ever lived. He is so consistent that I do not believe he has changed much in his basic conceptions since his adolescence. His separate acts may appear to be baffling, but they are all parts of a large pattern which has a beginning, a middle, and an end. There is complete unity. Take his stand on Communism, for instance. No one can say that he has deviated from the stand he made in 1923. At times that stand has not been obvious, as in the early Borodin days in Canton, out of deference to other considerations; but it is all painted in one color.

So also his strategy. Snow, in the same article, thinks that Chiang "lacks the long-range vision and the unity of concept necessary to make a military genius." My own feeling is that Chiang's plans are based upon such long-range vision and unity of concept that his strategy does not convey the impression of being strategy in the usual sense of the word. A study of his strategy in the Sino-Japanese War will show that he is one of the most extraordinary military geniuses that ever lived. It is obvious that without having planned a first-rate strategy the war could not have been sustained over a long period of time. As a matter of fact, it is because such masterly strategy has been used that we can now feel confident of victory in spite of the many shortcomings and difficulties with which the Chinese nation is clearly confronted in the prosecution of the war. It is not the strategy of single engagements or of isolated battles: it is the strategy for the entire war, based on considerations of all the available forces of both a national and an international nature.

One of the principal factors in the planning of that strategy is the full exploitation of the Japanese underestimation of Chinese strength. As Sun Tse said long ago, one must so conceal one's strength that the enemy will be totally misguided. The Japanese were correct in presuming that China was in no way prepared to meet them on the battlefield. Then Chiang's "long-range vision" played its part. Quietly and with great forbearance he laid the foundations of a new order in China. He was always prepared to yield and to produce the impression that he was not equal to the task of a large-scale war; but by 1936 the country had become sufficiently welded together to withstand foreign aggression. The Japanese did not realize that they themselves contributed in no small measure to the creation of this

Chinese national solidarity. If the south was inclined to be nationalistic and militant, the Japanese believed that the north was at least still imbued with the old war lord spirit. Influenced by General Doihara's reports, they thought they would meet with no difficulty in starting an autonomy movement similar to that in Manchuria and detach from the government at Nanking all that extensive area, which includes the provinces of Chahar, Suiyuan, Hopei, Shansi, and Shantung. Hence the Ho-Umetsu Agreement through which the Japanese hoped to create a new bloc of northern militarists under their protection that would work against Nanking. The scheme completely failed to produce the desired result. The north had learned to regard the problem of China as a whole in the same way as had the southern provinces. The military leaders themselves perhaps did not change their minds so rapidly, but an enormous change had come over the mentality of the people upon whom the militarists had to depend for their support. The Kuomintang ideology had so effectively taken root that the people's sympathy was completely with the government at Nanking. That was a new factor which the militarists in the north had to reckon with. Yen Hsi-shan, Han Fu-chu, and their kind could not now do anything against the wishes of Nanking without running the risk of losing their own power.

The fact is that by the summer of 1937, when the Japanese launched their drive against China, Chiang Kai-shek felt quite sure that he could fight back with a united country behind him. Warlordism, he was convinced, had become a thing of the past. Even his own sad experience in December 1936 at Sian was a clear indication to him that Chang Hsueh-liang might have been misguided, but that he had not used the usual war lord tactics. As Mme. Chiang very truthfully said in her account of the episode:

> What happened at Sian during the fortnight beginning December 12 last was not a rebellion as we know such politico-military upheavals in China. No question of money or increased power or position was at any time brought up. Indeed that aspect of the usual bargaining by recalcitrant military leaders was entirely absent from this mutiny. This is the first time on record that any high officer responsible for mutinous conduct had shown eagerness to proceed to the capital to be tried for his misdeed.

If the Sian incident provided proof that the system of feudal warlordism had definitely become a thing of the past, it also demonstrated the possibility that a united front could be established with the so-called Communists against whom Chiang had, without intermission, waged war for almost ten years. In the face of the national crisis an understanding was reached with the Communists, who issued an important declaration as soon as the Lukouchiao incident occurred. The declaration included the following stipulations: 1. Dr. Sun's Three Principles serve the needs of the present-day China and the Chinese Communist party is prepared to strive for their complete fulfillment. 2. They would abandon all violent action aimed at the overthrow of the Kuomintang and give up the movement for the propagation of Communism in China as well as the policy of violent confiscation of the holdings of landowners. 3. They would abolish the Chinese Soviet Government in the northwest and work toward a united democratic government for the entire country. 4. They would abolish the name and status of the Red Army and permit its incorporation into the National Revolutionary Army under the command of the National Military Council of the National Government.

That was a superb gesture and its announcement was an occasion for great rejoicing all over the country. Chiang Kai-shek was so pleased with this expression of solidarity that on September 24, 1937, he issued a statement to the people concerning the state of the nation.

Those who have in the past doubted the Three Principles [he said] have now realized the paramount importance of our national interests and have buried their differences for the sake of internal unity. The Chinese people, today, fully realize that they must survive together or perish together, and that the interests of the nation must take precedence over the interests of individuals or groups.

The manifesto recently issued by the Chinese Communist party is an outstanding instance of the triumph of national sentiment over every other consideration. . . . It declares that the Chinese Communists are willing to strive to carry out the Three Principles. This is ample proof that China today has only one objective in its war efforts. . . .

The Chinese Communist party, by surrendering its prejudices, has clearly recognized the vital importance of our national independence and welfare. I sincerely hope that all members of the Communist party will faithfully and unitedly put into practice the various decisions reached, and under the unified military command that is directing our resistance, will offer their services to the state, fighting shoulder to shoulder with the rest of the nation for the successful completion of the Nationalist Revolution.

With the establishment of complete unity within China the rest appeared to Chiang much simpler, for from the beginning it was his aim to make the war as long as possible by continual and dogged resistance, to spread it out over large areas, to attract the enemy into the interior of the country, and to make every foot of territory that the enemy occupied as costly as possible. In July 1934, three years previously, Chiang had said in Kuling: "Contempt for China on the part of the enemy is his weak point. Knowledge of this weak point is our strong point." He turned that knowledge to practical use; and as the war progressed he saw that the Japanese had fallen into the trap.

The Japanese staked everything on a quick, decisive victory. When that was not realized their original plan was weakened, and it soon became evident that new measures had to be improvised. When they struck at the Peiping-Tientsin area they believed that in a few weeks they would succeed in cutting off north China as they had Manchuria. But Chiang's best soldiers were in the south. To that part of the country, therefore, the Japanese were lured, and the war around Shanghai started on August 13. It was an integral part of the war. When fighting broke out in that place the Japanese called fresh reinforcements, and for three months some of the severest fighting took place there, to the surprise of the world and to the befuddlement of the Japanese. The Chinese losses were heavy, but Chiang was prepared for them. The Japanese losses were heavy also, and they were not prepared.

When the Chinese at last retreated in good order there was no alternative for the Japanese but to push on along the river to the capital at Nanking. They captured the city; and out of vicious spite, because they had been forced to expend so much of their military strength on a mere "incident" which they thought would be over in a few weeks, they committed some of the worst brutalities in the history of modern warfare and gave their latest version of *bushido* to an outraged world. They thought the war was then over, but Chiang simply moved the capital further inland along the river up to Hankow and continued to fight. Then came the famous battle of Taierchuang on April 8, 1938, in which Japanese forces were licked by Chinese forces for the first time. More reinforcements arrived, and the Japanese pushed further inland. Toward the end of October of that year the Chinese effectively evacuated Hankow and established their capital at Chungking, where it has remained ever since. The fall of Hankow nearly sixteen months after hostilities started at Lukouchiao marked the end of the first phase of the war for China.

Not long after the capital had been moved to Chungking Chiang reviewed the first eighteen months of the war and made plans for the future. "Our war," he said, "may be divided into two periods. During the first period which ended with the fall of Canton and Wuhan (Hankow, Wuchang, and Hanyang), we tried to wear down the enemy's strength and at the same time protect our rear so that solid foundations might be laid for the second period of protracted resistance." A pertinent question is: Did Chiang succeed in wearing down the enemy's strength as he had planned? To quote his own words, "To the enemy, eighteen months of war have meant the loss of all battlefields, of over seven hundred thousand men, and military expenditures of nine billion yen." And then Chiang continued with an observation that was within the purview of his planned strategy. "His [the enemy's] country is being impoverished, his agricultural development is being retarded, his social life is becoming corrupt, and his political stability is threatened by unrest. Since he launched his attack upon us, his military and political strategy, his ideas and calculation regarding us, his understanding of contemporary events have all been based on fundamentally false assumptions and consequently he has sunk deeper and deeper into error."

All that Chiang had planned had turned out as he wanted it to during the first phase of the war. Eighty-five per cent of Japan's armed strength had been poured into China, nearly three times more than she thought she needed, and the casualties had been appallingly large.

With China surviving the first phase of the war, Chiang not only became confident of the success of the second phase but also of eventual victory. It was true that China's ability to conduct the war during this phase would become correspondingly more difficult with the loss of the coast line and all the principal ports, for her supplies would be seriously reduced, but there would be other factors to compensate for this disadvantage. As Chiang had said long before: "It is not quite essential to match big guns for big guns, airplane for airplane. . . . It is quite possible for us to resist the enemy's powerful weapons with our old weapons, especially China's traditional, time-honored weapons and the knowledge of how to make use of whatever we can lay our hands upon, whether it be man power, manufactured articles, mountains, streams, trees, or even blades of grass. It is essential that we fully exploit the materials that are near us, that we have at our disposal."

This second phase of the war of resistance was going to be completely different in nature from the first phase. There were to be no fronts. The enemy would be drawn into the heart of the country where the terrain would become more and more difficult and the enemy would experience enormous hardships in maintaining communications and in securing supplies of food. He would have to send at least three men to one man on the Chinese side and spend three rounds to one round of Chinese ammunition. As Chiang surveyed the situation, he was able to say: "If Japan should emerge victorious in the present hostilities, then all existing military theories and principles of military strategy would be disproved. I will go further and say that all scientific theories and fundamental principles of cause and effect would be proved wrong." It was not necessary for Chiang to study Alexander or Napoleon or Clausewitz. He had one of the greatest of all strategists, Sun Tse, right at his elbow all the while. In Chiang's mind Sun Tse is on a higher level than other strategists because in addition to being able to plan war in a technical sense he was also a defender of the moral order. "A virtuous government has the support of the people; it can command life or death from the people without exciting fear or complaint," Sun Tse had said.

Chiang has been confident of the success of this second phase of the war because he feels that he has all the factors for success on his side. In the first place, from the point of view of topography, China is unconquerable. He can retire to Chungking and feel more or less relaxed. That part of the country, in the five thousand years of Chinese history, and in spite of constant invasions in other parts of China by barbarian hordes in the past, has never been invaded. It is protected by the most effective natural defenses. There are high mountains, mighty rivers where the cliffs rise a sheer thousand feet, and broad deserts on the south, east, and west, leaving only the north comparatively open to attack. The north is protected only by the unpredictable and loess-ridden Yellow River, which, even though it can be crossed, is still some distance from Chungking. The Japanese made about thirty attempts in 1941 and 1942 to penetrate this particular line of defense, but they have always failed, and now the two armies simply face each other across the river, some one thousand yards away from one another.

The only fighting done there is by radio, with the Japanese hurling unsavory epithets at the Chinese and the Chinese replying by telling the Japanese how hopeless their task is. At Tungkwan, one of the strategic cities south of the river, the farmers continue to till their fields actually within sight and sound of enemy guns, and although it is a front-line town the city is kept quite clean and orderly.

China also has the advantage of being an agricultural country. Whatever there was in the way of industry had either fallen into the hands of the enemy during the first phase of the war or was taken into the mountain fastnesses far back into the interior. There are no nerve centers that the enemy can put out of commission and thereby paralyze the country. The entire country is an enormous expanse of sprawling territory which has continued to yield bumper crops and to feed the population.

As regards the territory that is already under enemy occupation, a negative policy of attrition through guerrilla activity and scorched-earth tactics has been so successful that the Japanese have not been able to derive much benefit from the land. It is physically impossible to actually occupy the entire territory. All that the enemy can do is to keep possession of the main lines of communication between the larger cities, but even these are surrounded on all sides by the local population, which has been trained to harass and wear down the "dwarf soldiers" of the island empire. The Japanese might wish to assume the offensive, but there would be nothing to direct their offensive at. As soon as they relax, forces of opposition are once more around them. One apt comparison is that the Japanese are the swimmers and the Chinese are the surrounding water. The Japanese may swim around in the sea but they can never really occupy it. The invaders are continually being harassed. The moment they try to rest they sink. The guerrillas carefully see to it that the invaders are picked off one by one as they become exhausted. Vast numbers of Japanese soldiers are necessary to keep up this myth of occupation.

No wonder Prince Konoye, who was chosen as the Premier to prosecute the Chinese War, was a pathetic figure, when he addressed the Japanese Diet in the fifth year of the war which he had hoped to finish in three months. His voice trembled and was choked with emotion. Tears rolled down his face as he spoke the following words:

"This is the fifth year since the outbreak of the China conflict" (he sedulously avoided use of the word "incident") "and yet there is no sign of a solution. This is beyond the responsibility of the fighting services or that of any other person. It is entirely my own responsibility. Billions of yen have been spent from the state treasury and thousands of officers and men have been sacrificed on the continent, for which I must apologize to the Emperor and to the people at large."

Once they had launched upon the invasion, there was no turning back. As an old Chinese proverb says: "Once you are on the back of a tiger you can get down only with difficulty." So also Konoye, while shedding tears in the presence of the Japanese Diet and knowing already that his country was hopelessly bogged down, still had to proclaim the creation of a "new order in east Asia." On December 22, 1938, Konoye also declared that it was the aim of Japan to bring about a "rebirth of China" through this "new order" which would be based "on a triangular co-operation between the new China, Japan, and 'Manchukuo.'" As Chiang explained, this "reborn China [of Konoye's] is not an independent China but an enslaved China, a China that would have to take orders from Japan for generations to come." The second point in the Konoye declaration was "unity of east Asia," whatever that may mean. The explanation was given that this unity should be vertical, with Japan at the summit, and not horizontal. As Chiang again explained: "The system of relationship shall be patriarchal, with Japan as the head of the family and 'Manchukuo' and China as children. In other words, Japan is to be governor and master and China the governed and the slave."

The third point in the declaration regarded the creation of an "economic bloc" or "economic unity." This, too, is perfectly obvious. Japan wants to carry out a policy of economic exploitation of China so that all of China's natural resources would work for her, and the Japanese would sit back and enjoy the fruits of China's labor. So they proceeded to establish the North China Development Company and the Central China Development Company. Just because the British had the East India Company and conquered India, so the Japanese feel that they must have their equivalents of this company. No race has such an appalling lack of imagination. And finally, the last point on the declaration was the establishment of the Asia Development Board in Japan to take care of all Asia as a vast colony.

This scheme of conquest announced by Konoye on December 22, 1938, was in every way an extension of Koko Hirota's "Three Principles" made in January 1936. On April 30, 1941, another extension was made in what the Japanese called the "World Peace Plan." The Japanese sphere of conquest was widening in a series of concentric circles. This plan visualizes the conquest of the entire Pacific. It has four points: 1. It calls for the demilitarization of British and American naval bases in the Pacific. 2. The United States shall not seek to establish a hegemony over the American continent. 3. American influence shall not extend further west than Hawaii. 4. All islands in the Pacific, including Australia and New Zealand, shall become a part of the Japanese co-prosperity sphere. These demands were all publicly stated in the columns of the Japan *Times and Advertiser,* which is the mouthpiece of the Japanese Foreign Office.

Hirota's Three Principles were followed by Konoye's Four Points, which were followed by the four points of the Japanese Foreign Office. What was before secret in the Tanaka Memorial now became public property. The result was that Chiang Kai-shek could feel that he was winning a supreme diplomatic victory over Japan. He was positive that sooner or later the world was going to be divided into two distinct camps, one standing for law, order, justice, and humanity, while the other stood for aggression, barbarism, and darkness. On the eighth anniversary (1939) of the Mukden incident Chiang reiterated: "The Chinese nation believes that the successful completion of resistance and reconstruction in China is the most important factor in world peace and progress. Whatever changes take place in the international situation, the Republic of China will never absolve itself from the moral obligations which it has assumed. This we can tell the world." Chiang knew that it was only a question of time until the whole world would be embroiled. The logic of events was plain. And so when the attack on Pearl Harbor came and China declared war on all the Axis powers, the old Confucian saying, "Moral worth is never left alone; it will always find support," was again proved true. Chiang was thus able to say on December 10, 1941:

> Ours was the first country to suffer the inroads of aggression and also the first to assume responsibility for the vital task of putting bounds to the evil. Our faith is firm in the continuity of man's destiny and the indestructibility of his conceptions of equity. Nine tenths of mankind are striving to defend justice, peace, and the right to national freedom. The eventual overthrow of the aggressors is therefore a matter of certainty.[2]

We can imagine also the satisfaction which Chiang must have felt when on the sixth anniversary of the Lukouchiao incident, July 7, 1943, he could say: "As early as 1931, following Japan's invasion of Manchuria, I held that Japan's aggression would not be confined to China but would ultimately plunge the entire world into war. How-

[2]Generalissimo Chiang Kai-shek, *Resistance and Reconstruction* (Harper and Broth-

ever, I held even more firmly that in the end Japan's aggression could not but arouse all the progressive forces in the world and that its result would be the formation of a grand coalition of all peace-loving nations."

Chiang Kai-shek's plans for this war are based upon considerations of geography, the economic peculiarities of the country, the fundamental unity of the people, the lack of understanding on the part of the enemy, the diplomatic situation, and, above all, the infallibility of the moral law. Surely it is difficult for man to conceive a larger vision and a more embracing strategy.

38

Stiffening Resistance

WE ARE now in the seventh year of the Chinese-Japanese War. At the end of the sixth year, in July 1943, it was estimated that China had inflicted some 2,700,000 casualties on Japan. Not an especially large number as compared with what Russia has done to Germany, where the casualties have been twice as large, but the nature of the fighting is not the same. Since the fall of Hankow in the autumn of 1938, which marked the end of the first phase of the war in Asia, the Japanese in China have not met an enemy with whom they can come to grips, but rather they have been surrounded by a hostile nation that is in constant mobility. The war in China is just as much a people's war as it is in Russia, England, or the United States, but it is a people's war in a very special sense.

The second phase of the Chinese War, which will continue until it is terminated by a counter-offensive, has not been spectacular; it does not make newspaper headlines; but it is real and grim all the same. There is practically no distinction between the battle front and the home front. The whole country, every man, woman, and child, with the exception of a small number of collaborationists inevitable in a nation of four hundred and fifty millions, is at war with the enemy. Wherever there are Chinese, they are performing acts of hostility against the invaders in varying degrees of effectiveness. There is, in fact, no distinction between free China and occupied China, because in the so-called occupied China not only do the people wait to be delivered and nurse in their hearts the wish to get even with the enemy, but they are daily aiding in wearing down the enemy. The Japanese hold on occupied China is tenuous. They have entrenched themselves in a few big cities and hold on to the few main lines of communication between them. But immediately outside of these areas life goes on pretty much as it did before. Chungking orders are still being carried out, and the line of demarcation between the Chungking administration and the administration of the puppet regime is so faint as to be sometimes imperceptible.

A friend of mine recently journeyed from Shanghai to Chungking, taking three months to make the trip. From Chungking he came to the United States. He told me that, with the exception of trucks and carts, no other means of transportation is available in so-called occupied China. There was discomfort which was the result of disorder, but otherwise he was not conscious that he was traveling through territory occupied by an alien enemy. He seldom saw any Japanese soldiers after he left the neighborhood of Shanghai. The officials and police of the puppet regime chatted and befriended those of free China as if they belonged to two different local administrations, and the situation was much what it was in the days of the war lords. They were all Chinese. "Only," one of the puppet officials would come up to my friend and say, "don't let the grandson know." The "grandson" is used as a term of contempt for anyone whom they despise, and in this case it means the Japanese.

For hardheaded realism there is no one who can beat the common man of China. With him it is a question of getting three square meals a day, and if conditions are such that they cannot serve free China, what difference does it make if for the moment they are pressed into the services of the puppet regime so long as they are clear in their hearts that they are Chinese? The Japanese do everything in dead earnest, but the Chinese refuse to take them seriously and have the deepest contempt for them. This is one of the most galling experiences that the Japanese have to put up with. That is why their hold upon occupied China is so weak. Their influence is felt as far as their bayonets can reach and no farther, and in a large and populous country they need more bayonets than they have to make their influence felt in every corner of the territory they have occupied. After all, it is not for fun that the Japanese occupy Chinese territory. They hope to reap some benefit from it. Occupied China is not to be spoken of in

STIFFENING RESISTANCE

the same way as occupied Europe. In Europe the Nazis have able to control all the nerve centers and really oppress the population of the different countries, but in China, though the Japanese try to do as much, results have been disappointing. The fact that China is an agricultural country and has no industrial centers to be controlled by the enemy is an important factor.

Knowing that bayonets are limited and nothing can be done except with the bayonet, the Japanese have had recourse to one of the cruelest and most inhuman methods of subordination ever used. They rely upon the use of poison to exterminate the Chinese race or to weaken their resistance. That practice has been put into effect in Manchuria and also in other parts of China that fell after July 7, 1937. Accounts of this fiendish and diabolical method of blotting out or devitalizing a whole nation are legion. It is reliably reported that opium is grown under the compulsion and supervision of the Japanese soldiers in north China. Every family must by law consume it until the habit is formed. Every morning a certain quantity of the poison is deposited at the door of each house, and all the members of the household must pay for it and smoke it. Why, you may well ask, can't they throw it away or conceal it? The next morning a Japanese comes to make sure that the opium has been properly consumed. The inmates of the household must submit the ashes or residue of the opium for examination.

Another poison is heroin, which is injected into the skin. It is said that in Manchuria and north China there are rows of streets in which the shops are arranged in a systematic way. A person is first submitted to compulsory injection of this poison until he automatically goes for it himself. He spends all his money, and then, having no more to spend, he takes out all that he has in the way of worldly possessions and proceeds to the pawnshop at one end of the street. He gets a fresh supply of cash and goes along the street to the next shop where he can get his injection of the day. His spirits are artificially buoyed up for the moment, and he goes into a house of prostitution a few doors down the street. He contracts diseases and eventually has to go to a dispensary or hospital which is operated by a Japanese. He gets a few more injections and goes home to rest. This procedure is repeated many times. It doesn't take many repetitions before the poor man is no more than a walking corpse. Then finally there is a mortuary and cemetery at the other end of the street. The man's body, however, remains a treasure house for the Japanese. They extract the heroin which is supposed to have accumulated in the marrow of the dead man's bones and inject it into another victim. That is the Samurai spirit of the Japanese! That is their *kodo,* their *bushido!*

It is for the eradication of this and many other evils that Chiang Kai-shek must carry on the war against the Japanese. If he loses, it means the extinction of the race. If he wins, it means that he has saved mankind from the worst evils in history. That is why his movements were slow and deliberate, why he had to make the most elaborate preparations, the most careful calculations, so that once he took issue with these satanic forces he had to be certain that he could conquer them. This consideration is important because it leaves no room whatever for compromise until the war is brought successfully to an end. If this basic stand of Chiang Kai-shek's is clearly understood, then we need pay no attention to peace rumors, however widely they may be spread. As long as Chiang is at the helm of the Chinese ship of state there can be no peace with Japan, no matter what inducements are offered. "To seek compromise and peace now is equivalent to entering a trap or committing suicide," he said at the meeting of the Central Executive Committee of the Kuomintang on January 26, 1939, and the remark is truer today than at any period of the war. He knows that, in the full conception of his strategy, the longer the war is fought, the better are China's chances of winning. He depends upon Sun Tse again, who taught him, "In the beginning make it impossible for the enemy to win and then await the time for the enemy to be defeated."

Chiang also knows that the bulk of his people are intrinsically healthy and sound. He has nothing to worry about on that score, but there is one important lesson from history that he still must be ready to use. What occurred at the end of the Sung Dynasty (A.D. 960-1276), when the Mongols came in to conquer the reigning house, and what happened at the end of the Ming Dynasty (A.D. 1368-1644), when the Manchus came in, must not be repeated. "The fate of these two dynasties," he said, "was not caused by outside enemies with a superior force, but by a dispirited and cowardly minority in the governing class and the society of the time." These "dynastic falls were due to the cowardice, ignorance, lack of integrity, and selfishness of a small number of corrupt officials."

The outside world has spoken too often and too easily until very recent times of the lack of unity in China merely because the period of the war lords was still remembered. While there has been political disorder for many years, it is a superficial confusion. Fundamentally,

China has always been a united nation, not only now, but for the last two thousand years.

But, one may think, how can you say that there is unity in China when there is such a variety of languages? That is perhaps the most widespread misconception about China, but I can understand how it arose. Foreign merchants going to China have been confined to the coast, and the strip of coast line stretching from Shanghai to Canton, for some historical reason, has a rich variety of dialects, so dissimilar as to be quite often incomprehensible from one part of the coast to another. But there is no country in the world that has no dialects. It is the tendency of all languages to develop them. That is even true of so young a country as the United States.

Now in China the astonishing thing is that if one leaves this little coastal strip to go into the vast hinterland there is one dialect which can be understood almost everywhere. There are minor local peculiarities, but the dialect is to all intents and purposes a *lingua franca* and is a common medium of expression everywhere. Let us imagine a farmer from along the Amur River on the Russian border being flown in an airplane nearly three thousand miles to the southwest border in Yunnan Province and meeting another farmer there. What happens? Without having recourse to the written language, which for purposes of argument they are not supposed to understand, they can converse and discuss the climate and the methods of farming just as easily as any two farmers in the United States. The conclusion to be drawn is not that there are so many dialects in China, but that there are so few. And then, over and above the dialects, there is the written language, which has been the same for at least two thousand years, not only in China, but in Korea, in Indo-China, and even in Japan. I am not arguing that a unified language is essential to national unity. It frequently is, but Switzerland and Soviet Russia prove that it is possible to achieve national unity without a unified language. What I want to say about China is that not only is there only one language in the country but also that the *kuo-yu* or mandarin dialect, as it is popularly known among the foreigners, is spoken in the greater part of its territory. It is that heritage which has created the extraordinary unity of the Chinese.

There is another factor which has helped to create a common outlook upon life in China. There is no caste system of either the Hindu or British kind. What it is like in India we all know or think we know. In England the aristocracy is a very real institution. There was a law of primogeniture which once existed in China also, but it was abandoned two thousand years ago. Since then, there have been no social classes in China as such, though there are social distinctions. The Chinese, for instance, respect the scholar most of all, then the farmer, then the artisan, and lastly the merchant. And the reasons? The scholar is respected because through learning and understanding he cultivates the highest spiritual qualities; he is the physical embodiment of the virtuous and moral life, and things of the mind and soul must receive prior recognition. They are the *summum bonum,* the highest good. The farmer is respected because he is basically the most creative man. He puts in honest and honorable labor, and is rewarded not only by a bountiful crop upon which every person must depend for his sustenance, but also by the development of a simple, hardy, trustworthy character. Next comes the artisan, who does not work so much with his brain as with his muscles; but he, too, creates, although it is only objects which people use to carry on the everyday business of living. Last comes the merchant. There is scant respect for him because he does not create. He only carries the wares, which are the efforts of other people, from one part of the country to another. He may become rich, but is there much lasting value to what he has contributed to society as a whole? Very little as compared with the contributions of the others.

These are the four main social distinctions. They are not classes, for no one is born into any one of them without being able to shift from one to another. It all depends upon his own efforts and talents. A son born in a scholar's family has a better chance, it is true, to become a scholar. But he inherits no title, and if he does not work hard enough to secure his qualifications as a scholar there is nothing to prevent him from slipping to the ranks of the lowest. There are beggars in China today whose ancestors were distinguished people. On the other hand, children born into the family of a ricksha puller have less chance of achieving social distinction, but there is nothing to prevent them from doing so if they prove themselves worthy.

The Chinese system of civil service examinations introduced in the Han Dynasty (206 B.C.–A.D. 221) is one of the oldest democratic institutions the world has known. The civil service examination in China is a great leveler, since recognition is entirely the result of individual effort. On the benches of the examination halls princes and paupers literally had equal chance, and very frequently it was the pauper who won the laurels. There is, therefore, no myth about the old families in

China, for all families are old and all families are young. H. H. Kung must be amused every time an American newspaper correspondent insists upon calling him the direct descendant of Confucius, for everybody in China with the surname of Kung has an equal right to make such a claim, and there are thousands upon thousands of Kungs. As a matter of fact great heroes and founders of dynasties have always been proud of the fact that they sprang from the ranks of ordinary people. The founder of the Han Dynasty was himself from the ranks of the "coarse cloth." So was the founder of the Ming Dynasty. And both Sun Yat-sen and Chiang Kai-shek have likewise grown from plain, ordinary families, like any other of the tens of millions of families in China. Chiang has arrived where he is the hard way, and he is proud of it.

One reason I have thought it necessary to go into this background is that the present war and the sustained and stiffening resistance of the Chinese nation cannot be properly explained without this knowledge. Another reason is that out of it has emerged an unusual phenomenon: the common man in China. No one who has come to know him can fail to be impressed by him. As we have seen, Lieutenant General Stilwell, who has now been long associated with him, has nothing but the highest praise for this man. He is indeed the unsung hero of the Sino-Japanese War. No monument is big enough for this little man. It is he who has borne the brunt of the war. Whether it be in the home, the field, or in the front line of battle, he has asked for little and given much for the country. Chiang Kai-shek knows and understands this common man who is his compatriot.

In these more than six years of war, what heroic deeds has the common man in China performed. His building of the Burma Road, for instance, was a remarkable accomplishment. The outside world has heard about that achievement, but every day Burma Roads in other spheres of activity are being constructed without the knowledge of the outside world. The war started in July 1937. The decision was made at once to construct the Burma Road from Lashio on the Burmese side to Kunming on the Chinese side, which is a distance of three hundred and sixty miles as the crow flies. By October the work was well under way; and fourteen months afterward, in December 1938, the American Ambassador, Nelson T. Johnson, was able to drive from one end of the road to the other.

No modern machinery was used. The road had to pass over mountains more than seven thousand feet high, through deep gorges and ravines which are almost perpendicular, and across such mighty rivers as the Mekong and the Salween. It was to cover one of the most wildly beautiful portions of the world's surface. Besides, it had to run through the worst malaria-infested territory in China. It was thought that it could not be done. But along came the common man with his simple primitive adzes and picks. He brought his bamboo baskets to carry away the dirt and the rocks. He brought his meager supply of food. He came from nearly every village in China and in time his number swelled to over two hundred thousand. If the mosquitoes had undisputed possession of this territory at night, the common man worked during the day; and when he worked, he worked with such speed that within slightly more than a year a road seven hundred and twenty-six miles long, varying in width from nine to sixteen feet, along with some two thousand culverts and three hundred bridges, including two big suspension bridges, was constructed over the roof of one of the mightiest promontories of the world! They did something similar to that two thousand years before: they built the Great Wall of China. An American engineer visited the road after it was completed and exclaimed in bewilderment, "My God, they scratched these roads out of the mountains with their fingernails." That was precisely what they did. This road which the toiling masses opened up with their sweat and labor has made history, and we shall continue to hear about it. It will be heard about again when a vigorous counteroffensive conducted through the joint efforts of the Chinese soldiers and Lord Louis Mountbatten's forces succeeds in wresting Burma from the Japanese, and the Burma Road will again become the principal artery through which supplies and munitions can reach the heart of China from the outside world. It will be even more famous when the war is over and peace is established. For the Burma Road will contribute enormously to a new Asia, where its importance will be equivalent to the importance of the Suez Canal or the Panama Canal, linking two oceans. The Burma Road will be a land bridge linking two rich land masses with almost half the population of the world.

The Burma Road was only one of the many tasks which the common people of China have been called upon to perform when their land was being invaded. When the Japanese seized the principal cities on the coast and along the rivers a large percentage of the population simply moved into the interior to begin life anew. It was perhaps the largest migration in recorded history. Some fifty million people or the equivalent of the entire population of the United States west of the

Mississippi were on the move. Some one hundred and thirty thousand tons of steel and iron were taken down, and in the absence of the usual means of transportation which were either disrupted or put to more urgent use, all that metal was carried on the bare backs of the Chinese people into the heart of free China.

Also at the time of the fall of Shanghai the extent of the destruction of that city was enormous; but at the bottom of the heart of the people there was only contempt for the invaders. There were many who either could not or were too slow to move away from there, but there were still millions who were willing to break from everything, from the strongest of family ties, with their faces turned hopefully toward the west, and began their trek, if need be, on foot. The consequences of this enforced migration on so gigantic a scale are bound to be far-reaching in the future development of the nation.

The outlook is one of hope and faith in the future. Chungking and the new cities out in the Chinese west have many of the characteristics of the boom towns erected during the opening of the American West. I have met in the remote countryside of Chungking artisans, workmen, and even boatmen speaking the dialects of the lower Yangtze basin and of the coast, a phenomenon which would have been impossible other than through the cataclysm of this war. And what were the feelings of these men and women torn from the roots of the villages where their ancestors had lived for generations? The impression which I got was not one of resignation. They were not necessarily thinking of going back when the war is over. They looked forward to new work, new experiences, and to the enormous potentialities of the future.

In this enormous trek all sections of Chinese society are represented. You have the farmer, the artisan, the laborer, as well as the village blacksmith, the driver, the student, and the university professor, a great democratic throng. Nor were the animals forgotten. The chairman of the department of agriculture of one university decided to preserve his livestock from the Japanese. It took this professor and the animals eleven and a half months to trudge over a thousand miles from the doomed capital of Nanking. But the family, more numerous than ever, now thrives in the country outside of Chungking.

The pattern is now set. The war has brought untold destruction, privation, and suffering. That is one side of it which is ugly and unsavory. But there is another side of it which is much more impressive. It has also set free vast constructive forces out of which will grow a new nation of new powers.

Yet Chiang's strategy, brilliant as it is, sometimes appears to have its drawbacks. It was an essential part of that strategy to work until the democratic powers would join forces with the Chinese. They did. But no one believed that shortly after Pearl Harbor China would find herself worse off than ever before. The Burma Road, which was once closed by the British as a part of their policy of appeasement toward the Japanese, was at last captured by the enemy. China became almost completely isolated from the world. Not only did munitions and other supplies of war find it difficult to get in, but even the ordinary necessities of life were cut off. Neither soldiers nor civilians had enough to eat. By late spring of 1943 the strain was becoming so acute that reports began to come out of Chungking describing a state of virtual economic collapse and panic. They conveyed the feeling that the country was near the breaking point, and that disillusionment and dissatisfaction were spreading rapidly. The Japanese believed that. They believed it to such an extent that they thought the moment had arrived to give the Chinese a final blow, and the "China incident" would at long last be terminated.

So, toward the end of May, the Japanese launched a big offensive from the Hankow-Ichang area toward the west and the southwest. That is the rich rice-growing area around the Tungting Lake, which was overflowing with a good crop. The Japs thought they could take that area and cut off Chungking from its last available supply of food. Might not that further demoralize a despondent, despairing, and disillusioned country? Might not that even ultimately lead them to the gates of Chungking itself? Their ranking general, Harada, had flown to Hankow, and the headquarters of the Eleventh Army had been moved to Ichang. Between Hankow and Ichang, both of which cities are situated on the Yangtze River, is a highway less than two hundred miles long which the Japanese controlled. To the south of it is a curve in the river, the widest part of which is about one hundred miles from the highway. That area was in possession of the Chinese guerrillas. Toward the end of February the Japanese began pushing down from the south to the river. It took them three months.

On May 23 the Japanese crossed the river and attacked in force along five different routes in a westerly and southwesterly direction, in the direction of Chungking, which was only three hundred miles

Thomas Kuang—Chungking, Paul Guillumette, Inc.

The visit of Mr. Wendell Willkie with Generalissimo and Mme. Chiang Kai-shek. Figure in the rear is Fu Ping-sheung, then Vice-Minister of Foreign Affairs and now Chinese Ambassador at Moscow. Behind Mr. stands Clarence Gauss, U.S. Ambassador at Chungking.

away. They employed an army of one hundred thousand men equipped with heavy artillery, field artillery, and mountain guns. Their first objective was Shih Pai. If that was captured the Chinese capital would indeed be in danger. But for years the Chinese had been putting up defenses in that area. There were mountains which the invaders had to tackle, mountains only about fifteen hundred feet high, but high enough to be difficult to cross. The Chinese soldiers, numbering some one hundred and fifty thousand, were entrenched on the sides of these mountains. On the Japanese pushed, their front line getting farther and farther from their base. Finally the Chinese soldiers received orders to attack frontally and on the flanks. That was the famous "magnetic" strategy which had been used on the Japanese on previous occasions and had proved successful. The result of this assault was thirty thousand dead for the Japanese, who were completely routed. The Chinese pursued them hotly and took back all the territory that they had lost since March. In this engagement planes of the American Fourteenth Air Force made substantial contributions. There were Mitchell bombers and Warhawk fighters escorted by a squadron of Chinese fighters. The number of planes involved was small, but that engagement showed what could be accomplished with greater air strength distributed to all theaters of the war in China.

What is really significant about that engagement is that, even though he may be despondent, the common man of China could be depended upon to do a brave job. As the editorial of the New York *Times,* on June 6, correctly pointed out:

The backbone of China's resistance to Japan is the *chiupa,* the ordinary Chinese soldier. He is usually a peasant lad, honest, intelligent and cheerful. Inured to hardships from birth, he possesses an astonishing stamina. He fights on a diet of rice, noodles and vegetables and is paid six Chinese dollars a month, about thirty cents American. He is a very different person from the old-time Chinese mercenary who was recruited from the dregs of the population and whose main interest was loot. The *chiupa's* main strength lies in his courage and resourcefulness, backed by a morale built upon a new national consciousness.

The battle of May and June 1943 was a small one compared with the terrific battles in Europe and Africa, but it was nevertheless one of the major Chinese victories in six years of war with the invader. There have been large military engagements in China; but when one considers that some two million Japanese soldiers are being tied down by more than twice that number of Chinese soldiers, that fifteen million Chinese soldiers are in reserve units or training camps, that two and a half million casualties have been inflicted on the Japanese from the start of the war to October 1942, that five and a half million soldiers and civilians have been lost by China in six years, that millions of square miles of Chinese territory are involved, that some thirty thousand engagements of a major and minor nature have taken place, and that the war is being waged in the seventh year, then the epic rather than the dramatic qualities of the resistance become strikingly clear.

It is then that we realize the full significance of Wendell L. Willkie's words in his book *One World:*

> We do not keep sufficiently in our active consciousness that it might already be too late to defeat Japan's super-empire either militarily or politically, had it not been for the desperate resistance of the Chinese people through their long, heartbreaking years. So few realized the importance to our entire civilization of the Chinese resistance.

39

Constructing from Within

I BELIEVE that raising the economic level of the common man in China, especially when he has gone through such enormous sacrifices during the present war, is what Chiang has always worked for. We know what his feelings were when he was a mere boy.

In his latest book, *China's Destiny,* Chiang reminds the nation again of Article 2 of Sun Yat-sen's Principles of Reconstruction of the National Government:

> The basic aim of all reconstruction is the improvement in the life of the people. In the four main categories of the popular need, in food, clothing, housing and transportation, the government and the people should have the fullest co-operation. Together they should develop agriculture so that the granaries may be full; promote the weaving industry so that there may be an abundance of clothing material; carry out large scale housing projects so that the people may be comfortably protected; and construct highways and railways, and improve the water system so as to facilitate transportation.

Industrialization had scarcely begun in China when the war started. What there was in the way of modern industry was confined to certain isolated spots convenient to the foreigner and designed for his benefit. Incidentally it made a few Chinese entrepreneurs rich, but the whole system or lack of system had no essential bearing on the general economy of the people. That era has been terminated by the present war. When peace returns we shall find China entering a new era. The abolition of extraterritoriality and other special privileges will create—has, as a matter of fact, already created—a new situation in which China will proceed with her industrialization according to her own wishes and to meet her own specific needs.

Such a situation will also create new responsibilities. In the first place China will enjoy the advantage of being a late-comer into the industrial field. Modern industry all over the world has raised the level of existence for the great mass of people. But it is not an unqualified blessing: it has also raised many difficult problems which to this day have not been solved. These problems are disturbing and have been responsible for many social evils. The question is whether China, beginning with an almost clean slate, will be able to profit from the experiences of the more advanced industrial countries and avoid the pitfalls into which many of them have fallen. It is imperative, therefore, that there should be cautious planning, careful deliberation, of a nature that not only takes into consideration the industrial future of the nation, but also the whole of its social implications. For once the foundations are laid, the processes of industrialization will gather momentum and develop in a direction from which it will be difficult to deviate.

Chiang wants a modern China with all the wonders of scientific, technological, and industrial accomplishments, but he wants to have it through adaptation and assimilation rather than through substitution. Chinese culture and civilization are an integral part of an agricultural society, and in changing into a modern industrial society the serious problem arises as to whether it is possible to retain that culture without also introducing some radical changes both in its form and in its spirit. Wendell Willkie has reported a conversation with Chiang which is interesting. He said:

He [Chiang] hoped in the changes to retain the best of the old traditions and to avoid the social dislocations of large-scale western industrial development by the establishment of a great number of widely distributed small plants.

But Willkie explained to him that the social problems created by mass production in America and the large industrial combinations that Chiang wanted to avoid had not arisen, as he seemed to think, solely because of desire for power and the building of individual fortunes, though these elements undoubtedly contributed. They arose in part, at least, because of economic requirements: mass production greatly lowers costs. And the solution to the problem, Willkie pointed out, "did not consist in breaking up necessary large units into inefficient small ones." Chiang's answer was that he would find the solution in having these large units partly owned by the government and partly by private capital and that, in any case, he was sure that in the teachings of Sun Yat-sen "concerning a combined agricultural and industrial society he would find the way."

The close of the war will also find China in complete possession of her lost territories, the most important of which are Manchuria and Formosa. She will also regain her concessions and leased territories and will have to assume a full measure of control over such border provinces as Sinkiang. The area for industrialization will thus be an extensive one, larger than that of the United States. There will be no restrictions of a foreign nature. The whole matter will have to be handled through Chinese enterprise and initiative. The resources and the technical knowledge will also be supplied by the Chinese, regulated and controlled under Chinese auspices for specific Chinese purposes. The task will not be a simple one. It will, in fact, be quite complex. It will certainly be one of the most impressive pieces of work that the nation will be called upon to perform. There is reason to expect that it will be performed creditably. As Chiang once said, "If within the ten years between the establishment of the National Government and the outbreak of the war in 1937, China was able to accomplish so much in national reconstruction in spite of the many handicaps both of a domestic and international nature, surely we should look forward to this new work, gigantic as it is, with confidence and certainty." But he still wants to issue a note of warning. In *China's Destiny* he wrote:

> Up to the present when we could not proceed with our tasks of national reconstruction in the way which we wanted, we could always say it was because of the unequal treaties. But now these treaties are a thing of the past; and if we still cannot prosecute our program of reconstruction with vigor and expeditiousness, the responsibility will be entirely on

CONSTRUCTING FROM WITHIN

our own shoulders. In assuming this responsibility I wish all the citizens to ask themselves, first, the question whether their ability and power are equal to the task, and, secondly and more especially, whether they have confidence in themselves. Is there any task of reconstruction which does not require people who have the ability and the confidence in themselves? Do we have in China at present sufficient people to carry out these tasks of reconstruction? There must be a central focus for all our efforts. The five kinds of reconstruction [psychological, moral, social, political, and economic] which I have discussed should be undertaken simultaneously. No one of them should be ignored. But our focus should be on the economic task.

At this point Chiang proceeded to give an outline of his economic plans for the next ten years as regards the scope of the work to be accomplished and the volume of technical assistance that is required. To give a few examples:

	Total Plan	Total for the Next Ten Years
Railways	140,000 kilometers	20,000 kilometers
	(According to Sun Yat-sen's Plan of Industrial Development, the total mileage was 100,000 miles or 160,000 kilometers. There are at present already 20,000 kilometers.)	
Highways	1,500,000 kilometers	225,570 kilometers
	(Sun originally planned 1,000,000 miles or 1,600,000 kilometers. There are at present 100,000 kilometers.)	
Commercial Shipping	14,417,400 tons	3,043,300 tons
Motor Power	40,000,000 horsepower	10,700,000 horsepower
Electric Power	20,000,000 kilowatts	6,200,000 kilowatts
Telegraph Wires	36,000,000 kilometers	36,000,000 kilometers
Radios	18,000,000	18,000,000
Automobiles	7,677,210	451,570
Commercial Airplanes	120,000	12,000
Housing	50,000,000 rooms	10,000,000 rooms
Cotton Yarn	10,000,000 spindles	3,000,000 spindles
General Hospitals	200	100
Country Hospitals	2,000	2,000
Village Hospitals	160,000	80,000

Then as regards the number of technical assistants required for the next ten years:

	Graduates from Universities and Technical Colleges	Graduates from Vocational Schools
Civil Engineers	110,000	77,500
Mechanical Engineers	41,900	94,500
Electrical Engineers	12,400	20,400
Mining Engineers	8,600	23,300
Architectural Engineers	25,000	25,000
Chemical Engineers	7,200	8,100
Technical Engineers	3,600	8,200
Aeronautical Engineers	7,200	12,000
Medical Doctors	232,500	
Pilots	43,200	

The entire plan requires some thirty to fifty years of effort, and considering the population of the country and their needs the scheme is very conservative.

The question arises: Does China have the necessary natural resources to carry out this scheme? There was originally an impression that she was fabulously rich. That impression has now been corrected after careful scientific investigation. The resources are not scanty, but neither are they overabundant, especially in view of the large population. A measure of thrift and economy must be introduced. There are large coal reserves, estimated at two hundred and fifty billion tons, which should last thousands of years even when the country has attained a reasonably high degree of industrialization. Iron, the second principal mineral, is not too plentiful, but it is estimated at six to seven hundred million tons and should last another five hundred years. China's reserves in oil are not fully known. The estimated total at present is only about one per cent of the amount in the United States. But northwest China may have a large supply, and the National Resources Commission, which is one of the most energetic organizations, is sending out oil prospectors all over the country.

In the main it seems definite that there are four areas in the interior of China which can be marked for industrialization: 1. The Chungking area, which is situated in rich coal fields and iron deposits. 2. The Kiating-Loshan area, which has large power resources and coal reserves. 3. The Kunming area in Yunnan Province, which is famous for its tin and copper mines and is also richly supplied with coal.

4. Kansu Province, which produces raw cotton and excellent wool and has big reserves of coal and possibly also big oil reserves.

In other words, it appears quite definite that the western areas will receive an impetus in industrialization which will be comparable with the opening of the West in the United States. There is this difference, however. To the Americans of the pioneer days the wild West was in every respect virgin territory. In China the west was where the race had its origins. It was highly developed; it was, in fact, the meeting ground of many cultures. It was where the adolescent power and the early manhood of the Chinese race in the Han Dynasty found its fullest expression. It was through that region that China came into contact with the Roman Empire and with the races of southwestern Asia. Even as late as the Tang Dynasty the western parts of China were the outposts of a civilization where art and culture attained a high degree of development. The grottoes of Tunhuang have revealed the artistic wonders of that period.

This whole movement for the return to the west is creating a new epoch in Chinese history. It has all the romance of pioneer days. There will be the conquest of nature, the lure of distant horizons with their enormous possibilities. There will be a sense of adventure in following the course of the declining sun. Every inch of territory which will be harnessed for the use of man will yield the inward satisfaction that the human will is, after all, the most important of all forces. The effect on the youth of the country should be impressive. This is precisely what Chiang Kai-shek wants. "The development of the border," he said, "should be the ambition and the aim of all young men in the country. What I hope is that our vigorous young men will recapture the spirit of such men as Ma Yuan and Pan Chao. . . . The contributions which these young men will be able to make to the political development of the country and to the growth of a strong personality will be infinitely greater than what can be accomplished by remaining in the big cities."

In carrying out this gigantic industrial program, there are two nations which will capture the imagination of the Chinese. The first is obviously America, whose spirit of initiative has a special appeal to the Chinese. But the Russian experiment with its four Five-Year Plans which have proved so enormously successful in the present war against Germany will likewise receive sympathetic consideration. As a matter of fact, these two models, following two different social theories, completely agree with the principle which Sun Yat-sen laid down as far back as 1919, when he said: "The international development of China should be carried out along two lines: (1) by private enterprise, and (2) by national undertaking. All matters that can be and are better carried out by private enterprise should be left to private hands, which should be encouraged and protected by liberal laws. All matters that cannot be taken up by private concerns and those that possess a monopolistic character should be taken up as national undertakings." The basic question, however, still remains: where is China going to get all the capital necessary to carry out her industrial plans? The war has all but wiped out what there was in the way of capital in China. It never did amount to more than one and a half billion U.S. dollars, most of which was foreign capital.

There will be three main sources of capital. China must in the first place look for its own capital within the country, which is the property and credit of its bankers and merchants. A large amount of that is now in the United States for safekeeping, and it is hoped that when the war is over and peace and security are again established, it will go back to China. It is estimated to be between three and four hundred million U.S. dollars. It is suggested by one economist[1] that, "if necessary, [it] can be placed at the command of the government for the purpose of postwar industrialization, with property rights in the hands of owners who may draw interest on the capital so transferred." The Chinese banks which own a large portion of that capital have been largely commercial and speculative, and in the postwar period they will no doubt direct their credit to industrial, agricultural, and other economic activities so that at least they "can finance within China all the expenditure necessary to secure Chinese materials and to employ Chinese labor."

The second source consists of remittances from overseas Chinese which amount to over one hundred million U.S. dollars annually. Many of these Chinese have been hard hit by the war, and those in Malaya, the Dutch East Indies, and the Philippines are not only in no position to remit money to their homeland, but will have to be helped to regain the economic positions they held before Pearl Harbor. In 1939 and 1940 there was an especially large flow of money back to the homeland, owing to pressure being felt throughout the Southwestern Pacific area, although Japanese aggression was still largely confined to China. In 1939 the amount was two hundred and

[1] H. D. Fang, "The Postwar Industrialization of China," *Contemporary China*, March 23, 1942.

twenty-five million, while in 1940 it was one hundred and fifty million U.S. dollars.

The principal source of capital for postwar reconstruction in Asia will have to be from abroad. On this subject Chiang Kai-shek expressed himself very early. Away back in December 1926, just when he led his armies in victory to the banks of the Yangtze River, at a time when Borodin and his Communist friends exerted their greatest influence on China, he said to Bruno Schwartz, the New York *Times* correspondent:

"It [foreign capital] will always be welcome here. If foreign concerns wish to continue their factories in this country, or to open any other form of industrial enterprise, it will be given our hearty support in exactly the same manner as any Chinese enterprise. But it will only be permitted provided it is profitable to the Chinese people. The welfare of the worker comes first in our scheme of things, equally with the welfare of the enterprise itself."

The Atlantic Charter states that the United Nations are pledged "to bring about the fullest collaboration between all nations in the economic field with the object of securing, for all, improved labor standards, economic advancement and social security." This statement has now been substantiated by the Mutual Aid Agreements which, starting with Great Britain, have been extended to other powers. In the agreement between China and the United States Article VII pledges that the two governments are "not to burden commerce between the two countries, but to promote mutually advantageous economic relations between them and the betterment of world-wide economic relations."

Buttressed by these two instruments, it is likely that the Chinese Government will obtain the necessary foreign capital for its industrial schemes. There are already, in fact, the American credit of $500,000,000 and the British offer of £50,000,000. But even these amounts are not adequate, for as T. V. Soong, China's Foreign Minister, who works in close collaboration with Chiang Kai-shek, said on one occasion, China would require, to build up a solid national defense and to start a program of economic reconstruction, not $500,000,000 or even $1,000,000,000, but $5,000,000,000 or even $10,000,000,000. And he believed that the friendly powers would be willing to provide those amounts.

In a talk that he gave before the leading members of the American banking world in the fall of 1942, Soong said in effect that the economic reconstruction of China was one of the most hopeful and impressive undertakings for the improvement of mankind. In the past China was handicapped by many obstacles. In the first place, there was no strong, centralized government to co-ordinate the activities of the nation. There were also those unfair treaties which prevented the full realization of the plans of reconstruction. But out of these years of heroic resistance China had emerged as a new entity. The unequal treaties had now been abolished. There was at present a strong, centralized government, which was in a position to guide, to maintain, and to control all forms of productive enterprises. It was his belief that with ten years of sustained effort the productive capacity of the country would be at least three times what it was before the war.

Soong remarked to the American bankers that, when the war was over, China would settle down to a period of some twenty or thirty years of gigantic economic reconstruction and would put into practice Sun Yat-sen's ideas of social democracy. It would be for the friendly Allied powers to supply the resources which China would need, not only because she had been so closely associated with them, but also because of the permanent global peace which the United Nations hope to establish. The resources would be utilized for productive and not for unproductive enterprises so that there would be an adequate return on them. Soong also made the pointed remark that even though the friendly powers were unable or unwilling to provide the full measure of assistance which China needed, she must have recourse to other measures to develop her strength. He then referred to the Soviet Union. "When the Soviet Union began its plan of economic reconstruction," Soong said, "and approached the different powers for loans, no one responded. Whereupon Soviet Russia dug into its own resources, called upon its citizens to go through enormous sacrifices, and through perseverance and hard and bitter experiences completed its many Five-Year Plans. The people had to live through a period of tremendous shortage of the necessities of life, but the nation as a whole profited. It achieved remarkable success in the realization of its economic ideals. The fact that Soviet Russia has been able, during the present war, to rely upon its own military production to resist the most powerful army of the world is eloquent proof of the success of its enormous undertaking. The lesson is worth learning. With us in China also we are as firmly resolved to construct a new economic life as we are in resisting aggression. The two are one and indivisible."

The speech made a good impression on the American bankers. They understood that China's decision to industrialize is firm and irrevocable.

H. H. Kung, China's Minister of Finance, has also given the assurance that Americans and other foreigners would be "treated as if they were our own people," and that the Chinese Government would apply its laws to foreign guests with equity and consideration. And the Eleventh Plenary Session of the Central Executive Committee of the Kuomintang, held in the early part of September 1943, even passed a resolution that it expects to repeal the law demanding fifty-one per cent of Chinese capital and a Chinese manager in any joint enterprise, which was passed before the abolition of extraterritoriality, in order to show that China really welcomes the co-operation of foreign investors. China has not only decided to industrialize, but has decided also to carry that decision into the realm of realities.

40

And in Other Ways?

IT IS A PLATITUDE to say that the war is bringing profound changes to all the countries in the world. These changes vary with different countries; but in no country are the changes so extensive and fundamental as in China. The war caught that country when those changes were going on. In one sense they were interrupted, but in a truer sense it has brought those changes to a focus and has increased their tempo.

When the Kuomintang government was established at Nanking by Chiang Kai-shek upon the termination of the Northern Expedition in 1927, it was frankly announced as a "revolutionary" government. It was revolutionary in the sense that it at last had the opportunity of introducing those far-reaching reforms that were an integral part of the social and political faith of Sun Yat-sen and which became abortive as a result of the failure of the revolution in 1911. The energy with which those reforms were introduced filled the ten years which ended with the Japanese attack on July 7, 1937. The attack was in fact precipitated by those reforms. This explains why the present government is still known as a revolutionary government. This also explains why, in speaking about war and resistance, Chiang and his government lay much greater emphasis on internal reconstruction than does any other government.

Of the three basic principles which constitute the Sun Yat-sen ideology, that of nationalism was considered to have been fulfilled with the overthrow of the Manchu Dynasty in 1911; that of the social welfare or the economic well-being of the people forms an intrinsic part of the scheme of industrialization which we considered in the previous chapter. The problem remains whether the principle of political democracy is also being considered and carefully put into practice. It is a part of the program of reconstruction that is being undertaken in the course of the war. Are there indications, as the Archbishop of Canterbury once put it, that China "has made this challenge to her national life the occasion for a national rebirth and for setting on foot schemes of progress which will benefit the Chinese people throughout generations to come?"

The question is pertinent because there seems to be considerable doubt in the minds of many competent observers that the enforcement of democratic principles is being seriously considered by the present government in Chungking. The impression is found among many people that there is instead a growing tendency toward concentration of power, which is anti-democratic. In the absence of any formal declaration that Sun Yat-sen's principle of political democracy is being abandoned or even suspended for the duration of the war, the doubt should not be entertained, because in the prosecution of a large-scale war democratic institutions in any country may from time to time be overshadowed by measures which do not seem democratic; and in a country like China where these institutions are only being slowly evolved, it is in a way expecting too much that they should be functioning as if they had existed for a long time. Nevertheless, it is good that there is increasing concern over the future of democracy in China even though the same concern is not felt over other countries as, for instance, Soviet Russia. Russia is frankly a dictatorship, and that is the end of it. But in the case of China people somehow feel that the development of democratic institutions is a vital necessity not only for her own sake but for the future of the world.

Exactly why the development of democracy in China should be more important for the future of the world than in other countries which are fighting on the side of the United Nations is not clear. But it is presumed in any case that since China has had a strong democratic spirit all through her history, even though she was until recently a monarchy, and since she has professed to evolve modern democratic institutions, she must so justify herself.

It is true, however, that China has no other desire than to develop into a genuine working democracy, and I do not think for a moment that the resolution passed last September by the Central Executive Committee that constitutional government will be established one year after the end of the war was meant to allay the disquiet which has been recently expressed. If Chiang Kai-shek has been a consistent person and at the same time a sincere and devoted follower of Sun Yat-sen—we have no reason to believe otherwise—that resolution is a very logical step to take.

Still, it is interesting to observe that there was almost a timing to the recent crop of criticism of Chungking. In the April 25, 1943, issue of *Amerasia* there is an article, "Democracy versus One-Party Rule in China." Pearl S. Buck wrote an article entitled "A Warning about China" for the May 10, 1943, issue of *Life*. T. A. Bisson wrote "China's Part in a Coalition War" which appeared in the *Far Eastern Survey* for July 14. That was followed by Hanson W. Baldwin's "Resistance of Chiang Kai-shek's Army Keeps One Fourth of Japan's Land Forces Tied Up" in the New York *Times* on July 20 and a longer article, "Too Much Wishful Thinking about China," in the August issue of the *Reader's Digest*. Philip J. Jaffe wrote "China Can Win and Yet Lose" for *Amerasia* for July 25, which was followed by a radio talk about China by Raymond Gram Swing over the Blue Network on August 11. The views of Vincent Sheean in his recent book *Between the Thunder and the Sun* have also been expressed in his earlier *Personal History*, published in 1935, while Agnes Smedley, the author of *Battle Hymn of China*, has lived for a long period with the Eighth Route Army and for years has been frankly its protagonist.

These articles, written as they are by people of wide reputation, have been read and have naturally exercised some influence on the popular mind. Up to that time the American reaction to the Chinese in the war against Japan was one of praise. The American people know little about China and are too far away from the scene of hostilities to have an accurate view of the situation. But they do know that the Chinese people are peace-loving and, poorly equipped as they are, have shown enormous courage and success in holding a powerful invader at bay. When Pearl Harbor was attacked, they even had a vague feeling that, if it were not for the bravery of the Chinese soldier and of the Chinese people generally, the situation could have been even worse. That admiration remains; but it is true that this appearance of adverse criticism has made people wonder if they should not have been more restrained in their praise and if China really deserved all that encouragement.

In the meantime, the criticism appearing in the period between the end of April and the middle of August 1943 may have created a doubt in the American mind about both the military importance of the Chinese war against the Japanese in its relation to global strategy and the political competence of the Chinese people either to create a national unity or to develop a democratic form of government. For that is the main burden of the criticism.

Hanson W. Baldwin's two articles are entirely military. He has not been in China, but he does not hesitate to say that "China is not a nation in our sense of the word, but a geographer's expression." There is, of course, no reason why China should be a nation in any other sense than her own. The important thing is to have a consciousness of unity, and that unity was created by an identity of language, social manners and customs, laws, culture, art, literature, and philosophy which was in existence at least a millennium before such a thing existed in any other part of the earth.

The next piece of criticism by Baldwin is more serious. He thinks that Chinese troops lack training and have no leaders who are bound together by a common loyalty to a common cause. He still speaks about the existence of old war lords, "for whom war is a means for personal aggrandizement and enrichment." He speaks also about "loosely organized followers of some provincial general fighting chiefly for loot" and about discipline being "lax." If Chiang Kai-shek has accomplished anything at all in the twenty years that he has been an active political figure in China, it is precisely that he has created an army which is thoroughly indoctrinated with ideals and a sense of devotion and loyalty to the nation. Without that he could not have brought the whole country under his rule. When a common soldier, dying of his wounds, could still say to Mme. Chiang Kai-shek (a story which was related to Mrs. Roosevelt during Mme. Chiang's stay at the White House in 1943) that he fought not only for his own country but "for the liberation of all people who are downtrodden," there is certainly more than "loot" or "personal aggrandizement and enrichment" in his sentiments.

The drift of Baldwin's argument is to the effect that the Chinese military effort is of little or no value in the eventual victory over the Japanese in the Pacific, and that "there are many roads to Tokyo, but the one through China is perhaps the hardest." The subject of discussion is a military one, but the implication seems to be political. In this connection, it is well to recall that Admiral Ernest J. King stated on August 8, 1943, that China still held the key to final victory over Japan, adding that "you can imagine what the situation would be if China were out of the war."

Both Pearl S. Buck and T. A. Bisson have been residents of long standing in China and are warm friends of the Chinese people. They know conditions there well, and their observations deserve some close attention. Mrs. Buck laments the fact that "undemocratic forces" are becoming stronger, that there are signs that the war "is ceasing to be a people's war," that "the power of bureaucrats is growing," and that "there is now no real freedom in the press in China, no real freedom of speech." Mr. Bisson, while he would apparently patently agree with Mrs. Buck, goes further. He speaks of the existence of "two Chinas" as having "definitely emerged" even before Pearl Harbor. "One is now generally called Kuomintang China; the other is called Communist China." Up to this point he merely wishes to state facts. But when he goes on to say that "to be more descriptive, the one might be called feudal China; the other, democratic China," he frankly shows his preference. He then proceeds to describe conditions in "feudal" China where he discovers, like Mrs. Buck, that bureaucracy is having a tightening hold on the life of the people and that it makes no attempt to release democratic forces. On the other hand, he discovers that in Communist China there are signs of a working democracy. "The task of statesmanship is to merge these two Chinas into one." This act of merging would imply that Kuomintang China should go in the direction of Communist China and not vice versa. Mr. Bisson concludes correctly: "The future status of China as a healthy and vigorous nation, in which the people's livelihood is safeguarded by democratic processes, is at stake. Only such a China, moreover, can bring to the family of nations that level of constructive statesmanship that will be needed to guard the peace that the war has won."

There has indeed been a long list of foreign observers who have spoken sympathetically of the work of the Communists in China. Let us grant that many of them speak out of conviction. We are sometimes given to understand that the Communists have at long last brought the millennium to China. The territory under their control has been called "the Land of Five Withouts" by Lieutenant George Uhlmann—without beggars, without opium, without prostitution, without corruption, and without unjust taxes.

Granted that all this is true, though other reports do not confirm this impression, the fact remains that the Communists are sponsoring a secessionist movement; and so long as they do this, irrespective of the wonderful things they are reputed to have done or may do in the future, they are morally in the wrong. At a time when the country is going through a critical war and when national unity is of paramount importance, any effort to air party grievances through the creation of a separatist organization must be deprecated. When we bear in mind the fact that the Communists have their own armies—the Eighth Route and the New Fourth armies—which control large sections of territory bordering on Mongolia and covering the provinces of Hopei, Shensi, Chahar, Kansu, Shansi, Shantung, and Honan, no government can view the situation with equanimity. And when we recall that the Communists solemnly pledged themselves soon after the war with Japan was begun in earnest in July 1937 that they would abolish the name and the status of the Red Army and allow it to become a part of the National Army under the supervision of the Military Council, that they would abandon their government in the northwest areas and work toward a united democratic government, that they would abstain from any violent confiscation of landowners' holdings, and that they would strive meticulously to carry out Sun Yat-sen's Three Principles as the only means of salvation for China—then what they are doing at present constitutes a serious breach of faith. There was also the Program of National Resistance and Reconstruction which was accepted by all the parties including the Communist party at Hankow on March 29, 1938, in which the second of its thirty-one articles says: "All wartime powers and forces are hereby placed under the control of the Kuomintang and of General Chiang Kai-shek." Can the Communists honestly say that they have observed this article? Viewed in this light, the criticism which we frequently hear that the Chungking government is establishing a *cordon sanitaire* around the Communist areas and that it has been withholding funds and munitions which it has promised to the Communists becomes irrelevant.

We have not come to the point where we can calmly compare the accomplishments and defects of the two administrations. The mere fact that there are two separate administrations is an anomaly. If the one is by right and law the fully constituted government with authority to speak and act on behalf of the whole country, then all grievances should be aired and discussed within the framework of that government and not through the creation of a separate government which becomes in essence a seditious act. We must be logical; we cannot say that we are promoting the cause of democracy or constitutionalism when we condone, at the very outset, an act which is itself neither democratic nor constitutional. I think that on this subject as on others Chiang Kai-shek has at least the merit of consistency. The view which he holds today as regards Communism is the same view which he held back in the early days of the Northern Expedition. He has refrained from any overt military measures and will continue to do so not only as long as the national emergency lasts but even when peace is restored. The statement he made on March 6, 1941, before the People's Political Council still holds good. He said then, "In all matters—whether political, social, or party problems—not involving conflict with or obstruction to national order and authority, there is room for frank and open adjustment of differences in search of rational solutions. This has always been the policy and attitude of the government in relation to the Communist party—the achievement of unity by means of mutual concessions in the face of external aggression and the attainment of success in resistance and reconstruction."

This is a much more lenient and tolerant attitude than what he used to have. He speaks here of "mutual concessions." It may be that in these many years the Communists have themselves undergone a change and deserve to be given concessions. They may have improved, which is all to their good. As a matter of fact Mr. T. A. Bisson, in recounting the democratic measures they have introduced, came to the conclusion that "by no stretch of the imagination can this be termed Communism." This is all the more reason why the national ills should be removed by properly constituted instrumentation and not through a secessionist movement. Imagine a comparable situation in the United States if a group of people who were dissatisfied with the present administration should gather near the Canadian border and set up a government of their own in the states of Washington, Idaho, Montana, and the Dakotas, with a separate army, and enforcing its own social and economic measures with no reference to Washington. It is not entirely an analogous situation, but the principles involved are the same. The people would rise up against such a separatist movement. For the same reason the Communist regime should be abolished in China.

The truth of the matter is that the Kuomintang will rise and fall entirely on its own merits. The government today is frankly a one-party affair, but that does not mean that it is totalitarian. It is not the kind of one-party government which exists in Soviet Russia or in Germany or until recently in Italy. Chiang Kai-shek's official titles today include that of President of the Republic, Tsung-tsai or Leader of the Kuomintang party, President of the Supreme National Defense Council, President of the Executive Yuan, President of the Military Council, and Speaker of the People's Political Council. He is even President of the Central University and the Central Military Academy. But he is no dictator. Chiang's prestige is above any one of these separate posts or even a combination of them, but while he holds so many of these key positions in both the party and the government there is, as one observer said, "a good deal to be said in its favor, as it doubtless facilitates the handling of many urgent problems so often besetting a government in wartime."

The Kuomintang has committed itself to a democratic platform. It does so not only now, but has ever since Sun Yat-sen's political ideals became crystallized. That is a pledge to the nation and to the people. It cannot go back on its word without running the risk of losing faith with the people, which it cannot afford to do. As a matter of fact, totalitarianism is possible in China only if another party has the power to supersede the Kuomintang. The Kuomintang itself cannot become totalitarian without completely disowning the Sun Yat-sen faith: that it cannot do. The Kuomintang is a one-party government, but it is different from one-party governments in other parts of the world. It does not claim to play a permanent role; it is in theory and must also be in practice merely a custodian of the people's power until such time as they are able to exercise it themselves; its assumption of power is therefore temporary. It will have performed its historic mission when the constitutional period is reached. It may prolong the period of tutelage, but it cannot do so unduly without arousing the suspicion of the people. In fact, that period cannot now be stretched too long, because the Eleventh Plenary Session of the Kuomintang has placed itself on record as regards the time when constitutional enjoy any special privileges but occupy an equal status with the other political parties now existing or which may be formed in the future.

Then the question arises: What are the other political parties now functioning? We have discussed the Communist party. What other parties are there? On the printed page one party looks just as impressive as another. But actually almost without exception they are parties with party chiefs but no party members! This may sound unbelievable but is a well-known fact. An article in *Amerasia* for April 25, 1943, entitled "Democracy versus One-Party Rule in China" gives a list of five parties outside of the Communist party. They are: (1) the National Socialist party, (2) the Young China party, (3) the National Salvation Association, (4) the Vocational Education Group, and (5) the Rural Reconstructionists.

This sounds as if these parties are all well-organized political groups with large followings, struggling for power in the government, hoping perhaps eventually to supersede the Kuomintang, much in the same way as the Republicans, let us say, try to win power in the United States. Actually it is nothing of the sort. The National Socialist party heads the list and is deservedly considered the most important of these parties. It has a political and social platform, but in no way does it differ essentially from the platform of Sun Yat-sen. Its present party head, Carson Chang, studied under Rudolf Eucken in Jena and is passionately devoted to scholarship. He is a man of great integrity and has an irresistible personal charm. He is fully qualified to be a party leader. But if he has any quarrels with the Kuomintang, it is not because its political and social tenets are widely different from his own, for they are not, but because the Kuomintang has failed, in his judgment, to make its tenets a living reality in the government. Carson Chang has a few associates and friends who may be considered as belonging to his party, but even his secretary-general has deserted him to join the collaborationist government in Nanking. Chang still remains in Chungking as an almost one-man show. There is reason to believe that Chiang Kai-shek likes Carson Chang personally, for he is a likable man and was until recently the president of the Renascence Academy. He holds no position in the Kuomintang government and is on the presidium of the People's Political Council. The choice of the name of his party is unfortunate, and the fact that he has studied in Germany (although that was long before Hitler's day) seems also to convey the impression that it is the counterpart of the Nazis in China, though they have absolutely nothing in common.

When I last saw Chang in Chungking, we stood and talked on the sidewalk for quite some time. His deep concern was with the growth of the democratic spirit in China and he urged that everything should be done to stimulate it. One way was to keep the leading democracies as fully informed as possible concerning conditions in China, he said.

As regards the other groups, they are not in any strict sense political parties at all. But like Carson Chang's National Socialist party, they can all serve a useful purpose in urging the speedy realization of the Sun Yat-sen principles by the Kuomintang. The fact is that Sun, as a result of forty years of revolutionary agitation, developed so embracing a social and political faith that it leaves little opportunity for other parties to improve upon it. Even the Communists claim that they are simply putting into practice what has been neglected by the Kuomintang. There is, in fact, nothing basically in the Three Principles to which any sane, progressive, and patriotic Chinese can raise any objection. There are minor details which one or the other of the many so-called parties can elaborate upon and contribute to, but that is about all they can do. They can, however, do immense good by convincing the Kuomintang of the need for "self-analysis."

The final question is, therefore: To what extent has the Kuomintang really carried out or attempted to carry out the ideas which it professes? The progress toward democracy which is that party's ultimate aim has not, especially during a period of national emergency, been a steady one; but at the same time it cannot be denied that some effort has been seriously made. The People's Political Council is one of the principal efforts in that direction. That organization grew out of the Advisory Council of National Defense which started out as a small group of some seventeen people holding its first meeting four days after hostilities with Japan broke out at Shanghai on August 13, 1937. It consisted of some men who were not Kuomintang members and who were to act in an advisory capacity to the Kuomintang government. There was soon a demand to increase the membership, and finally there was a demand to transform it into something like a representative body of the people. Thus was the People's Political Council created in July of the following year. Its two hundred members were divided into four categories, one half of whom belong to the last category and are nominated by the Kuomintang from among the nation's cultural and economic organizations.

The majority of the members belong to the Kuomintang, which is fully to be expected, but the important thing is that the other groups, including the Communists, are all represented. The Council frankly acts in an advisory capacity and has no authority to pass resolutions which have the force of laws. It recommends proposals to the government and has the right to question the government on any scheme or policy which it desires to carry out. When properly used, this right of questioning can serve a useful purpose. The Council can at least air the views of the people which, if they are reasonable and good for the public welfare, are bound to have their influence on the policy of the government. It is not democracy in any full sense of the word, but it is on the road to democracy. It is a foregone conclusion that when the war is over the voice of the people to have a larger share in the government will increase in volume. They have already been assured a constitutional regime; and, depending on whether or not the Kuomintang fully lives up to the expectations of the people, other parties or a combination of the present parties will demand an increasing share in the conduct of the government. The Kuomintang has been in power since 1927 and has so far acquitted itself well, but the people are not blind to some of its shortcomings. Its power and influence in the days to come will depend entirely upon itself. If its accomplishments fully satisfy the wishes of the people it will continue to play an important part in the political and social life of China with such help as the non-Kuomintang elements may be able to contribute. That will be for the best interests of the country, for it guarantees steady evolution and improvement. On the other hand, if it becomes a source of disappointment to the people, then the demands for a limitation of its power will become insistent and new forces will appear on the scene. That may not necessarily be to the advantage of the nation, for it will mean new efforts for readjustment and a new turn of the political wheel with all its attendant dislocation and waste of power and energy.

The important thing is, therefore, the development of democracy within the Kuomintang itself and the continual realization of the principles upon which it is founded. That is the best guarantee of a modern China and the best invitation for all progressive elements within the country to offer their co-operation.

A survey of the present conditions shows that there is some room for improvement in the Kuomintang. It must try to improve the quality of its officials, for one thing. I would not be entirely frank if I said that its present quality is high: in fact it is mediocre. Chiang Kai-shek undoubtedly realizes this. Other Kuomintang leaders also know it. To quote from the article of my friend, T. S. Chien, "The Central Executive Committee, in a plenary session on March 1941, was quite unanimous that both the organization and the leadership of the party should be put on a more popular basis; that is to say that election from below should be substituted for appointment from above as a method of organization for the executive committees of the provinces and districts. If this comes true—as it has not for some twelve or thirteen years—the Kuomintang will easily secure a much broader basis of popular support, and may become more solicitous about democracy in general." This is a fine piece of constructive criticism. His observation is confined to the provinces and districts, but it is, of course, true generally.

What Chien means more specifically, I presume, is this: election implies some measure of wide and popular approval while appointment from above makes the government a personal matter. The Kuomintang so far has not strengthened or made full use of those two powers which, as Sun Yat-sen had the keenness to observe, were the distinguishing features of early Chinese political life, namely, the power of the people to control public officials and their power to admit officials into the government only through competitive examinations.

The history of China is full of extraordinary cases of men who had the courage to speak out and even to criticize the Emperor if it was thought that the Emperor's actions no longer promoted the best interests of the people. Wang Yang-ming of the Ming Dynasty, for whose philosophy Chiang Kai-shek has the highest admiration, was one of these men. His frank and open criticism led him into exile but, like others before him, he could not be deterred by any considerations of personal misfortune. That was in the days of the monarchy and at a period when there was no political machinery, as in modern democracies, through which popular sentiment could be expressed. But those people were nonetheless guardians of the democratic spirit and supplied vitality to the Chinese political system. They helped to maintain a high standard of public conduct. Those people strongly impressed Sun Yat-sen, and it is for this reason that he insisted upon creating the Control Yuan, which is on a par with the highest organs of the present government. But although the organization exists, the spirit of the ancient censorial officials is admittedly weak.

The same observation can be applied to the civil service examination which, if it is properly conducted, should be the strongest single factor in raising the quality of Chinese public life. If public servants enter the government through competitive examinations, as was consistently done in earlier days, it immediately creates an atmosphere in which merit and accomplishment take precedence over other considerations. That will at once place at the service of the nation a reasonably large supply of talent which today unfortunately is being more or less wasted. That is a great pity, as the country cannot afford not to make full use of all proven ability when it is going through a grave crisis. We continually hear complaints to the effect that the nation has no talent. That is in a sense true, as facilities for cultivating modern capacities are not as extensive in China as they are in other more advanced democracies. But it is also true that whatever available talent there is is not now being fully utilized.

"Appointment from above" implies a personal bond between appointer and appointee. Let us not go into the qualifications of some of the ranking officials in the government today. They are there, let us say, because they have rendered meritorious service to the cause of the Kuomintang. Now each of them has a large number of subordinate officials working for him. If the choice of these officials is made, as it is, on the basis of personal relationship, then it is clear that the field of choice becomes restricted. Talent, merit, ability, and integrity do not play any important part, for the appointing official is apt only to ask himself whether the subordinates whom he appoints are personally devoted to him. If the subordinate is both devoted and talented, all goes well; but devotion remains the primary consideration. The result is that official success depends not so much upon what one does or is but upon how ably one plays the game. In this game the able and talented do not play well: they have considerations of self-respect and personal integrity and consequently fall behind. Those who push themselves ahead are differently constituted, and once they are there they jealously guard their positions through fair means and foul. The quality of official life becomes naturally low.

It is to these two subjects that the present government would do well to pay careful attention.

Chiang Kai-shek himself has always looked for ability, because Chinese history has convinced him that final success has always attended those who have made wide use of all available talents. Chiang has today co-operating with him people of all kinds, including those who were formerly his political opponents. But that method has yet to be extended to all departments of the government. If the present government can utilize the country's men of ability and give them encouragement and security so that they can put their best into its service, then the tone and quality of Chinese public life will be so high that no one will think of challenging the right of the Kuomintang to even a permanent custodianship of the political power, for then the ideals of Sun Yat-sen will find their fullest expression and the people will be satisfied.

41

A Policy of Conciliation

THE IMMEDIATE PROBLEM that China expects Chiang Kai-shek to solve is the restitution of all the territory which China has lost in a century of spoliation. In doing this China will naturally have to adjust her relations with a number of powers. It is said that such an effort may be accompanied by a display of chauvinism. But I do not believe so; not, at any rate, until she considers that her legitimate demands have not been fully met. The Chinese boundaries as they existed a century ago were quite extensive, but it is not expected that the new China will claim all of them back. There will be no question, however, about certain areas which must come back into the fold.

The question of Manchuria and the northeastern provinces seems to be comparatively easy, because it is a question that affects the Japanese. With a defeated Japan, the thirty million Chinese inhabitants of Manchuria will regain their Chinese citizenship. On the twelfth anniversary of the Mukden incident, observed on September 18, 1943, Chiang said: "As we recall the humiliations our nation has endured during these twelve years and the untold misery and agony of our fellow countrymen in the northeast, we should offer to them our heartfelt sympathy. On the tenth anniversary of the Mukden outrage, commemorated on September 18, 1941, I plainly stated, 'Our sacred resistance will not end until the lost territory of our northeast is fully recovered and the liberty of our fellow countrymen there is regained.' The people of the northeast constitute an integral part and an indivisible section of the Chinese nation just as the four northeastern provinces constitute an integral and indivisible part of China's sovereign territory. Our war of resistance aims at preserving the independence of the Chinese people and the territorial sovereignty of the Chinese nation. This implies nothing short of the recovery of the territorial and sovereign rights in the northeast and the effacing of the insults and humiliations inflicted on us since September 18, 1931. This has consistently been our policy and determination. Military developments at present are bringing us closer to the attainment of our aim. We are more confident than ever in our ability to regain all our lost territory in the northeast and we will begrudge no sacrifice which the consummation of this task may entail."

It is significant that on the eve of that anniversary, in his message to Congress on the progress of the war, President Roosevelt almost pledged that Manchuria will be returned to China. He was speaking of the mandated islands in the Pacific. "It goes almost without saying," he continued, "that when Japan surrenders the United Nations will never again let her have authority over the islands which were mandated to her by the League of Nations. Japan obviously is not to be trusted. And the same thing holds good in the case of the vast territories which Japan has stolen from China, starting long before this war began." Manchuria is undoubtedly a territory to which China will attach the greatest importance. Its restoration to her sovereignty must be both complete and unconditional. The solution of this problem will, in fact, set the pattern for all subsequent Chinese policy. While Chiang Kai-shek is determined that that policy will be one of conciliation, any obstacles created for the recovery of Manchuria are likely to bring important changes in that position. As matters stand at present, the obstacles do not seem to exist. Soviet Russia's claim to any part of that territory would be most unusual even though ultimately she may go to war with Japan. As regards Great Britain, the only likelihood of her raising any difficulties for China will be one of general policy. It will be a test whether she is inclined to pursue a friendly policy or one of obstructionism.

Next to Manchuria, Japan will also have to give up Formosa and those islands, known as the Pescadores, on the China coast that stretch from Formosa to the mainland. Formosa had always been a Chinese province until it was taken away by Japan in 1895. She has since made the island into one of her most important naval and military bases.

With Great Britain there are two scores on which China will seek territorial adjustment. The first is Hong Kong. Up to the present time the Chinese Government, desiring to maintain the friendliest relations with her partners in a common war, has not raised the issue.

But it is clear that a nation which is determined to restore her prestige in a new world will hardly be satisfied if Hong Kong, whose cession to Britain in 1842 really started the century of spoliation, were to remain in British hands. Another consideration may perhaps induce Britain to satisfy Chinese wishes. Hong Kong was primarily a naval base and secondarily a commercial center. Its naval use has been proved in the present war to be entirely nonexistent, nor from now on can it be of any use as a naval base when there are hostile elements in the surrounding territory, especially when that hostility is expressed through the use of air power. If the surrounding territory is friendly there is no need for a naval base. As a commercial center, the bulk of the trade will naturally be with China. With China in the position that she held throughout the nineteenth century it could still have trade even though China might have been displeased, but a new China will look at the question in a different light.

A more serious matter that will concern Great Britain is Tibet. Although Tibet remains nominally under Chinese sovereignty, which Britain acknowledges, it is a matter of historical fact that Britain has had a deep interest in Tibetan internal affairs. The influence was strongest immediately after the revolution in 1911, when Chinese attention naturally could not be concentrated on that borderland. The last few years have seen a strong assertion on the part of China to make her sovereignty more than nominal. It is believed that as soon as Britain releases her pressure on Tibet the population will be glad to come back under the Chinese Government.

The only other major territorial adjustment is that with Soviet Russia concerning Outer Mongolia. Its position is analogous to that of Tibet. It was already a problem in the days of the closest Sino-Russian relationship. When Russia, following the success of its revolution, was professing the warmest friendship with China back in 1923, and was still unwilling to loosen its hold on Outer Mongolia, it is clear that it will be some time before Chinese suzerainty will go beyond the purely nominal stage. On the other hand, Russia does not intend to disclaim that suzerainty, which it acknowledged as late as 1941 in its Non-Aggression Pact with Japan. The Soviet Union has a so-called Mutual Assistance Pact with Outer Mongolia by which the Mongols remain technically outside of the Union though Red Army forces are stationed among them, and any infringement of their borders or of their interests is considered a direct threat to Soviet Russia itself. In view of the present policy of Soviet Russia toward the countries of eastern Europe, which she tries to prevent from forming any federation, the Mutual Assistance Pact with Outer Mongolia is interesting in that it is likely also to be applied to them as forming a group of satellites clearly within the orbit of Russian influence. The experiment has extended already to the Baltic States and to Czechoslovakia.

The questions of Kwangchowan and Macao are comparatively less important, but they need settlement all the same because a new China cannot remain indifferent to the maintenance of the vestiges of an era that has passed.

Chiang Kai-shek has not so far expressed himself quite as definitely on the need of these territorial adjustments, but there is no question that they are implied in the statements of broad principles which he has made from time to time on the aspirations of China in a postwar world. They represent, one may almost say, the consensus of opinion as being the irreducible minimum of Chinese irredentist policy: no intelligent Chinese can be satisfied with less. But at the same time they represent also the maximum demands. Chiang Kai-shek and other responsible Chinese leaders have made it quite plain that China has no desire at all for an inch of territory which is not her own. She is, however, interested in seeing that all the contiguous lands and those that are near her, including Korea, Indo-China, Thailand, Burma, and India, become fully independent countries. If the big countries need security the smaller countries need it even more. It is for this reason that Chiang Kai-shek said in his message to the *Herald Tribune* Forum of November 17, 1942: "China not only fights for her own independence, but also for the liberation of every oppressed nation." When the, proper time comes Chiang will obviously become the medium through which Chinese public opinion will be expressed. But it is typical of the Chinese in general and of Chiang Kai-shek in particular that, knowing as they do their desires on the subject, they have not seen fit to have them widely publicized.

Having regained the territory which she has lost, China will be prepared to work enthusiastically for general security. It will be security for herself extending to the whole Pacific area and finally security for the whole world. Obviously the country that has threatened her security more than any other is Japan. The question immediately arises: What stand will China take toward a defeated Japan? Will China insist upon Japan's complete disarmament? Will China insist upon Japan being placed, at least for a specified period, under the military or police control of the United Nations? To what extent will the internal affairs of Japan be controlled by the United Nations? Will China ask for reparations?

There will be two main schools of thought. One will lean toward severity and harshness, and the other toward a more generous arrangement. On the whole, I am inclined to believe that the second alternative will be more sympathetically considered, as it is more in consonance with the Chinese spirit. That does not mean that the criminal military leaders and officers of Japan can escape the supreme punishment. They will be put in the same category as their associates in the other Axis countries, and their punishment will be equally severe. It must also include the complete elimination of all the savage elements of a mentality that has been steeped in primitive barbarism.

The next step will be the complete disarmament of Japan. The details can be worked out later, but it will have to be so complete as to insure a permanent elimination of militarism as a cult from Japan. The military class must disappear from Japanese society, and although liberal elements in Japan amount to practically nothing as a force, Japanese educational life will have to be so molded that the least obstacle to the growth of liberalism will be removed. The Japanese constitution, as it exists today, which makes the military and naval leaders directly responsible to their Emperor must be abandoned; in fact the whole institution of the Emperor must be shaped so as to bring it into accord with democracy and constitutionalism in other parts of the world.

Whatever the details may be, the aim of the United Nations should be to eliminate once and for all any opportunity for the military class to re-establish its ascendancy over the Japanese nation, and to mold popular sentiment in Japan so as to make it feel that it is to the best interest of the Japanese nation to live in harmony with a democratic world. It is only on such a basis that it is possible to construct any organization for the attainment of an all-round security. In spite of varying degrees of faith in an ultimate global organization for the establishment of a general peace, some attempt in that direction will have to be made when the war is over. A global organization must work through its regional representatives, but its workability will not depend upon its constitution and machinery, to which people seem to attach so much importance, as upon the spirit behind it. In any regional organization in the Pacific area the part of China will naturally be an important one. But it calls first of all for a basic understanding with the three other leading members of the United Nations which will play an equally important part.

First, there will be an understanding with the United States. Through sheer geography, any security in the Pacific must depend upon complete agreement between China and America, two large land areas situated respectively on the western and eastern shores of that ocean. Other countries are also interested in the Pacific, but not in quite the same way. It is fortunate that between China and America there have always been the best of relations. I am not denying that there are issues that have caused friction, but they are unimportant in the large background of friendly intercourse which has been a basic historic fact. I believe that as time goes on the bond between the two countries will become firmer, and I believe also that it will become one of the strongest guarantees for the future peace of the world. All intelligent Chinese, from Chiang Kai-shek down, feel that way and speak about it, although they do so in a completely different sense from the way people speak about an Anglo-American alliance. Between China and America there will be a growing identity of ideals, while those who support an Anglo-American understanding, be they British or American, think primarily of their immediate common interests.

There is practically nothing more to be desired in the present state of feeling between the American and Chinese peoples. That in itself is a lesson to the world that genuine friendship does not have to depend upon those factors which are commonly held to be essential. That friendship has already gone beyond a mere cold-blooded consideration of an identity of practical interests upon which international friendship is usually based, and that is why it has a lasting quality which occasional friction cannot undermine. I think there is genuine admiration in America for the bravery of the Chinese soldiers in their war of resistance under the leadership of Chiang Kai-shek, and there is certainly a deep and warm feeling in China shared by Chiang toward the Americans who, they think, are the only people along with themselves that are exerting their efforts for the establishment of world peace which will be founded upon ideals and not upon power or any community of immediate practical interests.

With Russia, China desires to maintain the friendliest relations. Between them there is one of the longest boundaries in the world— longer by about one third than that between the United States and Canada—and no country having so intimate a geographical contact with another country can afford to have anything but a most friendly relationship. But the issue of Communism has for years been an obstacle to any understanding. If the Chinese Communists, as it is generally believed, are still inspired by Moscow, it will be a long time before that understanding can be reached. If, on the other hand, the Chinese Communists are entirely on their own, so long as their views are sound and their practices are really for the welfare of the country, they constitute mainly a political problem which the present government in Chungking will ultimately solve. The way will then be cleared for some approach to Russia.

Aside from the question of Communism, it is believed there is something hard and metallic in Soviet policy. There is a feeling that Soviet policy today is an extension of the policy of Ivan the Terrible, of Peter the Great and Catherine the Great, and that it is frankly expansionist. The war has brought untold suffering on the Russian people and one should not expect the country to be soft and sentimental over the prospects of world peace. But has not China gone through as much? It is because there has been so much torment and suffering that we must have a better and saner world. The Chinese are fortunate in having a large reservoir of urbanity, rationalism, and humanism to draw upon. The lessons in the past have taught them that power and force can never be the ultimate solution to human problems. Sooner or later, therefore, the Chinese come back to the long-range view that human relationships, whether they be between individuals or nations, must be guided by moral laws. The Russians are perhaps skeptical of this view. They may see little in their own past, or at least in the behavior of other European countries, to convince them that their policy should be based upon any other consideration than that of power politics.

But there is also reason to believe that, once her confidence has been won, Russia is prepared to be as constructive as any country. That is why it is gratifying to know that the problem of Sinkiang in northwestern China, which has been the cause of so much anxiety to China, is being peacefully and amicably settled with Russia. Sinkiang is an immense area of deserts and oases covering some half a million square miles. The word "Sinkiang" means "new territory" and that territory became a part of the Chinese Empire in the Han Dynasty (206 B.C.–A.D. 221); through it caravans carried on a brisk trade in silks and teas between China and the countries on the other side of Central outside world, but the suspicion prevailed that it was simply another field for Soviet penetration like Outer Mongolia. The construction of the Turksib Railway skirting around that territory increased that suspicion, as indeed it helped Russia to control Sinkiang's economic life. But the latest developments seem to indicate that Russia's interest in that part of China has been conditioned by a sense of her own security and that, since the defeat of Japan is a foregone conclusion, she is prepared to withdraw her influence over China's northwestern region. The result has been most encouraging. The Kuomintang government has re-established its authority over the whole area, and China feels satisfied that her historic entity has been restored. If the reports are true, the change is one of the most significant events in contemporary Chinese history. It not only augurs well for friendly relations between China and Russia, itself a stabilizing factor in the world of the future, but it should also become one of the outstanding examples of international relations being conducted on the basis of reasonable and peaceful negotiation. If Russia continues to show this new spirit and this constructive statesmanship and foresight, one is tempted to say that a new international order is almost assured, even though there be other countries that look longingly toward the past. Russia is destined, one way or the other, to play a leading role in the world of the future.

Into the history of Sino-British relationship we need not go. From the time of the Opium War to the Mukden incident Britain has been steadfastly guided by the desire to create a large empire with scant consideration for others, and she has been enormously successful. She has tact, subtlety, and diplomatic finesse compared with which other empire-minded powers appear to be crude, but the aim of self-aggrandizement and the repudiation of moral values have long been present From that policy the Chinese have suffered. Within the memory of those still living there was the Anglo-Japanese Alliance that helped make Japan what she is today and powerful British circles in China and elsewhere in the East long regretted the demise of that alliance. Even as late as just before the attack on Pearl Harbor the opinion was widely expressed by some British that Japan was only establishing law and order in China, which would mean eventually the preservation and development of British interests in that part of the world. It is surprising that a nation with such rich and wide political experience could have been so mistaken in its judgment. Obviously the Chinese and other peoples in Asia are not to blame if they are suspicious of British intentions. They are not sure that the precipitate fall of Hong Kong and Singapore has necessarily produced any change in a mentality that considers only its own interests as of paramount importance. The policy of appeasement can, after all, assume many shapes and forms, and the doctrine of balance of power may take a new lease on life.

For, all things considered, the British are a great race of people and although between them and the Chinese there is no common background, all educated Chinese have genuine respect for the cultural accomplishments of the British. They admire their literature from Chaucer to Masefield, for it has expressed some of the finest and noblest sentiments of the human heart. They admire their system of orderly government and the spirit of freedom that inspires it. They admire their urbanity, their sanity, their sense of proportion, their "sweet reasonableness," which are all a part of the Chinese way of life. The British deprecate revolutions as they are commonly understood. "The greatest revolution in England was a revolution which never took place," Mr. Chesterton once said. The Chinese like that; for their own revolution, although it did take place, was one in which the usual attendant horrors were conspicuously absent. The British are conservative and have a deep respect for tradition. The Chinese are much the same, for those qualities speak for steadiness and character.

Between the Chinese and the British there are, therefore, many points of contact; and yet the pity of it is that the Chinese have only doubt and suspicion of the British. The Chinese sometimes wish that the suspicion was not justified, because it hurts them to feel that they cannot work in harmony with a country which obviously has so many worthy qualities. They go back into history trying to discover some incident or episode that might be singled out to support a new attitude, but they invariably come to the conclusion that, even though Britain might have occasionally made a concession or two as, for instance, their abandonment of the Hankow and Kiukiang settlements in 1927 or the statement of their policy known as the so-called Christmas gift of Austen Chamberlain, they were made because Britain could not do otherwise. They can find no instance in which British statesmen had the vision to see the direction in which events were developing and to anticipate them by a direct action on their own initiative that would make the Chinese really grateful for what they did. The wide difference in the wording of Chiang Kai-shek's messages to the United States and Britain on the identical measure taken

Paul Guillumette, Inc.

Generalissimo and Mme. Chiang Kai-shek visiting India. Between them stands Gandhi. First person on the right rear is Jawaharlal Nehru.

by the two countries for the abolition of extraterritoriality on October 10, 1942, is a case in point. Chiang praised the British for "winning a moral victory" over themselves while his message to the United States was one of joy and gratitude. There was no reason why Chiang should express two different points of view, and yet all intelligent Chinese believed that he fully represented the feeling of the nation. Britain has never issued so magnificent an expression of cordiality as the one given by President Roosevelt, who had the statesmanship and the greatness of soul to say that the repeal of the Chinese Exclusion Acts was the removal of "a historical mistake." These few words completely won the heart of all Chinese. If only the British leaders could express themselves in a similar way on the subject of Hong Kong! There would then be a basis for a new attitude, but British political behavior has never been of that kind. When the day comes that Britain is forced to give up Hong Kong, there will be no appreciation, let alone any sense of gratitude.

From the British point of view, I presume they are satisfied that the doctrine of the balance of power that has helped in the expansion of British interests for at least two centuries has been enormously successful, and that there is no reason why it should be discarded in favor of a new policy. In Asia and in the colonies the old policy was easy to apply. With what alacrity did Japan seize the proffer of an Anglo-Japanese alliance! So long as their interests could be kept intact, the British considered it foolhardy to follow what would seem to them any quixotic policy. If Britain's preoccupation is to make those interests as unassailable as possible, there is scant reason to believe or hope that she is prepared to follow a new policy in Asia after the present war. If she does not follow a new policy it unfortunately means another war. Professor John Dewey once said to me that the whole of British policy in Asia was conditioned by the desire to keep India in subjection, and his implication was that this desire could be met only when other parts of Asia were also kept weak.

I am afraid that Britain will learn to her deep regret that the present war is the end of an era and that the inflexible policy projected by a fossilized nineteenth-century mentality will no longer work. I am not denying that there are younger minds in Great Britain that regard the future of the world in a different light. There are intelligent people who may yet save the situation, who are working for "no return to a democracy which was little but an oligarchy of property owners; no relapse to a type of capitalism which measured production by profit and put wealth before welfare; no reversion to an imperialism based upon pagan theories of usury and racial superiority." They wish "to re-define democracy in terms of social duty, capitalism in terms of welfare, imperialism in terms of trusteeship instead of extortion." But in the meantime the Churchill-Amery complex remains the dominant factor in practical British politics, even though eventually it may be superseded. But with or without the present war, although the war has immensely accelerated the process, Asia is no longer a passive agent but has become a positive factor whose leaders are exercising as much influence on the development of the future of the world as are leaders elsewhere. For the moment the greatest of all these leaders is Chiang Kai-shek, and what he says and does is determining the course of events in all Asia to an extent unknown before. The destiny of Asia is in his hands, and in the shaping of that destiny he is immeasurably contributing to the sum total of the world's future.

It is a test of British political sagacity to realize the existence of this immense historical fact before it is too late. It is a platitude to say that Asia under the leadership of China is going through enormous changes. The changes in the political, economic, and industrial life of Asia are only incidental to the enormous changes in mental attitude, and for the British leaders to bury their heads, ostrichlike, in the sand is to court sure disaster. To be more specific, it is impossible to have a Free China on one side of a line and expect that people on the other side will remain in a colonial status as they did before the war. Even under the present Japanese rule these people are enjoying a measure of freedom that was denied them before, although intelligent persons know that the freedom is entirely specious and has no lasting value. But the people of the East have a new political weapon all the same; and when the war is over, with the defeat of Japan, they are not going to revert to their former political servitude and wait to be harnessed for exploitation. The phenomenon of a new China ready to assert her will and play an important part in the community of free nations is having as exhilarating an effect on other Eastern peoples as it is on the Chinese themselves. There will be an osmosis between free China and the rest of Asia as sure as there is osmosis in the realm of chemistry, and Asia will no longer be the happy hunting ground of imperialism as it has been in years past. The handwriting on the wall should be clear enough.

42

China Looks Ahead

CHIANG KAI-SHEK and Mme. Chiang visited India in the early days of February 1942. Jawaharlal Nehru had visited Chungking in 1938, but the visit of the Chiangs was more than a return courtesy. Singapore and the Malay States had fallen to the Japanese, and Burma was in imminent danger of suffering the same fate. There were definite measures touching upon the military situation which Chiang Kai-shek thought it necessary to fulfill. He wanted to see for himself how the factories which have been turning out ammunition for the Chinese soldiers on the other side of the Burma Road were functioning, and how well they were being defended against a possible Japanese attack. He also wanted to know about the possibilities of a new road connecting India with Chungking in the event the Burma Road fell into the hands of the Japanese. And lastly he wanted to see for himself the relationship between the British and the Hindus and how the whole problem of India was being managed. It is useless to say that Chiang is not concerned with the welfare of a neighboring country with which China has had a close relationship for nearly two thousand years. But he desired to have firsthand knowledge of the problem itself. It was his first trip to a foreign country since he went to Soviet Russia in 1923.

During the official banquet held by the government of India in honor of the visitors, Lord Linlithgow made some fine and appropriate remarks. He even quoted a saying from Confucius: "Is it not delightful to have men of kindred spirit come to one from afar?" To which Chiang replied by quoting another Chinese saying: "To have one look at things is a hundred times more satisfactory than hearsay."

The train carrying the Chiangs and their entourage pulled into the railway station at New Delhi in the early afternoon of February 9. A reception in honor of the distinguished guests was held in the Durbar Hall of the Viceroy that afternoon. The Viceroy called the occasion "a turning point of history" and affirmed also that "India's heart is one with China." He paid a warm tribute to Chinese unity in which "is enshrined a jewel of great price, a precious hope and inspiration for all men in a discordant world." Lord Linlithgow also touched the heart of the Chinese visitors by referring to the history of China and India in which mutual influences, religious, cultural, and political, "have made themselves felt from the earliest times to the present day." Chiang Kai-shek expanded on the subject in his reply and said: "In days almost legendary, Chinese seekers after truth found their way to India after years of perilous travel through arid deserts and over sky-reaching mountains to drink at the inexhaustible fountain of Indian philosophy. They took back to their motherland, in the face of indescribable dangers and difficulties, the priceless volumes which embodied the wisdom of India."

On this phase of the relationship between two neighboring countries the average Chinese has indeed much to say and can even wax eloquent. Chiang was no exception. China in her long history has really only known two foreign contacts, the first with India since the early days of the spread of Buddhism into China and the other with the Western countries from the eighteenth century onward. The relationship with India was a fine example of what international relationships should be. It was marked by mutual respect of each other's cultural accomplishments although they are widely different in character. India was to China a land of inspiration whose profound philosophic thought and wide range of religious teachings made a deep intellectual and emotional appeal. There was no need for any effort at proselytizing, for moral and spiritual grandeur can stand on its own feet and is its own recommendation. If it has sufficient illumination it will spread its light without militancy or recourse to any measures of coercion. Perhaps in the history of no two countries in the world has the relationship been kept on such a consistently high level. In that relationship there was a certain amount of trade and commerce, but the prospects of material gain became something pleasant in the background of mutual intellectual and spiritual admiration.

When China came into contact with the Western nations, a certain amount of this kind of friendly relationship was maintained. The Jesuit fathers, for instance, still had a sense of discrimination. They showed respect for the great accomplishments of other civilizations. They brought the best that Europe had to contribute but also carried away with them from China fertile ideas which exercised a profound influence on Locke, Leibnitz, Quesnay, Rousseau, and the other thinkers who in one way or another were responsible for the French Revolution and the shaping of the world thereafter. The extent of Chinese influence on Europe and America was much wider than is commonly acknowledged. But that period was short and was completely overshadowed by what came afterward. From the beginning of the nineteenth century the relationship was frankly conducted by the Western nations on a basis of material gain and economic exploitation through the use of more effective weapons of war than China was able to manufacture. Anything that had to do with the mind and the spirit was completely forgotten. Asia's value was then conceived entirely in terms of the amount of wealth that it was able to contribute to the coffers of Europe. To a mind as sensitive as Chiang's the enormous differences between these two types of international relationship are only too palpable. He would not be true to himself if he did not attempt to re-establish the cordial international relationship that China and India enjoyed through many centuries. But an essential condition for that relationship is the restoration of freedom and independence. What Chiang saw in India must have depressed him—not so much the economic and social evils in India, for they exist in varying degrees in other parts of the world also, as the spectacle of a master race holding another race in bondage. This can give no comfort to a self-respecting onlooker, for he sees an irreparable damage being done to the soul of both the oppressed and the oppressor. The problem of India became for Chiang no longer a local problem; it merged into the larger problem for which this war is being fought and for which he has himself fought all his life. Therefore, before he left India he gave a vigorous farewell message on February 21 in which he frankly said that "should freedom be denied to either China or India there could be no real peace in the world."

The message is a historic document of the first importance and a landmark in the present struggle for freedom all over the world. "The present struggle," he said, "is one between freedom and slavery, between light and darkness, between good and evil, between resistance and aggression." And then it went on with this peroration: "In these terrible times of savagery and brute force the people of China and their brethren, the people of India, should, for the sake of civilization and human freedom, give their united support to the principles embodied in the Atlantic Charter and in the joint declaration of twenty-six nations, and ally themselves with the anti-aggression front. I hope they will wholeheartedly join the Allies, namely, China,

Great Britain, America, and the Soviet Union, and participate shoulder to shoulder in the struggle for the survival of a free world until complete victory is achieved and the duties incumbent upon them in these troubled times have been fully discharged.

"Lastly, I sincerely hope, and I confidently believe, that our ally, Great Britain, without waiting for any demands on the part of the people of India, will as speedily as possible give them real political power so that they may be in a position further to develop their spiritual and material strength and thus realize that their participation in the war is not merely an aid to the anti-aggression nations for securing victory, but also a turning point in their struggle for India's freedom. From an objective point of view, I am of the opinion that this would be the wisest policy, which will redound to the credit of the British Empire."

No person who has any sense of justice, including even the British themselves, can deny that Chiang's farewell message to India is one of vision and statesmanship. It was an appeal to the British to take a long-range view of the international situation, to avoid being compelled to act at some future date when to act now would immensely increase her prestige and place her in a new position of leadership. Britain would, in fact, have little to lose and everything to gain by playing a new role in a new world, even insofar as India is concerned, for did not one of her nationalist leaders say: "We will send the British out of India as masters, but before the boat is out of the harbor we will call them back as friends"? I am afraid, however, that it will be some time before Britain will turn a fresh page in history. Even when progressive thinkers everywhere are trying to find a new formula so that the problem of India may be brought into consonance with the principles for which human blood is being shed all over the world, Mr. Leopold Amery, in a speech before the American Outpost in London on May 6, 1943, said, "Ever since the opening up of the high seas India's contacts with Asia, whether for trade or for defense, have mattered far less to her than her contacts overseas. Her mountain frontiers are a serious obstacle alike to trade and to invasion. Her long coast line is a standing invitation to both." Mr. Amery did not stop to think whether these contacts have made India happy or miserable. And then he went on to say: "There is no such thing really as an Asiatic, and of the great racial and cultural divisions of the old world, India's racial origins and her historical and political associations and traditions have linked her, from the days of Alexander the Great, through the long centuries of Moslem infiltration and the subsequent two centuries of British influence, far more closely with the world of Europe and the Middle East than the fundamentally different history and outlook of the Mongolian Far East." Again Mr. Amery did not consider that India would at any moment be willing to renounce the two centuries of association with Britain and to continue, expand, and prolong the twenty centuries of contact with what he calls the "Mongolian Far East." During the short association with Britain India has completely lost her soul and forgotten even the simple dignity to which all human beings are entitled, while in her long association with China India was a free agent, proud of her spiritual heritage and dispensing her wisdom and her experience with a prodigality and generosity which only a nation conscious of the fullness of its powers can show. India had then a rich and abundant life while today she is starved, for no nation or race can feel otherwise than poor, abjectly poor, when its freedom has been taken away from it.

This is not the place to go into the usual stock arguments advanced by the Britain of imperialism to strengthen its hold on India. There is the perennial argument of the antagonism between the Hindus and the Moslems. There is the argument of the caste system and the untouchables. And there is the argument of the different languages. If these arguments are accepted, then India will never be free, for the differences of religion, of social status, and of languages will exist in India a thousand years from now as they exist in other countries. But no independence can wait upon the fulfillment of homogeneity, and no independent country in the world today has that homogeneity. If Britain had said to the colonies on the North American continent that they would have no freedom until they were united, the chances are that the Americans would not have freedom yet. Or if, at the time when the United Kingdom was being formed, someone should have said: "You English, Welsh, Irish, and Scotch are too divided and are sure to have civil war and cut each other's throats, and so we cannot grant you freedom," what would the English have said? The truth is that unity grows when freedom has been achieved and not before. And in India, in spite of the many differences, the people, whether they be Moslems or Hindus, are united in one thing —their desire for freedom from British rule.

The Britain of democracy was anxious to sign the Atlantic Charter and subscribe to the Four Freedoms while the Britain of imperialism quickly renounced these instruments without any feeling of compunction or even any awareness of the contradiction and absurdity of the situation. That, to the Chinese mind, is a discrepancy which must be eliminated before there can be any real peace in the world. Chiang Kai-shek willingly accepts this as a challenge. "There will be neither peace nor hope nor future for any of us unless we honestly aim at political, social, and economic justice for all peoples of the world, great and small." The New York *Herald Tribune* Forum of November 17, 1942, to which Chiang sent this message contains a number of ideas which will eventually, I think, help to solve many of the perplexing problems with which the world is confronted. "Among our friends," it also said, "there has been recently some talk of China emerging as the leader of Asia, as if China wished the mantle of an unworthy Japan to fall on her shoulders. Having herself been a victim of exploitation, China has infinite sympathy for the submerged nations of Asia, and toward them China feels she has only responsibilities, not rights. We repudiate the idea of leadership of Asia because the 'Fuehrer principle' has been synonymous with domination and exploitation, precisely as the 'East Asia Co-prosperity Sphere' has stood for a race of mythical supermen lording over groveling subject races."

One of the most important contributions which China has made to the future of the world through this war is the complete destruction of the myth that there is an inevitable race antagonism which can be suppressed only by the emergence of one race destroying all the others. In Europe it has been the talk of Nordic superiority, while in Asia it is the Pan-Asian movement, both of which are no more than fraud under whose mask it is intended to further designs of aggression. Through centuries of emphasis upon what is strictly fundamental in life and upon the realization of the moral law as the only criterion of man's worthiness China has fortunately been completely oblivious of racial differences, considering them no more than a mere accident of nature, and she stubbornly raises the question of cultural and moral fulfillment as the only norm of human behavior. As Confucius said: "There is no class or race distinction among mankind; the only differences are in education and cultural accomplishments." By extending this attitude to the present war China has thus made the issues clear-cut. They become pure moral issues, and the nations of the world, of whatever race, fall within two distinct camps —those that fight for the vindication of the moral law and those that

General Sir Archibald Wavell, now Viceroy of India, and General George Brett, of the U.S. Air Corps, with Generalissimo and Mme. Chiang Kai-shek. Sitting on the extreme right is Sir Archibald, behind

Thomas Kuang, Chinese News Service

attempt to repudiate it. By bravely fighting on the side of the morally right, from the days when she was quite alone, China has thus transcended all superficial racial considerations.

Such a position, which is inspiring because of its utter simplicity, cannot allow duality for any country, even though it may be a stanch supporter of the United Nations, for unless there is complete integration and unity of outlook the line of demarcation between the two opposite camps may become indistinct. This question of duality which expresses itself, for instance, in a Britain that devotes itself to the realization of man's highest ideals and a Britain that seeks to perpetuate its rule over subject peoples is indeed one of the most perplexing questions for which the modern mind must provide an adequate answer. As a Chinese I cannot reconcile two opposing attitudes existing side by side in the same person or in the national policy of the same country.

It has seemed to me that this bifurcation between ideals and actual practice has had a longer history in Europe than we ordinarily realize and helps to explain the inconsistencies in the national policies of its principal states. As a non-European I am deeply concerned with this problem, which is basically an intellectual and moral one, and unless it is solved it seems to me that all the economic and political plans and devices, now being advanced with the utmost sincerity, will fail to produce the desired result.

With all the unity provided by a common heritage, it is unfortunate that Europe has tended, in her historical development, to division and disintegration. The impulse to discriminate and to seek differences has somehow always been stronger than the impulse to identify and to find out the common grounds on which men are united. The first major difference was made between the church and the state, a difference quite unknown in the whole course of Chinese history. In Europe, with the establishment of this difference which became all but complete in the time of Machiavelli, human consciousness learned to have a split allegiance to two sources of power which are frequently irreconcilable. And this consciousness of distinction has extended to many fields, including languages, religious denominations, races, and nations, until it has created within the last four hundred years this astounding medley known as European civilization. It is impossible to find a counterpart elsewhere in the civilized world, where twenty to thirty different nations are separated from one another by so many different languages and racial distinctions. The principle of self-determination of peoples has helped to multiply rather than to diminish the national groups. Now and then a philosopher or a statesman as, for instance, the late Aristide Briand, deeply aware of the underlying spiritual and cultural unity of Europe, would show the courage and initiative to call for a united states of Europe, but no scheme of that nature has endured for any length of time for the simple reason that the forces of discrimination have proved to be too strong for the forces of cohesion.

Now it is interesting to recall that there was a similar situation in China before and during the time of Confucius. There was then in China, as there is now in Europe, a number of racial groups speaking a variety of languages. When the Chou Dynasty (1122–255 B.C.) began to disintegrate, there arose a conglomeration of states in what is known as the Age of Spring and Autumn and the Age of the Contending States, which were strikingly similar to conditions in contemporary Europe. There was the same emphasis on military conquest, on rivalry for power. One result was the remarkable book on military strategy written by Sun Tse of the state of Chi. There was the same emphasis on *realpolitik*, on expediency, on the expansion of national interests at any cost. The exponent of this view was Han Fei, who antedated Machiavelli by fully eighteen hundred years.

It was reserved for the great minds of the age to see its folly and to demonstrate that militarism and conflict and expediency, without the restraining influence of a higher impulse and without the acknowledgment and establishment of a moral order, would lead to the eventual destruction of all. It was then that Lao Tse, Confucius, and their followers came on the scene and created a really new order, one in which the ideas of any ultimate value are moral values to be accepted by all for the guidance of the conduct of individuals as well as of nations. From that time on the question of a national double standard—one for the individual and another for national policy—ceased to exist. The very first chapter of Mencius began with the following story. That distinguished follower of Confucius arrived at the Kingdom of Liang. The King greeted him and said: "Sire, you have not considered a distance of a thousand *li* as being too far to come to me. I presume you have some advice to give to me so that my kingdom may derive profit therefrom." To which Mencius replied: "Why must you speak about profit? It is much more important that you have virtue and high moral accomplishments. Now if you, as a King, begin to speak about profit for your kingdom, your officials will speak about profit for their families, and your citizens will speak about profit for themselves. Both the high and the low will then be contending for profit, and your kingdom will be in a dangerous situation." Mencius then went on to explain to the King that if he made profit the basis of his policy it could only lead to contention, struggle, and ultimate murder. "Please think about virtue and moral accomplishments and forget your profit."

That sentiment for the need of moral ascendancy steadily grew so that when the Han Dynasty came into existence in 206 B.C. the great empire builders became convinced that the strength of a nation was to be measured not by the extent of its military force but by that of its moral influence. Even when there was occasional recourse to military expeditions, the observation by Mencius in another part of his book that no enemy is really conquered by force but only when his heart is conquered, was never forgotten. This recognition of the supremacy of the moral law finally produced a civilization in which it may be truly said that the cultivation of the moral instinct became the primary consideration in all phases of its activity. Physical differences of race, language, and nation became unimportant and minor factors; and for over two thousand years the process of cohesion and harmony under the influence of the moral law, in which the superficial differences between mankind were first tempered and then eliminated, has worked until it has created a nation with an astounding basic unity. Succeeding periods of chaos and confusion in Chinese history do not invalidate the steady unfolding of this principle, and there is only one language in China, much as Latin was the universal language in the Middle Ages in Europe. But while the Chinese language remains a cohesive force through the centuries, Latin has long been dissolved into many languages and dialects.

It seems to me that the problem confronting the world today, with which Europe and America should be deeply concerned, is how to make moral ideas prevail over man's actions not only as an individual but also as a nation. There is in the Occident, even at the present moment, one set of values for a person's conduct as an individual and another set for his conduct as a member of a corporate group or nation, and normally it does not appear to him to be unusual that he is a servant of two laws which are often at variance with each other.

This double standard has been implied in a good deal of Western political thinking stretching back over a long period of time. One begins to see it as early as Thomas Aquinas, and it becomes more and more pronounced when we come down to Dante, to Marsiglio of Padua, to William of Occam and finally to Machiavelli, who was quite unashamed to speak about statecraft as being completely divorced from any moral consideration and whose views, I believe, have never been seriously challenged in the last four hundred years of European political thinking.

Let me give this one quotation from a man who was himself a great leader of the religious reformation, Martin Luther. "It must be noted," he said, "that the two classes of Adam's children, the one in God's kingdom under Christ, the other in the kingdom of the world under the state, have two kinds of law. . . . Worldly government has laws which extend no farther than to life and property and what is external upon earth. But over the soul God can and will let no one rule but Himself." Which means, in effect, that the state has always been left to take care of itself. It has no necessary reference to Christian thinking. It need not be guided by any of the moral and spiritual concepts which are a part of that thinking. "Life, property, and what is external upon earth" happen to be man's principal concern wherever he may be, in Asia or in Europe. And if God does not rule over them, who does? It should really cause little surprise that there has been so much chaos in the world. The occidental conception of the state has at best been mechanical; international relations have been based upon power and expediency and not upon the feeling of right or wrong. We often hear of "enlightened self-interest" as if self-interest can ever be noble. This view should now be rectified if we hope to create a new world order. That is the fundamental problem. If that is not solved, all the subtleties and niceties put forward about this or that form of international organization become only a game of words.

My contention is that Christian ideals, beautiful as they are, have not been effective in the shaping of national policies. There is no denial that Christian thought is among the noblest that the human mind has conceived and that it has evolved some of the highest types of humanity, but it has been confined to the individual, leaving national policy to be formulated by Machiavelli and his followers. We come back ultimately to this basic problem of dichotomy which Luther brought out with such clarity. How can we, as it has been done in Chinese thought, bridge that gulf and eliminate force, expediency, and self-interest as the final arbiter in international affairs and place the relations between nations on the same high moral plane which we consider essential in the lives of individuals? The state, according to the Chinese view, is merely an extension of the individual. And so it is said in the *Higher Learning:* "If things are thoroughly investigated, then your knowledge is complete. If your knowledge is complete, then your thoughts are sincere. If your thoughts are sincere, then your heart gains equilibrium and is in its proper place. If your heart has gained equilibrium and is in its proper place, then your whole person may be said to be cultivated. When you have become cultivated, then your families are properly regulated. When your families are properly regulated, then the country becomes well governed. When your countries are well governed, then the whole world becomes peaceful and happy." There is an amazing coherence and harmony in this scheme of things. There is not the least suggestion of a double standard of conduct; there is only one set of values that has been consistently applied to national policy. I have told the story of Chu-ko Liang and his release for the seventh time of the tribal chief Meng Ho. To this day the tribes of southwest China speak of Chu-ko Liang in terms of the deepest affection, and legends have been woven around him about his generosity and solicitude for the aborigines. There is one part of the Yangtze River in Szechuan where it comes to a narrow gorge in the middle of which is a mighty cliff on which is inscribed a memorial to the Meng Ho episode. It may take longer for Chinese culture to absorb the aboriginal tribes than it generally takes a European nation to conquer her neighbor by force, but there is no bitterness, because once they accept the culture they are on a completely equal footing with the rest of the nation. In this kind of imperialism there is little danger, since there is no subject people, no master-and-slave relationship. The only difference will be one of cultural and moral accomplishments.

The situation in the West is thus a serious challenge to the Christian religion to make its ideals effective in the conduct of national groups. The whole of Christendom must feel that challenge and that responsibility. I cannot forget an occasion when I was having dinner once with five bishops. After dinner I, as a non-Christian, solemnly and in a respectful manner asked them what they thought the church could contribute to the world after this terrible holocaust was over. Never did I see men more perplexed. There was an absolute silence that embarrassed me, and each of the bishops looked at the other, wondering what to say. The silence was not broken until another person felt that the strain was too much for everybody and led the conversation to some less exacting and more neutral subject. Of course not all church dignitaries are as silent on the subject. On the question of India, for instance, the Metropolitan whose position in India is equivalent to that of the Archbishop of Canterbury in London, in a letter to *The Statesman* on April 14, 1942, made a beginning toward the solution of the Indian problem that might well be followed through by the British everywhere.

While we may recognize [he said] the unselfish spirit in which many British administrators have done their work in India and while the blame for the strained relationship now existing cannot be attributed to one side alone, yet there undoubtedly have been faults on the part of the British. These ought to be frankly acknowledged and, when possible, reparation should be made. Our great fault has been the calm assumption of a superiority inherent in the British race. . . .

If through our past mistakes we have left India deficient in certain respects and so unable to discharge alone the duties which must fall upon an independent nation, we must be ready now to the utmost of our power to render such services as she may desire.

The Hindus' response to that letter was immediate and warm.

So also, on the general subject of a future world, the interfaith declaration by prominent members of the Catholic, Jewish, and Protestant faiths issued on October 6, 1943, calling for the establishment of a world order based on the moral law, must be hailed as one of the most significant documents of the time. It was a vigorous attempt to create a unified consciousness instead of the double standard which, as I said, has been responsible for so much of the world's woes. No country welcomes such an eventuality with so much enthusiasm as does China, since that would bring European thought into line with the whole trend of her own historical thought. Chiang Kai-shek, by embracing the Christian faith, and yet with his whole being so deeply immersed in Chinese ideals, is trying to create that larger unity in which all the peoples of the world will become harmonized under those basic moral concepts which are all manifestations of the same divine law. He is indeed Asia's man of destiny, but is it not possible that he becomes also the man of destiny for the new world that is now coming into being?

As I write these closing words, news comes from Moscow that out of the conference of the three Foreign Ministers there has emerged a Four-Power Pact signed by the United States, Britain, Soviet Russia, and China pledging their united action, not only in the prosecution of the war against their common enemies, but also "for the organization and maintenance of peace and security" after the war. This is one of the greatest triumphs of the entire war. It is the most substantial contribution to the creation of a world based on general welfare and not on the selfish interest of particular nations. It is a moral victory of the first importance. We now feel reasonably justified in hoping to see unroll before our eyes a calm and tranquil era of world peace. The words of Isaiah may yet come true:

For out of Zion shall go forth the law,
And the word of the Lord from Jerusalem.
And he shall judge among the nations,
And shall rebuke many people:
And they shall beat their swords into plowshares,
And their spears into pruningforks:
Nation shall not lift up sword against nation,
Neither shall they learn war any more.

An Appendix on the Cairo Conference

SINCE the preceding chapters were written, the momentous conference at Cairo was held during the Thanksgiving season of 1943. In a series of sessions beginning on November 22 and ending on November 26 President Chiang Kai-shek met the two great leaders of America and Britain for the first time. They all traveled long distances in order to assemble under the shadow of the Pyramids. Unless an urgent need arises, all three leaders will probably not meet until the war is over. The Cairo Conference was in every sense a historic assembly. The immediate problem presented for discussion was one of military strategy in the Pacific theater of the war, but diplomatic questions of the first importance were also raised and, on the whole, satisfactorily settled. Chiang was accompanied by a small military staff, for as a military man he did not have to depend upon expert military advice. He also knew where he stood on the diplomatic issues, although he had by his side Mme. Chiang, who had only recently returned to China after an extended and triumphant tour of the United States, and Dr. Wang Chung-hui, who is an international lawyer of world-wide repute and whose views on foreign affairs perhaps carry more weight with Chiang than do those of any other person in the Chinese government today, not excepting the Minister of Foreign Affairs himself. The fact should not be overlooked that the Foreign Minister, Dr. T. V. Soong, who had returned to Chungking from Washington less than two months before, was not included in the Chinese delegation at Cairo.

There is reason to believe that, aside from an agreement on general principles which had already been taken for granted, little was accomplished in the military discussions at the Cairo Conference. The declaration which was issued at the close of the meeting merely said:

> The several military missions have agreed upon future military operations against Japan.

The three great Allies expressed their resolve to bring unrelenting pressure against their brutal enemies by sea, land and air. The pressure is already rising.

It was generally thought that, with the creation of a separate Allied Southeast Asia Command under Lord Louis Mountbatten at the Quebec Conference in August 1943, a decisive step was made to retake Burma and open the Burma Road, through which vital military supplies could again be transported into China. Mountbatten visited Chungking shortly after his appointment and began discussions with the Chinese military authorities; but the Cairo Conference, although agreeing "upon future military operations against Japan," gave no indication that the reconquest of Burma was seriously considered. It is believed by some observers that when the proper time comes the British Navy will probably by-pass Burma and strike directly at Singapore, while the American naval forces strike from the east in an effort to recapture the Philippines.

But in the diplomatic field the accomplishments of the Cairo Conference were substantial and encouraging from the Chinese point of view. The declaration further stated:

The three great Allies are fighting this war to restrain and punish the aggression of Japan.

They covet no gain for themselves and have no thought of territorial expansion.

It is their purpose that Japan should be stripped of all the islands in the Pacific which she has seized or occupied since the beginning of the first World War in 1914 and that all the territories Japan has stolen from the Chinese, such as Manchuria, Formosa and the Pescadores, shall be restored to the Republic of China.

Japan will also be expelled from all other territories which she has taken by violence and greed.

The aforesaid three great powers, mindful of the enslavement of the people of Korea, are determined that in due course Korea shall become free and independent.

In these clauses the leaders of the three great Allied powers bind their respective governments, during the war instead of in the usual postwar peace conference, to specific territorial adjustments without which it would be difficult indeed to maintain peace and stability in the Pacific area. The concreteness of these proposals makes them, in a sense, more important than the articles of the Atlantic Charter. We now know definitely that the territories which Japan has taken

AN APPENDIX ON THE CAIRO CONFERENCE   347

from China since 1894, through repeated acts of military coercion, will be restored to the Chinese, that Japan will never be in a position to fortify the Caroline and Marshall islands, that Korea will in due course be independent, and that all the territory and island possessions in the Southwest Pacific will be taken away from the Japanese, leaving the details of their status to be discussed and decided upon at a later and more opportune time. The resolution to reduce the present Japanese Empire of three million square miles, enormously rich in natural resources, and three hundred million people who are intelligent and hard-working, to an area of a hundred and forty-eight thousand square miles and a population of eighty million is surely one of the momentous decisions of the entire war. The Cairo Conference, on paper at least for the time being, marks the end of the Japanese Empire and enforces the principle of "Japan for the Japanese." It removes the menace which for exactly half a century has been a source of anxiety to the peaceful neighbor on the Asiatic mainland. It was an expression of constructive statesmanship by Chiang Kai-shek as well as by those who were associated with him. Both President and Mme. Chiang were reported to be "jubilant" and "in a happy frame of mind" upon their return to China. On December 2 Chungking issued an official statement on the Cairo Conference:

Chinese official circles are of the opinion that the Three-Power Conference in North Africa was a great success of the United Nations.

In a congenial and harmonious atmosphere, the leaders of the three Powers gathered at the meeting were able to attain a significant achievement, especially with regard to the strengthening of common efforts for a counter-offensive against Japan until she surrenders unconditionally.

This decision will mean not only a serious blow to the Axis aggressors, but also a great comfort and inspiration to all the people under the domination of the aggressors.

The farsightedness of President Roosevelt and Prime Minister Churchill is particularly held in high esteem by all the Chinese people.

Index

Adams, John, 143
Advisory Council of National Defense, 316
Alexander the Great, as a pupil of Aristotle, 54; mentioned, 283
Amerasia, articles on China, 309, 315
Amery, Leopold, speech before the American Outpost in London, 334–35
Anti-imperialism, proclaimed by Sun Yat-sen, 140–41
Aquinas, Thomas, 339
Archbishop of Canterbury, quoted, 308; 342
Aristotle, 54
Arrow War, 7
Art of War, by Sun Tse, 38; quoted, 52–56, 171, 275
Associated Press, love message of Miss Soong, 186
Atlantic Charter, 305, 333, 335, 346

Baldwin, Hanson W., on Chiang's army, in New York *Times*; on China, in *Reader's Digest*, 309–11
Battle Hymn of China, by Agnes Smedley, 309
Bauer, Max, German military adviser to Chiang, dies, 270
Bisson, Thomas Arthur, writes on China in *Far Eastern Survey*, 309; 311, 313
Bonaparte, Napoleon, 54–55; mentioned, 283
Book of Poetry, quoted, 77
Book of Prophecy, Chinese, 98
Boone, Daniel, mentioned, 105
Borodin, Michael, Russian diplomat, 126; reorganizes Chinese Kuomintang party, 133–34; makes himself dictator in Canton, 158–61, 163–65; his downfall, 180; 136, 138, 140, 144, 168–70, 172, 176, 178–79, 181–82, 196, 305
Boxers (I-ho Tuan, or the Group of Righteous Harmony), their rebellion, 31, 33, 50, 69; indemnity paid to Russia returned by Soviet, 139
Briand, Aristide, 338
British-American Tobacco Co., and its monopoly of the cigarette market in China, 157
British Parliamentary Mission to Chungking, 68
Buck, Pearl Sydenstricker, writes on China for *Life*, 309, 311
Buddhism, its spread over China, 79, 238
Buddhist belief, 12
Burma Road, its building by the Chinese, 293–94; captured by the Japanese, 296; steps to retake it, 346
Bushido, Japanese cult, and its origin, 275, 281, 290

Cairo conference, 345–47
Canton, republic established by Sun Yat-sen, 117; trouble over customs revenue, 140; Communist strength, 164; government moved to Wuchang, 168; Chen Chi-tang revolts, 235
Caste system, non-existent in China, 291; and the untouchables of India, 335
Catherine the Great of Russia, 326
Central China Development Co., established by Japan, 285
Central Military College, at Nanking, 120
Chamberlain, Austen, 328
Chang, Carson, head of National Socialist party in China, 315-16
Chang Chien, Chinese explorer, 81, 238
Chang Chih-tung, his essay "Persuasion to Learn," 31
Chang Ching-kiang, 200
Chang Chung-chang, war lord, 106, 196, 198
Chang Fa-kwei, 194

349

INDEX

Chang Hsueh-liang, in the Sian incident, 242–57, 259; pardoned for his part, 260; 196, 235, 261–63, 279

Chang Hsun, defender of Nanking against revolutionists, 96–97; flees and city is taken over by them, 98

Chang Tso-lin, war lord, killed when his train is blown up, 106, 198, 242; 121, 157, 178, 196–97

Chan Kuo, writer, 221

Chapman, Herbert Owen, his *The Chinese Revolution 1926-27* quoted, 170–71

Chaucer, Geoffrey, mentioned, 328

Chen, Eugene, Minister of Foreign Affairs of the Hankow government, 168, 173

Chen Chi-mei, Chinese revolutionary, 47, 67–68, 91–93; captured but released when revolution succeeds, 95; made military commander of Shanghai, 96, 101; assassinated, 115; 99, 103, 108, 112, 114, 116

Chen Chi-tang, revolts in Canton, 235

Chen Chiung-ming, his treachery against Sun Yat-sen, 114, 117–18, 123; attempts to murder him, 119–20; 121, 125, 130, 135, 137, 158, 161–62, 169, 181

Cheng Chien, 176

Cheng Ju-chen, commands Chinese naval force at Shanghai against revolutionists, 113

Chen Ko-fu, 47

Chen Kung-po, of the puppet government at Nanking, 172

Chen Li-fu, 47

Chen Ming-shu, revolts in Fukien, 237

Chesterton, Gilbert Keith, quoted, 328

Chiang Kai-shek, his response to relinquishment of extraterritorial rights in China by U.S. and Great Britain, 3–4; Chou-tai in youth, 7–8; his task in creating a new China, 9; school days, 23–26; plays ghost, 29; mother changes his name to Chungchen, adding Kai-shek, its meaning, 34–35; goes to the School of Law and Politics in Hangchow, 36–37; determines on a military career, 45–46; his liquidation of China's modern feudalism, 53; association with Sun Yat-sen, 72–76; speech on nationalism, 80–81; on official corruption, 82–83; enters the revolution, 93; captures Hangchow, 94; trains new Chinese army, 96; death of his mother, 117; mission to Moscow, 121, 125–26; president of Whampoa Military Academy, 121, 126; opposes admitting Communists into Kuomintang, 136–37; launches Northern Expedition, 160 *et seq.*; press interview, 167; moves to suppress Communists, 177; resigns as Commander-in-Chief, 180–83; marries Miss Mei-ling Soong, 185–87; re-elected Commander-in-Chief, 195; campaign against Communists begins anew, 216–20; literary tastes, 221; his Christianity, 223–24; promotes New Life Movement, 226; his eight-point program, 231–33; resigns but is called back, 235–36; fiftieth birthday celebration, 239–41; Sian incident, 241–63; comments on the Lukouchiao incident, 272–73; establishes capital at Chungking, 281; his book *China's Destiny* quoted, 298–301; his official titles, 314; message to the *Herald Tribune* Forum, 323, 336; visit to India, and farewell message, 331–34; at the Cairo Conference, 345

Chiang, Mme., her visit to the U.S., 185; her account of the Sian incident, 279; visit to India, 331; 19, 23, 190, 192–93, 226, 231, 237, 248–51, 254–56, 261, 310. *See also* Soong, Mei-ling

Chiang Po-li, of the Paoting Military Academy, 247, 254

Chiang Ting-wen, General, 250

Chicherin, Grigoryi Vassilyevich, 125

Chien, T. S., quoted, 318

Chien Lung, Emperor of China, his greeting to the embassy of George III of England, 5, 153

Chikow (Mouth of the Brook), Chiang's birthplace, 10; becomes a national shrine, 14; its school, 16

China, treaties with U.S. and Great Britain give up extraterritorial rights, 3, 152, 211; war with France and Japan, 8; defeated by Japan, 30; pays indemnity, 46; country as a melting pot, 82; defeated by France, 86; monarchy overthrown and republic established, 88; betrayed by Yuan Shih-kai, 103; Second Revolution fails, 113–14; republic re-established at Canton, 117; declares war on the Axis powers, 271, 286; industrialization forecast, 299–306

Chinese Communist party, 138

INDEX 351

Chinese Eastern Railway, returned to China by the Soviet Government, 139
Chinese Exclusion Acts, repealed by the U.S., 329
Chinese Republic established, 88, 99
Chinese Revolution, betrayed by Yuan Shih-kai, 103; Second Revolution fails, 113–14; republic established at Canton, 117; 61, 86–91, 94–98, 124, 134, 151, 156, 162, 164
Chinese Revolution, The, by Herbert Owen Chapman, quoted, 170–71
Ching Dynasty, 79, 218, 221
Ching-kuo, Chiang's son, 224
Chin Kuei, Chinese minister, 38–40
Chin-ming festival, 17
Chinputang, opposition Chinese party created by Yuan Shih-kai, 103
Chiu Chin, Miss, Chinese revolutionary, executed, 67
Chou Dynasty, 81, 116, 338
Chou-tai, *see* Chiang Kai-shek
Chow En-lai, guerrilla leader, 262
Christian movement in China, opposed by Communists, 173
Chuan Tse, philosopher, 221
Chu-ko Liang, 57, 221, 341
Chun Chiu Period, 81
Chungking, Chinese capital, 281
Churchill, Winston Spencer, British Prime Minister, 347
Ciano, Count Galeazzo, 243
Civil service in China, 292
Classic on Filial Love, Chinese school book, 25–26, 36
Clausewitz, Karl von, mentioned, 283
Comintern, dissolved, 179, 261
Committee system in Chinese Government, abolished, 217–18
Communism in China, 136 *passim.*
Communist party in Russia, 135
Confucius, his concept of China, 9; his sayings, 15, 18, 25, 222, 286, 331, 336; *Li Chi* quoted, 77; 50, 84, 252, 338
Contending States, Age of, 52, 104, 338
Convention of 1787 at Philadelphia, 143
Cornwallis (H.M.S.), 3
Cort, David, 53 *n.*

Daily News (Moscow), edited by Borodin after his downfall, 180
Danes, their invasion of the British Isles, 82

Dante Alighieri, 340
Dewey, Professor John, 173, 329
Dialects in China, 291
Diary-keeping, enjoined on Chinese soldiers, 220
"Dictatorship of the proletariat," Soviet conception, 142–43
Diplomatic Quarter of Peking, its unconventional goings-on, 209–10
Doihara, General Kenzi, Japanese emissary, 105, 263, 279
Dollar, its revaluation in the U.S., 225
Donald, William Henry, friend of the Chiangs, 250, 254–55

"East Asia Co-prosperity Sphere," 336
East India Co., mentioned, 285
Empress Dowager of China, her control, 31–32, 100
Ethiopian conquest, 277
Eucken, Rudolf, German philosopher, 315
Extraterritorial rights in China, relinquished by U.S., and Great Britain, 3, 152, 211, 328–29; 299, 307

Falkenhausen, General Ludwig von, 270
Fang, H. D., 304 *n.*
Far Eastern Crisis, The, Secretary Stimson's book, quoted, 211–12
Far Eastern Survey, T. A. Bisson on China, 309
Federation of Farmers, Workers, Soldiers, and Students to Promote the Revolutionary Movement, 159
Feng Kuo-chang, quells an attempt at Chinese revolution, 94; 116, 157
Feng-shui, among Chinese, 18–19
Feng Yu-hsiang, called "Christian general," 105, 121, 164, 194, 197, 199; sang "Onward, Christian Soldiers" with his troops, 202; 204, 236, 242, 270
Fitzgerald, Charles Patrick, 56 *n.,* 77 *n.*
Five Classics, of Chinese literature, 26
Five-Year Plans of the Soviet, 303, 306
Flag of China, and its origin, 230
Forbidden City, 88, 102
Four Books, of Chinese literature, 26, 221
Four cardinal virtues of Chinese, 227–28
Four Freedoms, 335
Four-Power Pact, 342
Fourteen Points of President Wilson, 53
Franco-Prussian War, 221

French Revolution, 88, 333
Fu Tso-yi, 245

Galen, General (Vasily Konstantinovich Bluecher), 126, 135
Gandhara art in China, 238
Gannett, Lewis Stiles, his estimate of Chiang, 166-67
Gellhorn, Martha, on the charm of Mme. Chiang, 190
Genghis Khan mentioned, 241
George III, result of his first embassy to the Chinese Emperor, 4-5; 153
George, Henry, American economist, 133
Giles, Lionel, translator of Sun Tse's *Art of War*, 56 n.
Golden Hordes, 38
Gold standard, abandoned by the U.S., 225
Great Britain, treaty with Chinese Republic gives up extraterritorial rights, 3, 152
Great Commonwealth, 77, 80
Great Wall of China, 79, 198, 262, 293

Hamilton, Alexander, 143
Han Dynasty, introduced civil service in China, 292; 78, 153, 238, 293, 303, 326, 339
Han Fei, philosopher, 221, 338
Hangchow, former capital of China, 36-38; its character, 44; captured by revolutionists led by Chiang Kai-shek, 94-95; taken again by Nationalist Army, 168
Han Yu, philosopher, 79
Harada, General Kumakichi, 296
Hart, Sir Robert, opinion of the Boxer Rebellion, 31
Hayashi, Baron Tadasu, his government resigns, 277
Hedin, Sven Anders, Swedish explorer, 268
Herald Tribune (N.Y.) Forum, message from Chiang, 323, 336
Heroin, its injection compulsory in China by Japanese, 289
Hideyoshi, Toyotomi, Japanese ruler, 265
Higher Learning, quoted, 341
Hirota, Koki, Japanese Foreign Minister, 267; his "Three Principles," 285-86
Hitler, Adolf, 213-14, 277, 315
Holcombe, Professor Arthur Norman, 179-80
Ho-Umetsu Agreement, 279

Ho Ying-chin, Minister of War, 176, 203, 239, 249, 254
Hsingchunghui, *see* Society for the Regeneration of China
Hsu Chien, joins anti-Communists, 180
Hsu Hsi-ling, Chinese revolutionary, executed, 67, 72
Hsu Shi-chang, 116
Huang Hsin, fails in attempt at revolution, 90-92, 94
Hu Han-min, Chinese revolutionary, 65, 90; lecturer at Whampoa Military Academy, 126; disagreement with Chiang, 234-35
Hu Lin-yi, in Taiping Rebellion, 218; 221
Hull, Cordell, U.S. Secretary of State, on the Manchurian incident, 212
Hu Tsung-nan, 244

I-ho Tuan, or the Group of Righteous Harmony, *see* Boxers
Isaiah quoted, 343
Ivan the Terrible of Russia, 326

Jaffe, Philip J., on China, in *Amerasia*, 309
Jamieson, Sir James William, British Consul General at Canton, 140
Japan, defeats China in war over Korea, 7-8; defeats Russia, 32; its Twenty-one Demands upon China, 115; attacks Mukden, occupies Manchuria, 211, 234-36; Lukouchiao incident at Marco Polo Bridge starts war with China, 272; Nanking captured, 281
Jefferson, Thomas, 143
Joffe, Adolf, Soviet emissary to China, 123-25; his joint statement with Sun Yat-sen, 132; 136, 139-41, 144, 146, 159, 169
Johnson, Nelson Trusler, American Ambassador to China, 206, 293

Karakhan, Leo, first Soviet Ambassador to China, 124-25, 169
King, Ernest Joseph, American admiral, quoted on China, 311
Konoye, Prince Fumimaro, Japanese Prime Minister, 277, 284-85; his Four Points, 286
Koo, Dr. Vi Kuyuin Wellington, Chinese diplomat, 122
Korea, war over, between Japan and China, 7
Kriebel, General Hermann, 270

INDEX

Kuang Hsu, Emperor of China, 31, 100
Kung, H. H., Chinese Minister of Finance, 248, 250, 293, 307
Kuominchun, or People's Army, 105
Kuomintang, 35 *passim.;* dissolved, 114–15; reorganized, 133–34; Communists filter in and seek to wreck it, 137–38; China united under its flag, 203
Kwangfu Society, 67
Kwan Yu of the Three Kingdoms, 14

Lampson, Sir Miles Wedderburn, British diplomat, 172, 210
Land ownership in China, 145
Languages in China, 291
Lao Tse, Chinese philosopher, 338
League for the Freedom of the Race, 159
League of Common Alliance, *see* Tung-menghui
League of Nations, 197, 212–13, 215, 321
Liebnitz, Gottfried Wilhelm, cited, 332
Lenin, Vladimir Ilyich Ulyanov, 125, 141, 174
Liao Chung-kai, follower of Sun Yat-sen, assassinated, 126
Liberty Bell in Independence Hall, Philadelphia, rings to commemorate signing of treaty with Chinese Republic by the U.S., 3
Li Chi-sen, 204
Lien-tso, law of, 128–29, 171
Life, Pearl Buck on China, 309
Li Hung-chang, 30–31, 49, 110
Lin Sen, President of China, dies, 205; 239, 258
Linlithgow, Victor Alexander John Hope, Lord, receives Chiang Kai-shek and Mme. Chiang, 331–32
Li Shih-tsang, 200
Li Tsung-jen, 194, 204, 270
Li Yuan-hung, Chinese revolutionary, 64, 116
Locke, John, cited, 332
Lu Hsiu-fu, 128
Lukouchiao incident, at Marco Polo Bridge, starts war, 269–70, 272, 277, 280–81, 286
Luther, Martin, quoted, 340
Lynch, George, quoted on the Chinese soldier, 50; interview with Sun Yat-sen, 70–71, 82
Lytton Commission, 268

Macartney, George, Lord, first British envoy to China, 5
Machiavelli, Niccolò, mentioned, 337–38, 340
Manchu Dynasty, 8, 22; overthrown, 51, 61, 68, 72–73, 112, 308
Manchuria, and the war between Japan and Russia, 32; its occupation by Japanese troops, 211, 214–16, 225, 262, 265–66, 273, 286; President Roosevelt's pledge of its return to China, 321
Marsiglio of Padua, 340
Marx, Karl, Sun Yat-sen's description of him, 145
Masefield, John, mentioned, 328
Ma Yuan, 303
Meadows, Thomas Taylor, 6
Mencius, Chinese philosopher, 21, 56; quoted, 84; and the King of Liang, 338–39; 244
Meng Ho, 57–58, 341
Metropolitan of India, letter in *The Statesman*, 342
Military Preparedness, Japanese pamphlet, quoted, 269
Military studies for Chinese soldiers, 271–72
Military Voice, The, magazine, 108
Ming Dynasty, 11, 32, 99, 153, 188, 290, 293, 318
Mirrors of History, 221
Mountbatten, Lord Louis, visits Chungking, 346; 294
Mouth of the Brook, *see* Chikow
Mukden incident, and occupation of Manchuria, 211, 234–35, 273, 276, 286, 320, 327
Mussolini, Benito, 213, 243
Mustapha Kemal, President of the Turkish Republic, 158
Mutual Aid Agreements of the Atlantic Charter, 305

Nagaoka, General Gaishi, quoted on Chiang Kai-shek, 64–65
Names of Chinese, their origin, 34
Nanking, captured by revolutionists and proclaimed capital of the new China, 98, 102
Nanking incident, 177, 196
Napoleonic Era, relation to nationalism in Europe, 75
Napoleonic Wars, 221

National Resources Commission, 302
National Socialist party in China, 315–16
Nehru, Jawaharlal, visit to Chungking, 331
New Life Movement, promoted by Chiang Kai-shek, 226–28, 230–31, 234, 238
New Masses, on Communists in China, by Lieutenant George Uhlmann, 262
Nine-Power Treaty, Secretary Stimson quoted, 212–13
Nineteenth Route Army, 236–37
Non-recognition principle of Secretary Stimson, 212
North China Development Co., established by Japan, 285
Northern Expedition, 61 *passim.*

O'Malley, Owen, counselor of the British legation in China, 172
Opium, its use in China made compulsory by the Japanese, 289
"Opium for the people," Communist designation of Christianity, 173
Opium War, its end, 3, 5–7, 155, 327
Order of the Students, 159
Organic Law of the National Government of the Republic of China, 205

Pact of Paris, 213
Pai Chung-hsi, 168, 176, 194, 204
Panama Canal, 294
Pan Chao, Chinese explorer, 238, 303
Pan Ku, Chinese explorer, 81
Paoting Military Academy, 47–49, 51, 58, 61, 74, 100–01, 121, 247
Pearl Harbor, attacked by Japan, 270–71, 286, 296, 304, 309, 311, 327
Pei-yang, military party in China, 49
Peng Yu-lin, 218
People's Political Council, 78, 313–17
"Persuasion to Learn," Chinese essay, 31
Peter the Great of Russia, 326
Polo, Marco, on China, 153
Program of National Resistance and Reconstruction in China, 312
Puyi, Henry, puppet Emperor of Manchuria, 275

Quesnay, François, cited, 332
Quo Tai-chi, Chinese Foreign Minister, declares war on the Axis powers, 271

Randolph, John, 143
Reader's Digest, Hanson W. Baldwin on China, 309

Record of Self-Analysis, A, by Chiang Kai-shek, 108
Reorganization Loan to China, 112
Revolutionaries in China, 51–52
Revolutions in China, *see* Chinese Revolution
Righteous Harmony, Group of, *see* Boxers
Roman Empire, contact with China, 303
Roosevelt, Franklin Delano, President of the U.S., pledge to return Manchuria to China, 321; on the repeal of the Chinese Exclusion Acts, 329; 347
Roosevelt, Mrs. Eleanor, 310
Roosevelt Administration, and the great depression, 225
Rousseau, Jean-Jacques, cited, 332
Roy, Manabendra Nath, Indian Communist, 179
Russell, Bertrand, 173
Russia, defeated by Japan, 32
Russian Revolution, 88, 117, 124, 133, 136–37, 144–45, 158
Russo-Japanese War, 33, 110, 221

San-min chu-i, see Three Principles of the People
San Min Principles, 180–82
School of Law and Politics, in Hangchow, 36–37
School of the Keeper of the Phoenix, attended by young Chiang, 24
Schools in China, 24, 26–28
Schwartz, Bruno, New York *Times* correspondent, interview with Chiang, 305
Seeckt, General Hans von, 270
Seventy-two Heroes, 88
Shanghai, captured by revolutionists, 95
Sheean, James Vincent, 159 *n.,* 174 *n.,* 309
Shidehara, Kijuro, Japanese diplomat, 213
Shih Ko-fa, national hero, 128, 221
Shih Yu-shan, war lord, starts rebellion in Shantung, 235
Shinbo Gokyo, military academy, 62–63, 65, 92
Sian incident, 14, 19, 223, 241–64, 267, 279
Silver, embargo a blow to China, 225
Simon, Sir John, 212–14
Sino-Japanese War, 86, 110, 144, 263, 267, 278, 287, 293
Smedley, Agnes, her *Battle Hymn of China,* 309

INDEX 355

Snow, Edgar, his description of Chiang, 277–78
Social distinctions in China, 292
Social structure of China, 153–55
Society for the Regeneration of China (Hsingchunghui), 66, 72
Soong, Miss Mei-ling, marries Chiang Kai-shek, 185–87, 190–91, 193
Soong, T. V., Foreign Minister of China, 168, 184; statement on Economic Conference, 201; Sian incident, 250, 255–56; 305–06, 345
Soong, Mrs., mother of the two preceding, 185
Soviet regime established in Russia, 117, 123–24; returns Chinese Eastern Railway and Boxer indemnity to China, 139; disclaims responsibility for Sian revolt, 260; its Five-Year Plans, 303, 306
Spheres of influence, in China, established by foreign powers, 30
Ssu Ma Chien, historian, 221
Stalin, Joseph, 174–75
Statesman, The, letter of the Metropolitan of India, 342
Stepanoff, Nikolai, Russian journalist, 164
Stilwell, Lieutenant General Joseph Warren, his tribute to the Chinese soldier, 271; 293
Stimson, Henry Lewis, U.S. Secretary of State, his book *The Far Eastern Crisis* quoted, 211–12; on the Nine-Power Treaty, 212–13
Su-an, father of Chiang, 13, 16, 19
Suez Canal, 294
Sui Dynasty, 81
Sun, Mme., sister of Mme. Chiang, 168, 190
Sun Chuan-fang, war lord, 168, 171, 194, 196, 198
Sun Fo, son of Sun Yat-sen, 168, 206; his government falls, 236; 237
Sung Chiao-jen, member of the Kuomintang, his assassination instigated by Yuan Shih-kai, 112, 115
Sung Dynasty, 14, 37, 79, 290
Sun Tse, author of *Art of War,* 38, 52–55, 128, 171, 221, 275–76, 278, 283, 290, 338
Sun Yat-sen, at Medical College in Hong Kong, 7; 8 *passim.;* graduates, 65; his Three Principles, 80; 82–83, 85–86; leads Chinese Revolution, 87–88; becomes President of the Republic of China, but is superseded by Yuan Shih-kai, 99–100; returns to presidency, 108; established in Canton, 117; anti-imperialist platform proclaimed, 140; his idea for the national flag, 230; his death, 4, 61, 69, 122, 151
Swing, Raymond Gram, radio talk on China, 309
Sze Ko-fa, 252

Tada, Hayao, Japanese general, 262
Tai Chi-tao, lecturer at Whampoa Military Academy, 126
Taierchuang, battle of, 281
Taiping Rebellion, 7, 13, 128–29, 218, 268
Takada Regiment, 64, 73
Tanaka, Baron Giichi, his proposal to Sun Yat-sen for breaking treaties, 274; 276
Tanaka Memorial, a plan for Japanese-aggression, 265, 276, 286
Tang Dynasty, 11, 37, 79, 81, 98, 153, 206, 303
Tangku truce, 236, 262
Tang Sheng-chih, defeated in attempt on Hankow, 194
Tao Huan-ching, Chinese revolutionary, 67
Temple of the Jade Clouds, first tomb of Sun Yat-sen, 207
Teviot, Charles Ian Kerr, Lord, tribute to Sun Yat-sen, 68–69
Third International in China, 136; in Moscow, 174
Three Eastern Provinces (Manchuria), 198
Three Kingdoms, 14, 56, 79, 153, 166
Three Principles of the People (*San-min chu-i*), 66 *passim.*
Three-Word Classic, Chinese school book, 24–26
Times (London), on the Sian incident, 244, 259
Times (New York), 166; message on Chiang's love affair, 186; editorial on the Chinese soldier, 297; interview with Chiang, 305; Hanson W. Baldwin on Chiang's army, 309
Tota, Ishimaru, Japanese writer, 275–76
Trans-Siberian Railway, 116
Treaties with China, 3, 152–55, 210–11
Treaty of Nanking, 3, 5–6
Treaty of Tientsin, 7

INDEX

Treaty ports of China, their exploitation, 153–54
Trotsky, Lev Davidovich, quoted on Communism in China, 125, 161, 174–75; 185
Tsai Ao, begins uprising against Yuan Shih-kai, 115
Tsai Ting-kai, commander of the Nineteenth Route Army, 236; joins Fukien revolt, 237
Tsai Yuan-pei, chancellor of Peking National University, 124; reads wedding address to Chiang Kai-shek and Miss Mei-ling Soong, 187–200
Tsao Kun, 157
Tseng Kuo-fan, statesman, 128; in Taiping Rebellion, 129, 218; 221, 225, 227, 230
Tseng-tse, disciple of Confucius, 25
Tsieh Chi-kuang, national hero, 221
Tsin Dynasty, 78, 153
Tso Chuan, writer, 221
Tso Tsung-tang, road builder in Taiping Rebellion, 218, 268
Tsui Shu-chin, 132 n.
Tsung-li (Sun Yat-sen), 128, 136–37, 162–63
Tuan Chi-jui, 121
Tuchuns, or war lords, in China, their origin, 104; 109
Tungmenghui (League of Common Alliance), Chinese revolutionary party, founded by Sun Yat-sen, 47, 66, 68, 72, 74, 83–84, 88, 90, 92–93, 100
Turksib Railway, 327
Twenty-one Demands, made by Japan upon China, 115, 266

Uhlmann, Lieutenant George, on Chinese Communists in the *New Masses*, 262; 312
United States, negotiates treaty with Chinese Republic, giving up extraterritorial rights, 3, 152
Uxbridge, Henry William Paget, Earl of, at Battle of Waterloo, 54

Valley Forge, mentioned, 142
Versailles, 53

Wang, C. T., Foreign Minister of China, 208–11
Wang Ching-wei, Chinese quisling, 66, 126, 194, 236, 275
Wang Chung-hui, Dr., 345
Wang family of Fenghua, 19
Wang Yang-ming, philosopher, 221, 318
Washington, George, his revolutionary activities, 142
Washington Conference, 197
Water-drinking as a symbol, 64
Waterloo, Battle of, 54
Weichow, captured by Chiang's forces, 122
Wei-kuo, Chiang's son, 224–25
Wellington (Arthur Wellesley), Duke of, at Battle of Waterloo, 54–55
Wen Tien-hsiang, national hero, 128, 221, 252
West Point, mentioned, 269
Wetzell, General Georg, 270
Whampoa Military Academy, Chiang made president, 121, 126–27, 135, 160; now located in Chungking, 131; 130, 132, 134, 160, 162, 170, 269
William of Occam, 340
Williams, Maurice, British economist, 133
Willkie, Wendell Lewis, on Mme. Chiang, 193; his book *One World* quoted, 298–300; 225
Wilson, Woodrow, and the Fourteen Points, 53; opposed loan from U.S. to Yuan Shih-kai, 111
Women in China, 189
Women's Northern Expeditionary Force, attempts to capture Nanking, 96–98
World's Students Christian Federation, 173
World War I, starts, 115; 221
Wu Chao-chu, Canton Foreign Minister, 140
Wu Pei-fu, war lord, 104; his death, 105; 118–19, 121, 162, 165–66, 198
Wu Te-cheng, mayor of Shanghai, 239
Wu Tse, writer, 221
Wu Tse-hui, 200–01

Yang Hu-cheng, in the Sian incident, 242, 244–48, 253–57, 263; his demands on Chiang, 264–65
Yen Hsi-shan, terminates Northern Expedition by taking Peking, 198–99, 202; 197, 242, 245, 270
Yo Fei, of the Sung Dynasty, 14, 37; his military career and death, 38–40; 41–44, 52, 67, 128, 221, 252

INDEX

Snow, Edgar, his description of Chiang, 277-78
Social distinctions in China, 292
Social structure of China, 153-55
Society for the Regeneration of China (Hsingchunghui), 66, 72
Soong, Miss Mei-ling, marries Chiang Kai-shek, 185-87, 190-91, 193
Soong, T. V., Foreign Minister of China, 168, 184; statement on Economic Conference, 201; Sian incident, 250, 255-56; 305-06, 345
Soong, Mrs., mother of the two preceding, 185
Soviet regime established in Russia, 117, 123-24; returns Chinese Eastern Railway and Boxer indemnity to China, 139; disclaims responsibility for Sian revolt, 260; its Five-Year Plans, 303, 306
Spheres of influence, in China, established by foreign powers, 30
Ssu Ma Chien, historian, 221
Stalin, Joseph, 174-75
Statesman, The, letter of the Metropolitan of India, 342
Stepanoff, Nikolai, Russian journalist, 164
Stilwell, Lieutenant General Joseph Warren, his tribute to the Chinese soldier, 271; 293
Stimson, Henry Lewis, U.S. Secretary of State, his book *The Far Eastern Crisis* quoted, 211-12; on the Nine-Power Treaty, 212-13
Su-an, father of Chiang, 13, 16, 19
Suez Canal, 294
Sui Dynasty, 81
Sun, Mme., sister of Mme. Chiang, 168, 190
Sun Chuan-fang, war lord, 168, 171, 194, 196, 198
Sun Fo, son of Sun Yat-sen, 168, 206; his government falls, 236; 237
Sung Chiao-jen, member of the Kuomintang, his assassination instigated by Yuan Shih-kai, 112, 115
Sung Dynasty, 14, 37, 79, 290
Sun Tse, author of *Art of War,* 38, 52-55, 128, 171, 221, 275-76, 278, 283, 290, 338
Sun Yat-sen, at Medical College in Hong Kong, 7; 8 *passim.;* graduates, 65; his Three Principles, 80; 82-83, 85-86; leads Chinese Revolution, 87-88; becomes President of the Republic of China, but is superseded by Yuan Shih-kai, 99-100; returns to presidency, 108; established in Canton, 117; anti-imperialist platform proclaimed, 140; his idea for the national flag, 230; his death, 4, 61, 69, 122, 151
Swing, Raymond Gram, radio talk on China, 309
Sze Ko-fa, 252

Tada, Hayao, Japanese general, 262
Tai Chi-tao, lecturer at Whampoa Military Academy, 126
Taierchuang, battle of, 281
Taiping Rebellion, 7, 13, 128-29, 218, 268
Takada Regiment, 64, 73
Tanaka, Baron Giichi, his proposal to Sun Yat-sen for breaking treaties, 274; 276
Tanaka Memorial, a plan for Japanese-aggression, 265, 276, 286
Tang Dynasty, 11, 37, 79, 81, 98, 153, 206, 303
Tangku truce, 236, 262
Tang Sheng-chih, defeated in attempt on Hankow, 194
Tao Huan-ching, Chinese revolutionary, 67
Temple of the Jade Clouds, first tomb of Sun Yat-sen, 207
Teviot, Charles Ian Kerr, Lord, tribute to Sun Yat-sen, 68-69
Third International in China, 136; in Moscow, 174
Three Eastern Provinces (Manchuria), 198
Three Kingdoms, 14, 56, 79, 153, 166
Three Principles of the People (*San-min chu-i*), 66 *passim.*
Three-Word Classic, Chinese school book, 24-26
Times (London), on the Sian incident, 244, 259
Times (New York), 166; message on Chiang's love affair, 186; editorial on the Chinese soldier, 297; interview with Chiang, 305; Hanson W. Baldwin on Chiang's army, 309
Tota, Ishimaru, Japanese writer, 275-76
Trans-Siberian Railway, 116
Treaties with China, 3, 152-55, 210-11
Treaty of Nanking, 3, 5-6
Treaty of Tientsin, 7

356 INDEX

Treaty ports of China, their exploitation, 153–54

Trotsky, Lev Davidovich, quoted on Communism in China, 125, 161, 174–75; 185

Tsai Ao, begins uprising against Yuan Shih-kai, 115

Tsai Ting-kai, commander of the Nineteenth Route Army, 236; joins Fukien revolt, 237

Tsai Yuan-pei, chancellor of Peking National University, 124; reads wedding address to Chiang Kai-shek and Miss Mei-ling Soong, 187–200

Tsao Kun, 157

Tseng Kuo-fan, statesman, 128; in Taiping Rebellion, 129, 218; 221, 225, 227, 230

Tseng-tse, disciple of Confucius, 25

Tsieh Chi-kuang, national hero, 221

Tsin Dynasty, 78, 153

Tso Chuan, writer, 221

Tso Tsung-tang, road builder in Taiping Rebellion, 218, 268

Tsui Shu-chin, 132 n.

Tsung-li (Sun Yat-sen), 128, 136–37, 162–63

Tuan Chi-jui, 121

Tuchuns, or war lords, in China, their origin, 104; 109

Tungmenghui (League of Common Alliance), Chinese revolutionary party, founded by Sun Yat-sen, 47, 66, 68, 72, 74, 83–84, 88, 90, 92–93, 100

Turksib Railway, 327

Twenty-one Demands, made by Japan upon China, 115, 266

Uhlmann, Lieutenant George, on Chinese Communists in the *New Masses*, 262; 312

United States, negotiates treaty with Chinese Republic, giving up extraterritorial rights, 3, 152

Uxbridge, Henry William Paget, Earl of, at Battle of Waterloo, 54

Valley Forge, mentioned, 142
Versailles, 53

Wang, C. T., Foreign Minister of China, 208–11

Wang Ching-wei, Chinese quisling, 66, 126, 194, 236, 275

Wang Chung-hui, Dr., 345

Wang family of Fenghua, 19

Wang Yang-ming, philosopher, 221, 318

Washington, George, his revolutionary activities, 142

Washington Conference, 197

Water-drinking as a symbol, 64

Waterloo, Battle of, 54

Weichow, captured by Chiang's forces, 122

Wei-kuo, Chiang's son, 224–25

Wellington (Arthur Wellesley), Duke of, at Battle of Waterloo, 54–55

Wen Tien-hsiang, national hero, 128, 221, 252

West Point, mentioned, 269

Wetzell, General Georg, 270

Whampoa Military Academy, Chiang made president, 121, 126–27, 135, 160; now located in Chungking, 131; 130, 132, 134, 160, 162, 170, 269

William of Occam, 340

Williams, Maurice, British economist, 133

Willkie, Wendell Lewis, on Mme. Chiang, 193; his book *One World* quoted, 298–300; 225

Wilson, Woodrow, and the Fourteen Points, 53; opposed loan from U.S. to Yuan Shih-kai, 111

Women in China, 189

Women's Northern Expeditionary Force, attempts to capture Nanking, 96–98

World's Students Christian Federation, 173

World War I, starts, 115; 221

Wu Chao-chu, Canton Foreign Minister, 140

Wu Pei-fu, war lord, 104; his death, 105; 118–19, 121, 162, 165–66, 198

Wu Te-cheng, mayor of Shanghai, 239

Wu Tse, writer, 221

Wu Tse-hui, 200–01

Yang Hu-cheng, in the Sian incident, 242, 244–48, 253–57, 263; his demands on Chiang, 264–65

Yen Hsi-shan, terminates Northern Expedition by taking Peking, 198–99, 202; 197, 242, 245, 270

Yo Fei, of the Sung Dynasty, 14, 37; his military career and death, 38–40; 41–44, 52, 67, 128, 221, 252

Yuan Dynasty, 79
Yuan Ming Yuan, his Winter Palace burned by British and French troops, 98
Yuan Shih-kai, leader of the Pei-yang military party, 49; becomes President of the Chinese Republic, 100, 108, 111; instigates assassination of Sung Chiao-jen, 112; declares himself Emperor, 114–15; his death, 115; 47, 62, 73–74, 101–04, 107, 113, 116, 121
Yu Hsueh-chung, 245
Yung Lu, 188
Yu-piao, Chiang's grandfather, 12–13, 16

Zinoviev, Grigori Evseyevich, Russian diplomat, 164

www.ingramcontent.com/pod-product-compliance
Lightning Source LLC
Chambersburg PA
CBHW021815300426
44114CB00009BA/185